University of London Historical Studies

XXV

UNIVERSITY OF LONDON HISTORICAL STUDIES

This volume is published with the help of a grant from the late Miss Isobel Thornley's Bequest to the University of London

THE YORKSHIRE GENTRY

Burton Constable Hall, East Riding.
A seventeenth-century painting of the Elizabethan manor-house which was
mainly the work of Sir John Constable.

THE
YORKSHIRE
GENTRY

From the Reformation to
the Civil War

by

J. T. CLIFFE

UNIVERSITY OF LONDON
THE ATHLONE PRESS
1969

Published by
THE ATHLONE PRESS
UNIVERSITY OF LONDON
at 2 *Gower Street, London* WC1

Distributed by Tiptree Book Services Ltd
Tiptree, Essex

Australia & New Zealand
Melbourne University Press

Canada
Oxford University Press
Toronto

U.S.A.
Oxford University Press Inc
New York

485 13125 0

Printed in Great Britain by
WILLIAM CLOWES AND SONS LTD
London and Beccles

PREFACE

THIS BOOK has its origins in a London Ph.D. thesis entitled 'The Yorkshire Gentry on the Eve of the Civil War' which was submitted and approved in 1960. Although I have substantially rewritten and expanded the thesis (which covered only the early seventeenth century) its date is of some significance in relation to the appearance of other works concerned either wholly or in part with that celebrated historical controversy, 'the storm over the gentry'.

It will be obvious from the Bibliography that I have made extensive use of family papers, most of them now in the care of local record offices. In this respect I wish to acknowledge my great indebtedness to the following owners of manuscript collections which I have consulted: the Duke of Norfolk, the Earls of Dartmouth, Mexborough, Swinton and Wharncliffe, the Earl and Countess Fitzwilliam, Viscount Galway, the Lords Crathorne, Gisborough, Hotham and Savile, and Baroness Beaumont; Sir Henry Beresford-Peirse, Sir Alvary Gascoigne and Sir William Pennington-Ramsden; Mr R. A. Bethell, Mr John Chichester-Constable, Lieutenant Colonel R. E. Crompton, Mr S. W. Fraser, Captain Myles Hildyard, Mr Richard Howard-Vyse, Major A. J. Hutton Squire, Commander G. B. Palmes, Captain Marcus Wickham-Boynton and Captain V. M. G. and Mrs Wombwell; the Executors of the Will of the Marchioness of Crewe, the Battie Wrightson Trustees, the Trustees of the Will of Sir Somerled Bosville Macdonald of Sleat and the Trustees of the Winchilsea Settled Estates. I am also very grateful to the staff of the libraries and record offices listed in the Bibliography, and not least to Mr C. K. Croft Andrew, the former North Riding County Archivist, Miss A. G. Foster, formerly librarian of the Yorkshire Archaeological Society, Mr N. Higson, the East Riding County Archivist, and the archives staff of the Leeds and Sheffield Central Libraries.

I have received valuable help and advice from a number of fellow workers in this field, among them Mr G. C. F. Forster, Dr A. Gooder, Dr R. T. Spence and Mr P. Tyler, and I wish to record my gratitude

to them. For the map I am indebted to Dr June A. Sheppard and
Mr G. R. Brannon of the Department of Geography, Queen Mary
College, London University.

My greatest obligation is to Professor S. T. Bindoff who has guided
and encouraged me in this work ever since I first decided to embark on
a study of the Yorkshire gentry. Without his wise counsel, so
generously given, this book would never have seen the light of day.

Finally, I must thank the trustees of the Isobel Thornley Bequest
Fund for the grant which they have provided to assist in the publication of this volume.

Twickenham   J.T.C.
November 1968

CONTENTS

LIST OF PLATES

MAP

at the end

ABBREVIATIONS
USED IN FOOTNOTES

Al. Cant.   *Alumni Cantabrigienses. A biographical list of all known students, graduates and holders of office at the University of Cambridge, from the earliest times to 1751.* Ed. J. and J. A Venn. 4 vols. 1922–7

B.M.   British Museum

Cal.   *Calendar*

Cholmley Memoirs   *The Memoirs of Sir Hugh Cholmley…in which he gives some account of his family, and the distresses they underwent in the Civil Wars &c.* 1787

Clarendon   *The History of the Rebellion and Civil Wars in England…by Edward, Earl of Clarendon.* Ed. W. D. Macray. 6 vols. 1888

Clay   *Dugdale's Visitation of Yorkshire, with Additions.* Ed. J. W. Clay. 3 vols. 1899–1917

C.R.S.   *Catholic Record Society Publications*

D.N.B.   *Dictionary of National Biography*

Fairfax Correspondence   *The Fairfax Correspondence. Memoirs of the Reign of Charles the First.* Ed. G. W. Johnson. 2 vols. 1848

Foley   *Records of the English Province of the Society of Jesus.* Ed. H. Foley. 7 vols. 1877–83

H.M.C.   *Historical Manuscripts Commission Reports*

Knowler   *The Earl of Strafforde's Letters and Dispatches.* Ed. W. Knowler. 2 vols. 1739

N.R. Records   *The North Riding Record Society: Quarter Sessions Records.* Ed. J. C. Atkinson. vols. i–iv. 1884-6

P.R.O.   Public Record Office

Rushworth   John Rushworth, *Historical Collections of Private Passages of State, Weighty Matters in Law, Remarkable Proceedings in Five Parliaments.* 8 vols. 1721 edition

Slingsby Diary   *The Diary of Sir Henry Slingsby of Scriven, Bart.* Ed. D. Parsons. 1836

S.P.Dom.   State Papers Domestic, Public Record Office

V.C.H.   *Victoria County History*

Y.A.J.   *Yorkshire Archaeological Journal*

Y.A.S.R.S.   *Yorkshire Archaeological Society Record Series*

NOTE

In quotations from contemporary sources the original spelling has been retained but abbreviated words are given in full.

Except where otherwise stated (see Appendix A) the year is taken to begin on 1 January and not on 25 March which was still the practice in the period covered. In the footnotes, however, the dates of letters are shown in both styles.

CHAPTER I

The Social Fabric

IN THE sixteenth and seventeenth centuries, as today, the county of York was noted for the rich variety of its landscape. 'If in one place the soil be of a stony, sandy, barren nature', wrote William Camden, the celebrated Elizabethan antiquary, 'yet in another it is pregnant and fruitful; and so it be naked and exposed in one part, we find it cloathed and sheltered with great store of wood in another; Nature using an allay and mixture, that the entire County, by this variety of parts, might seem more pleasing and beautiful.'[1] To the contemporary traveller the shire seemed to consist of a virtually limitless countryside, in some places liberally sprinkled with villages and hamlets but also including large areas of moorland, forest and mountainous terrain which had few inhabitants. While road communications throughout England were generally poor the hard facts of topography added substantially to the difficulties of travel in a county which surpassed all others in size. Writing of his journeys in the summer of 1639 John Taylor the poet relates that on 5 September he left Wortley, near Penistone, with a guide whose services he had hired and 'rode to Hallifax 16 miles, the ways were so rocky, stony, boggy and mountaynous, that it was a days journey to ride so short a way'.[2]

Although Yorkshire was still a predominantly rural county the West Riding was the scene of a minor industrial revolution which in some areas was transforming the structure of the local economy and, to a certain extent, the face of the landscape. Sheffield was already nationally famous for its cutlery while in many places there were coalmines, sometimes driven horizontally into hill-sides, and iron mills, with their furnaces, quarries and water-courses, which made heavy demands on the surrounding woodlands. The most important industry, however, was the manufacture of cloth which provided employment for thousands of cottagers in the area around Leeds, Halifax, Bradford and

[1] William Camden, *Britannia*, 706.
[2] John Taylor, *Part of this Summers Travels*, 26.

Wakefield. In 1639 a report on the food situation in the wapentake of Agbrigg and Morley (an administrative division which broadly corresponded to the main clothing region) emphasised that 'above two partes of that whole division doe consist of tradeing, and for the rest, the Corne that doth growe on itt is not able to sustaine itt...for butter and cheese they are weekly supplyed from Ripon, Knaresborough and other places 30 miles of'.[1]

By present-day standards Yorkshire was sparsely populated. According to a modern estimate the total population at the end of the sixteenth century was probably rather more than 300,000[2] or roughly the size of the current population of Hull. In spite of the comparatively rapid growth of industry most Yorkshiremen were country-dwellers who depended, either directly or indirectly, on agriculture for their livelihood. None of the urban communities was as yet particularly large: in 1639, for example, John Taylor could write that Leeds was one of the most populous towns in England, 'it hath in it above 12,000 people'.[3] To contemporaries in southern England the inhabitants of Yorkshire (and indeed of the northern counties generally) seemed a wild race of people, unlettered, lawless and economically backward. When, shortly before the Civil War, a petition was drawn up seeking the establishment of a university at York the authors felt obliged to admit that 'we have been looked upon as rude and barbarous people'; they might truthfully have added, however, that over the preceding century there had been a spectacular increase in the number of grammar schools in the county.[4]

At the upper level of Yorkshire society were the nobility and gentry with their manor-houses (in some cases medieval castles) and their parks 'greatly stored with red and fallowe deer with conyes hares and fesannts partridges and whatsoever beastes or foules for game or use'.[5] During the sixteenth century the English aristocracy were a comparatively small class, partly because of the losses which they had sustained in the Wars of the Roses and partly because the Tudor monarchs kept a tight control over new creations. At the accession of Queen Elizabeth in 1558 six noblemen were actually seated in Yorkshire, men such as

[1] P.R.O., S.P.Dom., Charles I, S.P.16/cdxiv/125.
[2] A. G. Dickens, 'The Extent and Character of Recusancy in Yorkshire 1604', Y.A.J., xxxvii, 32–3.
[3] John Taylor, Part of this Summers Travels, 22.
[4] Fairfax Correspondence, ii, 278. See below, 67.
[5] James Ryther's description of Yorkshire, 1588 (B.M., Lansdowne MSS 119, f.115).

Henry Clifford, Earl of Cumberland, whose family had owned Skipton Castle since 1310 and who held property not only in Yorkshire but also in Cumberland, Westmorland, Northumberland, Derbyshire and Nottinghamshire.[1] In the early seventeenth century, as a result of the lavish creations of the Stuart kings, the nobility received a substantial infusion of new blood from the ranks of the wealthier gentry. In Yorkshire the process began in 1620 when Sir Henry Constable of Burton Constable was created Viscount Dunbar, a Scottish title, and before the outbreak of the Civil War no fewer than ten Yorkshire gentlemen in all had been raised to the peerage. [2]

In the aftermath of the Wars of the Roses the great nobles had to a large extent lost the old feudal power which had enabled them to behave like independent princes and the suppression of the Northern Rebellion in 1570 marked its final extinction. With the military decay of the aristocracy their prestige and influence came to depend primarily on other factors, on their social position and wealth, their court connections and their office-holding. Henceforth the most powerful nobleman north of the Trent was the lord president of the Council of the North who exercised the functions of viceregal government from the King's Manor at York and who had considerable resources of patronage at his disposal. During the early Stuart period (in sharp contrast with the practice in Elizabeth's reign) the lord president was invariably a member of the Yorkshire nobility.

Next in importance to the nobility, in terms of social status, were the gentry. The official badge of gentility was the coat of arms and for the purposes of this study the term 'gentry' has been taken to cover all families beneath the peerage which had a specific right to bear such arms. As a class symbol coats of arms were proudly displayed over manor-house doorways and on ceilings, windows, chimneypieces, family portraits, collections of plate and signet rings. In addition, such heraldic devices were often incorporated in church memorials: in the parish church of Boynton, for example, a number of monuments to members of the Strickland family are decorated with the turkey-cock crest which commemorates the fact that William Strickland, who was

---

[1] For the Cliffords, see J. W. Clay, 'The Clifford Family', *Y.A.J.*, xviii, 355 and R. T. Spence, 'The Cliffords Earls of Cumberland, 1579–1646' (unpublished London Ph.D. thesis, 1959).

[2] G.E.C. (ed.) *Complete Peerage*, iii, 27, 406, iv, 513, v, 229, 234, 264, xi, 461, xii, part ii, 516. Of these two were Scottish peers and four were Irish peers who were not entitled to sit in the House of Lords.

granted arms in 1550, was associated with the introduction of the turkey from America.

From the fifteenth century onwards the kings of arms (or chief heralds) were responsible for determining the authenticity of coats of arms and for granting armorial bearings to men whom they deemed worthy of the honour. In discharging these responsibilities they began in 1530 to undertake formal visitations of the counties, the primary object being 'to severe and distinguishe the worthie from those of the baser and vulgar sorte which unjustlie... usurpe and without true grounde assume and take upon them titles not due unto them'.[1] At these visitations the gentry were required to furnish proof that they were entitled to bear arms, either by a specific grant or by prescription. Opinion seems to have varied as to what constituted long usage in this context but according to a seventeenth-century note on the visitation procedure a gentleman who claimed to have a prescriptive right had to show that his lineal ancestors had made use of the same coat of arms for 'above 80 Yeares last past at the least'.[2] As the visitation system developed it became the normal practice for the heralds to hold their sittings in the most convenient towns but if necessary they were often prepared to visit the gentry in their own houses. 'And those', declared the herald at the Staffordshire visitation of 1583, 'that may not comodiously bringe with them such theire evidences, auncient writinges, and monuments as would serve to prove the antiquitie of theire race and familye, but shalbe desirous to have me home to theire houses, upon the significatyon of such theire desires, for the furtherance of Her Majesties service, I will make my repaire unto them soe soon as conveniently I maye.'[3] Gentlemen who successfully passed the test had their pedigrees and arms recorded in the official book of the visitation, though only if they were willing to pay the prescribed fees. Others who failed to satisfy the heralds were disclaimed in a proclamation forbidding them to use the style of gentleman and requiring the sheriff and other county officials to forbear from describing them by that title. In addition, the offending coats of arms were destroyed or defaced.[4]

[1] College of Arms: MS C.13, Yorkshire visitation book, 1612, f.1.
[2] Sir Anthony Wagner, *Heralds and Heraldry in the Middle Ages*, 3.
[3] *William Salt Archaeological Society: Collections for a History of Staffordshire* iii, The Visitation of Staffordshire 1583, 3.
[4] Sir Anthony Wagner, *Heralds and Heraldry in the Middle Ages*, 3–4. J. Foster (ed.), *The Visitation of Yorkshire in 1584–5 and 1612*, 406–7.

The first heraldic visitation of Yorkshire took place in 1530 and the last in 1665–6. Between these years there were several visitations, of which the most comprehensive were Robert Glover's visitation of 1584–5 and Richard St George's of 1612.[1] The pedigrees recorded on these occasions represent the main source of evidence in calculating the size of the Yorkshire gentry. They do not, however, provide us with a full catalogue of the gentry, partly because of the irregularity of the visitations (there was, for example, no visitation between 1612 and 1665) and partly because some men who were fully entitled to bear arms either failed to respond to the visitation summons or refused to pay the fees which were demanded for the entering of pedigrees. Consequently it has been necessary to supplement the visitation material with other sources of evidence, including records of grants of baronetcies, knighthoods, coats of arms and crests, private collections of pedigrees, parish registers, marriage licences, wills and administrations, and Exchequer subsidy rolls.[2]

From this evidence it can be said that in 1642 the Yorkshire gentry consisted of 679 families,[3] excluding families which owned property but were not seated in the county. In broad geographical terms these families were distributed as follows:

North Riding	195
East Riding	142
West Riding	320
York	22
Total	679

Within this class there were a number of groups of families which shared a common surname and were descended from the same family

---

[1] The Yorkshire visitation records are printed in *Surtees Society* xli, cxxii, cxxxiii and cxlvi, *Harleian Society* xvi, J. Foster (ed.), *op. cit.* and J. W. Clay (ed.), *Dugdale's Visitation of Yorkshire, with Additions.*

[2] The following list is not intended to be exhaustive. *Harleian Society* xxxvii–xl, lxvi, lxxxviii, xciv–xcvi. G.E.C. (ed.), *Complete Baronetage.* W. A. Shaw (ed.), *The Knights of England.* Y.A.S.R.S., i, ix, xi, xxvi, xxxii, xxxv, xl, xliii. *Yorkshire Parish Register Society* publications. P.R.O., Exchequer, Lay Subsidy Rolls (E.179).

[3] For statistical purposes the family unit includes the head of the family, his wife and children, his younger brothers and unmarried sisters, and the widow of any previous head of the family. Where, however, the head and a younger brother both had adult sons these have been counted as two separate families.

In the case of Kent it has been estimated that in 1640 there were at least 800 and possibly more than 1000 gentry (A. M. Everitt, *The Community of Kent and the Great Rebellion, 1640–60*, 33–4).

2—Y.G.

stock. In 1582 William Camden noted that the Saviles were 'a very numerous family in these parts'[1] and sixty years later there were eight distinct branches still surviving. The Constables, however, surpassed even the Saviles in this respect: in 1642 they consisted of twelve separate families, not including the Constables of Burton Constable who had been raised to the peerage.

If the gentry represented one of the upper segments in an essentially hierarchic society they also had their own internal stratification. From 1611, when the order of baronetcy was created, they embraced four distinct social categories: baronets, knights, esquires and plain gentlemen. The following table shows the basic structure of the Yorkshire gentry in 1642.

Families in which
(a) the head was a baronet	28
(b) some member other than the head was a baronet	2
(c) the head was a knight[2]	61
(d) some member other than the head was a knight	9
(e) the head was styled 'esquire'	256
(f) the head was styled 'gentleman'	323

In the reign of Elizabeth knighthoods were granted sparingly. One of the factors responsible for the indebtedness of Sir Thomas Reresby of Thrybergh (we learn from the family history) was 'his following the Court without any other recompence then empty knighthood (though very rare and consequently of great honor in thos days)'.[3] During the early Stuart period, however, the situation was radically different. In 1603, following the accession of James I, no fewer than sixty Yorkshiremen were knighted, many of them at York where the new king lodged on his way to London. In the main these were representatives of the major squirearchy but they also included such men as George Palmes of Naburn and Ingleby Daniell of Beswick who were of comparatively modest estate.[4] Although the creation of knights on this scale was exceptional (the king was anxious to gain the support of the gentry for his succession) the Stuart monarchs continued to inflate the currency up to the time of the Civil War. In these circum-

1 William Camden, *Britannia*, 710.
2 This excludes one family, the Dawneys of Cowick, in which the head, Sir Thomas Dawney, was a knight and his grandson Sir Christopher a baronet.
3 B.M., Additional MSS 29442, f.46.
4 W. A. Shaw (ed.), *The Knights of England*, ii, 100–29.

stances the order of baronetcy provided that special type of distinction which a knighthood had once conferred, particularly since the new title was hereditary. At the outset the Crown promised to control the grant of baronetcies in such a way as to create a comparatively small élite of prime gentry. In the first place, the number of baronets was not to exceed 200 for the whole country. Secondly, the honour would only be granted to men with estates worth £1000 a year or more whose paternal grandfathers had possessed coats of arms. In practice the first of these undertakings was ignored but in spite of this the baronets never amounted to more than a small minority of the gentry. Between 1611 and 1642 thirty-five Yorkshiremen were made baronets (a figure which includes three Nova Scotia baronets as those instituted into the Scottish order were called).[1] Although the earlier recipients generally paid for the honour at the normal rate[2] rather more than half these men were discharged from payment. The free grant of baronetcies, which was particularly common in the reign of Charles I, reached a peak in the years 1641 and 1642 when fourteen Yorkshire gentlemen were favoured in this way. Like his father in 1603 Charles I was using the honours system in an attempt to muster support among the squirearchy.[3]

During this period many gentlemen were said to be using the style of 'esquire' without justification. Although there was some disagreement over the precise definition the heralds appear in practice to have recognised three broad categories of persons who could be classed as esquires. In the first place, there were the heirs male and descendants of baronets, knights and noblemen's younger sons. Secondly, there were the heads of ancient families who had a prescriptive right because they could show that their lineal ancestors had used this title over a considerable period. Thirdly, sheriffs, justices of the peace and other officials who were not otherwise entitled could use the style of 'esquire' for as long as they remained in their appointments.[4] Not surprisingly, the esquires were on the whole possessed of larger estates than the plain gentlemen, many of whom were the heads of cadet branches or families

---

[1] For the order of baronetcy see F. W. Pixley, *A History of the Baronetage*.
[2] See below, 111.
[3] G.E.C. (ed.), *Complete Baronetage*, ii, 115, 128, 136, 149, 156, 161, 174, 176, 185, 187, 189, 194. The inflation of honours is discussed in L. Stone's *The Crisis of the Aristocracy, 1558–1641*, 65–128.
[4] See Sir Anthony Wagner, *Heralds and Heraldry in the Middle Ages*, 5.

which had comparatively new coats of arms. This fact was well understood by contemporaries who saw a close link between social rank and
landed wealth. In the middle years of Elizabeth's reign a Catholic
prisoner at Hull was obliged to pay 6s. 8d. a week for the rent of his
cell if he was an esquire and 5s. a week if he was a mere gentleman.
Similarly, when the House of Commons decided in June 1641 to
introduce a poll tax it was agreed that baronets should be charged £30,
knights £20 and esquires £10, while gentlemen worth £100 a year
were to pay £5.[1]

In a society which was so stratified it is hardly surprising that
excessive importance should have been attached to questions of
social rank. Writing to his father-in-law in June 1611 Sir Henry
Savile of Methley, who had decided to purchase a baronetcy, explained
his wishes with regard to the insertion of his name in the book of
baronets: 'For my place amongst my Cuntriemen I desyre neither to be
first nor laste; I can be content to followe Mr Wentworth and Sir
Henry Bellasis, for any other I yet heare of I may without any great
incongruitye be rankt afore them.' As a subsequent letter makes clear,
however, he was not a little concerned about the reaction which his
acquisition of the honour might provoke, at least 'amongst my better
kyndred and neighbors who will thinke much to see me leape before
them, our byrthes beinge equall and my state [estate] inferiour'.[2] In
May 1612 the king issued a decree announcing that baronets would be
regarded as next in degree to the younger sons of barons. On the
strength of this ruling Sir Henry Savile and Sir Henry Bellasis, both of
whom were members of the Council of the North, claimed precedence
over their legal colleagues on the board notwithstanding the fact that
it was considered necessary on practical grounds to have the lawyers
seated near the lord president. In a letter to Lord Sheffield, the lord
president, they argued that since there were only two baronets on the
Council they could not 'much depress the feed [salaried] counsellors in
their sittings by the interposition of one single man betwixt the President and them'. If (they told Lord Sheffield) their request was turned
down they would prefer to be left out of the Council rather than serve
the king to his prejudice and their own dishonour. Although the king
was inclined to favour the claims of the lawyers the baronets continued

---

[1] Borthwick Institute of Historical Research: High Commission Act Book, 1576–80,
RVII/AB/6, f.58. *Lord Somers's Tracts*, iv, 298–9.
[2] J. J. Cartwright (ed.), *Chapters in the History of Yorkshire*, 345, 347.

to press their case and in the end a compromise was worked out which was apparently satisfactory to both parties.[1]

This emphasis on degree and precedence gave rise to considerable litigation in the Court of Chivalry which, to judge from its surviving records, was particularly active in the reign of Charles I.[2] Not long before the Civil War John Constable of Catfoss, an East Riding landowner, was put to great trouble in seeking to prove his right to style himself 'esquire'. In 1639 his kinsman Christopher Constable of Great Hatfield, also described as 'esquire', brought an action against him, alleging that he had recently assumed this style and as a result had 'taken place and used precedency' in both York and London. He had done this (the plaintiff related) in spite of the fact that he had no right or just claim to the title, not being descended of any knight of his family. Between 11 and 14 January 1640 an inquiry was held at Beverley and evidence taken from numerous witnesses. Some men testified to having seen old deeds in which ancestors of John Constable had styled themselves knights or esquires; others referred to an inscription on a tombstone in the church of Sigglesthorne (the parish church of Catfoss): 'Hic jacet Johanes Constable de Catfoss armiger qui obiit xxiiijto mensis...' On 23 April 1640 Garter, Clarenceux and Norroy kings of arms certified that the defendant and his ancestors had employed the title of 'esquire' over a long period and that he was the lineal heir male of Sir John Constable of Freshmarsh who was living in the reign of Richard II; consequently in their view he had a just right to the style of 'esquire'. At the same time they confirmed that Christopher Constable was the lineal heir male of Sir William Constable who had lived in the reign of Henry VIII and therefore he too was entitled to call himself 'esquire'. In the light of this report it comes as a surprise to find that John Constable was required to pay £20 damages and £30 costs and to make submission. This, however, was not the end of the matter. As the result of subsequent cross-proceedings the earlier verdict was reversed and Christopher Constable was fined £60 damages and £60 costs.[3]

More often the Court of Chivalry was called upon to deal with the type of case in which one man was alleged to have cast aspersions on

[1] *H.M.C. Various*, ii, 113. R. R. Reid, *The King's Council in the North*, 375–6.
[2] See G. D. Squibb, *The High Court of Chivalry*, 56.
[3] *Harleian Society*, cvii, 35–9, 48. G. Poulson, *The History and Antiquities of the Seigniory of Holderness*, i, 438.

another's gentility with 'scandalous words provocative of a duel'. In 1640 Thomas Keresforth of Dodworth, an attorney, presented a bill against Robert Scamadine of Barnsley. This referred to an earlier suit which he had commenced against Gervase Eyre who had claimed that he was neither a gentleman nor a Keresforth. In August 1639 (Keresforth alleged) Scamadine had repeated Eyre's statement, saying that he knew all those who were of the house of Keresforth and that the coat of arms which the plaintiff had exhibited did not belong to him. According to one witness Scamadine had argued that the plaintiff's name was Kesforth and not Keresforth and that consequently he was not entitled to bear arms. In addition, he had declared that Keresforth was not a gentleman and indeed could not be a gentleman because his father was a tailor. Unfortunately no record of the final verdict has survived but the probability is that Keresforth won his case since the pedigree registered at the visitation of 1665–6 shows him to be descended from a younger brother of Richard Keresforth of Keresforth Hill who was certainly armigerous.[1]

In view of the importance of status and degree in the eyes of the gentry it was natural that they should take a close interest in their personal ancestry and kinship. Men with social pretensions who had purchased coats of arms tended to be regarded with amusement or derision: ancient lineage, on the other hand, was a source of pride and respect. Shortly after the visitation of 1612 Thomas Meynell of North Kilvington, the head of a North Riding Catholic family, wrote in his commonplace book: 'TIME will produce with the grace of god an orderly pedigree out of the Court of honour: the way is layd, and the evidences will attest the truth. I dare boldly say no family of England can more exactly fetch and derive them selves, even from the Conquest.' In describing his ancestry Meynell refers to the great debt which he owed his mother, who was a daughter of Anthony Catterick of Stanwick: 'I had by hir some lands in Thornton in the Streete and other good prefermente: but which I more esteeme, I had also by hir ffyve worthie Cote Armors and as many Crestes, viz. twoo by Cathericke, twoo by Tempest, one by Umfrevill.' After listing his ancestors Meynell goes on to delineate the complex marriage alliances through which his family was connected with many families of quality not only in the North Riding but also in the West and East Ridings. Even the most distant relationships were considered worthy of inclusion if they

[1] *Harleian Society*, cvii, 48. Clay, i, 40–1.

involved families of eminence: 'There was ever an ancient league of friendshippe betwixt the Constables of Burton Constable and mine Auncesters. The Cause is now greater then before for Sir John Constable grandfather to Sir Henry that now is maried one of the daughters of ... Lord John Scrope', the grandfather of Meynell's first wife. 'Sir Henrie that now is and my children are third and third in bloud.'[1]

Kinship was not simply a matter of genealogical interest. Contemporary opinion held that ties of blood, however tenuous, involved special obligations and loyalties and this concept of clan solidarity was an important factor not only in normal social intercourse but also in public life. A great personage such as the lord president of the Council of the North felt entitled to the support and allegiance of his kinsmen as a matter of course while they in turn expected him to reward them with offices and other favours. When Lord Scroope became lord president in 1619 Sir Richard Cholmley of Whitby, 'being cousin-german to him half removed, held himself obliged, not only to wait upon him, but to appear in such a posture as was suitable to their relation, and the quality of Sir Richard's person, who was now looked on as the head of his family, his father being dead'. On Lord Scroope's entry into Yorkshire Sir Richard met him near Doncaster with a retinue of twenty mounted servants. This gesture did not go unacknowledged: soon afterwards Lord Scroope made him a deputy lieutenant and appointed him to the Council of the North.[2] Twenty years later Sir William Strickland of Boynton recalled in a letter to Lord Wentworth (the then lord president) that his lordship had not only honoured him with a commission as deputy lieutenant but had been

pleased to acknowledge me as a partaker of your bloode, as being descended of a Wentworthe, in which respecte, if your lordships affaires doe require it, nothing shall be more visible, then that my veines are filled with your bloode, which is but reserved to be employed in your service: and I hope this felicitie shall be transmitted to my posteritie for my boye will be alltogeather Wentworthe, deriveing one halfe from his mother and the reste from my selfe.[3]

In his work *The Blazon of Gentrie*, published in 1586, Sir John Ferne emphasised that a gentleman should never marry outside his own class:

it is the unequall coupling in yoke of the cleane Oxe, and uncleane Asse, an

---

[1] *C.R.S.*, lvi, 2, 4–13. [2] *Cholmley Memoirs*, 21–2. See also 237 below.
[3] Sheffield Central Library: Strafford Letters, xviii. Sir William Strickland to Lord Wentworth, 3 February 1638(–9).

iniurie not onely done to the person of the yong Gentleman, but eeke a dishonor to the whole house from which he is discended...Are we carefull then, from what tree our plant is taken? Of what kind our dogs come? And of what race our horses are bred? And shall we hold it nothing to the purpose of what parents a Gentleman is begotten?[1]

Christopher Wandesford of Kirklington also believed that a gentleman should take a wife of similar degree to himself but more for practical reasons than because of any theoretical considerations about the mixing of gentle and ignoble blood. In advising his son about the choice of a wife he wrote:

For her Birth, certainly the wisest Rule that can be, is to affect Parity according to that Degree you shall be in when you marry. This is within the excellent Rule of Mediocrity; many Inconveniencies follow upon either Extream. Those above you *too much*, commonly expect more Regard from you, and more Expence upon her Person, than your Contentment, or Estate can well yield to her. On the other Side from a Match too inferior, however she may think Obligation calls upon her to respect you the more, yet thereby may fall *some Contempt* upon your Children and Posterity.

At the same time Wandesford recognised that there were other factors to be taken into account, including the size of her marriage portion: 'the greater her Fortune is, (where the Rest of the requisites be had in a reasonable Manner,) the more Cause of Comfort you bring to yourself in present, and hereafter a great Acknowledgement from your Posterity'.[2] For gentlemen with competent estates social rank could never be the sole criterion: indeed the marriage of an heir did not normally take place until the two families had reached agreement on the terms of a formal settlement specifying the amount of the bride's portion and the jointure which was to be provided for her widowhood.[3] In the main the prime gentry intermarried either with the nobility or with gentle families of comparable social and financial status. Occasionally a major landowner took as his bride, or married his eldest son to, the widow or heiress of a city merchant but this was still rare enough to merit comment. In contrast, the inferior gentry were far less exclusive in their marriage alliances, at least in social terms, and at this

---

[1] Sir John Ferne, *The Blazon of Gentrie*, 9–10, 12.
[2] Christopher Wandesford, *A Book of Instructions*, 51–2.
[3] For marriage settlements see L. Stone, *The Crisis of the Aristocracy, 1558–1641*, 589–671 and H. J. Habakkuk, 'Marriage Settlements in the Eighteenth Century', *Transactions of the Royal Historical Society*, Fourth Series, xxxii, 15.

level there was frequent intermarriage with commercial and yeoman families. Throughout the gentry it was customary for a marriage to be arranged between the respective families without too much attention being paid to the wishes of the young couple; nevertheless there were undoubtedly cases where a father gave his consent to a love match even though from his point of view it was hardly an advantageous marriage. In his memoirs Sir Hugh Cholmley of Whitby relates that his ancestor Sir Richard Cholmley, who was one of the wealthiest squires in Elizabethan Yorkshire, had intended that his daughter Katherine should marry Lord Lumley but she fell in love with Richard Dutton, 'a gentleman but a younger brother', who was her music teacher. In spite of the difference in station Sir Richard allowed her to marry Dutton and at his death left her a substantial portion in land and money.[1] On the other hand, parents were not inclined to be so understanding in the case of a runaway marriage, especially if the other partner was of humble origin. During the reign of Charles I (we learn from a Chancery suit of 1650) Isabel Acclom, a daughter of Sir William Acclom of Moreby, went to live with her grandfather Sir Thomas Dawney and while residing at Cowick Hall 'overthrew her fortunes' by marrying one of Sir Thomas's serving men. As a result she was banished from his house and disowned by her family and kinfolk.[2]

2

Even in the reign of Charles I there were many country squires who could trace their ancestry back to the medieval knightly class from which the gentry had evolved. Of the 679 families of 1642 at least 270 had been represented in the ranks of the Yorkshire gentry as early as 1500. Some families like the Vavasours and the Maleverers had Norman surnames; others like the Wortleys and the Arthingtons were still seated in the villages from which they derived their names. Typical of this group of ancient gentry was Sir William Ingleby of Ripley, near Harrogate, who was created a baronet in 1642. The family had acquired Ripley Castle (which is still in their possession) in the fourteenth century, apparently as the result of an advantageous marriage by Sir Thomas de Ingilby, one of the justices of the common pleas. Had the

[1] *Cholmley Memoirs*, 8–9.
[2] P.R.O., Chancery Proceedings Six Clerks' Series, C.9/6/146.

antiquity of his family ever been questioned Sir William could have pointed out the tomb of Sir Thomas de Ingilby, with its recumbent effigy, and the other monuments to his ancestors (among them his grandfather who had rebuilt the castle) in the parish church of Ripley.[1]

In the reign of Henry VIII an event occurred which was to have a profound impact on the gentry. At the time of their suppression the monasteries owned vast estates which must have represented a substantial proportion of the total land area of England. As a result of the dissolution all this property came into the possession of the Crown which in turn sold (or exceptionally gave away) the greater part of it, a process which continued beyond the end of the sixteenth century. Most of this land passed in the first instance into the hands of noblemen, courtiers and central government officials, often in large blocks which might include the possessions of several monasteries. Occasionally one of these purchasers took the opportunity to lay the foundations of a country estate: Sir Thomas Chaloner, for example, bought Guisborough Priory in 1550 and settled it on his son and namesake who made it the family seat.[2] As a general rule, however, such men sold their acquisitions in smaller parcels to members of the local gentry or to persons of substance who were seeking to enter the gentry. According to the family history Sir Richard Cholmley of Roxby 'was a great improver of his estate, and purchased lands of great value, within the county of York; amongst others, the manors of Whitby, Whitby Laythes and Stakesby, with the demesne lands belonging to them, parcel of the monastery of Whitby'. These manors had originally been granted to the Earl of Warwick in 1550 and he in turn had sold them to Sir John Yorke, treasurer of the Mint, who already owned a considerable amount of former monastic property in Nidderdale. In 1555, after putting up the rents of his tenants, Sir John conveyed the Whitby estates to Sir Richard Cholmley and in the next generation the Cholmleys took up residence in a new house adjoining the abbey.[3] In south Yorkshire Nostell Priory and its estates changed hands in similar fashion. In 1540 Dr Thomas Leigh, one of the commissioners who had carried out a visitation of the monasteries on the eve of their dissolution, paid the Crown £1126. 13s. 4d. for the house and site of

[1] J. J. Sheahan, *History and Topography of the Wapentake of Claro*, 228–31.
[2] *V.C.H.*, *N.R.*, ii, 358.
[3] *Cholmley Memoirs*, 6–7, 12. *Cal. Patent Rolls, Edward VI, 1549–51*, 372 and *1550–3*, 34. *Cal. Patent Rolls, Philip and Mary, 1554–5*, 257–8. *Selden Society*, xii, 198–205.

Nostell Priory and extensive property which had formerly belonged to the priory. These estates passed by marriage to Lord Mountjoy who in 1567 sold the priory and some of the neighbouring lands to Sir Thomas Gargrave of Kinsley, vice-president of the Council of the North, for the sum of £3560.[1]

If the local gentry were buying land on an impressive scale from speculators and middlemen they were also represented among the original grantees of monastic property. Those who obtained direct grants from the Crown often had positions of influence in the county. They included several of the gentlemen who had been appointed commissioners for surveying the lands and goods of the Yorkshire monasteries: Sir Marmaduke Constable of Everingham who bought Drax Priory for the sum of £200; Sir William Babthorpe of Osgodby who significantly increased his East Riding estates; and Sir Leonard Beckwith of Selby, receiver of the Court of Augmentations in Yorkshire, who secured various manors and rectories which had formerly been in the possession of Selby Abbey.[2]

Many of the religious houses and granges which passed into private hands took on a new role as family seats. At Nostell Priory the Gargraves converted part of the monastery buildings into a manorhouse and embellished the walls with heraldic devices.[3] In other cases a new house was built on an adjoining site with masonry taken from the deserted ruins. At Fountains Abbey, for example, Sir Stephen Proctor pulled down one of the domestic buildings and used the stones to construct a fine Jacobean mansion close to the abbey gatehouse.[4]

By the end of the sixteenth century most of the landed property of the Yorkshire monasteries was in the possession of the country gentry. This major transfer of land, which included valuable mineral resources, resulted in a spectacular increase in the economic wealth of the squirearchy, not least since many of the new owners were soon engaged in the development and exploitation of the premises. Some idea of the extent of this process may be gained from the fact that over one-quarter of the gentle families of 1642 (182 out of 679) owned property which had

[1] J. Hunter, *South Yorkshire*, ii, 210. *Letters and Papers of the Reign of Henry VIII*, xv, 175. *Cal. Patent Rolls, Elizabeth I, 1566–9*, 118.

[2] *Letters and Papers of the Reign of Henry VIII*, x, 304, xiii part i, 569, xvii part ii, 60 and xix, 17. *Cal. Patent Rolls, Edward VI, 1550–3*, 133.

[3] J. Hunter, *South Yorkshire*, ii, 219.

[4] J. J. Sheahan, *History and Topography of the Wapentake of Claro*, 67.

been seized from the monasteries. While many ancient families benefited from the dissolution of the monasteries (in some cases substantially enlarging their estates) the availability of land on this scale also opened the way for the entry of new families into the ranks of the gentry, families such as the Armitages of Kirklees Priory, the Ramsdens of Longley and the Hutchinsons of Wykeham Abbey.

During the reign of Elizabeth and beyond the Yorkshire gentry continued to grow in strength, the number of families increasing from 557 in 1558 to 679 in 1642. This net increase, however, gives no real indication of the highly complex and fluid situation which existed. On one side of the balance sheet there were heavy losses to be recorded:

> total number of gentle families, 1558–1642   963
> number of families which
>   (a) entered the nobility[1]   9
>   (b) died out in the male line   181
>   (c) left the county   64
>   (d) disappeared without trace   30
>   Total   284

In view of the high rate of infant mortality, the prevalence of epidemics and the primitive state of English medicine it is hardly surprising to find so many families dying out in the male line. On the face of it, the danger was greatest in the case of Catholic families which were in the habit of sending their younger sons abroad to become priests and monks; in practice, however, such families showed a remarkable capacity for survival.

Families which left the county were often in severe financial straits. Having disposed of their estates to meet the demands of their creditors they were no doubt strongly averse to the idea of living in humiliating poverty among men whom they had been accustomed to treat as their social inferiors.[2] Some gentlemen (not necessarily in financial difficulties) hoped to advance their fortunes in Ireland either by acquiring lucrative offices or by securing grants of land under the scheme for the plantation of Ulster. When Sir Hugh Wyrrall of Loversall was summoned to appear at the herald's visitation of the county in 1612 the herald was informed that 'This Sir Hugh Wyrrall hath sould Levershall, and is

---

[1] In the case of one family (the Saviles of Howley) the father and his heir were both raised to the peerage in 1628.
[2] See below, 157–8.

become one of the undertakers of Ulster in Ireland, and hath wholie planted himself and his families'.[1] Another Yorkshire squire, Oswald Bankes of Whixley, had similar intentions but was drowned when the ship on which he was travelling sank in St George's Channel; unfortunately for his heir he had with him the proceeds from the sale of his estate.[2] When Lord Wentworth took up his duties as lord deputy of Ireland in 1633 a number of Yorkshire gentlemen accompanied him or subsequently went out there and were granted offices or benefices.[3] In the main these were mere birds of passage who eventually returned to Yorkshire but a few intended to settle themselves and their families permanently in Ireland. In 1635 Sir Edward Dodsworth of Troutsdale arrived in Dublin with his wife and family, having sold a great part of his estate for their maintenance in the expectation that Wentworth would appoint him to some profitable office. In a letter of introduction which he brought with him from Richard Marris, Wentworth's steward in Yorkshire, the latter asked his master to allow him a plantation in Lower Ormonde and suggested that he might make good use of his services in the government of Coleraine or Derry.[4]

During this period a number of Yorkshire gentry went to live abroad for religious reasons. After the failure of the Northern Rebellion in 1570 several Catholic landowners who had taken up arms against the Crown sought refuge in Spain, Italy or the Spanish Netherlands.[5] In 1612 Sir Ralph Babthorpe of Osgodby, a recusant squire who had been persecuted by the Northern High Commission, settled with his wife at Louvain where, it was reported, he lived so religious a life that he was held up as an example to his fellow Catholics who were domiciled there. After his death in 1617 his wife Lady Grace Babthorpe entered the convent of St Monica at Louvain.[6]

These Catholic refugees had their counterparts in the Puritan gentry who, discontented with the prevailing trends within the Church of England, decided to seek religious freedom in New England or the Dutch Netherlands. Of the Yorkshire Puritans who emigrated to America the most socially distinguished was a substantial West Riding landowner, Sir Richard Saltonstall of Huntwick Grange. At a

[1] J. Foster (ed.), *The Visitation of Yorkshire in 1584–5 and 1612*, 349. Sir Hugh had received a grant of land in Ireland in 1610 (P.R.O., Signet Office Docquets, Index 6803, no pagination).
[2] B.M., Harleian MSS 4630, 71.   [3] See below, 87.
[4] Sheffield Central Library: Strafford Letters, xx. Marris to Wentworth, 28 May 1635.
[5] See below, 171.   [6] Foley, iii, 192, 198–9. See below, 177.

conference held in Cambridge on 26 August 1629 twelve members of
the Massachusetts Bay Company, including Sir Richard, resolved
that within six months' time they would go to New England with
their families and establish a plantation there. Having disposed of his
estates Sir Richard set off with his family in March 1630, travelling
in the *Arbella* from Cowes. Although he is regarded as the founder of
Watertown he did not remain there for long: within a year of
his arrival he had returned to England (though not to Yorkshire)
leaving several members of his family behind him.[1] In March
1631 Sir Richard's steward in Watertown described in a letter how
the Saltonstalls were faring in their new environment. 'The Country',
he wrote,

is very good, and fitt to receive Lords and Ladies, if there were more good
houses, both for good land and good water, and for good creatures to hunt
and to hawke, and for fowling and fisheing...besides his great family [Sir
Richard] hath many Cattle and kyne, and horse and swine, and some Goats
and poultry, he hath also much building at his owne house, and fenceing,
ploweing and planteing, and also to helpe build the new Citty, and first for
a house for God to dwell in, these things will require my best diligence.[2]

Although the Yorkshire gentry sustained heavy losses in this period
these were more than counterbalanced by the emergence of new cadet
branches, the grant of coats of arms to the socially ambitious and the
infusion of gentle families from other counties. In the main, cadet
branches sprang from the wealthier families which had land to spare:
further down the scale younger sons tended to leave the county (and
sometimes the kingdom) in pursuit of a career. Gentlemen who came
and settled in Yorkshire fall into three broad categories: lawyers and
other professional men who took up Crown appointments, usually at
York; fortune hunters who married Yorkshire heiresses; and moneyed
men who bought up estates in the county.

Between 1558 and 1642 a total of 102 Yorkshiremen obtained
coats of arms. In the patents recording such grants the heralds tended
to stress the personal qualities of the recipients: thus in 1563 Norroy
king of arms noted that Robert Sotheby of Birdsall was 'descended of
a house undefamed and hath of long used himselfe so honestly and

---

[1] *Massachusetts Historical Society Collections*, Second Series, iv, 454–6, and Fifth
Series, i, 216. F. Rose-Troup, *The Massachusetts Bay Company and its Predecessors*, 19,
153. C. E. Banks, *The Winthrop Fleet of 1630*, 20, 53, 90.
[2] B.M., Egerton MSS 2645, f.245. See also below, 306–8.

discreetly that he hath well deserved to be, in all places of honour, admitted, numbered, and taken in the number and company of other nobles and gentils'.[1] Moral worth, however, was not a sufficient qualification in itself. Above all the herald needed to be satisfied that the aspirant could maintain himself without manual labour and that he was wealthy enough to uphold a style of living appropriate to the status of a gentleman. In December 1641 Stephen Bright of Carbrook received a grant of arms from Sir John Borough, Garter king of arms, who (it was recorded at the visitation of 1665–6) considered him 'to be a man of £1000 a yeare estate, and of credit and respect in the affections of the gentrye and extraordinary merits'.[2] If, however, the would-be gentleman was normally expected to have landed property it was un-necessary for him to be so richly endowed; indeed some yeomen who were granted arms at the visitation of 1612 owned estates worth no more than £50 or £100 a year.

Sir John Ferne wrote in *The Blazon of Gentrie* that knowledge of the law was considered sufficient cause

to aduaunce the professour to nobleness, and the bearing of Armes...If any person be aduaunced into an office or dignity, of publique administration, be it eyther Ecclesiasticall, Martiall, or Ciuill: so that the same office compre-hendeth in it...either dignitie (or at the least) a title of dignitie: the Heralde must not refuse, to devise to such a publique person, upon his instant request, and willingnes to beare the same without reproche, a coate of Armes.

On the other hand, he contended that it was wrong for persons en-gaged in trade to be granted arms: 'Merchaundizinge is no competent or seemelye trade of lyfe, for a gentleman.'[3] In Yorkshire the recipients of arms included not only lawyers and professional servants of the Crown but successful merchants who saw nothing incongruous in continuing in business after entering the ranks of the gentry. Occasion-ally a steward or bailiff in the employment of a great nobleman was also honoured in this way: in 1586, for example, William Ferrand was granted arms at the request of his master Francis, Earl of Cumberland.[4] In the final analysis, however, it was the yeomanry who represented the greatest source of recruitment and in fact roughly half the York-shiremen who bought their way into the gentry in the period 1558–1642 can be identified as yeoman farmers.

[1] *Surtees Society*, xli, Appendix, xl.   [2] Clay, ii, 12.
[3] Sir John Ferne, *The Blazon of Gentrie*, 38, 58–9, 69, 72.   [4] Clay, iii, 95.

3

Although the Yorkshire gentry were basically a rural class it would be misleading to picture them simply as a backwoods squirearchy immersed in country pursuits and unmindful of trends and developments outside their own narrow world. During the assize week many gentlemen from all over the county converged on York where they attended the high sheriff and the judges, enjoyed the sheriff's hospitality and exchanged the latest news and gossip. Besides this well-established custom it was also not unusual, at least in the early seventeenth century, for the more substantial families to make frequent visits to York and even to take up residence there for a time. Some families were primarily interested in the social pleasures afforded by the northern capital while others were anxious to avoid the expense of country housekeeping during a period of financial difficulty.[1] In addition, a family seated in a remote part of the county might prefer to sojourn in York rather than endure a long hard winter on a windswept coast or in a bleak moorland area cut off by snow or flooding.[2] In 1634 a party of travellers from Norwich noted in their journal that there were a number of gentlemen residing in York, among them Sir Arthur Ingram of Temple Newsam and his son and namesake, Sir William Lister of Thornton, Sir William Ingram of Little Cattal, Sir Henry Jenkins of Great Busby and Sir Thomas Danby of Masham. Sir Arthur Ingram owned a splendid mansion which he had built on the site of the archiepiscopal palace adjoining the Minster. In 1639 another visitor to the city wrote of this house, rather grudgingly, that it was 'low, noe extraordinary building, but very commodious and stately and spacious enough, though not suitable to his estate'; in the same year, however, the vice-president of the Council of the North described it as the only house in York fit to receive the king.[3] Other houses in the general neighbourhood of the Minster belonged to Sir William Savile of Thornhill and Sir Henry Slingsby of Scriven. Towards the south side of the medieval city Sir Henry Goodricke of Ribston owned a house known as Trinity's in Micklegate while his son-in-law Sir Richard Hawksworth of Hawks-

---

[1] For the latter practice see below, 151.
[2] See, for example, Knowler, i, 60.
[3] L. G. Wickham Legg (ed.), *A Relation of a Short Survey of 26 Counties*, 17, 21. *Surtees Society*, cxviii, 4. *H.M.C. Coke MSS* ii, 212.

worth had a residence in Walmgate which he had bought in 1632.[1] Sometimes a gentleman lent his town-house to a relative or leased it to a merchant or lawyer who earned his living in the city. In 1601 Philip Constable of Everingham granted a lease of his house near Monk Bar for forty-one years but included the proviso that he and his heirs should have the use of a lodging parlour as the need arose.[2]

In this period many Yorkshire gentry had occasion to journey southward for one reason or another. Not infrequently these were adolescents who were entering the universities or the inns of court or taking up apprenticeships with London merchants and tradesmen. In addition, a gentleman might find it necessary to travel up to London to sit in the House of Commons, or render his accounts as sheriff of the county or, more often, prosecute a lawsuit in one of the courts at Westminster. Another reason for travel was a desire to test the efficacy of the waters at Bath or Buxton. References to such journeys can be found as early as the reign of Elizabeth: William Hussey of North Duffield, for example, was temporarily released from custody (he was a Catholic prisoner) to visit Buxton in 1567 and Bath in 1569. As its amenities improved Bath gained in popularity with the gentry and in the early seventeenth century it was relatively common for a Yorkshire squire in failing health to go there in search of a cure.[3]

Clarendon writes of his father, Henry Hyde of Dinton in Wiltshire, that 'from the Death of queen Elizabeth, He never was in London, though He lived above thirty Years after; and his Wife, who was married to him above forty Years, never was in London in her life; the Wisdom and Frugality of that Time being such, that few Gentlemen made Journies to London, or any other expensive Journies, but upon important Business, and their Wives never'.[4] This observation which primarily referred to the Wiltshire gentry may be applied, as a broad generalisation, to the Yorkshire gentry but only in the reign of Elizabeth. In the early seventeenth century the picture is rather different: gentlemen of substance were tending to visit London more frequently and to remain there for longer periods, often with their wives and

---

[1] *Y.A.S.R.S.*, cxviii, 13. Y.A.S. Library: Slingsby MSS, Box B8. P.R.O., Chancery, *Inquisitions Post Mortem*, Charles I, C.142/dcclxxiv/19. Sheffield Central Library: Bright MSS, BR 89(b).

[2] Beverley County Record Office: Maxwell–Constable MSS, DDEV/35/3 and 4.

[3] Borthwick Institute of Historical Research: High Commission Act Books, 1566–R.VII/AB/15, f.107 and 1568–9, R.VII/AB/12, f.78.

[4] Edward Earl of Clarendon, *The Life*, i, 5.

children accompanying them. To a large extent this development must have been due to the emergence of the private coach as a common mode of conveyance for the wealthier members of the community. For the first time women and children were able to travel if not in luxury at least with a reasonable degree of comfort. During the early Stuart period many of the leading Yorkshire gentry owned coaches and there is ample evidence to show that they were being used on occasion for journeys to London: indeed there was a considerable traffic problem created by the multitude of gentlemen's coaches which filled the streets.[1]

In some cases a Yorkshire squire took his wife and children to London for medical reasons. In 1637 William Rokeby of Skiers had six of his children under treatment for rickets, a clear indication that the rich as well as the poor had deficiencies in their diet.[2] Two years later Sir Henry Slingsby of Scriven noted in his diary that his wife 'not perceiving any recovery of her health after so many tryalls with physitians of our country' (that is to say, in Yorkshire) had expressed a desire 'to go to London where the best are'. After they had tried several London doctors she at last became a patient of Sir Theodore Mayerne, the king's physician 'and from him she hath reap'd the most benefit for her health'. This proved expensive, however, because Sir Henry later writes that Sir Theodore 'was rich, and the Kings phycitian, and a Knight, which made him more costly to deal with all'.[3]

Although their journeys to London were often undertaken primarily for business or medical reasons the gentry were far from indifferent to other aspects of life in the capital. According to their personal inclinations they visited the court, dined with their friends (and sometimes with the great), walked in the gardens of Kensington, heard the sermons of celebrated preachers, went to the theatre and gambled their money in the gaming-houses. In addition, they went shopping and bought such luxury goods as hangings of tapestry, fine linen, plate and jewellery. In an age which was remarkable for sumptuous clothes they often felt obliged to keep abreast of contemporary fashion by patronising London tailors. In 1639 John Goodricke related that a tailor called Livingston had been making clothes for his father, Sir Henry Good-

---

[1] F. J. Furnivall (ed.), *Harrison's Description of England*, part iii, 252-3.
[2] *Cal.S.P.Dom. 1637-8*, 17.
[3] *Slingsby Diary*, 45, 48, 70. For this study the printed version of the diary (D. Parsons (ed.), 1836) has been used. The original manuscript is in the Galway of Serlby MSS (Nottingham University Library).

ricke of Ribston, and other members of his family for about the last ten or twelve years. Similarly we find Sir Henry Slingsby writing in his diary: 'In 1641 I sent from London against Easter a suite of cloathes for my son Thomas, being the first breeches and doublet that he had ever had, and made by my tailor Mr Miller'.[1]

The growing fashion among the nobility and the richer gentry for sojourning in London was a matter of serious concern to the Crown and from time to time proclamations were issued commanding such persons to return to their country estates. According to the authorities this practice had various harmful consequences: the decay of hospitality in the counties, the neglect of public duties, tax avoidance, heavy expenditure on foreign luxuries and rising food prices in the capital. During the early seventeenth century the proclamations came thick and fast. Between 20 November 1622 and 26 March 1623 there were no fewer than three such proclamations, of which the second is of particular interest. This decreed that the prohibition against persons of quality residing in London would apply to all seasons of the year and although men who had to visit the capital during the law terms were specially exempted they were nevertheless required to leave their wives and families in the country.[2] In spite of the Crown's efforts to stem the tide many country gentlemen continued to make protracted visits to London with their families. Sir Hugh Cholmley of Whitby writes in his memoirs that his family lived there from 1620 until the beginning of 1623 when they obeyed the king's proclamation and returned to Yorkshire. In 1622, however, Sir Hugh had married Elizabeth Twisden, the daughter of Sir William Twisden of Peckham in Kent, and until she had borne him two sons they resided in the house of his father-in-law in Redcross Street, not far from St Paul's. During the winter of 1630–1 Sir Hugh and Lady Cholmley and their two children were again living in London, this time with their relatives the Yelvertons of Northamptonshire. In 1633 Sir Hugh travelled up to the capital to negotiate the purchase of some Crown property in the North Riding. On this occasion he apparently left his wife in Yorkshire but at Eastertide 1637 he took her to London to visit her mother and they remained in southern England until the autumn. Two years later the whole family went up to London and sojourned there throughout the winter. In 1640

---

[1] P.R.O., S.P.Dom., Charles I, S.P.16/cdxiv/55. *Slingsby Diary*, 71–2.
[2] *Cal.S.P.Dom.* 1619–23, 462, 470, 484, 540, 554.

Sir Hugh was elected first to the Short Parliament and then to the Long Parliament and one of his sons afterwards recalled that between 1640 and 1642 he had lived sometimes in Yorkshire and sometimes in or near London as his father's occasions required.[1]

[1] *Cholmley Memoirs*, preface iii, 22–3, 39, 50–1, 53, 58, 59.

CHAPTER II

The Gentry as Landowners

TAKEN as a whole the Yorkshire gentry were essentially a landed class. In 1642 there were only seventy families (out of a total of 679) which could be regarded as urban gentry in the sense that a town-house was the normal place of residence. Even then, there was no clear-cut division between the urban gentry and the country gentry. In the first place, a few families like the Copleys of Doncaster and the Percys of Beverley were dependent, in the main line at least, on the rents and profits of agricultural property. More important, a considerable number of families engaged in urban pursuits had country estates which afforded them a respite from the hurly-burly of town life. For the new armigerous families of the towns usually had aspirations to become country gentry and with this end in view we find them purchasing the estates of bankrupt squires, inter-marrying with established county families and often, within a generation or two, severing all connection with the original source of their wealth.

Some heads of families were merchants, lawyers and royal officials, while not a few held stock in trading companies or lent money at interest.[1] Most of the gentry, however, derived their income entirely from the land. In the sphere of landownership the basic unit was the manor and the revenue which issued from it might consist of various elements: the perquisites of the manorial courts, the rents and other payments from tenants of the lord of the manor, the profits from direct farming or the exploitation of minerals, and such casual receipts as the proceeds from the sale of timber. Although many gentry farmed at least a part of the manorial demesne the main bulk of their revenue usually took the form of rent. The following example[2] illustrates this point:

---

[1] See below, 85–92.
[2] P.R.O., S.P.Dom., Committee for Compounding, S.P.23/lviii/ff.48–53. The manor belonged to Charles Thimbleby of Snydal.

Manor of Snydal	Survey January 1653		
	£	s	d
chief rents	1	1	6
profits of Court Baron		6	8
windmill	3	0	0
profits of lands in the lord's possession (108 acres)	51	0	0
rents from tenants of remaining property (539 acres)	295	1	1
total revenue per annum	350	9	3
out rents	2	13	7½
net revenue per annum	347	15	7½

Broadly speaking, there were three main types of rent: chief rents or free rents, customary rents and leasehold rents. Chief rents were small fixed sums payable by the holders of freehold land within the manor; in total they rarely exceeded a few pounds. Customary rents were the rents of tenants holding land according to the ancient custom of the manor: either tenants-at-will who (as their name implies) had little security of tenure or copyholders whose tenements were held 'by copy of the court roll'. Associated with them were fines payable on entry to a holding or on the death of the lord or tenant.[1] By the time of the Civil War customary rents were of far less importance than leasehold rents in most parts of Yorkshire. In the case of leasehold property the tenant sometimes paid a fine on the granting or renewal of a lease but the normal arrangement, certainly in the seventeenth century, was a straighforward rent with no form of premium.

In his treatise on *The State of England Anno Dom. 1600* Thomas Wilson gives us a contemporary view of the wealth of the gentry. Knights (he relates) 'for the most part are men for living betwixt £1000 and £2000 yearly'. Esquires 'are men in livinge betwixt £1000 and £500 rent. Especially about London and the Countyes adoyning, where their landes are sett to the highest, he is not counted of any great reckning unless he be betwixt 1000 marks or £1000, but Northward and farr off a gentleman of good reputacion may be content with 300 and 400 yerly'.[2] That there were important regional variations is

---

[1] For customary tenure see, for example, R. H. Tawney, *The Agrarian Problem in the Sixteenth Century*, and J. Thirsk (ed.), *The Agrarian History of England and Wales, iv, 1500–1640*.

[2] Thomas Wilson, *The State of England Anno Dom. 1600* (ed. F. J. Fisher, *Camden Miscellany*, xvi), 23–4. A mark was 13s. 4d.

beyond dispute. In the reign of Charles I the Devonshire gentry consisted mainly of families with incomes of £100 to £200 a year, while across the border in Cornwall there was a similar profusion of small estates. In Kent, on the other hand, the average income appears to have been significantly higher: in the period between 1640 and 1660, for instance, a sample of 135 families has been shown to have had a total revenue of £88,578.[1] In view of this contrast between the home counties and the remoter provinces a detailed survey of the Yorkshire gentry might be expected to reveal a close affinity, in terms of income, with the landed families of the western counties. For this type of analysis there is a wealth of material available. First in importance are the collections of family estate papers which have survived in considerable quantity. These contain rentals, account books, indentures of leases, surveys, wills and particulars of estates drawn up for such purposes as a marriage settlement. Another major source consists of the records of the various parliamentary and county committees which dealt with the estates of delinquents and recusants: estate surveys, sequestration papers and the compounding papers of royalist gentry. Some of these compounders undervalued their estates and managed to escape detection: in the main, however, the information provided in the royalist composition papers can be relied upon and not least in cases where the local committee undertook an independent assessment. Before the Civil War the valuation of private land for official purposes, whether fiscal or otherwise, was rarely undertaken with any real pretence at accuracy. Consequently the land values given in the subsidy rolls, recusant rolls and *inquisitions post mortem* bear little resemblance to the actual values. In the general field of taxation the most accurate type of assessment was the survey carried out by the Court of Wards feodary of the estates of a minor who was declared in ward to the Crown. During the early seventeenth century the feodaries often performed this task with commendable efficiency and their surveys represent a useful source of evidence provided they are treated with discrimination. In addition, a vast amount of information about landed property is to be found in the records of lawsuits in the Courts of Chancery, Requests and the Exchequer. Most of these lawsuits concerned land and not infrequently the value is given. Finally, since many gentry either

---

[1] W. G. Hoskins and H. P. R. Finberg, *Devonshire Studies*, 337, 346. M. Coate, *Cornwall in the Great Civil War*, 4. A. M. Everitt, *The Community of Kent and the Great Rebellion, 1640–60*, 41.

owned or held leases of impropriate rectories and tithes, mention must also be made of the parliamentary surveys of ecclesiastical benefices.[1]

The table of income which follows relates to the year 1642 and covers all landed property descending in the main line of a family, including property settled as a jointure or for the payment of debt. The term 'annual income' in this context signifies the net revenue after deduction of the normal outgoings from a landed estate (for example, chief rents or leasehold rents payable to another landlord). On the other hand, annuities to relatives and annual rents employed in the repayment of loans or the provision of marriage portions have been regarded as ordinary items of expenditure out of income and have not therefore been excluded from the net revenue.

Annual income 1642	Number of families within each income bracket[2]
£	
4000 and over	2 (1)
3000	4 (4)
2000	9 (2)
1000	58
750	23
500	70
250	151
100	124
under 100	238
	679

In his *History of the Worthies of England*, which he began during the Civil War, Thomas Fuller relates that most of the ancient gentry of the kingdom 'were middle-sized persons as are above two-hundred and beneath a thousand pounds of annual revenue'.[3] This is a reflection of the contemporary method of classifying the gentry according to their income: upper gentry, middling gentry and lesser or inferior gentry.

[1] A detailed account of sources will be found in the Bibliography. The reliability of the royalist composition papers is discussed in more detail in my thesis ('The Yorkshire Gentry on the Eve of the Civil War', London, 1960), 77–81. For the feodary's survey see below, 131–2.

[2] The figures in brackets denote the income of those families which had risen into the peerage during the early Stuart period and were still seated in Yorkshire in 1642.

[3] Thomas Fuller, *History of the Worthies of England*, i, 63.

On the same broad basis the Yorkshire families of 1642 may be grouped in the following way:

Annual income £	Number of families	General description
1000 and upwards	73	upper gentry
250–1000	244	middling gentry
under 250	362	lesser gentry

In all, this represents a total income from land of some £270,000 a year made up as follows: upper gentry £120,000, middling gentry £120,000, lesser gentry £30,000.

Some gentlemen of modest estate were attorneys, tradesmen and government officials but these constituted a small minority. The fact remains that within the Yorkshire gentry there were great inequalities of wealth which in turn had their impact on social position and standard of living. Materially, the richer families were scarcely distinguishable from the resident nobility of the county (most of whom had recently sprung from the ranks of the gentry) while the large group of families at the lower end of the income scale had much in common with the yeomanry, however ancient the coat of arms which proclaimed their gentility. Against this background the traditional concept of the gentry as a tightly-knit class of well-to-do landowners is clearly in need of revision.

The wealthy families which have been labelled 'the upper gentry' had estates of 5000, 10,000 and even 20,000 acres and upwards. Not infrequently they owned land in other counties: Sir Michael Warton of Beverley Park, for example, had property in London, Middlesex and Lincolnshire as well as the East Riding of Yorkshire.[1] Such large estates could not be run single-handed and a substantial landowner found it necessary to employ a steward and bailiffs to help him manage his property, enforce his manorial rights and collect the rents from his tenants. As a general rule this type of family had at least two manor-houses, one of which might be used as a dower-house or as a residence for the eldest son and his family. The principal manor-house was usually a richly-furnished Elizabethan or Jacobean mansion (though occasionally a medieval building with a modern interior) which stood in its own park and required a large establishment of household servants. In addition, the family might own or rent a town-house in York or London.

[1] P.R.O., S.P.Dom., Committee for Compounding, S.P.23/clxxxvii/289.

As major landowners the upper gentry occupied a leading position in Yorkshire society. They served as deputy lieutenants, sheriffs and justices of the peace, sat on the Council of the North and attended the House of Commons as county and borough representatives. They were also well endowed in terms of social rank: in 1642, for example, most heads of families were baronets, knights or sons of knights.

At the head of this group, far outstripping the rest in landed wealth, were two sharply contrasted families, the Ingrams of Temple Newsam and the Saviles of Thornhill. The Ingrams owed their position entirely to the financial skill and ruthless self-interest of Sir Arthur Ingram (c. 1565–1642), a London businessman and revenue farmer, who built up vast estates and established himself as a prominent figure in Yorkshire society. In 1642 he and his eldest son, who was commonly known as Sir Arthur Ingram the younger, held property yielding an income of over £9000 a year while additional property worth £3000 a year was in the possession of other members of the family. These estates were mainly situated in Yorkshire but also included extensive possessions in Lincolnshire, Derbyshire and Suffolk. In keeping with their wealth the Ingrams maintained several fine residences: in particular, the magnificent house at Temple Newsam which still testifies to their opulence, a large town-house near York Minster, and the house in Sheriff Hutton Park which has also survived.[1]

In contrast, the Saviles of Thornhill were one of the most ancient families in Yorkshire, as their monuments in Thornhill church still bear witness. On the eve of the Civil War they had landed possessions in a number of counties: first of all, there were the ancestral estates in the West Riding which provided the bulk of their income; secondly, the Lincolnshire and Nottinghamshire estates which they had acquired through marriage in the sixteenth century; and finally the estates in Derbyshire, Staffordshire, Oxfordshire, Shropshire and Wiltshire which they had inherited from Edward Earl of Shrewsbury in the reign of James I. By marriage and inheritance the Saviles greatly improved their fortunes yet Sir George Savile (1551–1622) was for a time in financial difficulties and had to sell substantial property in Yorkshire. Probably this was due in the main to poor estate management: at all events there was a dramatic increase in the revenue after his death, apparently as the result of a new leasing policy. When Sir William

---

[1] Leeds Central Library: Temple Newsam MSS, estate papers. See A. F. Upton, *Sir Arthur Ingram*.

Savile (1612–44) died at the height of the Civil War he left an estate of over 50,000 acres producing an income in normal conditions of £7000 a year. Included in this property were three main residences: Thornhill Hall (which was destroyed by the parliamentarian forces), Rufford Abbey in Nottinghamshire and a house in York. In addition, there was a baronetcy to be passed on to the heir for Sir George Savile had been one of the first Yorkshiremen to purchase this honour when James I instituted the order in 1611.[1]

As a group the middling gentry had broadly the same purchasing power as the upper gentry but there was a substantial difference in terms of average income. In general, their estates varied in size from 1000 to 5000 acres and usually included several manors. Although such families could rarely compete with the upper gentry in the outward manifestations of wealth their income enabled them to maintain a high standard of living, to engage in housebuilding on a considerable scale and to send their sons to the university and the inns of court. In 1648 Henry Tempest of Tong, who had an estate worth some £600 a year, told his son, in emphasising the primacy of spiritual riches, that he had been left a goodly heritage in a plentiful country, had delighted in building and had gold and silver in great plenty.[2] Within this section of the gentry there were a number of knights and an occasional baronet but most heads of families were styled 'esquire'. If the highest offices in the county were normally reserved for the major landowners, the middling families were nevertheless represented in strength on the commission of the peace.[3]

The inferior gentry were mainly freeholders with estates of between 50 and 1000 acres which sometimes included a small manor. In addition, they might have leasehold and even copyhold property. Gentlemen of this sort were almost invariably farmers as well as landlords and in many cases agricultural profits represented a significant proportion of the total revenue. The estate of John Vavasour of Willitoft, which was surveyed in 1653, may be taken as an illustration. This consisted of a house known as Willitoft Hall and 532 acres of land, 164 acres in his own possession which yielded £30 a year and 368 acres in the hands of

---

[1] Nottinghamshire County Record Office: Savile of Rufford MSS, estate papers.
[2] Cartwright Memorial Hall, Bradford: Tempest MSS, Henry Tempest's advice to his son, 16 February 1647(–8), and estate papers.
[3] See below, 245–6.

tenants who paid some £50 a year in rent.[1] With their limited income
the minor gentry could rarely indulge in luxury spending; their houses
were plainly built and unpretentious in size, while their domestic
establishments usually conformed to the same modest scale. In general,
as befitted their economic status, they used the ordinary style of
'gentleman'.

Whatever the size of their estates the Yorkshire gentry had a common
economic problem to contend with in the century before the Civil War.
The phenomenon known as the Price Revolution has been attributed
to various factors, in particular, the influx of Spanish silver from the
New World and the growth of population which led to increased consumption. Irrespective of its causes the price movement was real enough
to contemporary Englishmen who experienced its effects. The precise
rate of increase is still a matter of controversy but on the evidence so
far assembled it seems probable that in this century of inflation grain
prices rose fourfold and the general price level about threefold. In
Yorkshire the same trend is discernible. In the period of some eighty
years between the accession of Elizabeth and the outbreak of the Civil
War agricultural prices may be said to have roughly trebled while the
price level of manufactured goods and raw materials tended to rise more
steadily.[2]

Since agricultural prices led the inflation the country gentry, as a
class of landed proprietors, were potentially in a more sheltered situation than the great majority of town-dwellers. Nevertheless the continuing decline in the value of money brought a growing awareness that
good husbandry, in every sense of the word, was essential if they were
to safeguard their economic position. In combating the problems of
inflation one of the first requirements was to keep a strict account of
income and expenditure. 'As in other Things', Christopher Wandesford advised his son, 'so especially a good Order is to be kept in your
Rentalls: an exact Accompt of your domesticall and all other Expences;
the more plain and particular, the better; and under the more Heads

---

[1] P.R.O., S.P.Dom., Committee for Compounding, S.P.23/lviii/ff.81–3.

[2] G. Maynard, *Economic Development and the Price Level.* J. E. T. Rogers, *A History
of Agriculture and Prices in England.* E. Kerridge, 'The Movement of Rent 1540–1640',
Economic History Review, Second Series, vi, 16. Sir William Beveridge and others, *Prices
and Wages in England,* vol. i. P. Bowden, 'Agricultural Prices, Farm Profits, and Rents',
The Agrarian History of England and Wales, iv, *1500–1640* (ed. J. Thirsk), 593–695.
The Yorkshire material has been taken from probate inventories, the reports of justices
of the peace and such works as Henry Best's farming book (*Surtees Society,* xxxiii).

you distribute your Receipts and Disbursements, you will find it more familiar, and less subject to Confusion.'[1] In many cases a Yorkshire squire insisted on exact methods of accounting, either maintaining his own records or carrying out a regular check on his steward's accounts. Efficient book-keeping, however, was not enough in itself: more important was the constant search for ways and means of improving the revenue. In 1633 Lord Wentworth told his nephew Sir William Savile of Thornhill: 'take your own Accompts, and betimes inure yourself to examine how your Estate prospers, where it suffers, or where it is to be improved.' From the evidence of rent-books and other estate papers it is clear that many gentry regarded this as an essential function of land management which demanded their close attention. In February 1622 Gervase Bosvile of Warmsworth drew up a valuation of his property, noting the improvements which had recently been made and the further improvements which he intended to make. Several parcels of land in Warmsworth and Doncaster had lately been enclosed and one of these closes worth £4. 10s. 0d. a year he hoped would yield £5 within a few years. Another close which he valued at £8 or £9 a year would, if well husbanded, be worth £10 a year. In Tickhill there were 45 acres of arable land which were let at 4s. 3d. an acre but (he noted) the rent could be increased to 6s. 8d. an acre. On such painstaking attention to detail the whole future of the estate might well depend.[2]

For the business-minded landlord there was no lack of guidance available. During the century of the Price Revolution many books of husbandry were published which provided information on new farming methods and practices. In addition, a Yorkshire gentleman who was anxious to make improvements often took the advice of a lawyer or a surveyor before embarking on a major reorganisation or development scheme. In such cases the opinion of counsel might be sought on the legal implications of a projected enclosure or the feasibility of introducing new leasing arrangements. The surveyor, for his part, had the task of drawing up a detailed particular of the estate and advising the owner on the measures which were necessary to realise the full potential value. In John Norden's work *The Surveyors Dialogue*, first published in 1607, the Farmer complains to the Surveyor: 'customes are

---

[1] Christopher Wandesford, *A Book of Instructions*, 79. See Appendix A for the expenditure accounts of Sir Henry Slingsby of Scriven.
[2] Knowler, i, 169. Leeds Central Library: Battie Wrightson MSS, BW/R/4.

altred, broken, and sometimes perverted or taken away by your
meanes: And above all, you looke into the values of mens lands,
whereby the Lords of Mannors do rack their tenants to a higher rent
and rate than ever before.'[1]

If some gentry raised their income purely through rack-renting
others showed considerable enterprise in developing waste land,
draining marshes and increasing the productivity of the soil. After
purchasing the manor of Roundhay early in the reign of Charles I
Stephen Tempest of Broughton improved the estate 'at great charge',
clearing wooded ground and erecting buildings, walls and fences. At
the same time he began to quarry the limestone deposits, setting up
sixteen kilns in summer and three in winter which yielded profits of £80
to £100 a year. The Gascoignes of Barnbow, another Catholic family,
were also keenly interested in this type of activity, as we can see from
their estate papers. In 1642, for example, Sir Thomas Gascoigne noted
on a particular of his estate that within the wastes and commons of
Barwick, Scoles, Bramham and Clifford 'there is good possibilitie of
improvement by Inclosure, planting of Connye Warrens, and by the
Quarries of stone and lymestone thereof'. Sometimes a landowner
began to experiment with new agricultural techniques after he had
seen them applied on a neighbouring estate. In 1638 Sir Henry
Slingsby of Scriven wrote in his diary:

I am now about a point of Husbandry, new grown in fashion, of burning the
swarth they mean to plough, the ashes whereof by experience they find to
yeild a greater increase of corn than any other manure of lime Malr [marl] or
Dung...hereafter I will try it upon a peice of ground which they call the
out Gang...the gain is great they make by this husbandry, when as they
refuse not to give 20s. by the year an acre for 3 crops which before they gave
little rent at all.[2]

Besides investing their own capital some landowners used another
means of developing their estates: the improvement lease. In 1627
James Maleverer of Ingleby Arncliffe granted a long lease of closes in
Manston for a rent of £10 a year. By this indenture the lessee was given
liberty to stub all the roots of the underwoods and all other dead and
dry roots except the hedgerows and to convert the grounds into arable,

---

[1] John Norden, *The Surveyors Dialogue*, 3.
[2] Leeds Central Library: Temple Newsam MSS, TN/PO 1/111 and Gascoigne of
Barnbow MSS, estate papers. Y.A.S. Library: MS 381 (t). *Slingsby Diary*, 27. For Sir
Henry's expenditure on husbandry see below, 55–6.

meadow and pasture. In 1628 Sir William Hungate of Saxton made a lease for three lives of property in Sherburn in Elmet, Huddleston and Newthorpe — most of it 'barren, boggy or bushy ground' — at a total rent of £79. 3s. 2d. a year. At the same time he leased to the tenant, Robert Hewes, a further 120 acres in the parish of Sherburn in Elmet, also for three lives, in consideration of his work and charges in repairing Sir William's mills and other buildings, the expenditure which he would incur in developing the property and a yearly rent of £46. 2s. od. In 1665 the lessee's son claimed that he had spent at least £200 on improving the grounds and had taken great pains in digging, draining, stubbing and manuring all or most of the 120 acres, thereby increasing the annual value from 5s. or 6s. to 20s. an acre.[1]

One of the main obstacles to improved efficiency was the medieval open field system which had survived to a marked extent in Tudor Yorkshire. In manors where this system flourished the lord's property was distributed in narrow strips (or 'lands', as they were called in the East Riding) which were intermingled with the strips belonging to other freeholders. To the progressive landowner strip cultivation was an anachronism: modern agricultural practice demanded the replacement of scattered holdings by compact fields held in severalty and enclosed with hedges, fences or ditches. That this would increase the profitability of the land was generally recognised: thus in 1651 Christopher Legard of Anlaby noted on a rental of his estate that certain plots of land in Tranby fields would, if enclosed, yield nearly double the rent.[2] On occasion the squire concluded an agreement with his freehold tenants for a general redistribution and enclosure of their holdings in the town fields. This happened in 1595 when the open fields of Ingleby Arncliffe were enclosed, the preamble to the agreement reading: ',That whereas the severall grounds do ly in the said township dispersed, that they shall be laid together, viz. the chefe lord's land and every freholders' land by themselves, that is to say, the tillage by itself, medow by itself, and pasture by itself.' Similarly, in 1602 Gabriel St Quintin of Ganstead, Michael Constable of St Sepulchre's and other landowners who had freehold property in the manor of Ganstead were parties to an indenture which recorded that they 'had procured all the land arable and grass ground in the fields of the land arable, and the meadow in Southinges and Westinges and the town's pasture' within the manor

[1] *Y.A.J.*, i, 114–5. P.R.O., Chancery Proceedings, Six Clerks' Series, C.10/117/64.
[2] Beverley County Record Office: Legard of Anlaby MSS, DDBL/20/17.

'to be measured, and divers books of every acre, where it lay and to whom it belonged, to be made thereof, and to the same books had set their hands, and sithence had made divers and sundry exchanges and allotments of the same, and thereupon had made, bounded, pitted, or divided every ones part of the same, where it by the exchange and allotment lay or should lie'.[1]

Generally the enclosure of the open fields was a more gradual process involving the piecemeal exchange and purchase of holdings. Often the lord of the manor sought, as a first step, to consolidate and enclose the demesne lands (which could be as widely scattered as the tenanted lands) in order to facilitate his own farming activities. By the time of the Civil War the transformation of the open fields was well advanced in some Yorkshire manors but in others had hardly begun. This can be seen from the Commonwealth surveys of royalist estates: in Roundhay, for example, the lord's property was almost completely enclosed while in Beswick much of the estate consisted of 'lands' lying dispersed in the open fields. Probably the situation in the manor of Snydal was the most representative: here the great majority of tenants had leases of both enclosed grounds and strips in the town fields.[2]

In seeking to increase their revenue many landlords turned their attention to the common pasture and the common waste which in the northern counties especially represented an extensive area of undeveloped land. In Yorkshire the enclosure of common land, often piecemeal but sometimes on a major scale, was becoming a familiar sight, so familiar indeed that when Thomas Anlaby of Etton related, in a Star Chamber bill of 1620, that he and his ancestors had allowed the wastes and commons of Etton to lie open for the benefit of the commoners he clearly regarded this as a remarkable act of forbearance.[3] In many cases, and particularly where only a few acres were involved, the lord of the manor considered it unnecessary to consult the freeholders and tenants who had rights of common. On occasion, however, it was deemed prudent to obtain some form of legal consent. In 1631 Sir William Constable of Flamborough had a deed of enclosure drawn up as a preliminary to taking in part of the common in his manor of Holme on Spalding Moor. This document had one specific purpose: to record the

[1] Y.A.J., xv, 506 and xvi, 173. Y.A.S.R.S., lxv, 74–6.
[2] P.R.O., S.P.Dom., Committee for Compounding. S.P.23/lviii/ff.48–53 and lviii (A)/ff.278–83, 360–2.
[3] P.R.O., Star Chamber Proceedings, Star Chamber 8/36/11.

formal agreement of the freeholders and commoners to Sir William's proposal to 'take improve enclose and kepe in severaltye, one parcell of the sayd Holme more called Arghan conteyninge by estimation Threescore Acres or thereabouts'.[1] Sometimes two neighbouring squires might enter into an agreement for the division and enclosure of the waste which separated their manors; sometimes the lord might join in a general agreement for the partition of the common, each man's share being assessed in accordance with the size of his holdings within the manor. Finally, there were cases where the tenantry apparently took the initiative: in 1627, for example, John Ingleby of Lawkland authorised the tenants of his manor of Clapham to enclose, improve and till the commons in return for a payment of £500.[2]

Enclosures might be made on the commons for various purposes, the increase of tillage, the depasturing of the squire's cattle and sheep, the preservation of woodland, the mining of coal and lead. Often the ground was broken up and put under cultivation. When George Butler of Ellerton enclosed twelve acres on Laytham common in the reign of Charles I he burnt off the grass and furze, ploughed the soil and sowed oats and rye; the yield he valued at 4s. an acre.[3] Not only was the amount of productive land increased but in many cases cottages were erected for the housing of tenants. In 1585 witnesses in an Exchequer suit testified that James Hebblethwaite of Norton had already built one house and set up the frame of another on pasture known as Norton Outgang. Similarly, in a lawsuit of 1623 William Ramsden of Longley was said to have constructed ten houses and made divers closes of good yearly value on the wastes and commons of Quick.[4]

In the period 1558–1642 there was a considerable body of enclosing gentry to the number of at least 130 families. In general, their activities aroused far less controversy than the large-scale enclosures of the early sixteenth century, when many tenants were evicted to make way for sheep-walks, or the contemporary enclosures in the Midland counties which led to the peasant rising of 1607. Cases of depopulation were not unknown in Elizabethan Yorkshire: in the North Riding, for example, the villages of Gristhwaite, Maunby and North Kilvington appear to

---

[1] B.M., Additional MSS 40132, ff.35–42.　　[2] T. D. Whitaker, *Richmondshire*, ii, 349.

[3] P.R.O., Chancery Proceedings, Six Clerks' Series, C.10/4/143.

[4] P.R.O., Exchequer Depositions, E.134, 26 and 27 Elizabeth I, Michaelmas No. 32, and Chancery Proceedings, Series II, C.3/334/6.

have suffered this fate. Nevertheless there were comparatively few depopulating enclosures over the period as a whole. In 1633 the justices of the peace throughout the county were required to submit reports on this question and the returns which have survived invariably claim that the divisions concerned were wholly free of depopulations. In their report for Agbrigg and Morley the magistrates, Sir John Ramsden and John Kaye, added that 'generallye where Inclosures are made with us Howses are erected upon them'. No doubt Sir John recalled his father's improvements on the commons.[1]

If there was little depopulation in this period the enclosure of common land could yet provoke strong resistance from freeholders and commoners whose grazing rights were threatened. Piecemeal encroachments usually went unchallenged but when the landlord sought to take in a substantial area for his exclusive use this might lead to the bringing of a lawsuit or, more often, the destruction of fences and hedges. In a Star Chamber bill of 1617 Sir William Acclom of Moreby Grange informed the court that, having resolved to enclose certain waste ground called the Little Moor 'for that thereby a greater proffitt and comoditie would arise to your said subject', he wrote to Sir Ralph Ellerker, who owned Stillingfleet moor adjoining this stretch of land, giving him advance notice of his plans. After performing this act of courtesy he fenced and ditched a great part of the Little Moor — apparently 80 out of a total of 100 acres — intending to complete the work by planting trees and quickset. To his dismay Sir Ralph Ellerker took strong exception to the enclosure on the grounds that his rights were being infringed and (it was alleged) called for its overthrow in both speech and writing, declaring that £400 or £500 would be collected if necessary to maintain suits and troubles against him. On 18 February 1617 a large crowd, including a number of Sir Ralph's tenants, assembled on the Little Moor armed with staves, pitchforks and other weapons and proceeded to throw down the fences and ditches. Such incidents were not uncommon in Yorkshire.[2]

Since the Yorkshire gentry derived the bulk of their income from the rents of tenants the possession of a static rent-roll in a period of inflation could lead inexorably to a financial crisis. To avoid this danger it was necessary for the landlord to restrict the length of his leases and maintain his rents at a level commensurate with, or at least not too far

---

[1] *N.R. Records*, i, 78. P.R.O., S.P.Dom., Charles I, S.P.16./ccl/47, ccli/14 and ccliv/8.
[2] P.R.O., Star Chamber Proceedings, Star Chamber 8/40/9.

behind, the rise in farming profits. In practice, however, this might prove difficult if copyhold was the prevailing tenure on his estate. According to a modern estimate customary tenants formed nearly two-thirds of the entire landholding population in Tudor England, freeholders about one-fifth and leaseholders between one-eighth and one-ninth.[1] How far this is true of Yorkshire it is difficult to judge in the absence of any detailed study but in the reign of Elizabeth there were undoubtedly many copyholders as well as the more easily removable tenants-at-will. From the landlord's point of view the worst feature of copyhold tenure was the fixed rent, hallowed by custom, which in the course of time had ceased to bear any relation to the true value of the tenement. If the squire found it impossible to increase the rents he might be able to secure a greater yield from the fines payable on specified occasions. This depended on whether the fines were fixed and certain or arbitrary and variable according to the will of the lord. In his treatise on surveying published in 1577 Valentine Leigh tells us that in most manors fines were 'uncertain and at the Lordes will' and other contemporary writers testify to this fact. Sometimes there was a dispute as to what the custom of the manor permitted but wherever possible the landlord took steps to augment his income through the raising of fines. As a result the copyholders might be required to pay fines representing four years' rent and upwards, although practice varied widely; in contrast, two and a half years' rent was held to be an unreasonable fine by the reign of Charles I.[2]

One Yorkshire squire who demanded heavy fines was Sir Henry Savile of Methley. In 1612 he brought a Chancery suit against the copyhold tenants of his manor of Methley who had allegedly refused to pay any more fines unless these were assessed by a jury. In his bill he claimed that the fines payable on the alienation of land (other than to the heir) were 'arbitrable' at the lord's will, that even so he had never charged more than two and a half times the annual value, and that since the tenants were allied to most of the freeholders in the area no jury could be expected to look at the matter objectively. He therefore asked the lord chancellor to act as arbitrator and set down a reasonable rate for the copyhold fines. In reply the customary tenants argued that when a

---

[1] R. H. Tawney, *The Agrarian Problem in the Sixteenth Century*, 24.

[2] Valentine Leigh, *The Most Profitable and Commendable Science of Surveying of Landes, Tenementes and Hereditamentes* (no pagination). R. H. Tawney, *The Agrarian Problem in the Sixteenth Century*, 296.

copyholder died or alienated his land to someone other than the heir the fine had never been above 12d. an acre at the most, and usually only 4d. or 6d. an acre, until Sir John Savile (the lord's father) bought the manor and increased the rate by 4d., 8d. or exceptionally 12d. Sir Henry, on the other hand, had imposed 'very excessyve and unconsionable ffynes on the pore Copieholders', the increases amounting to eighty- or a hundredfold more than the former rate. In the case of one customary holding which the lord valued at £30 a year Sir John Savile had assessed the fine at 20s. but his son had demanded no less than £70. Sir Henry (they alleged) was a harsh landlord and many of the copyholders wished to go and live under 'some better and more conscionable lorde then the plaintyfe ys'. As a further example of his greed he had offered to make their copyhold fines fixed and certain in return for a composition of forty-five years' rent which was nearly as much as his father had paid for the whole lordship. In fact the customary rents were a minor element in the total revenue for in 1607 the manor had been valued at £240 a year and this included demesne lands reputed to be worth £200 a year. How unrealistic were these rents may be seen from the compounding papers of John Benson, a royalist tenant of the parliamentarian lord of Methley. In 1648 he had 48 acres of copyhold land for which a fine of £100 (three times the annual value) was owing to the landlord. According to his own particular the annual rent was a mere £2. 19s. 6d. and the holding yielded him a profit of £33. 0s. 6d. (and in normal conditions £49) a year over and above this sum. Small wonder, therefore, that Sir Henry Savile was discontented with his revenue.[1]

The raising of fines was one method of tackling the problem of uneconomic customary rents. A more radical solution (apart from enfranchisement) was to break free from the archaic restrictions of copyhold tenure altogether and put the estate on a sounder commercial footing. If the copyholders had possession for a period of years or for one, two or three lives the squire could decline to renew their copies when the term expired and instead make leases at a substantially higher rent. If, on the other hand, the customary tenants were copyholders of inheritance their holdings could be passed on indefinitely from one generation to another provided they observed the basic conditions of their tenancies. In the northern counties, including Yorkshire,

[1] P.R.O., Chancery Proceedings, Series I, C.2/S.6/20, and S.P.Dom., Committee for Compounding, S.P.23/clxxix/95, 103, 111, 115. B.M., Additional MSS 12497, f.429.

this hereditary kind of tenure sometimes took the form of tenant right which, in theory at least, involved military obligations associated with the defence of the border regions; this apart, its main characteristic was the right of succession which continued 'so long as there is any of the same stocke'. Faced with this situation the ruthless landlord used every means to evict his tenants. First of all, he showed no mercy when a copyholder was found guilty of a breach of the customs which rendered him liable to forfeiture, for example, the felling of trees or the alienation of land without the lord's consent. In *The Surveyors Dialogue* John Norden has his Surveyor exclaim: 'I know many Lords too forward in taking advantage of forfeitures upon small occasions',[1] and this was certainly happening in Yorkshire. Secondly, the squire might deliberately set out to harass his tenants, either through litigation or through physical acts of intimidation. Finally, the exaction of heavy fines, while helping to increase the revenue, was also employed as a means of forcing the copyholders to relinquish their tenements.

The struggle between the landlord and his tenants could be long and bitter as the Elizabethan lawsuits concerning the manor of Ingleton clearly demonstrate. This property was situated in a remote corner of the West Riding, near the Lancashire border, where copyholds of inheritance were the commonest form of tenure. In the middle years of Elizabeth's reign Sir Richard Cholmley was alleged to have taken great and unaccustomed fines from the tenants (whereas they were only liable to pay a fine of one year's rent every seven years) and to have resorted to litigation in an attempt to deprive them of their holdings. When his son Richard Cholmley inherited the property in 1583 this campaign of attrition was if anything intensified. In 1589 the tenants of Ingleton filed a bill in Chancery which contained a number of specific accusations against their landlord. Having persuaded them to grant him a benevolence of £400 he had arranged for a jury to be set up 'whereof the moste parte are cottages [cottagers] and of the simpleste sorte' and had encouraged them to find and present such unreasonable fines, amercements and forfeitures that if no remedy was forthcoming the customary tenants would be 'enforced to leave and yeelde up' their tenements 'to their utter undoynge for ever'. In addition, two of Richard Cholmley's servants had of late begun to drive their horses and cattle through the holdings of the tenants, 'thereby spoylynge eatinge wastinge and consumynge their said grasse'. Out of necessity

[1] Valentine Leigh, *op. cit.* John Norden, *The Surveyors Dialogue*, 60.

some of the tenants had been forced to alienate part of their holdings but the landlord had taken these grounds into his own hands and converted them to his private use. This was not all. Richard Cholmley, it was claimed, had evicted one family from a customary tenement and had pulled down the houses and buildings on the site. Furthermore, he had brought a number of lawsuits against the tenants in order 'to overthrowe theire saide Anncyent and lawdable custome of Tennant righte'. In reply Richard Cholmley denied that they held by tenant right: the customary tenements had been let for life, years or at will according to the pleasure of the lord. Similarly, the fines were not certain but subject to negotiation between the lord and his tenants.

Subsequently Richard Cholmley came to an agreement with the tenantry and this was recorded in a Chancery decree issued on 23 June 1592. The main provisions of this agreement were as follows: (1) the tenants were to occupy their holdings without let or hindrance from the lord, and to be allowed to surrender or alienate them at their pleasure; (2) the fine payable every seven years was to be the equivalent of two years' rent; (3) when a tenement descended to the next heir a fine amounting to seven years' rent was to be paid; (4) in all other cases where there was a change of tenant the lord would be entitled to a fine equal to fifteen years' rent; (5) in consideration of the benefits and privileges which the decree bestowed on them the tenants were to pay the lord a sum equal to five years' rent of their customary tenements.

After the squire's death in 1600 his son and heir claimed that the deceased was merely a tenant for life so that the decree was not legally binding on his successors. When the tenants refused to conclude a new agreement he sold the manor to a relative, Gerard Lowther, who promptly commenced suits against them. In 1660 there were still customary tenants in Ingleton but their numbers appear to have diminished. At that time the rents of the copyhold lands amounted to £33. 12s. 6d. a year, the fines for the period 1653–60 came to £38. 18s. od. and the total revenue of the manor was valued at £300 a year.[1]

Most Yorkshire landowners were spared the type of situation which existed in the manor of Ingleton. Since there were comparatively few

[1] P.R.O., Court of Requests, Requests 2/135/77, Chancery Proceedings, Series I, C.2/I.6/47 and C.2/I.3/72, and Six Clerks' Series, C.10/93/86. A. G. Ruston and D. Witney, *Hooton Pagnell*, 317–20.

manors with copyholds of inheritance the average squire was able, sooner or later, to rid himself of his customary tenants and the restrictions which this kind of tenure imposed. In a sample of fifty manors belonging to Yorkshire landed families in the period 1620–60 only fourteen were found to have copyhold tenants (and it is significant that these included several manors which had recently been purchased from the Crown). Even where copyhold tenure survived the yield from this source was often a minor item in the general rental and hardly more important than the chief rents which had long since ceased to have any real value. Thus when Henry Hildyard of Winestead, a royalist delinquent, compounded for his estates in 1646 he valued the total revenue at £2357 a year while the freehold and copyhold rents together amounted to only £4. 8s. 9d. a year.[1] The conclusion is inescapable: in the century preceding the Civil War a high proportion of customary land was being converted into leasehold property as the Yorkshire gentry sought to improve the revenue from their estates.

In describing the state of England in 1600 Thomas Wilson relates that it had been the practice for gentlemen to let their lands 'some for 30, some 40 and some 50 some 200 yeares' in return for fines and small rents. The devaluation of the coinage

and then the prise of corne, cattell and all farmers' Commodityes increasing daily in prise, and the gentleman who is generally enclined to great and vayne expence had no more then would keepe his howse and some small rent, and therefore could not spend away prodigally much of the welth of the land bycause he had no superfluity...but since these long leases are growne to expire the gentlemen by this beginne to be warr [beware] how to be so overreched.[2]

In the sixteenth century many Yorkshire landowners granted long leases of their property although twenty-one-year leases were not uncommon even at the beginning of Elizabeth's reign. In such cases the financial arrangements normally consisted of a fine, either on entry or renewal, and a fixed rent which was often uneconomic at the outset and became increasingly so as time went on. Before the end of the century this short-sighted leasing practice was giving way to more businesslike methods of estate administration. Some gentlemen took legal advice on the practicability of cancelling long leases which had been made in a

[1] P.R.O., S.P.Dom., Committee for Compounding, S.P.23/clxxvii/608.
[2] Thomas Wilson, *The State of England Anno Dom. 1600* (ed. F. J. Fisher, *Camden Miscellany*, xvi), 39.

previous generation and many tenants who hoped to renew their leases on favourable terms were faced with unprecedented demands from their landlords. When Christopher Wandesford of Kirklington succeeded to his father's estate in 1612 he found that much of the property was leased out at unrealistic rents or for merely nominal acknowledgements. According to his biographer, Thomas Comber, he bought in some of these leases in order to improve the grounds and resolved to await the expiration of others and then let the lands not on fines but for reasonable rents. As a result of this new leasing policy the rent-roll, which amounted to £560 a year in 1612, had risen to £1040 a year in 1640, the year of his death.[1] In the seventeenth century leasehold property was usually let for a period of twenty-one years (and sometimes for ten, twelve or fifteen years), the tenant paying an annual rent but no fine. On the whole, long leases and entry fines were the product of special circumstances: for example, where an improvident squire wanted to raise money quickly to clear his debts or where a mercenary guardian was seeking to exploit his ward's estate for his own financial gain.

For leasing purposes the manorial authorities distinguished between three main types of land: arable, meadow and pasture. As a general rule the highest rent per acre was obtained from the rich meadow land which provided hay for winter feeding and was also used for the grazing of livestock. In contrast, arable land not infrequently yielded the lowest rent per acre: in 1621, for example, Marmaduke Grimston of Grimston Garth claimed in a Chancery bill that his aunt and her new husband, Sir Henry Browne, had ploughed up 60 acres of meadow or pasture in the manor of Little Smeaton and as a result the rental value had fallen from 26s. to 5s. an acre. Over the period as a whole, however, arable rents increased at a greater pace than meadow or pasture rents.[2] In the case of leasehold property the rent level depended on various factors, in particular, the quality and productivity of the soil, the amount of competition for holdings from would-be tenants and the local market conditions which governed the price of farm produce. Naturally there were considerable regional variations in the average rent per acre. In the Wolds country of the East Riding, where the chalk hills dominated the landscape, the barren soil and low density of population offered little prospect of securing a high rent yield. In 1619 the executors of Christopher Maltby of Cottingham told the Court of Wards that his lands in Muston and Filey were of poor quality and 'the Cottages divers of them are not Inhabited, and such as be are in thoccupacion of poore fishermen, soe as they are of verey small value'. Similarly, the Court of Wards was informed in 1628 that the property which had belonged to Sir Thomas Norcliffe of Langton was of little value, 'for the greater parte thereof is upon the highe Woulds and Moores which are so barren that a greate quantity of it yeild but a small Rent'. Low rents were in fact a characteristic feature of the Wolds region: in 1653, for instance, certain property in Hunmanby was valued at 2s. an acre.[1] At the other extreme the fertile plains of the Vale of York and the river valleys leading from it represented an area of high rent. In 1640 Sir Henry Slingsby of Scriven noted in his diary: 'Lands as they are now rent'd yeild me a good revenue, and lett dear about Knasborough. I have plowing land that give me 18s. an acre according as they are now rent'd.'[2]

Whatever the accidents of geography the general tendency was to put up the rent on the expiration of a lease. In many cases a survey was undertaken with the express purpose of assessing the additional revenue which the tenanted lands could be made to yield: thus when Richard Remington of Lund had his estate at Catfoss surveyed in 1639 the current value was put at £144. 13s. 4d. a year and the potential value at £213. 6s. 8d. a year.[3] Substantial increases in rent were not uncommon, particularly in the early Stuart period. One Yorkshire squire who raised his rents to a high level was Sir Marmaduke Langdale of North Dalton: in 1628 the manor of Gatenby (which he had recently purchased for £3240) had a rent-roll of £234 but ten years later, when the leases expired, new rents were fixed which produced a total revenue of £378 a year. Even more dramatic was the rise in income from the Yorkshire estates of the Saviles of Thornhill. In 1619 the rents of twelve West Riding manors in their possession amounted to £399 a year; in 1651, however, the same manors had a rent-roll of £2049. Clearly this was due to a major reorganisation of the estate for

---

[1] P.R.O., Court of Wards, Wards 5/49. P.R.O., S.P.Dom., Committee for Compounding, S.P.23/ccxxv/139.
[2] *Slingsby Diary*, 61.
[3] Beverley County Record Office: Bethell of Rise MSS, DDRI/10/2.

Sir George Savile (1551–1622) seems generally to have preferred entry fines to economic rents.[1]

In 1648 Henry Tempest of Tong advised his son: 'Oppress not thy tenants, but let them live comfortably of thy hands as thou desirest to live of their Labours, that their soules may bless thee and that it may go well with thy seed after thee.'[2] Benevolent landlords could still be found even in the seventeenth century. One West Riding squire, Walter Hawksworth of Hawksworth, granted a number of leases for lives and in his will, which was drawn up in March 1619, required his son Richard to be good to his tenants and not to raise their rents. Sir Richard, who was noted for his unruly temperament, subsequently took legal advice on the possibility of breaking these leases. In a note which was apparently written in 1631 he recorded the opinion of counsel: 'I may dispose of these tenements for my father had no power to make any such leases for 3 leives.' Ironically enough, when Sir Richard prepared his own will in September 1652 he besought his son Walter to treat the tenants well 'and suffer them to continue upon their ould rents I haveing raysed them myselfe'.[3]

Although some gentlemen were reluctant to overburden their tenantry many others in the early seventeenth century thought only of exacting the highest possible rent yield, a policy which inevitably gave rise to a good deal of discontent. In 1617 Roger Dodsworth the antiquary contrasted the generosity of Sir Peter Middleton of Stockeld with the common attitude which prevailed among the landowning classes. This Catholic squire (he tells us) was greatly esteemed by his tenants while the tenants of neighbouring landlords, complaining of harsh treatment, said of him 'God bless Sir Peter Middleton'. To Dodsworth such paternalism was 'a rare example in this cold time'.[4] As supporting evidence the reports of sequestration officials on the estates of royalist landowners reveal a number of rack-renting gentry in this part of the West Riding: Sir John Goodricke of Ribston (whose whole estate was said to be 'upon the rack'), Sir Guy Palmes of

[1] B.M., Additional MSS 40135, f.5. Y.A.S. Library: MD 287(b) (rent-book of Sir Marmaduke Langdale). Nottinghamshire County Record Office: Savile of Rufford MSS, estate papers. Sheffield Central Library: Strafford Letters, xx, 95.

[2] Cartwright Memorial Hall, Bradford: Tempest MSS, Henry Tempest's advice to his son, 16 February 1647(–8).

[3] W. P. Baildon, *Baildon and the Baildons*, i, 414. Sheffield Central Library: Bright MSS, BR 80 and WWM D566. See also below, 371–2.

[4] B.M., Additional MSS 24468, f.138.

Lindley, Sir Richard Tankard of Whixley, William Vavasour of Weston and Michael Fawkes of Farnley.[1] At the same time the imposition of heavy rent increases was not a practice confined to the West Riding: thus in 1626 a number of Cleveland subsidymen alleged that they were unable to contribute to the 'free loan' which the Crown was demanding since the majority of them were poor farmers and tenants 'at rackt and enhanced rents'.[2]

In the period 1558–1642 it is clear that rents were in the main following an upward trend. This process was temporarily halted during the depression of the 1620's: Sir Hugh Cholmley of Whitby, for example, relates that £700 or £800 of his father's estate was at that time unlet and that because of the fall in commodity prices 'it would neither let nor raise the rent, by keeping in our hand'.[3] Even so, this represented only a brief interlude in the general movement of rent. In view of the differences in local conditions and methods of estate management the actual rate of increase varied from manor to manor but there is sufficient evidence to enable some broad conclusions to be drawn. In the early years of Elizabeth's reign the average rents on Yorkshire estates were usually of the order of 6d., 1s. or 2s. an acre (and it is interesting to note that in Valentine Leigh's book on surveying published in 1577 the following specimen rents are given: pasture 1s. per acre, arable 6d. per acre, meadow 1s. 9d. per acre[4]). In the reign of Charles I, on the other hand, most rents appear to have ranged between 5s. and 10s. an acre, although rents of 15s. and upwards can be found in the more fertile regions. On some Yorkshire manors the rent-roll increased eightfold and more in the period between 1558 and 1642, a development which may be illustrated by reference to the manor of Bonwick, an outlying property belonging to the Accloms of Moreby Grange. During the reign of Elizabeth the annual revenue consisted of £11 in money, ten quarters of seed barley and three quarters of wheat and rye (the total yield from the manor amounting to about £16 or £17). About 1600, however, John Acclom raised the rental to £60 a year, dispensing with the food rents, while at the death of his son Sir William in 1637 the

---

[1] B.M., Additional MSS 24468, f.138. P.R.O., S.P.Dom., Committee for Compounding, S.P.23/clxxvii/193, 255, clxxxii/485, cxci/175 and cxcviii/26.

[2] P.R.O., S.P.Dom., Charles I, S.P.16/xxxviii/88.

[3] *Cholmley Memoirs*, 44.

[4] Valentine Leigh, *The Most Profitable and Commendable Science of Surveying of Landes, Tenementes and Hereditamentes* (no pagination).

manor was worth £160 a year.[1] Such cases were more the exception than the rule but even at the other extreme rents were usually trebled and over the county as a whole the normal tendency was for rents to rise five- or sixfold, which corresponds with the rate of increase noted in such counties as Norfolk, Suffolk and Warwickshire.[2] In the most vulnerable position were the landowners who had a large number of copyhold tenants or whose predecessors had granted long leases. For a time the situation could be serious, possibly even desperate, but there were various measures which an energetic landlord might take to overcome or alleviate the problem: in particular, the vigorous exploitation of his demesne lands, the bringing of new land under cultivation, the raising of fines, the buying in of leases, the gradual conversion of copyhold to leasehold property as the tenancies expired. On the whole, it seems likely that on most Yorkshire estates the increase in the rent level over this period was higher than the increase in the general price level. And in the early seventeenth century there can be no doubt that rents were often forging ahead of prices.

[1] P.R.O., Chancery Depositions, C.21/D.16/3 and C.22/759/13. For further examples of rent movement see Appendix B.

[2] See E. Kerridge, 'The Movement of Rent 1540–1640', *Economic History Review*, Second Series, vi, 17.

CHAPTER III

Farming and Industry

IN TACKLING the problem of inflation the country gentry had other remedies at their disposal besides the exaction of higher rents from their tenants. Since agricultural prices were the spearhead of the Price Revolution landowners were able not only to protect themselves against the worst aspects of this inflationary trend but also to exploit the situation to their own advantage. Food rents (which were medieval in origin) represented one method of keeping down household expenditure. These were still relatively common in Yorkshire. During the reign of Elizabeth it was customary in the manor of Holme on Spalding Moor for tenants who held at least half an oxgang of arable land to pay each year two capons, two pigs, two geese, two hens, a dozen chickens and two dozen eggs on certain appointed days. Similarly, in 1619 Sir Peter Middleton of Stockeld granted a lease of property in Austby at a yearly rent of £4. 9s. 9d. together with four fat capons at Midsummer and four fat hens at Christmas.[1] Rents in kind could make a useful contribution to the provisioning of the household but from the evidence available they were rarely a significant factor in the management of a country estate. More important was the practice of direct farming, whether on a subsistence or a commercial basis. In 1587 William Harrison noted that 'men of great port and countenance are so farre from suffering their farmers to have anie gaine at all, that they themselves become grasiers, butchers, tanners, sheepmasters, woodmen and *denique quid non*, thereby to inrich themselves, and bring all the wealth of the countrie into their owne hands'.[2]

Few Yorkshire gentlemen were mere *rentiers* who lived entirely off the labours of their tenants. Inventories of goods and chattels which have survived almost invariably give details of ploughing implements, wagons and carts, farm animals and corn already garnered or growing

[1] B.M., Additional MSS 41168, f.18. *Y.A.S.R.S.*, lxv, 20. An oxgang usually amounted to fifteen acres or thereabouts.
[2] F. J. Furnivall (ed.), *Harrison's Description of England*, i, 243.

in the fields. In addition, the ancillary buildings adjoining the manor-house normally included several barns, a dairy, a bakehouse and a brewhouse. Naturally the activities of the home farm were concerned first and foremost with supplying the needs of the household. The average household consumed its own bread, its own milk, butter and cheese, its own meat and its own beer. In terms of basic necessities the country gentry could achieve a high degree of self-sufficiency; on the other hand, the richer families which had large establishments and catholic tastes in food might be put to a good deal of expenditure in supplementing the produce from their farms.[1]

According to one contemporary school of thought a country squire was ill-advised to engage in farming on a commercial scale. Christopher Wandesford of Kirklington contended that

no Gentleman whose Eye cannot be constantly upon the Labors of his Servants every Day, and consequently commits much to the Care of others doth ever gain or save by keeping much Ground under Stock...if the Countrey be so well planted and inhabited that Lands may be set at reasonable Rates, I Think it loss to keep more in your Hands than will serve for the Provision of your House. For the Negligence of Servants is so great, and there be so many Accidents, of Loss and Waste, to which Cattle (Corn especially) are subject, that your Loss in one Day by that Means may be greater than your Gain for a whole Year.[2]

Nevertheless, in spite of these hazards, many Yorkshire gentlemen kept more land in their own possession than was required for purely domestic purposes. In such cases the area of land belonging to the home farm usually amounted to between 50 and 200 acres of arable, meadow and pasture. Exceptionally, however, a well-to-do squire might be farming a significantly greater area than this: in 1578, for example, Sir John Constable of Burton Constable, one of the principal landowners in the East Riding, had 380 acres in his own hands.[3]

Although it was customary to practise a mixed type of farming there were some regions where the main emphasis was on the rearing of livestock. In 1631 the justices of the peace for Richmondshire informed the Privy Council that their division, 'the greatest part thereof being mountainnous and consisting of grazinge', could not be self-supporting so far as corn was concerned, while the magistrates for the liberty of

[1] See below, 116–17.   [2] Christopher Wandesford, *A Book of Instructions*, 83–4.
[3] Beverley County Record Office: Burton Constable MSS, DDCC/141/68.

Pickering Lyth described their part of the North Riding as 'consisting much of grasse, moorysh grounde, meadowe and feeding grounde'.[1] Similarly, there were extensive tracts of pasture country in the other Ridings, in particular the Wolds region of the East Riding and the Pennine region of the West Riding adjoining the Lancashire border. In such areas some of the wealthier gentry were engaged in meat and wool production on a major scale, at least in the reign of Elizabeth. To illustrate this the following examples may be quoted[2]:

	Date	Cattle	Pigs	Sheep	Total
Francis Wandesford of Hipswell	1559	201	6	954	1161
Sir Marmaduke Constable of Everingham	1575	159	38	1020	1217
Sir William Ingleby of Ripley	1579	178	12	1465	1655

In the early seventeenth century this type of large-scale pasture farming appears to have been much less common, primarily no doubt because of the slump in wool prices which began about 1610.[3] Thus in 1618 Sir William Ingleby's son and namesake, who must be classed as an enterprising landowner, possessed no more than 74 cattle, 27 swine and 81 sheep, a total of 183 farm animals.[4]

During the period of this study sheep-farming was popular in many parts of the county. Its attractions were obvious: not only did it yield a variety of marketable commodities — wool, mutton, tallow and skins — but the labour costs were comparatively modest. Although an individual landowner often had no more than 50, 100 or 200 sheep there were some major squires who invested heavily in this type of farming, especially in the Dales and Wolds regions which were noted for their wool production. In 1567 Thomas Rokeby of Mortham, the head of an ancient Richmondshire family, had a number of flocks on various parts of his estate. On Mortham moor a woman shepherd, Mrs Holme, appears to have been responsible for about 400 sheep and lambs (the inventory is unfortunately defective at this point). In 'blencking bus' field there were 20 fat wethers, 20 ewes and 13 old 'tale' sheep. On Rokeby moor there were 28 'taile' sheep and 38 lambs in the keeping of one Clerkson, while Ralph Barningham had

[1] P.R.O., S.P.Dom., Charles I, S.P.16/cxc/25 and 55.
[2] *Surtees Society*, xxvi, 133–6 and civ, 131. Beverley County Record Office: Maxwell–Constable MSS, DDEV/66/6.
[3] See E. Kerridge, 'The Movement of Rent 1540–1640', *Economic History Review*, Second Series, vi, 28. [4] *Y.A.J.*, xxxiv, 182, 198–9. See below, 373.

charge of 260 ewes and gimmers and 120 wethers. Finally, the inventory lists 35 wethers at Gilmonby in the keeping of one Anderson and 220 wethers at Stonesdale in the keeping of Thomas Todd. In all, Thomas Rokeby must have owned between 1100 and 1200 sheep, employing five or six shepherds to guard them.[1] As we have seen, Sir William Ingleby of Ripley had 1465 sheep at his death in 1579. These were kept on seven different pasture grounds, the smallest flock consisting of 45 hoggs and the largest of 391 wethers and other sheep. Another wealthy squire with a major interest in sheep-farming was Sir Henry Bellasis of Newburgh Priory: when in 1617 he settled his property in the parish of Hawnby on his son and heir he included in the conveyance approximately 1700 wethers, tups, ewes and lambs which were valued altogether at over £900.[2] These holdings of sheep are impressive yet they must be viewed in perspective for some of the great Norfolk sheepmasters had between 10,000 and 20,000 sheep.[3]

In his farming book, compiled in 1641, Henry Best of Emswell provides some interesting facts about the sale of wool. He writes:

Wee usually sell our wooll att hoame unlesse it bee by chance that wee carry some to Beverley on Midsummer day: those that buy it carry it into the West, towards Leeds, Hallifax and Wakefield; they bringe (with them) packe-horses, and carry it away in greate packes; these wool-men come and goe continually from clippinge time till Michaellmasse. Those that have pasture wooll, sell usually for 10s. and 11s. a stone; and oftentimes, when woll is very deare, for 12s. a stone.

In addition, he tells us that 'usually sixe of our ordinary fleeces make a just stone; if the fleeces bee very good, five of them will bee a stone, and if they bee bad, seaven'.[4] On this basis the owner of 1000 sheep in good pasture country could make between £80 and £100 a year from the sale of wool but besides this there were the receipts from the sale of meat, skins and (possibly) stock. From an examination of several East Anglian sheep-farming accounts it has been estimated that in the early seventeenth century the net profits from the keeping of 1200 sheep might amount to £140.[5]

The Yorkshire gentry had another important link with the woollen

[1] *Surtees Society*, xxvi, 204.
[2] B.M., Additional Charter 30,933.
[3] A. Simpson, *The Wealth of the Gentry 1540–1660*, 184.
[4] *Surtees Society*, xxxiii, 24, 26.
[5] A. Simpson, *The Wealth of the Gentry 1540–1660*, 194.

industry. A number of West Riding families owned fulling mills where the weavers brought their cloth to be cleansed and thickened in texture. In March 1629 a large body of clothiers submitted a petition of complaint against the aldermen and chief burgesses of Leeds, beseeching the king to refer the matter to such of the lords, knights and gentlemen of the county as best understood the clothing industry. When a commission was duly appointed it is significant that at least three of its members — Sir Henry Savile of Methley, Sir John Ramsden of Longley and John Kaye of Woodsome — had a direct connection with the industry through the ownership of fulling mills.[1]

On a number of estates the landlord had more land under cultivation than any individual copyhold or leasehold tenant. Often this amounted to between 50 and 100 acres, especially in the more fertile lowland regions. At the same time, there were some energetic squires who went in for arable farming on a considerably greater scale. One such was Sir Cotton Gargrave of Nostell Priory: in 1588 he had 92 acres of wheat, barley and oats at Nostell and 65 acres of barley, peas and oats at Upton. Another was Sir Thomas Wentworth of North Elmsall: in 1650 he was farming 216 acres of arable land, his crops consisting of wheat, rye, barley, maslin (a mixture of wheat and rye), oats and peas.[2] In addition, there are instances where a gentleman of modest estate extended his farming activities by securing a lease of arable land from a more substantial landowner. In 1632 we find William Copley of Wadworth handing over management of his estate to Christopher Copley, his eldest son, so that he could concentrate on farming the demesnes of the manor of Loversall, 'being of a great tillage', which he held from Sir John Wolstenholme. Another representative of the minor gentry, Thomas Barnby of Barnby Hall, had a seven-year lease of property in Kinsley from Lady Agnes Gargrave. In 1638 he sold the 'corn and oats' sown on these lands, together with all the profits and tithes for the year, to the new owner of Kinsley Hall who paid him the sum of £230 as consideration.[3]

Where a gentleman was managing his home farm as a commercial enterprise the total value of his crops might well amount to £100, £200 or £300. The following examples which have been taken from probate

---

[1] *Cal.S.P.Dom.* 1628–9, 500.

[2] P.R.O., Duchy of Lancaster, Special Commissions, D.L.44/442. Sheffield Central Library: Bright MSS 79(b).

[3] P.R.O., Chancery Proceedings, Six Clerks' Series, C.10/55/32. Nottingham University Library: Galway of Serlby MSS 9469.

inventories may be regarded as typical. In 1574 Roger Burgh of Brough Hall had 63 acres of wheat and rye worth £43 at Brough and Catterick while his barns and garners contained wheat, rye, barley, oats and peas valued at £189. 5s. 4d.; in addition, there was hay in the barns and fields worth £30. In 1638 George Wentworth of West Bretton, another landowner of medium income, had 6 acres of wheat (valued at £22), 20 acres of wheat and rye (£50), 68 acres of oats (£136) and 2 acres of barley (£8); besides the crops growing in the fields there were twenty-seven loads of corn in the garners worth £22. 19s. 0d. and forty loads of hay in the barn worth £30. The value of wheat and rye per acre in 1638 (50s.) may be compared with the value given in the inventory of 1574 (about 13s. 8d.) to show how cereal prices had been rising in the intervening sixty years. A more valid comparison, however, can be made between the crop values at West Bretton in 1638 and those at Nostell Priory in 1588 since the two estates were situated in the same general area of the West Riding. In terms of value per acre the figures are as follows: wheat 30s. in 1588 and 73s. 4d. in 1638; barley 24s. 3d. in 1588 and 80s. in 1638; and oats 13s. 4d. in 1588 and 40s. in 1638.[1]

The valuation of crops in probate inventories is an imperfect guide to the profits which were being made out of arable farming because a substantial quantity of corn and vegetables would be needed for the household. Few accounts relating to the sale of produce have survived from this period but the following example provides a glimpse of the commercial implications of large-scale crop cultivation. In the period 1638–42 Thomas Stringer of Sharlston kept a record in his memorandum book of the receipts which he had obtained from the sale of wheat, rye, barley and peas. These figures are set out in the following table:

		£	s	d
1638	wheat and rye	143	9	1
1639	wheat	104	8	8
1640	wheat and barley	166	4	5
1641	wheat	100	6	4

		£	s	d
1642	wheat	176	16	5
	barley	150	12	10
	peas	10	8	1
	total	337	17	4

[1] *Surtees Society*, xxvi, 247–8. Y.A.S. Library: Bretton Hall MSS 85. P.R.O., Duchy of Lancaster, Special Commissions, D.L.44/442.

Thomas Stringer was clearly not a typical representative of the country gentry. In the first place, his rent-roll (excluding property which he held on mortgage) was usually of the order of £40 to £50 in this period. Secondly, when he compounded for his estate as a royalist delinquent he claimed that the parliamentarian troops had taken from him cattle and corn worth £3700.[1]

Generally speaking, the charges of husbandry consisted of two main items, the purchase of stock and the payment of wages. Stock buying could involve heavy expenditure, particularly when a new herd or flock was being built up. Thus in 1587 Sir Robert Stapleton of Wighill claimed in an Exchequer suit that one of his servants had embezzled the sum of £150 which he had given him for the purpose of stocking his grounds with cattle.[2] Servants in husbandry could hardly be described as well paid even when due allowance is made for free board and lodging. A foreman might receive £3 or £5 a year in money wages, an ordinary labourer 30s. or £2.[3] In some cases the home farm employed as many as ten or fifteen men throughout the year: in August 1609, for instance, Sir Henry Bellasis of Newburgh Priory had eleven hinds and two millers at Newburgh alone, their half-yearly wages amounting to £11. 16s. 4d.[4] Besides the work-servants who had permanent employment there was also a requirement for extra labour at harvest-time. Henry Best writes in 1641:

They weare wont, in former times, to hire att Malton good and able mowers out of the Moores for 2s. 2d. and 2s. 4d. a weeke and finde them meate, drinke, and lodginge; they used likewise to hire there, able younge followers, for bindinge and stockinge, for 20d. a weeke and theire meate; and boyes, for lyinge out and traylinge of the sweathrake, for 15d. a weeke and theire meate; but nowe of late wee give to our mowers 3s., and finde them meate and drinke; and to the binders wee hire there 2s. 4d.; and for outliggers 20d. a weeke, and meate, drinke, and lodginge.[5]

To illustrate the amount of expenditure which might be incurred on husbandry we may turn to the accounts of a well-to-do squire, Sir

[1] Y.A.S. Library: MS 311 (no pagination). P.R.O., S.P.Dom., Committee for Compounding, S.P.23/ccxiv/155.
[2] P.R.O., Exchequer, Special Commissions, E.178/2693.
[3] For the fixing of wage rates see R. K. Kelsall, *Wage Regulation under the Statute of Artificers.*
[4] Y.A.S. Library: Newburgh Priory MSS, Box 3, Bundle 15: account book (no pagination).
[5] *Surtees Society*, xxxiii, 48.

Henry Slingsby of Scriven. In the period 1635–6 to 1640–1 his expenditure under this heading was as follows:

	£	s	d
1635–6	73	0	0
1636–7	104	15	0
1637–8	121	10	6
1638–9	160	0	10
1639–40	181	15	4
1640–1	141	7	11

His total expenditure in these years varied between £1568. 5s. od. in 1635–6 and £2082. 6s. od. in 1640–1.[1]

In the ranks of the minor gentry we occasionally find a landed proprietor whose income was derived entirely from his own farming activities. In 1653, for example, William Constable of Caythorpe was managing his compact estate as a single farming undertaking, the property being valued at £129. 7s. 4d. a year after the deduction of an out rent.[2] Nevertheless the gentleman who farmed his whole estate was no more typical than the gentleman who was completely dependent for his income on the rents of his tenants. A clearer picture of the relative importance of farming profits in the management of a country estate may be obtained from the following examples[3] which have been brought together as a representative selection:

	Year	Annual income from lands belonging to home farm £	Total annual income from estate £
John Constable of Kirkby Knowle	1653	20	65
John Vavasour of Willitoft	1653	30	81
Charles Thimbleby of Snydal	1653	51	400
William Rokeby of Skiers	1651	58	580
Henry Tempest of Tong	1642	40	658
Sir Philip Constable of Everingham	1642	144	1570

[1] See Appendix A, including the explanation of Sir Henry's accounting year.
[2] P.R.O., S.P.Dom., Committee for Compounding, S.P.23/lviii/ff.204–5.
[3] P.R.O., S.P.Dom., Committee for Compounding, S.P.23/lviii/ff.48–53, 58–62, 81–3 and Commonwealth Exchequer Papers, S.P.28/215, account book 1655, ff.48, 49. Beverley County Record Office: Legard of Anlaby MSS, DDBL/20/16. Cartwright Memorial Hall, Bradford: Tempest MSS, estate papers. C.R.S., liii, 433–5. P.R.O., S.P.Dom., Committee for Compounding, S.P.23/lxxv/615.

Naturally there were some landowners who had a greater enthusiasm for demesne farming than others, while in the more sparsely populated regions a landlord might be obliged to keep a sizeable proportion of his estate in his own hands. Nevertheless it may be said that as a general rule the larger the estate the smaller the percentage of income attributable to farming profits. For the lesser gentry direct farming often represented a substantial, and sometimes a predominant, source of income; for the wealthier gentry it was a valuable weapon in the Price Revolution even if it provided only a fraction of their revenue.

Francis Bacon wrote: 'I knew a nobleman in England, that had the greatest audits of any man in my time: a great grazier, a great sheep-master, a great timber man, a great collier, a great corn-master, a great lead-man, and so of iron, and a number of the like points of husbandry; so as the earth seemed a sea to him, in respect of the perpetual importation.'[1] Good husbandry could mean industrial as well as agricultural development and many Yorkshire gentry whose estates were favourably situated increased their revenue through the exploitation of mineral resources. On the whole, the county was well furnished in this respect. In the West Riding there were extensive deposits of coal, lead and ironstone. In the North Riding there was alum in Cleveland, lead and coal in Richmondshire. Only the East Riding was lacking in mineral wealth: 'coal-finders' who searched for coal seams in this region were ill-rewarded for their enterprise.[2]

Coal was being mined in Yorkshire at least as early as the thirteenth century.[3] The first major expansion of the industry had its beginnings in the reign of Elizabeth when hundreds of new pits were opened in the West Riding. To a large extent the rapid growth of the Yorkshire coal industry was due to the efforts of the gentry who owned much of the coalbearing land: indeed in the period 1558–1642 at least eighty families had coalmining interests. The enthusiasm which this type of industrial enterprise aroused may be judged from the activities of the principal landowners in Baildon, a township situated to the north of Bradford. These activities were described in some detail in the course of a Chancery lawsuit between Francis Baildon and his father-in-law Sir Richard Hawksworth which began in November 1652. According to depositions taken in 1654 coal had been dug on Baildon moor for

---

[1] *The Essayes or Counsels Civill and Morall of Francis Bacon Lord Verulam*, 108.
[2] J. U. Nef, *The Rise of the British Coal Industry*, ii, 72.
[3] *V.C.H. Yorkshire*, ii, 338.

about fifty years. At the beginning of the seventeenth century there were three gentle families with manorial rights in Baildon: the Fitz-williams of Bentley, the Baildons of Baildon and the Vavasours of Weston. A map of the township prepared by Robert Saxton in 1610 depicts a number of coalmines, some in the North Wood (which Sir Mauger Vavasour had enclosed for this purpose) and some in William Baildon's part of the common known as Glovershay. Several years previously William Baildon and Gervase Fitzwilliam had concluded an agreement whereby the profits of the coalmines (excepting the North Wood colliery) were to be divided equally between them. In 1615 Walter Hawksworth of Hawksworth acquired the Fitzwilliam manor and entered into a similar agreement with the Baildons. Between 1620 and 1640 the profits averaged £80 a year after the deduction of charges. In his Chancery bill of 1652 Francis Baildon claimed that shortly after the death of his father, which occurred in 1627, Sir Richard Hawksworth 'did digge and sinke severall cole pitts within the said waists, and gott and sold coles there, of the yearly value of two hundred poundes'. In his reply Sir Richard put the value at no more than £20 a year while testimony was produced that the clear profits of the new mines had varied between 14s. and 20s. a week. The coal-mining accounts which have survived among the estate papers of Sir Richard Hawksworth throw some further light on the subject. In the early months of 1658 his mines were producing coal at the rate of 350 loads, or roughly forty tons, a week and the net value, including the coal supplied to Hawksworth Hall, averaged 13s. a week over and above the charges. Sir Richard never lost his interest in coalmining and in the last years of his life he was developing new pits. An account drawn up in May 1657 contains the item 'ffor sinking one dep pitt £2. 18s. 8d.' while another account for 1658 records that £7. 16s. 8d. was owing 'for two deepe pitts sinkinge'.[1]

In some cases a 'gentleman collier' was interested only in supplying his own domestic needs. According to his family journal John Kaye of Woodsome caused pits to be sunk at Claverley which served the house there and would have furnished the county if necessary. In addition, he sought and found coal at Rowley for the use of Woodsome Hall.[2] Other gentlemen leased out their mines or coal seams and arranged for

[1] W. P. Baildon, *Baildon and the Baildons*, i, 538, 541 and ii, 305–8. Sheffield Central Library: Bright MSS, BR 37 and WWM D.569.
[2] Y.A.S. Library: MS 178, 19.

part of the rent to be paid in kind. In 1652, for example, Sir George Wentworth of Woolley granted a three-year lease of his pits on Stain-cross moor, the lessee paying £20 a year together with six wainloads or roughly as many tons, of 'well dressed sleck'.[1] On the other hand, many landed proprietors worked their mines on a commercial basis, usually with the assistance of a 'banksman' who was responsible for day-to-day management. If he had real enthusiasm for coalmining an energetic landlord might be found sinking pits wherever there were rich seams to be exploited: in the wastes and commons, in the demesne lands, in the park adjoining his house, even in the tenanted lands. Sometimes he took the precaution when granting a lease of reserving to himself full liberty to dig coal and carry it away across his tenant's holding; sometimes he compensated his tenants for the disturbance caused by his mining activities. Even so, the extensive working of coal frequently resulted in litigation. Neighbouring landowners brought actions for trespass; copyholders challenged the lord's right to extract minerals from beneath their tenements, while freeholders and other manorial tenants resisted encroachments on the commons which inter-fered with their grazing rights.

Besides working their own mines some gentlemen took leases of coalpits from the Crown or from private owners. In the case of Crown leases particularly the rent was often unrealistic and considerable profits could be made in this way. Among Elizabethan concessionaires who worked coal on duchy of Lancaster property we find Sir Thomas Bland of Kippax Park, John Mallet of Normanton and John Freeston of Altofts.[2]

In this period coal was rarely mined at any great depth. One of the main problems was the influx of water which might put a mine com-pletely out of commission: thus in 1582 it was reported that the Crown mines in Rothwell 'are drowned with water so as nether the said John Malet', who had a lease from the Crown, 'nor any othere have taken any proffet or commoditie...by the space of nyne yeres laste paste'.[3] For drainage purposes a colliery owner often relied on 'soughs' or tunnels driven into the adjacent hill-side which provided outlets for the water accumulating in the workings. In addition, there were various

---

[1] Brotherton Library: Wentworth of Woolley MSS, coalmining papers.
[2] P.R.O., Chancery Proceedings, Series II, C.3/382/14. J. U. Nef, *The Rise of the British Coal Industry*, i, 295, 298.
[3] P.R.O., Duchy of Lancaster, Special Commissions, D.L.44/317.

types of pumping machine which could be used for raising water from the pit-face.[1] How formidable was the problem of drainage may be seen from the following account which appears in a notebook kept by Sir Thomas Gascoigne of Barnbow. In 1638 (he writes)

I did...sinke the Ginn pitt deeper and added another Pumpe and did lenthen the Pumps 4 yeards and drew the water 4 yeards more, which will with greate ease be donn and the water drawn by both pumps. And after that time againe I sunke the same Ginn Pitt 10 foote deeper which went with much more difficulty in respect of the greate weight of the chaine...the Soughes, watercourses, Stanks, and Damms must be carefully attended to...From Parlington Hollins there is two rowes of bottom cole, and one rowe of hard-band to be gotten when the ginns shall draw 20 yeards which to recover there must be 2 water gates driven, one for the high cole and another for the low cole. The higher water gate must be taken out of the bottom of the Ginn pitt which is about 20 yeards deep.[2]

Coalmining could involve heavy capital investment, particularly if it was undertaken on a commercial scale. Before any profits could be made it was necessary to spend money on carrying out trial borings, sinking pits, digging water-courses, purchasing machinery and other equipment, and erecting colliery buildings. Sir Arthur Ingram's coalmining accounts for the year 1634 contain a number of items of capital expenditure. These include various payments to the colliers for boring operations at Altofts (for which the standard rate was 2s. 10d. a yard) and the sum of £4. 4s. 8d. 'for 3 great Ropes...being eache of them 50 yarde longe'.[3] Few Yorkshire colliery accounts have survived for this period but there are scattered references to mining expenditure in the records of lawsuits. According to a Chancery bill of 1623 Sir William Slingsby had invested at least £700 in developing the mines in Kippax and bringing them to a good performance. Similarly, in 1665 the co-partners of a colliery enterprise in Seacroft were said to have spent £800 in making a sough.[4] In view of the heavy development costs some landowners entered into arrangements for sharing both the expenditure and the profits. In August 1633 John Farrer of Ewood

---

[1] See J. U. Nef, *op. cit.*, i, 353–8 and ii, 449–51.

[2] *Thoresby Society*, xvii, 10–11. As used in mining a 'gin' was an apparatus for hauling up coal or waste material or (as in this case) for pumping out water. A 'stank' was a ditch or pond.

[3] Leeds Central Library: Temple Newsam MSS, TN/EA/15/1.

[4] P.R.O., Chancery Proceedings, Series II, C.3/382/4. Leeds Central Library: Gascoigne of Barnbow MSS, GC/C4.

concluded an agreement with Abraham Shaw of Northowram, described as a yeoman, for the mining of coal in the wastes and commons of Hipperholme and Sowerby. Under this agreement Shaw, who was the working partner, undertook to bear all the initial charges up to the sinking of the first pit but was to be allowed 'the fourth part of the said charges, except of boring with wimble for searching, out of the half of the profit accrueing to the said John Farrer forth of the premises'. It was further agreed that the whole charge of sinking any more pits, together with expenditure on tools, ropes and other items, 'shal bee equally borne betwixt the said parties, and all the cleare profitt equally devided betweene them'. In addition, Farrer and his heirs were to have yearly 'to his and their owne use three hundred horse loades of coles paying for getting thereof'.[1]

By modern standards the annual output at the average colliery can only be regarded as modest. In 1598 the Privy Council were informed that Hewett Osborne's mines in Wales Wood produced each year '2,000 lodes of coles', or roughly as many tons, 'towardes the furnishinge of the countries next adjoynynge'.[2] This rate of production may be compared with the output of the Colsterdale mines in Mashamshire which belonged to the Danbys of Masham. During the last quarter of 1622 (we learn from the banksman's accounts) coal was being mined at an average rate of about 500 corves a week which would have amounted to around 1200 tons a year.[3] In the northern counties pithead prices could vary considerably from one locality to another but normally they fell within the range of 1s. to 4s. a ton. According to a particular of Handsworth Park which apparently dates from 1659 the colliery had an annual output of 1600 loads or tons which sold at the rate of 3s. a load while the running costs averaged 1s. 2d. a load.[4] As a rule the recurrent expenditure mainly took the form of wages. In 1622 the labour force at the Colsterdale mines consisted, at its maximum, of twenty-three workmen besides the banksman. Over a nine-week period the coal extracted was valued at £45. 16s. 2d. while the total wages bill came to £38. 8s. od., leaving a profit of roughly 16s. a week.[5]

[1] W. Wheater (ed.), *Old Yorkshire*, Second Series, 274–5. A 'wimble' was an instrument for boring holes or scooping out earth and other waste material.
[2] *Acts of the Privy Council 1598–9*, 657.
[3] Cartwright Memorial Hall, Bradford: Cunliffe–Lister MSS, Bundle 16.
[4] Sheffield Central Library: Bright MSS, BR 53.
[5] Cunliffe–Lister MSS, Bundle 16.

A few Yorkshire gentlemen made large profits out of coalmining. One North Riding landowner, Sir William Gascoigne of Sedbury, had mines in Durham which in 1607 were said to be worth £400 a year.[1] In 1623 it was claimed that over a twenty-year period Sir William Slingsby had obtained £6000 from his mining venture at Kippax and that the profits had amounted to £600 a year 'for divers years together'. Some accounts relating to the Kippax colliery have been preserved. These show that in the unsettled conditions of the Civil War period the earlier profitability of the mines was seriously impaired. For example:

	Total receipts £	Expenditure £
year ending November 1647	691	405
year ending November 1648	300	388

Nevertheless the situation soon began to improve and in the year ending November 1650 the total receipts from the sale of coal had risen to £877. 16s. 1d.[2] If some landowners drew a substantial part of their income from coalmining they were in no way representative of the sizeable group of families which engaged in this activity on a commercial scale. After covering his expenditure a typical 'gentleman collier' might be left with clear profits of £50 or £100 a year although not infrequently a mining enterprise yielded no more than £20 or £30 a year. Even then, the need for further capital investment could mean a complete suspension of operations, perhaps for a lengthy period, or at least a heavy fall in profits. In general, coalmining profits were a useful supplement to the normal estate revenue rather than a source of great wealth.

Leadmining, an industry dating from at least the Roman occupation, also engaged the attention of Yorkshire landowners. The main lead-mining areas at this time were Ribblesdale, Wharfedale, Nidderdale, Wensleydale and Swaledale. In Nidderdale Sir Arthur Darcy and his son Henry were undertaking mining operations in their manor of Bewerley during the early years of Elizabeth's reign. In 1573 Sir Henry sold the manor to Thomas Benson who (it was said) made an annual profit of £160 from the leadmines. The moors and wastes of Bewerley adjoined the commons of Brimham and at some stage Benson entered

[1] *Surtees Society*, xvii, 207.
[2] P.R.O., Chancery Proceedings, Series II, C.3/382/4. Leeds Central Library: Temple Newsam MSS TN/EA/16.

into an agreement with Sir William Ingleby of Ripley, the owner of Brimham, their purpose being to 'ioyne together for digginge to gett leade, and have the equall benefytt, and beare the equall Chardge'. Towards the end of the sixteenth century Sir Stephen Proctor of Fountains Abbey acquired an interest in the Bewerley leadmines and in February 1611 was reported to have taken the profits for the space of twelve years. Sir Stephen worked the lead with characteristic energy, opening new mines and engaging in litigation over the mineral rights in Bewerley.[1] Another Nidderdale landowner who had leadmining interests was Sir John Yorke of Gouthwaite. At his death in 1634 his property included leadmines in the manor of Appletreewick (which were actually in Wharfedale) and smelthouses in Harefield, on the other side of the Nidd from Bewerley.[2]

Probably the most profitable leadmines in the county were the Marrick mines in Swaledale. These were developed by John Sayer of Great Worsall, one of the wealthiest squires in the North Riding, who held the estate from 1584 to 1635. In the Commonwealth period the mines were said to be worth £1000 a year and indeed the clear profits in the year ending 11 March 1651 amounted to £968. 6s. 2d.[3]

In Yorkshire the iron industry was almost completely in the hands of the nobility and gentry. During the period 1558–1642 they owned a considerable number of ironworks, some large but most of them relatively modest in size. These were mainly situated in the neighbourhood of Leeds, Huddersfield, Barnsley and Sheffield, at such places as Kirkstall, Attercliffe, Wadsey, Lascelles Hall, Colne Bridge, Honley, Cawthorne, Rockley, Wortley, Hunshelf, Midgley Bank and West Bretton. Basically there were two distinct processes involved: the mining of ironstone and the extraction of iron from the crude ore. As a general rule these mining and smelting operations were carried on side by side although an ironmaster was sometimes obliged to look further afield for his raw material: in 1575, for example, Matthew Wentworth of West Bretton secured a lease of a 'myne and dellff' of ironstone in the neighbouring township of Emley in order to supply his forge at West Bretton.[4] To work the hammers and bellows the

[1] P.R.O., Star Chamber Proceedings, Star Chamber 8/227/6 and 35.

[2] P.R.O., Court of Wards, Feodaries' Surveys, Wards 5/50 and Exchequer, Recusant Rolls, E.377/50

[3] P.R.O., S.P.Dom., Committee for Compounding, S.P.23/cxxii/67 and Commonwealth Exchequer Papers, S.P.28/215, order book 1651 seq., f.102.

[4] *Y.A.S.R.S.*, lxix, 40.

power of running water was required and for this reason an ironworks had to be built alongside a river or stream and equipped with dams and water-wheels. At this time charcoal was the only fuel which could be used in smelting: not until the early years of the eighteenth century was an effective method found of using coal (in the form of coke) as the basic fuel of the iron industry. This reliance on charcoal meant a great demand for wood which could represent a major item of expenditure. The estate papers of Thomas Barnby of Barnby Hall, who had an iron forge in Cawthorne, contain various documents relating to the purchase of wood. On 11 April 1626 (to quote one instance) George Wentworth of Woolley agreed to sell him all the spring wood growing on his Notton estate for the sum of £157. 10s. 0d. Under the terms of this agreement the purchaser was to cut down and take away all the wood before 1 May 1629; failing this, he would be required to pay 12d. for every acre of wood left standing on that date.[1]

One of the leading ironmasters of this period was Sir John Savile of Howley (later raised to the peerage as Lord Savile of Pontefract) who owned the great Kirkstall ironworks on the River Aire near Leeds. In 1631 the Court of Wards' feodary valued the works, together with some closes and woods, at 1000 marks a year while assessing the total revenue of the estate as £2200 a year. That this was a conservative estimate is made clear in a letter of Thomas Lord Savile (the eldest son of Sir John Savile) which is dated 12 September 1631. According to this letter his sister had been granted a two-year lease of the works but had agreed to sell him her interest in return for £4500 in cash. As the result of litigation all work had been brought to a standstill and Savile goes on to explain what measures he had taken in the meantime:

I have provided a stocke at least of £2000 most of it perishable commodityes, I have repayred the Iron workes, brought the sow Iron to the forge at £100 charge, I have mended the Dammes, I have sent up and Downe all the countrey to find out workemen to make new the Bellowes...and all the while the workemen have layd Idle so great a number also, I have been glad to pay as if they had wrought for feare if they had once gone away, I should never have gotten them together againe.[2]

Another Yorkshire squire who had a major stake in the iron industry was Sir Francis Wortley of Wortley. On his travels through York-

---

[1] Sheffield Central Library: Spencer Stanhope MSS, forge and furnace papers.
[2] P.R.O., Court of Wards, Feodaries' Surveys, Wards 5/49. Sheffield Central Library: Strafford Letters, xii. Lord Savile to Lord Wentworth, 12 September 1631.

shire in the years 1619–30 Roger Dodsworth the antiquary noted in his journal that the River Don 'leaveth Wharncliffe Chase...on the North, belonging to Sir Francis Wortley, wher he haith great iron workes' and subsequently he passed by the 'Midgeley Bank Smythies, being iron workes belonging to Sir Francis Wortley'.[1] Besides his own works Sir Francis had a share in the iron smithies and iron mines of Silkstone which were held on lease from the Crown: in Hilary term 1631 he was accused in the Exchequer court of attempting to deprive the other tenant of his profits. No accounts have survived for this period to show how much profit the Wortleys were making out of their industrial activities but some rough indication can be found in an agreement drawn up in May 1658. Under the terms of this agreement Sir Edward Wortley granted to John Spencer, a London merchant, a nine-year lease of a forge in Hunshelf and another forge called the 'New Hammer' or 'Lower Forge' lately erected in Wortley, allowing him 1800 cords of logwood a year. In return the lessee was to pay a rent of £510 per annum.[2]

We have seen how the Yorkshire gentry sought to increase their revenue in a period of inflation, whether as a direct response to the economic situation or simply as good businessmen. The methods which they employed fall naturally into three categories. In the first place, there were the measures which can be grouped under the heading of estate administration: the raising of rents and copyhold fines, the shortening of leases, the conversion of copyhold into leasehold property, the introduction of a proper accounting system. Secondly, there were the various types of agricultural improvement aimed at increasing farming efficiency and productivity: the enclosure and development of common land, the redistribution and consolidation of holdings in the open fields and the use of new techniques for promoting soil fertility. Finally, there was a considerable range of productive activities: demesne farming, coalmining, leadmining and iron manufacture. The general rate of increase in the rent level and the widespread practice of maintaining a home farm should in themselves have been sufficient to overcome the problem of inflation; in other words, there was no inherent reason why the Price Revolution should have proved too much for the country gentry who relied on normal methods of estate management. At the same time, there were some families

[1] Y.A.S.R.S., xxxiv, 16, 17
[2] Sheffield Central Library: Wharncliffe MSS, WM. 94, D.98 and D.576.

which stood out from the rest in the enthusiasm they displayed for agricultural improvement, large-scale farming or the exploitation of mineral resources. From the evidence available at least 120 families may be assigned to this category in the period 1558–1642. Often the same names occur in more than one context. John Sayer of Great Worsall was interested not only in leadmining but also in the possibilities of enclosure: in May 1607, for example, he was reported to have taken up part of the common of Marrick. George Shilleto of Heath was a colliery owner and an enclosing landlord. Thomas Stringer of Sharlston not only went in for arable farming on an extensive scale but also owned coalmines and stone quarries.[1] Some of the most energetic landlords, like Sir Arthur Ingram of Temple Newsam and Sir Stephen Proctor of Fountains Abbey, were representatives of the new families which were acquiring estates and social position. It is impossible, however, to equate the 'improving gentry' with the *parvenu* gentry: of the 120 families which showed particular enterprise only seventeen had been granted arms since 1558. In short, an ancient coat of arms did not necessarily signify an outdated approach to the problems of estate management. At a later stage we shall be considering how successful, in terms of material advancement, the landed gentry really were when they had no other source of income to sustain them.

[1] *Surtees Society*, xvii, 206–7. *Thoresby Society*, xvii, 227. Sheffield Central Library: Strafford Letters, xx(a), papers relating to Roundhay and Seacroft. Y.A.S. Library: MS 311 (no pagination). P.R.O., S.P.Dom., Committee for Compounding, S.P.23/ccxiv/155. Nottingham University Library: Galway of Serlby MSS 9309.

CHAPTER IV

Education and the Pursuit of a Career

'THERE IS nothinge that can more advaunce the florishinge and constant happines of any Kingdome or common welth, then in the advancement of divine and humane knouledge, the undoubted mother of all good pollicie in the magistrate, and of all right obedience in the people.' So begins the preamble to the first statutes of Wakefield Grammar School which were drawn up in July 1607.[1] During the century before the Civil War the growing awareness among the propertied classes of the value of education, both to the commonwealth and the individual, resulted in a striking expansion of educational facilities in Yorkshire. Grammar schools were founded and endowed not only in such populous towns as Sheffield, Wakefield and Halifax but also in many rural townships and villages.[2] In this process the gentry played a significant part, providing money and land, securing foundation charters and serving as governors and trustees. In the major towns the establishment of a grammar school was usually a community effort but in country districts a village school often owed its existence to the generosity of a local squire: in 1570, for example, Sir Nicholas Fairfax of Gilling made arrangements in his will for the building of a free school in the parish of Gilling and bequeathed an annuity of £10 for the support of a schoolmaster.[3] At the same time this interest in education extended far beyond the realm of philanthropy. During this period the gentry frequently made provision in wills and settlements for the upbringing of their children at school and other establishments of learning. In 1578 Sir William Ingleby of Ripley settled an annuity of £20 on his son Francis 'for his exhibicion and maintenance of his studie', expressing the wish that he should take up a legal career. In 1593 George Savile of Wakefield (who more than anyone else was

---

[1] M. H. Peacock, *History of the Free Grammar School of Queen Elizabeth at Wakefield*, 54.
[2] See W. K. Jordan, *The Charities of Rural England, 1480–1660*, 299–350.
[3] *Y.A.J.*, xix, 189.

responsible for the foundation of Wakefield Grammar School) gave directions that his nephew George should be 'mainteyned at schoole till he be fitt for the universitie' and granted him an annuity towards the cost of his university education. In 1618 Tristram Carliell of Sewerby stipulated that his son John should receive an allowance of £20 a year to keep him at school during his nonage. 'My will', declared Thomas Stockdale of Bilton Park in 1651, 'is that my sonne William Stockdale be educated in learninge at the universitie and Inns of Court.'[1] One of the major factors in this context was the belief which had gained currency within the gentry that their position in society demanded a certain standard of education: thus it was not unusual for a gentleman to talk of educating his children 'according to their degree and quality'. There was, however, another important consideration: in the case of younger sons particularly, education was highly prized for more prosaic reasons in that it represented the gateway to a career.

School records which have survived from this period rarely mention the names of pupils. At some Cambridge colleges, however, new entrants were required to furnish brief particulars of their previous education and this information sheds considerable light on the schooling of gentlemen's sons.[2] Further evidence is to be found in family histories, memoirs and correspondence. In addition, there are frequent references to Catholic schools and schoolmasters in the York ecclesiastical visitation books, in the records of the Northern High Commission and in the registers of the English seminaries on the Continent.[3]

The following table represents an analysis of the schooling received by a substantial number of Yorkshire gentlemen in the period 1558–1642. In the light of this evidence it is clear that most Protestant gentlemen were in the habit of sending their sons to public grammar schools within the county. This is not true, however, of the upper gentry with their superior financial resources and their extensive connections which often transcended county boundaries. Among the Protestant families

---

[1] *Surtees Society*, civ, 129. Borthwick Institute of Historical Research: York Wills, will of George Savile, 6 October 1593. *Y.A.S.R.S.*, lxv, 140. Leeds Central Library: Bilton Park MSS 240.

[2] J. Peile (ed.), *Biographical Register of Christ's College*. J. Venn (ed.), *Biographical History of Gonville and Caius College. Admissions to the College of St John the Evangelist. Al. Cant.* (entries relating to Sidney Sussex College).

[3] Borthwick Institute of Historical Research: Court Books and High Commission Act Books. *C.R.S.*, x, xi, xxxvii and xl. H. Foley (ed.), *Records of the English Province of the Society of Jesus.* See also E. Peacock (ed.), *A List of the Roman Catholics in the County of York in 1604.*

at this level no marked preference was shown for any particular form of schooling: indeed their choice of schools or schoolmasters was extremely varied, ranging over the whole field of education, both inside and outside the county.

Protestant Education

public (endowed) grammar schools:
(a) in Yorkshire	114[1]
(b) Eton, Winchester, St Paul's, Westminster	17[2]
(c) other schools outside Yorkshire	13[3]

schools run as a private venture:
(a) in Yorkshire	32
(b) in other counties	5[4]
resident tutors	12
education simply described as 'private'	3

Catholic Education

Catholic schools:
(a) in Yorkshire	10
(b) preparatory schools at St Omer and St Gregory's Douai	34[5]
resident tutors	70
grand total of pupils comprised in this table	310

At this time it was still comparatively rare for a Yorkshire squire to enter his sons at such leading schools as Eton and Winchester. The small minority who did so usually had interests of some kind in southern England: they included, for example, William Pennyman of Marske, one of the six clerks in Chancery, whose heir was educated at Westminster School.[6] Between 1596 and 1622 Sir Henry Savile (a younger brother of Sir John Savile of Methley) served as provost of Eton and during these years several of his relatives and kinsmen in Yorkshire sent their sons to the college.[7] Among the papers of Sir Timothy Hutton of Marske there are various bills relating to the education of John Hutton, a younger son, at Winchester towards the end of

[1] Includes three who subsequently went to St Omer and three who received some private education.

[2] Includes two who also had some private education.

[3] Includes two who also had some private education.

[4] Includes one who subsequently went to St Omer.

[5] Includes four who also had some private education.

[6] G. F. Russell Barker and A. H. Stenning (ed.), *The Records of Old Westminsters*, ii, 732.

[7] Sir Wasey Sterry (ed.), *The Eton College Register*, 187, 296, 297.

6—Y.G.

James I's reign. These show that over a period of three years a total of £39. 3s. 6½d. was spent on such items as clothes, bedding and school books. In addition, there were tuition fees (unspecified) and the cost of food which amounted to £6 for one half-year.[1]

In many cases a gentleman's sons were educated at the local grammar school with the children of neighbours and tenants. Christopher Wandesford of Kirklington, the son of a knight, was brought up at the free school of Well, a small village school in the vicinity of Kirklington Hall, and subsequently his brothers also went there. Similarly, Lyon Bamford of Pule Hill studied for three years at Worsborough Grammar School, a few miles from his father's house.[2] When the son of a leading squire went to a public grammar school this was usually one of the larger establishments such as St Peter's York, Beverley and Ripon: thus Sir Hugh Cholmley of Whitby writes that at the age of eleven he was sent to the free school at Beverley where he remained for two years before going on to Cambridge.[3] If the master had a good reputation such schools might attract pupils from a wide area: hence a distinction was drawn between scholars from the town whose education was free and 'foreigners' who had to pay tuition and boarding fees. Sometimes the number of boarders was artificially limited in order to maintain sufficient places for the children of townspeople: at Wakefield Grammar School, for instance, a clause was included in the statutes forbidding the schoolmaster to accept more than twenty 'foreigners' at any one time.[4] In some major schools, however, a sizeable proportion of the scholars were the sons of gentry. This point is well illustrated in the admission register of Pocklington School which dates from an earlier period than any other Yorkshire school register known to have survived. Of the 165 pupils who were admitted to the school in the period 1650–7 when Edward Llewelyn was master exactly one-third came from families which were genuinely armigerous. In terms of social rank their fathers represented a broad cross-section of the Yorkshire gentry, ranging from baronets to mere 'gentlemen'.[5]

[1] *Surtees Society*, xvii, 237–44. T. F. Kirby (ed.), *Winchester Scholars*, 169.
[2] T. Comber, *Memoirs of the Life and Death of the Lord Deputy Wandesforde*, 7, 23. *Admissions to the College of St. John the Evangelist*, part i, 50.
[3] *Cholmley Memoirs*, 36.
[4] M. H. Peacock, *History of the Free Grammar School of Queen Elizabeth at Wakefield*, 70.
[5] H. Lawrance, 'Pocklington School Admission Register, 1626—1717', *Y.A.J.*, xxv, 53.

Perhaps the most celebrated private schoolmaster in England during this period was Thomas Farnaby who for some years kept a school in Goldsmiths' Rents, Cripplegate. This school normally had 300 pupils, most of whom were the sons of nobility and gentry.[1] In 1623 they included John Ingram, a younger son of Sir Arthur Ingram of Temple Newsam who was paying the sum of £20 a year for 'tabling and teaching'.[2] Another Yorkshire gentleman who received tuition at this school was Toby Swinburne, the son of a York diocesan official. On entering the English College at Rome in 1633 he described how he had been educated at a well-known London grammar school under Thomas Farnaby before entering Oxford.[3]

In Yorkshire there were a considerable number of private schools which took in boarders. At the time of the Civil War Thomas Smelt, 'an excellent grammarian, both of Latin and Greek', kept a school in the village of Danby Wiske, near Northallerton. Here (according to a former pupil of his) 'he taught about three score boys, the greater part of which were gentlemen's sons or sons of the more substantial yeomanry of that part of Yorkshire or the south parts of the bishopric of Durham'.[4] Not infrequently a parish priest augmented his income by teaching fee-paying pupils. Sir Henry Slingsby of Scriven mentions in his diary that he had been brought up at school with the Reverend Phatuell Otby, then parson of Foston, 'from the age of six until I was 15 years old'. Foston, a small village in the North Riding, was about twelve miles from Red House, one of the principal seats of the Slingsby family. To judge from entries in his father's accounts Henry and his brother Thomas appear to have resided at the parsonage while they were under Mr Otby's tuition: on 6 August 1613, for example, his father sent Mr Otby £5 'towardes the buyinge of Mr Henry Slingesbie and Mr Thomas Slingesbie some clothes and other nessissaries', together with a further sum of £8 for their 'dyet and learninge' over a period of six months.[5]

The practice of employing a resident tutor was mainly confined to the upper levels of the squirearchy, at least within the Protestant section of the gentry. Sometimes a domestic chaplain might be responsible for the early stages of the children's education: in the preface to his

[1] See *D.N.B.* for Thomas Farnaby.
[2] Leeds Central Library: Temple Newsam MSS, TN/EA/12/17.
[3] Foley, v, 693. [4] *Y.A.S.R.S.*, xxxiii, introduction, lxvii.
[5] *Slingsby Diary*, 3, 275.

father's memoirs one of Sir Hugh Cholmley's sons relates that he received instruction from a succession of chaplains until he reached the age of ten when he was placed at St Paul's School.[1]

Until the closing decade of the sixteenth century it was not unusual for even a hardened Catholic to enter his sons at such public grammar schools as St Peter's York, Ripon and Pocklington: indeed there is evidence that in the early part of Elizabeth's reign some of these schools had teachers with popish sympathies.[2] As the religious division sharpened, however, English Catholics saw no alternative but to develop their own system of education with private tutors who shared their beliefs and with clandestine schools and continental seminaries. This system of education will be discussed in detail in a later chapter.[3] The only point which needs to be made here is that while the continental foundations earned a considerable reputation as academies of learning the educational resources available in Yorkshire were probably more satisfactory from a religious than a strictly academic point of view. To provide for his children's education Sir Thomas Reresby of Thrybergh, a secret Catholic, employed a resident schoolmaster who was described in 1604 as a recusant. According to the family history Sir George Reresby, his son and heir, derived little benefit from this form of schooling. Sir Thomas (we are told) 'gave him private Education and not much learning though he could not but be very capable of it haveing...a good Natural witt and Judgement'. Sir George, 'finding the defect of schollership in himselfe, repaired it as to the education of his eldest son, whome he brought up at school, and sent him to Cambridge'.[4]

Whatever the precise kind of schooling the main emphasis in the field of education was on the teaching of Latin and Greek. At a time when Latin was still extensively used not only in works of literature but also for official and legal purposes no one could afford to regard himself as an educated man unless he had a good working knowledge of the language. Such was the importance attached to it that some gentlemen began to teach their children Latin before they had mastered

---

[1] *Cholmley Memoirs*, preface, iii-iv.
[2] At Ripon, for example, there were two Catholic masters: Edmund Browne and John Nettleton (*Y.A.S.R.S.*, xxvii, introduction, lxxii and 194).
[3] See below, 194-9.
[4] B.M., Additional MSS 29443, ff.2, 6. E. Peacock (ed.), *A List of the Roman Catholics in the County of York in 1604*, 6.

their native language. In 1640 Sir Henry Slingsby noted in his diary that he had committed his son Thomas

into the Charge and Tuition of Mr Cheny whom I intend shall be his school-master, and now he doth begin to teach him his primer; I intend he shall begin to spell, and read Latin together with his english, and to learn to speak it, more by practise of speaking than by rule; he could the last year, before he was 4 years old, tell the Latin words for the parts of his body and of his cloaths.[1]

At such schools as Wakefield, Rotherham and Giggleswick the pupils were taught Hebrew in addition to the basic classical subjects. In the statutes of Giggleswick School which were drawn up in 1592 it was stipulated that the master should 'not use in schoole any language to his schollers which be of ryper yeares and proceadinges but onely the lattyne, Greeke and Hebrewe, nor shall he willingly permitt the use of the English tonge in the schoole to them which are or shalbe able to speake lattyne'.[2]

After completing their schooling many Yorkshire gentlemen went on to a university or to one of the inns of court. The following table shows the higher education (including Catholic seminary education) received by the men who were heads of families in 1642[3]:

heads of families who went to
(a) a university only		79
(b) an inn of court only		70
(c) both a university and an inn of court		92
(d) a Catholic college only		4
(e) a Catholic college and an inn of court		1
(f) a Catholic college, a university and an inn of court		1
		247
Total number of families in 1642		679

On the whole, it can be said that the larger the family estate the greater the prospects of receiving some form of higher education. Thus a Protestant squire with an estate of £500 a year or more normally sent

---

[1] *Slingsby Diary*, 53.

[2] *Y.A.S.R.S.*, xxxiii, 256.

[3] The main sources are as follows: J. and J. A. Venn (ed.), *Alumni Cantabrigienses*. J. Foster (ed.), *Alumni Oxonienses*. H. A. C. Sturgess (ed.), *Register of Admissions to the Honourable Society of the Middle Temple*. *The Records of the Honorable Society of Lincoln's Inn i. Admissions from A.D. 1420 to A.D. 1799. Students Admitted to the Inner Temple 1547–1660*. J. Foster (ed.), *The Register of Admissions to Gray's Inn, 1521–1889*.

his heir (and not infrequently his younger sons) to a university or the inns of court.

Of the heads of families of 1642 a total of 172 received a university education, as follows:

Cambridge	134
Oxford	33
Aberdeen and Cambridge	1
St Andrews	1
Leiden and Cambridge	1
Padua	1
Rheims	1
	172

That so many Yorkshire gentlemen went to Cambridge was due to such factors as its geographical position, the strength of its Protestantism and the links which it had with various grammar schools in the county.[1] In March 1641 a petition seeking the establishment of a university at York was submitted to Parliament by a large number of signatories describing themselves as the nobility, gentry, clergy, freeholders and other inhabitants of Yorkshire. In this petition they claimed that since many of their habitations were 'one hundred miles, and some two hundred, from Oxford and Cambridge...many gentlemen send their sons unto the Scotch universities, or only unto country schools'.[2] The petitioners must have been thinking primarily of the North Riding because most Yorkshiremen would have had a shorter journey to Oxford or Cambridge than to any of the Scottish universities. Even then, there is little evidence to substantiate the reference to university education in Scotland. Only three Yorkshire gentlemen are known to have been admitted to Scottish universities during this period: John and Francis Goodricke, sons of Sir Henry Goodricke of Ribston, who were educated at Aberdeen University, and Guildford Slingsby, the heir of Sir Guildford Slingsby of Hemlington, who went to St Andrews. Sir Henry Goodricke, it may be noted, sent his sons to Aberdeen because he considered the discipline there to be stricter than in the English universities.[3]

At Oxford and Cambridge the student was placed, as now, under the

---

[1] See below, 266–7.
[2] *Fairfax Correspondence*, ii, 275.
[3] C. A. Goodricke, *Ribston*, 36. P. J. Anderson (ed.), *Roll of Alumni in Arts of the University and King's College of Aberdeen 1596–1860*, 12. Rushworth, viii, 774.

care of a tutor. In June 1637 we find Robert Gell, a fellow of Christ's College, Cambridge, writing to William Frankland of Great Thirkleby:

I have received your sonne into my tuition, and twenty pounds of your servant Duke for his use; also I have provided him gowne, sirplice or whatsoever is for the present needful; and shall, through Gods blessing, take such care of him as is fit in what belongs unto the office of a Tutour. As for a bed I cannot yet hear of any. Duke tells me, he is to inquire at Sydney-colledg, according to your direction. If thear he cannot get bedding, I know no remedie but you must send some from home.

In a postscript he added: 'Your son Matthew, I hope will do well.'[1]

The main subjects taught at the English universities were Latin, Greek and Hebrew, theology, philosophy and logic, mathematics (which included geometry and astronomy), medicine and civil law. Many gentlemen's sons (and particularly heirs) left the university without taking a degree, in some cases after spending no more than a year in residence. For the heir to a large estate the acquisition of courtly accomplishments was often regarded as having at least the same importance as the study of academic subjects. While Sir Henry Slingsby the diarist was at Queens' College, Cambridge, he spent part of his free time in improving his fencing skill and riding the great horse. In addition, his father's accounts record the payment of various sums to a private tutor who was teaching him the French language.[2] While some undergraduates made the most of their opportunities others completely misspent their time at the university. Writing about the universities in 1636 Christopher Wandesford of Kirklington told his son that he would 'find many who instead of Diligence and Study are conversant together in mean Delights and Fashions. Many instead of Learning and good Behaviour, affect Vanity and the Habits of Liberty'.[3]

The sons of well-to-do gentry were usually admitted as fellow-commoners, that is, the fee-paying students who represented the most privileged class of undergraduate. Others went as scholars, pensioners or sizars. For the gentleman who maintained his son at a university entirely out of his own pocket the cost was by no means insignificant. Towards the end of Elizabeth's reign Robert Kaye of Woodsome allowed his heir John £40 to £50 a year while he studied for two years

---

[1] Y.A.S. Library: Payne–Gallwey MSS (no catalogue number).

[2] *Slingsby Diary*, 307, 312. Y.A.S. Library: Slingsby MSS, Box D5, account book 1619–1623 (no pagination).

[3] Christopher Wandesford, *A Book of Instructions*, 16.

as a fellow-commoner at Queens' College, Cambridge, and subsequently for four to five years at the Middle Temple.[1] In 1622 the widowed mother of John Robinson of Ryther, who was then in ward to the Crown, asked the Court of Wards to grant her an exhibition of 100 marks a year for his maintenance. The Court (she related) had only allowed her £30 a year on this account which was insufficient, 'he beinge nowe 15 yeeres of age and a fellowe Commoner in Cambridge where he cannot be well mainteyned under 100 markes per annum'.[2] One further example may be quoted. In the accounts of Sir Francis Monckton of Cavil there are details of the sums which he had given to his son Philip or disbursed on his behalf since his entry to Oxford in May 1638: these amount to a total of £88. 5s. od. over a two-year period.[3]

Most of the gentlemen's sons who entered the inns of court had no intention of becoming lawyers: they were sent there to acquire a legal grounding which would be of value to them in the management of their estates and in carrying out their duties as sheriffs or justices of the peace. From the evidence available the cost was broadly comparable to the expenditure involved in maintaining a fellow-commoner. When Sir George Radcliffe of Overthorpe was studying at Gray's Inn he had a basic allowance of £40 a year. In 1613 he wrote to his family:

If you can provide me 20 pounde I can buy a fair Chamber therewith, together with what my good friends will lend me. For my other allowance it were as good for me to take it quarterly onelye: my desire is, that I might have 20 nobles paid at Midsummer and Christmas, and 20 markes at Michaelmas and Easter. For these two quarters I have more use for money to fournish me with apparel and other accessories, than I have the two other.[4]

Among the richer gentry it was becoming fashionable for the heir, or sometimes a younger son, to travel on the Continent in order to complete his education. Often in such cases the entry in the Privy Council register which records the grant of a pass states that the person concerned was going abroad for his 'better experience'.[5] Occasionally,

---

[1] Y.A.S. Library: MS 178, 18.

[2] P.R.O., Court of Wards, Entry Book of Petitions, Wards 9/clxxvi/f.62.

[3] Nottingham University Library: Galway of Serlby MSS 12149, seventeenth-century account book (no pagination).

[4] T. D. Whitaker, *The Life and Original Correspondence of Sir George Radcliffe*, 92. A noble was 6s. 8d.

[5] There are many references to passes in the *Acts of the Privy Council*, P.R.O., Privy Council Office Registers (P.C.2) and Signet Office Docquets (Indexes). See also P.R.O., S.P.Dom., Elizabeth, S.P.12/cliv/5.

however, the official record is a little more specific: in 1616, for example, Henry Witham of Ledston signified his intention to sojourn in France for three years in order to learn or improve his knowledge of the language.[1] In some cases, as we shall see, a gentleman sent his heir abroad to be schooled in the arts of war (although not, as in the case of many younger sons, to become a professional soldier). This, however, was not the usual meaning of the term 'better experience'. Christopher Wandesford of Kirklington expressed the most widely held view on the purpose of foreign travel in the book of precepts which he bequeathed to his eldest son: 'To view all Countries, to observe the Situation and Structure of the Towns and Buildings Abroad; to know their Laws and Forms of Government; to learn their Language, to compare those Things which you have heard or read of the Places where you shall be, with what you find now in Presence, is the most prudent Use and Application of that Thing which we call Travell.'[2]

During the period 1558–1642 over a hundred Yorkshire gentlemen travelled on the Continent for their 'better experience'. This is in addition to the Catholic youths who were sent to continental seminaries and monasteries[3] and the younger sons who became professional soldiers. It is significant that most of these travellers undertook their journeys in the early seventeenth century. Although some members of the nobility and gentry were already beginning to send their sons abroad for 'experience' in the middle years of Elizabeth's reign the Grand Tour did not really come into fashion until after the conclusion of the Anglo-Spanish peace treaty of 1604.

Passes granted by the Privy Council were normally valid for three years which was sufficient for most persons undertaking the Grand Tour. France and Italy were the principal countries visited although Germany, Switzerland, Holland and the Spanish Netherlands occasionally figured in the itinerary. Few Yorkshire gentlemen travelled into Spain, however, apart from Catholic exiles and youths seeking admission to the English seminaries.

Not infrequently the son of a wealthy squire was entrusted to the care of a tutor who was responsible both for his education and his general welfare. When Thomas Wentworth (later Earl of Strafford) went to France in December 1611 he was accompanied by Charles Greenwood, a fellow of University College Oxford, who was to be-

---

[1] *Acts of the Privy Council 1615–16*, 194.   [2] *A Book of Instructions*, 32.
[3] See below, 195.

come one of his closest friends.[1] In the reign of Charles I John Good-ricke, the son and heir of Sir Henry Goodricke of Ribston, spent eighteen months in France in the company of George Anderson, a Scotsman, who had probably taught him at Aberdeen University. This was almost certainly the same George Anderson who was described as the tutor of George Wandesford of Kirklington in a pass issued in April 1642.[2]

In 1610 Sir Henry Slingsby of Scriven decided to send his eldest son William on a tour of France. Sir Henry chose one Mr Snell as his son's tutor and on 31 March 1610 gave him a set of instructions for the 'guidinge of his pupil'. In these instructions great emphasis was placed on the young man's spiritual welfare. During his travels abroad he was to learn the principles of religion, say his prayers daily and, as opportunity afforded, 'resorte to the service sermons and Sacramente of the reformed Churche'. From 'his first landinge in ffrance' (Mr Snell was enjoined) he was not to 'speake anithinge to him but either latinge or in ffrencht excepte when you shall have occacion to give him some holesome precepte which cannot be understood by him but in English'. Besides the formal academic studies which his father had prescribed for him William was also to learn fencing, dancing and riding. In addition Mr Snell was to ensure that he kept a journal of his travels. Sir Henry had a low opinion of the French: his son (he declared) should 'take heed what companie he keepes in too familiar a fashion for the frenche are of an ill conversacion and full of many loathsome deseases'. Towards the end of his French tour the young traveller spent some time at the famous riding academy in the Rue St Honoré in Paris: in his father's accounts there are references to various sums of money which were sent over to Monsieur Benjamin, the manager of this establishment. William appears to have returned to England early in 1613 but before long preparations were being made for a more ambitious venture. In June 1613 Sir Henry's accounts record the purchase of a black nag in Smithfield for his son's journey into Italy. Clothes and shoes were also bought for him together with a book of Italian grammar. In July Mr Philip Burlamachi, the well known international financier, was given the sum of £50 'to be repaid at fflorrence the first of octobre next to Mr William Slingesbie for his Chardge

---

[1] Knowler, ii, 430.
[2] C. A. Goodricke, *Ribston*, 36. P.R.O., Signet Office Docquets, Index 6811, April 1642 (no pagination). *Surtees Society*, lxii, 40.

and expences in Italie uppon a lettere of Credite'. Little is known of William's sojourn in Italy except that it ended in tragedy: in 1617 he fought a duel with another Englishman in Florence and was slain.[1]

Occasionally the emphasis was not so much on experience through travel as on military experience, though there might also be an opportunity to acquire other accomplishments at the same time. In February 1629 Sir Ferdinando Fairfax of Denton wrote to his father: 'My Lord of Clare adviseth to send my son to my Lord Vere's company, at Dort; he saith he may there practise arms, fencing, dancing, and study the mathematics; my Lord Houghton promiseth his best care over him whilst he is there.' Shortly afterwards Thomas Fairfax (together with John Hotham, the son and heir of Sir John Hotham of Scorborough) went to join the English forces in the Netherlands but did not remain there long. In obedience to his grandfather's wishes he travelled into France and spent some eighteen months there; in 1633, however, he complained to his grandfather that during his sojourn in France he 'only learned the language, and knew war only by an uncertain relation'. Not until the English Civil War was he able to use his military talents to the full.[2]

The Grand Tour was not without its hazards. During this period a number of Yorkshire travellers died on the Continent, either through sickness or misadventure. Another danger which a Protestant squire could not afford to dismiss too lightly was the possibility that his son might be converted to Catholicism. In May 1626 a Dutchman under interrogation at Newcastle testified that he had served Thomas Fairfax, the heir of Sir Thomas Fairfax of Gilling, 'for the space of three years together in the tyme of his travaile beyond seas' and had then accompanied him to England 'to a place called Walton in Yorkshire' which was one of the family seats. Sir Thomas, however, 'taking dislikeing to his said sonne for his popish recusancy would not suffer him to stay there' and he had been obliged to take up residence with a Catholic relative in Newcastle.[3] A further source of anxiety was the problem of keeping the young traveller supplied with money. In 1614 John Savile

[1] *Slingsby Diary*, 259–66, 269, 272–4. Y.A.S. Library: Slingsby MSS, Box D5, account book 1613–1615 (no pagination). *Acts of the Privy Council 1613–14*, 104. J. W. Stoye, *English Travellers Abroad 1604–1667*, 57–8.

[2] *Fairfax Correspondence*, i, 160–3, 228. *Acts of the Privy Council 1628–9*, 371.

[3] P.R.O., S.P.Dom., Charles I, S.P.16/ccvii/34.

of Methley had to borrow £20 from Sir Dudley Carleton, the English ambassador at Venice, 'his own moneyes fayling him through his neglect of giving his frendes in England certayne Advertisement of his remove from place to place'. In writing to thank the ambassador, his brother Sir Henry Savile went on:

Hereafter during his aboade in Italy or else where he shall not fayle God willing in this kynde so as he exceede not his allowance of a £100 per Ann. His frendes heare must intreate your Lordshipp to have an eye to his government and afforde him your best advyse and dyrection in his courses for though wee cannot expect much from his Education, whom nature did more enclyne to make a ploddinge common lawyer than an accomplisht traveller, yet... we would be glad he should returne worthie his expence of tyme and money.[1]

Some gentlemen returned from foreign travel with little to show for it except perhaps a certain affectation in gesture or attire. Others used their time more profitably. Thomas Wentworth (who, as we have seen, embarked on a tour of France in 1611) diligently kept a journal in which he made notes about the people, the towns, the institutions and the customs. He also bought a large number of books, including French comedies and historical and theological works, from which he some-times copied extracts into his diary.[2] In the case of a younger son who had to make his way in the world there was obviously a greater incen-tive to exploit the opportunity of foreign travel to the full in order to fit himself for a career. In May 1635 Michael Wentworth of Woolley wrote to his kinsman Thomas Wentworth (now Viscount Wentworth):

my sonne John Wentworth is (I thank god) well returned from his travell: wherein he spente above 3 yeares, much in Italy, more in France (which langinges he hath) and some in othere Countryes: and truly I thinke and others saye, thatt he hath not ile bestowed his tyme therein. He is nowe (my lord) growne to some ripnesse in yeares, when yf experience (by imploymente) may be added to his partes, by nature and education, I thinke he will make a man serviceable. Good my lord make me furthere bounde unto you to take him into your servyce [that is, in Ireland] or othere wyse dispose of him as you please, to sett him in a way of beginninge.

No doubt through the lord deputy's influence John Wentworth

---

[1] P.R.O., S.P.Dom., James I, S.P.14/lxxx/9.
[2] Sheffield Central Library: Strafford Letters, xxx. See J. W. Stoye, *English Travellers Abroad 1604–1667*, 64–9.

became secretary to Lord Littleton who in 1640 was appointed to the office of lord keeper.[1]

2

In view of the emphasis placed on education in this period it would be surprising to find that the Yorkshire gentry conformed to the traditional image of the provincial squire as a rough unsophisticated countryman who was interested only in the state of his rent-roll and the pleasures of the chase. There is in fact a good deal of evidence to show that among the richer families particularly an interest in cultural pursuits was by no means uncommon. In the first place, the inventories which were made of household possessions not infrequently mention books (in one case valued at £100[2]) and on occasion a testator, in settling his bequests, paid special attention to the disposal of his library. Among the papers of Sir William Fairfax of Gilling, an Elizabethan squire, there is a list of his books 'remayning at Gilling' (phraseology which suggests that the bulk of his library may have been at Walton Hall, the other family seat). To judge from this list Sir William was a man with catholic tastes in literature. In all, the titles of thirty-nine books are mentioned, half in English and the rest in French or Latin. Apart from the inevitable book on hawking there were works by a wide range of authors, among them St Augustine, Tacitus, Plutarch, Machiavelli, Chaucer, Froissart and Holinshed. The last item in the inventory testifies to his genealogical interests: this was a book listing all the coats of arms depicted on the walls and windows of the great chamber at Gilling Castle for which Sir William had been responsible.[3] Secondly, many Yorkshire manor-houses were visited by bands of strolling players who performed not only traditional morality plays but in some cases plays by contemporary authors. In 1616 two of these groups were indicted for vagabondage at the North Riding quarter sessions and also presented with them were a number of squires who had entertained them in their houses, men such as Ralph Rokeby of Marske,

[1] Sheffield Central Library: Strafford Letters, xv. Michael Wentworth to Lord Wentworth, 13 May 1635. *Y.A.J.*, xii, 160. John Wentworth had been granted a pass in May 1631 (P.R.O., Privy Council Registers, P.C.2/xl/545).

[2] Leeds Central Library: MSS of Lord Mexborough, inventory of the personal estate of John Savile of Methley, 1659.

[3] *Archaeologia*, xlviii, 152–3. The book of arms is printed in J. Foster (ed.), *The Visitation of Yorkshire in 1584–5 and 1612*, 639–51. See also below, 105.

William Chaytor of Croft and Thomas Barton of Whenby.[1] Thirdly, music-making was a common pastime among the gentry, the most popular instruments being the virginals, the regals and the orpharion. Even a strait-laced Puritan might have a love of music: thus in January 1600 Lady Margaret Hoby of Hackness noted in her diary that 'to refreshe my selfe beinge dull, I plaied and sunge to the Alpherion'.[2]

We have already met a number of Yorkshire gentry who wrote family histories, diaries or books of precepts for their sons, in particular Sir Thomas Wentworth (the future Earl of Strafford), Sir Hugh Cholmley, Sir Henry Slingsby, Sir John Reresby and Christopher Wandesford. In addition, there were the poets, among them Sir Francis Wortley of Wortley, a friend of Ben Jonson, who was also the author of various prose pamphlets;[3] Sir John Jackson of Hickleton, who is described as 'very studious, a good scholar, as also a good poet for Latin';[4] and Sir John Reresby (not the family historian but his father) who was learned both in Greek and Latin.[5] Finally, we should not overlook the gentlemen who were responsible for works of a more technical nature: legal writers like William West of Firbeck and Henry Swinburne of York and scientific writers like John Field of East Ardsley and William Gascoigne of Thorpe on the Hill.[6]

Altogether at least forty members of the Yorkshire gentry who were living in the period 1558–1642 essayed the writer's craft, either for the amusement or edification of themselves and their families or (less frequently) with a view to reaching a wider readership.[7] Of the families represented two in particular stand out: the Saviles of Bradley and Methley, and the Fairfaxes of Denton. Henry Savile of Bradley, a lawyer, had three distinguished sons. The eldest, Sir John Savile of Methley, who became a baron of the Exchequer, was one of the original members of the Society of Antiquaries and a friend of William Camden.

---

[1] *N.R. Records*, ii, 111, 122, 136. P.R.O., Star Chamber Proceedings, Star Chamber 8/19/10. *The Ancestor*, iii, 148–9.

[2] D. M. Meads (ed.), *The Diary of Lady Margaret Hoby 1599–1605*, 99.

[3] See *D.N.B.* and Sir Francis's *Characters and Elegies*.

[4] J. Hunter, *South Yorkshire*, ii, 137. Sir John died in 1637.

[5] B.M., Additional MSS 29443, f.8. A manuscript volume of Sir John's poems, essays and epitaphs is in the Yorkshire Archaeological Society Library (MS 329).

[6] See A. G. Dickens, 'The Writers of Tudor Yorkshire', *Transactions of the Royal Historical Society*, Fifth Series, xiii, 49 and *D.N.B.*

[7] A. G. Dickens, *op. cit.*, includes a number of writers not mentioned here.

At his death he left a number of writings but only one of these, a collection of law reports, achieved publication, at least in the seventeenth
century. Sir Henry Savile, provost of Eton, was a celebrated mathema-
tician and Greek scholar who founded the Savilian professorship of
astronomy and geometry at Oxford. Of the works which he published
the most notable was his sumptuous edition of the writings of St
Chrysostom. The third son, Thomas Savile, who was a fellow of
Merton College, Oxford, had a considerable reputation as a specialist
in British antiquities.[1]

Although the Fairfaxes produced no one of the same academic
stature as Sir Henry Savile there are several members of the family who
have an honourable place in the history of scholarship and learning.
Sir Thomas Fairfax (later created Lord Fairfax of Cameron) wrote
treatises on horsemanship and other subjects. His brother Charles is
said to have been 'an excellent scholar, but delighted most in antiquities,
and hath left many valuable collections of that kind'; he is now chiefly
noted for his annals of the Fairfax family. Another brother, Edward,
was a poet and scholar who was highly esteemed for his translation of
Tasso. One of Sir Thomas's younger sons, the Reverend Henry Fairfax, followed the example of his uncle Charles and applied himself to
antiquarian and genealogical studies. Finally, Thomas Lord Fairfax
the parliamentarian general was not only the patron of such men as
Roger Dodsworth and Andrew Marvell but also the author of a
number of poems and translations as well as two autobiographical
works relating to the Civil War.[2]

3

At one time or another all gentle families had to face the problem of
providing the younger sons with a means of livelihood. Among the
richer gentry it was not unusual for them to be given parcels of landed
property for their financial support. More frequently, however, a
younger son was granted a life annuity which varied in amount
according to his father's resources and the number of children for
whom provision had to be made. At one extreme he might receive £5

[1] J. W. Clay and J. Lister (ed.), *Autobiography of Sir John Savile, of Methley, Knight,*
Y.A.J., xv, 420. *D.N.B.*
[2] *Fairfax Correspondence*, i, introduction lxxi and ii, 40–1. *D.N.B.* See also A. G.
Dickens, *op. cit.*, 69–70.

or £10 a year; at the other, £50 or even £100 a year. On occasion a capital sum was paid instead of, or exceptionally in addition to, an annuity.

In April 1613 Sir Thomas Wentworth (subsequently Earl of Strafford) asked his father 'what Course of life' he would like 'everie of his brethren trained upp in'. In a memorandum which was drawn up Sir William expressed the wish that his second son William should 'continue his studye at law'. John Wentworth, 'after convenient tyme at Cambridge', could also study the law if he so wished: 'other wyse', Sir Thomas was informed, 'he may lyve in the Countrye and be your frend and Companion...yf he have a desyre to travaile and cann fynd good Companye he may spend some tyme therin.' Robert, the fourth son, was 'to be brought up at Cambridge and so to the Inns of court. Yf his disposition serve for a lawyeare he may followe it, yf not, then to take suche other profession as he more affecteth and as by yow allowed'. Michael, the fifth son, was 'to be kept at schoole tyll 15 yeares that he may understand lattin and wryt well, then one yeare to learne to do those things that belonges to a marchants profession, then bound prentice and in the meane tyme he to have a plentyfull maintenance duringe his minority'. As for his other three sons they were 'to be brought up at Schoule, Cambridge, and Inns of Courte and then to take such profession upon them as yow shall advise them consideringe their naturall disposition and their own desire'.[1]

Younger sons who had their living to make might become lawyers, royal officials, clergymen, tenant farmers, soldiers of fortune (and in the case of Catholic families Jesuits, missionary priests or monks). In addition, they sometimes entered the households of noblemen or wealthy gentlemen where they were employed as servants of the first rank.

In spite of the claim by some contemporary writers that 'merchandising' was not a fit occupation for persons of quality[2] many young men from Yorkshire manor-houses sought to make their fortunes as merchants or tradesmen, either in London or in such towns as York, Leeds and Hull. These came from every section of the gentry (though rarely from the Catholic group of families). In the records of the Skinners Company of London there are references to a number of Yorkshire-born apprentices who were the younger sons of gentlemen. In

---

[1] Sheffield Central Library: Strafford Letters, xxi, 8.   [2] See above, 19.

terms of rank and wealth their fathers represent a broad cross-section of the country gentry: at one extreme there was Sir Richard Darley of Buttercrambe, a leading North Riding landowner; at the other, such men of modest estate as Henry Banke of Bank Newton and William Savile of Copley.[1] An apprenticeship (which might cost several hundred pounds in fees if the master had a high reputation) usually lasted for a period of seven or eight years. Some youths, however, failed to stay the course: in 1621, for example, Sir Thomas Norcliffe of Langton related how his brother William, 'a man of ill government', had departed out of his apprenticeship five years before his time.[2]

While a younger son normally had his living to make the eldest son was destined, as a general rule, to inherit a landed estate. In spite of the law of primogeniture, however, heads of families appear relatively frequently in the ranks of what might be loosely described as the professional and commercial gentry:

total number of heads of families in 1642	679
number of heads of families in 1642 who were or had been:	
(a) physicians	3
(b) clergymen	6
(c) counsellors at law, recorders, attorneys	29
(d) merchants, tradesmen	34
(e) stewards of private estates	1
(f) holders of offices of profit, whether full-time or part-time	35
	108[3]

If we extend this examination to cover all families which can be found within the Yorkshire gentry during the period 1558–1642 the proportion of families with other sources of income besides land increases significantly: in fact, rather more than one-quarter of these families (265 out of 963) fall at one time or another within the scope of the above table.

Such families were in the main new gentry or minor gentry with little inherited wealth. The office-holders, however, often came from families of ancient lineage and included a considerable number of gentlemen (most of them local officials) who were already of good

[1] The apprenticeship records of the Skinners Company are printed in *Miscellanea Genealogica et Heraldica*, Third Series, i, 41–6, 76–80, 102–5, 149–52, 172–6, 194–6, 246–53.

[2] Y.A.S. Library: MD 237(c).

[3] This includes twenty-five heads of families who had not been heirs at birth.

estate before they entered the public service. Taking the period as a whole the office-holders were a sizeable group:

number of heads of families who held offices of profit, 1558–1642   168
number of families represented
   (a) once   108
   (b) more than once   27

During the early seventeenth century there were several Yorkshire landowners who held important offices either in the royal household or in the central government. In the reign of James I Sir David Foulis of Ingleby, a Scotsman who had settled in the North Riding, acted as cofferer or treasurer to both Prince Henry and Prince Charles, while his brother-in-law Sir Thomas Chaloner of Guisborough was first governor and then chamberlain to Prince Henry. Both these gentlemen obtained grants of Crown property: Sir David's estate, for example, included the manor of Greenhow, worth £500 a year, which had been given to him (it was claimed in 1632, when he was busily stirring up opposition to the knighthood scheme) *pro servitio impenso et impendendo*.[1] Another North Riding gentleman holding a key appointment under James I was Sir George Calvert of Danby Wiske (subsequently created Lord Baltimore) who served as one of the principal secretaries of state from 1619 until 1625 when he retired after declaring himself a Catholic. Among his financial rewards was a pension of £1000 a year granted out of the customs.[2]

Sir George's career in the public service was a particularly distinguished one but there were other Yorkshiremen who, without matching his achievement, nevertheless managed to gain lucrative appointments for themselves within the central bureaucracy. In 1637 Sir Rowland Wandesford (the eldest son of Michael Wandesford of Pickhill) was made attorney of the Court of Wards, an office which was probably worth at least £1500 a year.[3] For some time two Cleveland gentlemen, James Morley of Normanby and William Pennyman of Marske, worked together in Chancery where each held one of the

---

[1] *Cal.S.P.Dom. 1603–10*, 7, 30, 72, 142, 155, 169, 176. Sheffield Central Library: Strafford Letters, xii. Sir William Pennyman to Lord Wentworth, 22 August 1632.

[2] Dr Williams's Library: Morrice MSS, 'A Chronological Account of Eminent Persons, &c', vol. iii (no consistent pagination).

[3] Knowler, ii, 116. G. E. Aylmer, *The King's Servants: The Civil Service of Charles I 1625–1642*, 309.

six clerkships. During the reign of James I the customary price for a six clerkship was £6000 and the profits of the office amounted to about £1400 a year on average.[1] Although William Pennyman's office was lost to the family after his death in 1628 the heir eventually resolved to make a career in the central administration. In December 1638 Sir William Pennyman told his friend Lord Wentworth that he had secured an office in the Star Chamber and intended to officiate in person; the profits had averaged nearly £2000 a year over the previous seven years and he had been granted three lives of his own nomination. Mrs Hutchinson states in the biography of her husband, Colonel John Hutchinson, that the gentleman who held the next office to Sir William Pennyman's was 'careless and debauched, and thereby a great hindrance of Sir William's profits, who apprehended that if he could get an honest man into that place, they might mutually advantage each other; whereupon he persuaded Mr Hutchinson to buy the place', but before the transaction could be completed the Star Chamber was abolished.[2]

During his term of office as lord deputy of Ireland Wentworth entrusted a number of senior and junior posts to members of the Yorkshire gentry. These included Christopher Wandesford of Kirklington, Sir George Radcliffe of Overthorpe (two of his closest friends), Sir Richard Scott of Ecclesfield and Sir Richard Osbaldeston of Hunmanby. One of the most profitable of the Irish offices was the mastership of the rolls: in 1637, four years after his appointment, Christopher Wandesford was able to purchase an estate at Castlecomer worth £2000 a year and subsequently spent over £14,000 on its development, building a market town and erecting several ironworks. It is significant that when Sir John Temple became master of the rolls in 1641 directions were given that the fees of this office should be reduced 'to a moderation'.[3] In 1633 Sir George Radcliffe, an Irish Privy Councillor and formerly king's attorney in the North, was granted a pension of £500 a year for the duration of his employment in Ireland: this was

---

[1] N. E. McClure (ed.), *Letters of John Chamberlain*, ii, 193. Knowler, ii, 141. G. E. Aylmer, *op. cit.*, 71, 210.

[2] Knowler, ii, 258. P.R.O., Signet Office Docquets, Index 6811, January 1638(–9) (no pagination). Lucy Hutchinson, *Memoirs of the Life of Colonel Hutchinson*, ii, 67–8.

[3] H. B. McCall, *Family of Wandesforde of Kirklington and Castlecomer*, 78, 141–2, 144–7, 275–7. P.R.O., Signet Office Docquets, Index 6811, January 1640(–1) (no pagination). For Wentworth as lord deputy of Ireland see H. P. Kearney, *Strafford in Ireland, 1633–41*.

in compensation for the loss of his 'practice and profession of the law' in England.[1]

Some offices of profit in Yorkshire such as the legal places on the Council of the North were reserved for career lawyers. There were, however, many remunerative appointments for which no professional qualifications were required. The duchy of Lancaster in particular employed a considerable number of officers for the purposes of administering the Crown estates in the county: receivers, stewards and bailiffs of royal manors, bowbearers, foresters, masters of game, keepers of parks and constables of royal castles. In addition, there were similar posts in the gift of the archbishop of York. In the main such offices were granted to members of the nobility and gentry who usually delegated the more onerous work to servants or salaried deputies.

Local offices of this kind were highly prized and eagerly sought after, not least by gentlemen of rank and substance. In 1584 Sir Henry Gate of Seamer, who was himself an office-holder, solicited a grant of the constableship of Scarborough Castle for his son Edward, emphasising that the manor of Northstead usually went with the appointment. The Queen was 'well pleased' to approve the request and Edward Gate was granted the office for life, together with a lease of the manor.[2] In 1629, not long after becoming lord president of the Council of the North, Wentworth persuaded Sir Thomas Hoby of Hackness to relinquish the office of chief seneschal of the manor of Ripon (a church appointment which Sir Thomas had held since 1617) so that his friend Christopher Wandesford could take it over.[3] In 1641 Sir Henry Slingsby of Scriven noted in his diary that 'about the latter end of August I made a Journey to Scipton, unto my Lord Chaimberlain's house, to move his Lordship for the Understuard of the Castle Court of Knasboroug, having formerly his promise; but Robaltome his man had chang'd his mind and when I came he deny'd me; at the same time came Mr Matthew Hutton, and obtain'd of his Lordship the Understuardship of Richmond'. And Sir Henry added, rather plaintively: 'I have not yet learnt the way how to prevail, nor what weapons to bring

---

[1] P.R.O., Signet Office Docquets, Index 6809, May 1633 (no pagination).

[2] *Camden Society*, Old Series, xii, 103–4. R. Somerville, *History of the Duchy of Lancaster*, i, 535–6.

[3] H. B. McCall, *Family of Wandesforde of Kirklington and Castlecomer*, 75, 260, 270–1. Sheffield Central Library: Strafford Letters, xii. Sir Thomas Hoby to Lord Wentworth, 22 September 1629.

to assail a wilful refusal, nor what more on my part to be seen than a clear intention and a thankful heart.'[1]

The main attraction of these local offices was not so much the fees (which were generally modest) but the perquisites which might be associated with them, in particular, leases of Crown property which could be extremely profitable. About the beginning of the seventeenth century the mills and bailiwick of Wakefield, which were normally granted with the stewardship of the manor, were worth £450 a year to the lessee.[2] In 1615 Sir Henry Slingsby, the father of the diarist, was deprived of the offices of receiver and collector of the honor of Knaresborough, keeper of Bilton Park and forester of the forest of Knaresborough. Subsequently, in claiming compensation for his dismissal, he gave details of the clear annual profits which he had enjoyed:[3]

	£	s	d
the fees	100		
lease of Hay-a Park	280		
bailiwick of Knaresborough	2		
herbage of Bilton Park	80		
certain closes	13	6	8
	475	6	8

It seems unlikely that Sir Henry was exaggerating his losses: indeed profits of this order were probably not unusual where there was an accumulation of offices. On the other hand, a minor office such as a bowbearership or a forestership could be worth no more than £20 or £30 a year to the holder.

Although there were few hereditary offices (that is, offices granted to particular families in perpetuity) a gentleman sometimes managed to secure possession of an office for two or three lives. Similarly, an established office-holder might use his influence to obtain another remunerative appointment for one of his sons or a close relative. Among the Yorkshire gentry who had dynastic ambitions of this kind there was one family which stood out above all the rest: the Slingsbys

[1] *Slingsby Diary*, 72. For a general discussion of this subject see W. T. MacCaffrey, 'Place and Patronage in Elizabethan Politics' (*Elizabethan Government and Society*, ed. S. T. Bindoff, J. Hurstfield and C. H. Williams, 95).

[2] Nottinghamshire County Record Office: Savile of Rufford MSS DD.SR A5/11/1. The Saviles of Thornhill retained the lease after the stewardship had been granted to a kinsman, Sir John Savile of Howley. This led to a dispute between the two families (see, for example, *Cal.S.P.Dom. 1603–10*, 419, 467).

[3] Y.A.S. Library: Slingsby MSS, Box A10.

of Scriven. During the reign of Elizabeth Francis Slingsby served as feodary of the honor of Knaresborough and master forester, keeper and paler of Bilton Park. His grandson Sir Henry Slingsby, who succeeded to his estate in 1600, held a number of offices belonging to the honors of Knaresborough, Pontefract and Tickhill. In addition, he was receiver of the manor of Wakefield and receiver of the issues and profits of the late colleges, chapels and chantries in the county of York which were in the possession of the duchy of Lancaster. In May 1635, not long after his death, these two receiverships were granted to his son-in-law Brian Stapleton of Myton with the reversion to Stapleton's eldest son. Among Sir Henry's younger brothers were Sir William Slingsby of Kippax, a courtier, and Sir Guildford Slingsby of Hemlington who served as comptroller of the navy during the reign of Charles I. Of the latter's children Guildford, the heir, became one of Lord Wentworth's chief secretaries in Ireland while Robert, his second son, was granted the office of comptroller of the navy at the Restoration.[1]

For men who had influence at court the fees and perquisites associated with office-holding were not the only source of profit available: revenue farming and monopolies granted by the Crown could also provide opportunities for profit-making although on a more speculative basis. A project which aroused particular interest among the Yorkshire gentry was the North Riding alum industry. Towards the end of the sixteenth century Sir Thomas Chaloner found alum deposits on his estate at Guisborough and subsequently further discoveries were made at Mulgrave and Sandsend on property belonging to Lord Sheffield, lord president of the Council of the North. In 1607 Lord Sheffield and Sir Thomas Chaloner, together with Sir David Foulis of Ingleby and Sir John Bourchier of Hanging Grimston, secured a patent of monopoly for the sole manufacture of alum, borrowing the capital required for the initial development work from a group of London merchants. Two years later, following an investigation, the Crown took over the industry but agreed to compensate the patentees with annuities amounting to £6000 a year which were to be paid from 1616 to 1638, when the original grant was due to expire. Out

---

[1] R. Somerville, *History of the Duchy of Lancaster*, i, 518, 526, 531. Y.A.S. Library: Slingsby MSS, Box A10. P.R.O., Signet Office Docquets, Index 6810, May 1635 (no pagination). *Slingsby Diary*, 403, 406. Rushworth, viii, 774. *Cal.S.P.Dom. 1660–1*, 214. G. E. Aylmer, *The King's Servants: The Civil Service of Charles I, 1625–1642*, 81.

of this Sir Thomas Chaloner and his heirs were to receive £1000 a year: in fact they appear to have been paid no more than £1250 in spite of frequent attempts to persuade the authorities to honour their obligations.[1]

Between 1613 and 1625 Sir Arthur Ingram played a leading part in the development of the Yorkshire alum industry, first as joint manager on behalf of the Crown, then as member of a syndicate which managed the enterprise as Crown tenants and finally as sole farmer of the works. Although Sir Arthur was accused of fraud and misappropriation it is doubtful whether he made any great profit out of the industry.[2]

In 1630 Sir John Gibson of Welburn was granted a reversionary lease of the mines (subsequently modified) which was to commence in January 1638 under a rent of £12,500 a year to the Crown.[3] Sir John was in fact acting on behalf of Lord Wentworth whose papers contain many references to the alum business. In 1637 the lord deputy apparently assigned the lease to Sir Philip Burlamachi and an agreement was concluded under which two North Riding gentlemen, Sir William Pennyman of Marske and Richard Winne of Guisborough, were to be responsible for the actual manufacture of the alum. Sir William, a close friend of Lord Wentworth, owned the land on which the Slapewath and Selby Hagg works were situated while his prospective partner had long experience in the production field. Shortly after this assignment, however, Sir Paul Pindar acquired the lease and, according to Thomas Fuller, covenanted to pay annual rents of £12,500 to the Crown, £1640 to the Earl of Mulgrave (who, as Lord Sheffield, had been one of the original patentees) and £600 to Sir William Pennyman.[4] The vice-president of the Council of the North, Sir Edward Osborne of Kiveton, also derived some financial benefit from Wentworth's lease: in 1649 his

---

[1] For accounts of the North Riding alum industry see R. B. Turton, *The Alum Farm*, W. H. Price, *The English Patents of Monopoly*, C. J. Singer, *The Earliest Chemical Industry* and *V.C.H. Yorkshire*, ii, 381–7. There are a number of documents relating to the alum business in the muniments of the Chaloner family (Northallerton County Record Office: MSS of Lord Gisborough).

[2] For Sir Arthur's activities see A. F. Upton, *Sir Arthur Ingram*, 107–47.

[3] *Cal.S.P.Dom. 1629–31*, 291. R. B. Turton, *op. cit.*, 161, 164. W. H. Price, *op. cit.*, 98.

[4] Sheffield Central Library: Strafford Letters, xv. Sir William Pennyman to Lord Wentworth, 9 March 1635(–6), xvi. William Robinson to Wentworth, 25 January 1636(–7), Pennyman to Wentworth, 17 February 1636(–7), xvii. Pennyman to Wentworth, 4 April and 24 July 1637. Turton, *op.cit.*, 162. *H.M.C. Various*, viii, 17, 24. Thomas Fuller, *History of the Worthies of England*, iii, 393.

widow sought to compound for a rent of £200 a year issuing out of the alum patent.[1]

Another form of speculation which had attractions for the richer gentry was the purchase of shares in companies engaged in overseas trade and colonisation schemes. During the early seventeenth century the Virginia Company (one of the major joint-stock companies) included among its shareholders at least sixteen Yorkshire gentlemen. Some of these were merchants or businessmen but there were also a number of country squires who, apart from this, had no direct connections with the mercantile world, men such as Sir Guy Palmes of Lindley, Sir Hugh Wyrrall of Loversall and Sir John Mallory of Studley.[2] At his death in 1645 Sir John Hotham of Scorborough left stock in money, goods and merchandise in the East India Company and elsewhere 'employed in the way of trade or at interest'.[3] In certain sections of the gentry moneylending for profit was a relatively common activity which was carried on not only by merchants and lawyers but also by some of the more prosperous landlords. Among the papers of Sir Henry Slingsby the diarist there is an account book giving particulars of the loans which he had advanced in the years 1635–8: these loans were secured with bonds and subject to the statutory rate of interest which then stood at eight per cent.[4] If country gentlemen of ancient lineage were granting loans on a commercial basis moneylending had indeed become a respectable occupation.

---

[1] *Cal. Committee for Compounding*, 1027.

[2] Lists of Virginia Company stockholders are to be found in P.R.O., State Papers Colonial, General Series, C.O.1/iii/33, A. Brown, *The Genesis of the United States* and S. M. Kingsbury (ed.), *The Records of the Virginia Company of London*.

[3] P.R.O., Chancery Proceedings, Six Clerks' Series, C.6/191/20.

[4] Y.A.S. Library: Slingsby MSS, Box A11, rent-book (no pagination).

CHAPTER V

The Affluent Society

ACCORDING to one school of thought the century which preceded the Civil War was a period of great prosperity for the gentry. Mainly as the result of improved methods of estate management they were able to increase their landholdings at the expense of the Crown and the aristocracy. On the other hand, it has been suggested that the rising gentry consisted largely of office-holders, merchants and lawyers: in contrast, the 'mere landowner' had little hope of advancing his fortunes and often experienced serious financial difficulties.[1]

At this stage we are concerned only with the Yorkshire gentry who were enlarging their estates. Apart from family papers the main sources of evidence for property transactions are two categories of legal records: the close rolls and the feet of fines. In addition, there are the special papers relating to the sale of Crown land.[2]

From the most superficial examination it is clear that there was a thriving market in land virtually throughout the period 1558–1642. This state of affairs may be attributed to various factors. In the first place, a significant amount of former monastic property was still changing hands during the reign of Elizabeth.[3] Secondly, the Crown was selling land on an impressive scale in an attempt to bridge the gap between revenue and expenditure. In the reign of James I the sale of Crown property realised £775,000 while Charles I raised over £650,000 by this means in the first decade of his reign.[4] Thirdly, many private

---

[1] R. H. Tawney, 'The Rise of the Gentry, 1558–1640', *Economic History Review*, xi, 1. H. R. Trevor-Roper, *The Gentry, 1540–1640*, *Economic History Review*, Supplement 1. J. H. Hexter, *Reappraisals in History*, 117–62. L. Stone, *The Crisis of the Aristocracy, 1558–1641*, 129–98. I. Roots, 'Gentlemen and Others', *History*, xlvii, 233. See also the Bibliography.

[2] P.R.O., Chancery, Close Rolls (C.54), Common Pleas, Feet of Fines (C.P.25(2)) and Exchequer, Particulars for Grants (E.147). Guildhall Library: Royal Contract Estates. The Yorkshire fines for the period 1558–1625 are printed in *Y.A.S.R.S.*, ii, v, vii, viii, liii and lviii.

[3] See above, 15.

[4] R. H. Tawney, 'The Rise of the Gentry, 1558–1640', *Economic History Review*, xi, 25.

landowners in financial straits were finding it necessary to realise their capital assets. These men included members of the aristocracy, the gentry and the yeomanry. In this situation it is possible to trace a substantial redistribution of land within the Yorkshire gentry as some families prospered and others declined. At the same time the total holdings of the gentry were steadily increasing, partly through the accession of new families but mainly through the acquisition of property from outside sources.

As a general rule the more intensive land-buying occurred within that section of the gentry which was growing rich through the medium of office-holding, commerce or the legal profession. Capital accumulated in this way was often employed in the purchase of land while in some cases an estate was acquired as the result of speculative money-lending. Sir John Savile, a baron of the Exchequer and justice of assize, was one lawyer whose career had a major influence on the economic fortunes of his family. The eldest son of a West Riding gentleman, he had inherited only a modest estate in the parish of Halifax. In 1590, however, he purchased the manor of Methley near Leeds and began to rebuild the house. At his death in 1607 he left an estate worth £850 a year, two capital mansions and a town-house in London. In the next generation the family secured a baronetcy.[1] Sir John Lister, a Hull merchant, had also been born into the minor gentry, succeeding his father in 1617. Three years later he bought a competent estate at Thirkleby and Linton on the Wolds from a bankrupt squire and made Linton Grange his country seat. Further property was purchased in the East Riding, the West Riding, Durham, Lincolnshire and Derbyshire and at his death in 1640 his landed income amounted to over £1000 a year.[2] During the early seventeenth century William Pennyman of Marske, one of the six clerks in Chancery, used the profits of his office to build up a substantial estate in Cleveland; in 1628 his landed posessions (which included former Crown property) were valued at £954 a year.[3] A colleague of his, James Morley of Normanby, amassed an estate worth £2500 a year but in the process he overstrained his re-

[1] Leeds Central Library: MSS of Lord Mexborough. B.M., Additional MSS 12497, f.429. H. S. Darbyshire and G. D. Lumb, *The History of Methley* (*Thoresby Society*, xxxv), 21–2, 98. Sir Henry Savile, the heir, was created a baronet in 1611 (see above, 8.)

[2] P.R.O. Chancery Proceedings, Six Clerks' Series, C.6/153/85. *Y.A.S.R.S.*, lviii, 162.

[3] P.R.O., Court of Wards, Feodaries' Surveys, Wards 5/49.

sources and on the eve of the Civil War he and his eldest son were heavily in debt.[1]

As a result of this great flow of capital into the land market a considerable number of professional and commercial families (some of ancient stock, others with new coats of arms) advanced at a striking pace into the front rank of landed proprietors. In 1642 there were seventy-three gentle families with property worth £1000 a year or more and of these no fewer than nineteen had acquired at least the bulk of their estates in this way since the beginning of the century. Most spectacular of all was the achievement of Sir Arthur Ingram of Temple Newsam. In 1607 he bought his first Yorkshire property, Castleford Mills; in 1625 his estates in the county were worth between £4000 and £5000 a year, while in 1642, the year of his death, the family's Yorkshire possessions were yielding a total income of some £9000 a year. Some of his individual transactions help to illustrate the extent of his capital resources: the manor of Temple Newsam, for example, cost him £12,000, Walton in Derbyshire £16,000, Hatfield over £20,000. At the same time he was completely without scruple in his business dealings and on occasion managed to keep back part of the purchase money.[2]

As we have seen, many landowners in this period were improving their estates and engaging in farming on a commercial rather than a subsistence basis. In addition, the rate of increase in rents compared favourably with the general trend in the price level.[3] In these circumstances an efficient landlord was in a strong position economically and it would be surprising, therefore, if the weight of evidence supported the proposition that without external aid the country gentry had little prospect of increasing their estates. In fact it is clear from a detailed examination of the property market that a distinction must be drawn between the minor gentry on the one hand and the upper and middling gentry on the other. Generally speaking, the smaller landed families with incomes of £50 or £100 a year (and in the early seventeenth century £200 a year) were making comparatively little headway in terms of land-buying. Where, exceptionally, such a family made an

---

[1] P.R.O., S.P.Dom., Committee for Compounding, S.P.23/lxxx/9 and lxxxiv/451, 457, 466, 473.

[2] Leeds Central Library: Temple Newsam MSS, estate papers. Sheffield Central Library: Strafford Letters, xx. Richard Marris to Lord Wentworth, 13 March 1633(-4). Y.A.S. Library: Duke of Leeds MSS, Box 13. A. F. Upton, *Sir Arthur Ingram*, 51-2.

[3] See Chapters II and III.

impressive ascent up the economic scale this was usually the result of special circumstances: either the family had inherited property or the head of the family had taken up a professional or commercial career. At the higher income levels, however, a different picture emerges: here a substantial amount of land-buying was being financed from the rents and profits of country estates.

Landed families with rent-rolls of £1000, £2000 or above often had a considerable surplus available after meeting their basic expenses. This was not necessarily used for the purchase of land: it might be spent on such items as housebuilding, luxury goods or agricultural improvement. Nevertheless a significant number of landowners at this financial level were enlarging the estates which they had inherited. During the reign of Elizabeth Sir William Bellasis of Newburgh Priory, an enclosing landlord, bought extensive property which included the manors of Yearsley, Oulston and Yafforth, Old Byland Grange and part of the manor of Coxwold. His son Sir Henry, who succeeded in 1604, also engaged in land-buying on a major scale: in 1608, for example, he acquired the manor of Thornton on the Hill and the residue of Coxwold manor for the sum of £8256. According to his account book Thornton and Coxwold alone were worth £650 a year while the estate which he left in 1624 was producing an income of nearly £4000 a year.[1] Another wealthy landowner who substantially increased his possessions was Sir Michael Warton of Beverley Park, the head of a predominantly Catholic family. His most notable acquisition was the Crown estate at Beverley which he bought in 1627 for £3593. This property was formally valued in the Exchequer at £184 a year although the Exchequer officials who were concerned with the transaction had heard that it was reputed to be worth over £800 a year. In 1642 Sir Michael had a clear income of £1197 a year from these lands, his total estate revenue amounting to £2600 a year.[2]

Within the middling gentry the more businesslike squires were also buying land out of their estate income although in their case the normal pattern was a piecemeal accumulation of property over a lengthy period. This process can be followed in the family journal (now surviving only as a transcript) which was kept by successive generations

[1] *V.C.H.*, *N.R.*, i, 175 and ii, 4, 15, 19–21, 86. Y.A.S. Library: Newburgh Priory MSS, Box 3, Bundle 15, account book of Sir Henry Bellasis (no pagination). *H.M.C. Various*, ii, 110–11. P.R.O., Chancery Proceedings, Series II, C.3/364/41.

[2] P.R.O., Exchequer, Particulars for Grants, E.147/3/14 and S.P.Dom., Committee for Compounding, S.P.23/clxxxvii/283, 310.

of the Kaye family of Woodsome, near Huddersfield. On the evidence
of this journal the Kayes were industrious and enterprising landowners
who developed unproductive land, mined coal and worked iron forges.
John Kaye (1530-1594), whose portrait bears the inscription

> I lyve at home in howsbandrye,
> Wythowte office or fee trulye,
> As servithe myne abylitie,
> I manteyne hosspitalytie,

bought the manor of Honley, together with corn and fulling mills in
Burton and Honley. His son Robert (c. 1550–1620) acquired property
in Farnley Tyas, Honley, Flockton and elsewhere; this cost him
£1400 in all and was valued at £60 a year. In the next generation
John Kaye (1578–1641) added considerably to the family possessions,
his purchases amounting to £279 in annual value; in addition, he built
Denby Grange and made improvements at Woodsome Hall. In 1642
Sir John Kaye (1616–62), the first baronet, had an estate worth about
£1000 a year.[1] A few miles from Woodsome, in the township of
Almondbury, was Longley Hall, the Ramsden family seat. Like the
Kayes, the Ramsdens were improving landowners who were rising
from the middle ranks into the upper stratum of the country gentry.
Not only did they make large-scale enclosures but they were also
interested in various types of industrial activity, owning collieries,
iron forges and fulling mills. William Ramsden (1558–1623) can be
found buying land year after year in the Huddersfield district; in 1599
he secured half the manor of Huddersfield from the Crown for the
modest sum of £965. His son Sir John Ramsden (1594–1644)
continued to build up the estate: his purchases included the manors of
Almondbury and Byram (where he established a second family seat)
and the remainder of the manor of Huddersfield.[2] To the north of
Huddersfield was Kirklees Hall, the home of the Armitage family.
The site of Kirklees Priory had been acquired by John Armitage, a
merchant and clothier, in 1565 but his armigerous descendants went
on buying land out of their estate revenue. During the period 1580–1640
they spent around £10,000 on the purchase of land in addition to

---

[1] Y.A.S. Library: MS 178. Lord Dartmouth Estate Office: seventeenth-century rent
book. T. D. Whitaker, *Loidis and Elmete*, 331–2.
[2] Leeds Central Library and Huddersfield Town Hall: Ramsden MSS. P. Ahier,
William Ramsden II, 1558–1623.

building a new mansion at Kirklees. In 1641 their efforts were crowned with a baronetcy.[1]

Land-buying was not always financed out of normal income. Sometimes a marriage portion was used for the purchase of property while loans were another means of financing land transactions. Among the private papers of Sir Edward Osborne of Kiveton, vice-president of the Council of the North, are some rough notes, written in his own hand, concerning a large estate in Hatfield Level which he intended to buy. In all he calculated that the purchase would cost him the formidable sum of £12,278. This was obviously beyond his immediate resources because he noted that it would be necessary for him to borrow £4930 from Humphrey Shalcrosse, a well-known London scrivener who had a number of Yorkshire gentlemen on his books.[2]

At the same time there were other ways of acquiring land besides purchase. Many gentlemen sought to increase their estates by marrying a wealthy heiress or a widow with a competent jointure. When a man of property died without heirs male there was no lack of suitors for his daughters if they were as yet unmarried. At his death in 1619 Thomas Talbot of Bashall left two infant daughters, Elizabeth and Margery. In 1627 Thomas Lewis of Marr, the son of another West Riding squire, secured the hand in marriage of Elizabeth Talbot who was then thirteen. Subsequently, in 1629, a friend of the Lewis family who had made inquiries about the other sister was informed that the manor of Bashall amounted to 2230 acres long measure or about 4000 statute acres, the land being held in free socage of the honor of Pontefract. 'The gentlewoman', wrote Lewis's father, 'is but little of growth, and if the gentleman you move for be of stature or years unfit, I doubt it will be a great difficulty to proceed.' The younger sister eventually married William White, a clerk in the Court of Wards who appears to have had no previous connection with Yorkshire.[3]

For the small landowner there was not much prospect of benefiting from an advantageous marriage because he had so little to offer in a material sense. Occasionally, however, a family of minor gentry managed to achieve a great leap forward as the result of a successful

---

[1] *A Catalogue of the Muniments at Kirklees.* It may be noted that Woodsome Hall, Longley Hall and Kirklees Hall have all survived and that the Armytage family (as the name is now spelt) still resides at Kirklees.

[2] Y.A.S. Library: Duke of Leeds MSS, Box 13. M. Beloff, 'Humphrey Shalcrosse and the Great Civil War', *English Historical Review*, liv, 686.

[3] P.R.O., Court of Wards, Feodaries' Surveys, Wards 5/49. *H.M.C. Coke MSS*, i, 392.

marriage negotiation. In 1599 Henry Savile, the heir of William Savile of Copley, took as his wife Anne Darcy, sister to John Lord Darcy of Aston who was to die childless in 1635. By contemporary standards this was an unusual match in view of the great disparity in both wealth and social position. The Saviles had only a modest estate which in the reign of Charles I was said to be worth between £160 and £180 a year and the jointure which was settled on the bride amounted to a mere £80 a year in her widowhood. After Lord Darcy's death the bulk of his estates passed elsewhere but the Saviles were by no means forgotten. In his will Lord Darcy had made generous provision for his sister's younger sons while the eldest son Thomas inherited through her the manors of Rothwell and Roundhay which were worth £600 a year.[1]

When a landowner died childless there was often a bitter dispute among his relatives over the descent of the estate. Even if a settlement had been made this did not necessarily prevent a family argument. Shortly after the death of Godfrey Copley of Sprotborough in 1633 a friend of his, Francis Nevile, described in a letter how he had assisted in resolving a quarrel between William Copley (a cousin of the deceased) and Edmund Hastings and his wife (who was William Copley's sister):

I tooke uppe my lodgeing at Sprodburgh where I miste the best friend that ever man had, and instead of him found differences betwixt all those to whom he left his estate, and most implacable and unnatural ones betwixt the brother and sister: my ever honoured kinsman buried (or I have heard) if with christian, yett I dare say not with decent buriall. I labored to reconcile these swelling and blustering discordes of my kindred, but being a taske too great for me and a busines that hung of soe many stringes, I desired them to nominate freinds, tyme and place for that purpose; which they did.

Eventually, 'after three dayes debate', the arbitrators produced a settlement which was acceptable to both parties. 'And thus you see a good man's estate miserably anatomized, whose funerall expenses (if he have any) must be discharged by them both equally, I meane the brother and sister.'[2]

Of all the families which increased their holdings through marriage or inheritance none could match the good fortune, or good management, of the Darcys of Hornby. Early in the reign of Elizabeth Thomas

[1] P.R.O., Court of Wards, Book of Affidavits, Wards 9/dlxxii/403, 451, Chancery Depositions, C.22/822/58, and S.P.Dom., Committee for Compounding, S.P.23/ccxv/613. Y.A.S. Library: Savile of Copley MSS.

[2] J. Hunter, *South Yorkshire*, i, 342–3.

Darcy secured a large estate in the North Riding by his marriage to Elizabeth Conyers, one of the co-heirs of John Lord Conyers of Hornby. His son Sir Conyers Darcy, who succeeded in 1605, also acquired substantial property at the stroke of a pen. In 1635 John Lord Darcy of Aston died seized of an estate worth £4000 a year; having no surviving issue he had settled the bulk of his lands (subject to his wife's jointure) on Sir Conyers, a kinsman and fellow Puritan. During the Civil War period the marriage of Thomas Darcy and Elizabeth Conyers brought further benefits to the family. Sir William Pennyman of Marske and his wife (a granddaughter of John Lord Conyers) died childless and left most of their property to Sir Conyers (now Lord) Darcy whom Lady Pennyman had acknowledged to be her heir. In the time of the Commonwealth the Darcy family had an estate worth between £4000 and £5000 a year.[1]

In seeking to augment their income many gentlemen secured leases of property belonging to the Crown or the ecclesiastical authorities. Church leases were normally granted for three lives or twenty-one years[2] while Crown leases frequently involved terms of thirty, forty or fifty years. Since the rent charged was generally well below the true value, even at the outset, such tenancies were often extremely profitable. In 1616 Sir Timothy Hutton of Marske, whose father had been archbishop of York, valued his estate at £1449 a year and of this no less than £573 a year was derived from church leases. Similarly, Sir Lancelot Alford of Meaux Abbey and his son Sir William held long leases of Crown land which in 1650 were valued at £320 a year above the rent.[3] On the outbreak of the Civil War some ninety families drew part of their revenue from Crown or church leases.[4]

Altogether 340 families appear in the ranks of the Yorkshire gentry in both 1558 and 1642 and of these, 144 (or roughly two-fifths) increased their landed possessions over the period as a whole. Such

---

[1] B.M., Egerton MSS 3402 (Duke of Leeds papers). P.R.O., S.P.Dom., Committee for Compounding, S.P.23/ccxv/613–14, 617–18, and Chancery Depositions, C.22/822/56. J. W. Pennyman (ed.), *Records of the Family of Pennyman of Ormesby*, 62.

[2] 13 Elizabeth I, c.x.

[3] Northallerton County Record Office: Hutton MSS, note entitled 'A coppie of myne estate which I delyvared unto Sir Coniers Darcye'. P.R.O., Exchequer, Parliamentary Surveys, E.317/35.

[4] The following are the main sources which have been used. Lambeth Palace MSS 918, 919. B.M., Harleian MSS 6288 and Egerton MSS 925. P.R.O., Exchequer, Parliamentary Surveys (E.317). Guildhall Library: Royal Contract Estates. See *P.R.O. Lists and Indexes*, xxv, 356–93.

1. Sir Hugh Cholmley (1600–57).

2. Sir John Hotham (*c.* 1589–1645).

figures, however, exclude a large number of families which entered or left the Yorkshire gentry in these years (for example, families which died out, entered the peerage or were granted arms).[1] If all gentle families are taken into account we find that altogether 308 (out of a total of 963) families enlarged their estates within the period 1558–1642. It is clear, therefore, that while the total holdings of the Yorkshire gentry were increasing this in no way reflected a general advance but was attributable to a minority of rising families. Even within this group there were a considerable number of families which experienced financial difficulties at one time or another,[2] despite the overall increase in their landed property:

families which sold land on a significant scale	55
families which fell heavily into debt but avoided any significant sale of land	38

Within the 'rising gentry' there were 122 families which owed their advance at least in part to other sources of income besides the ownership of land. However, if such families were in a minority they probably bought almost as much property as the families which were dependent on their estate revenue. The following table, which relates to the period 1625–42, underlines this point:

	Number of manors	Total annual value
(a) total number of manors purchased by members of the Yorkshire gentry from landowners outside their ranks	41	£9300
(b) manors bought by families with other sources of income besides land	15	£4500
(c) manors bought by 'mere landowners'	26	£4800

As a footnote it may be added that the figure of £4500 includes three manors worth £1300 a year acquired by one man, Sir Arthur Ingram of Temple Newsam.

In his *Description of England*, first published in 1577 and revised a decade later, William Harrison comments on the rise in living standards which was taking place:

The ancient manours and houses of our gentlemen are yet, and for the most part, of strong timber...Howbeit such as be latelie builded, are commonlie either of bricke or hard stone, their roomes large and comelie...The furniture

---

[1] See above, 16, 18.   [2] For sources see below, 144–5.

8*

of our houses also exceedeth, and is growne in maner even to passing deli-
cacie: and herein I doo not speake of the nobilitie and gentrie onelie, but
likewise of the lowest sort...in the houses of knights, gentlemen, merchant-
men and some other wealthie citizens, it is not geson [rare] to behold
generallie their great provision of tapistrie, Turkie worke, pewter, brasse,
fine linen, and thereto costlie cupbords of plate, worth five or six hundred
or a thousand pounds, to be deemed by estimation.

Farmers and artisans 'have for the most part learned also to garnish
their cupbords with plate, their ioned [joined] beds with tapistrie and
silke hangings, and their tables with carpets and fine naperie, whereby
the wealth of our countrie...dooth infinitelie appeare'. All this was
happening 'in a time wherein all things are growen to most excessive
prices'.[1]

William Harrison was writing primarily about the more prosperous
home counties, and particularly about Essex where he spent most of
his life: it does not necessarily follow, therefore, that the same trend was
in progress in the remoter provinces. To judge from the evidence of
probate inventories taken in the early part of Elizabeth's reign[2] the
Yorkshire gentry were at that stage lagging well behind their fellow
squires in the southern counties in living standards. If, however, the
improvement in material conditions had a slow beginning the pace
undoubtedly quickened as time went on: indeed one of the most
characteristic features of this period (at least among the upper and
middling gentry of the county) is the large-scale expenditure on new
houses, plate, tapestry and other household goods. In this upsurge of
luxury spending two factors must have played an important part: first
the greater emphasis on 'good husbandry' which enabled a landowner
not only to overcome the problems of inflation but also to increase his
purchasing power and, secondly, the growing fashion for visiting
London which helped to develop a taste and appetite for the fruits of
prosperity.[3]

In Yorkshire, as in other counties, the period between the accession
of Elizabeth and the outbreak of the Civil War was a great era of housebuilding.[4] From the evidence available it can be said that at least 280
manor-houses were either built from the ground or substantially

---

[1] F. J. Furnivall (ed.), *Harrison's Description of England*, i, 238–9.
[2] *Surtees Society*, xxvi, civ, cx.   [3] See above, 21–3.
[4] For housebuilding see W. G. Hoskins, 'The Rebuilding of Rural England, 1570–
1640', *Past and Present*, iv, 44 and E. Mercer, 'The Houses of the Gentry', *Past and
Present*, v, 11.

improved (and in all probability the actual figure was much greater than this). In a society which loved display the country mansion represented one of the most conspicuous forms of wealth. Lawyers, merchants and government officials who were entering, or rising within, the ranks of the gentry were anxious to provide themselves with houses affording visible proof of their financial stature. Some of these houses which proclaimed new wealth still remain today. Kiplin Hall was the work of Sir George Calvert who started on its construction three years after his appointment as one of James I's principal secretaries of state. The magnificence of Temple Newsam, which had few equals in northern England, testifies to the success of Sir Arthur Ingram's shrewd business methods. Of other fine houses which have survived Goldsborough Hall was built by Sir Richard Hutton, the celebrated ship money judge, and Marske Hall by William Pennyman, the Chancery official whom we have already encountered.[1]

This enthusiasm for housebuilding was in no way confined to the *nouveaux riches*: on the contrary, most of the families engaging in this type of activity were well established gentry who financed their building operations from the rents and profits of their estates. Even if it was structurally sound the ancestral manor-house often failed to satisfy contemporary standards of comfort and convenience; moreover, there was an increasing demand for greater style and splendour in domestic architecture. Such was the spirit of the age that the well-to-do gentry were expected (and in many cases felt compelled) to build themselves houses which more adequately reflected their position in society. Thus in 1633 Lord Wentworth advised his nephew Sir William Savile of Thornhill: 'Considering that your Houses in my Judgment are not suitable to your Quality, nor yet your Plate and Furniture, I conceive your Expence ought to be reduced to two Thirds of your Estate, the rest saved to the accommodating of you in that kind.'[2]

Some men built out of competition or simply because they wished to copy a style or technique which they had admired on their travels. In 1639 Sir Henry Slingsby of Scriven recorded in his diary: 'That which I have done in matter of building is not much, but here and there a piece, which one summer hath begun and finish'd: I should never endure nor have the patience to begin a tedious work; and I shall ever

---

[1] Marske Hall is sometimes attributed to Sir William the son but he was only sixteen when the house was completed in 1625.
[2] Knowler, i, 169.

disuade my son from affecting building unless it be with good moderation.' When, however, he was up in London attending the Short Parliament he had supper one evening at Lord Holland's house in Kensington and, he relates,

I was much taken with the curiosity of the house; and from that house I took a conceite of making a thorough house in part of Red-house which now I build; and that, by placing the Dores so against another and making at each end a Balcony that one may see clear through the house. Yet [he adds] I may by this see the vanity of all worldly things which men do so much rest upon.[1]

The new manor-houses which were going up in this period varied widely in both size and quality, as might be expected in a class which embraced substantial differences in wealth. At one extreme there were such great mansions as Wighill Hall, built by Sir Robert Stapleton in the reign of Elizabeth, 'a Palace the model whereof he had brought out of Italy ... fitter for a lord treasurer of England than a knight of Yorkshire';[2] at the other, there were the modest houses of the minor gentry, many of them little more than farm-houses. The commonest design at this time was the E-plan: two projecting wings and a porch representing the centre stroke. Other characteristic features were tall chimneys, gables and mullioned windows. Timber-framed houses were still being erected in the reign of Elizabeth but the main building material was stone, in particular, millstone grit, limestone and sandstone. In some cases (for example, High Sunderland[3]) an existing wooden structure was covered with a stone facade. From the closing years of the sixteenth century the use of brick in domestic architecture was gaining in popularity among the Yorkshire gentry although it never challenged the supremacy of stone. The brick-built houses of this period were generally of the larger sort; they included Temple Newsam and Goldsborough in the West Riding, Burton Constable and Burton Agnes in the East Riding, and Kiplin in the North Riding.

In a typical manor-house the most important rooms were the hall and the great chamber. The hall (which was medieval in origin) was usually reached through a passage (known as the 'screens passage') leading from the main entrance door. Although the squire and his family no longer took their meals in the hall it retained its importance as a common meeting-place where visitors were received and as a

---

[1] *Slingsby Diary*, 45, 51.   [2] *Y.A.J.*, viii, 416.
[3] *Halifax Antiquarian Society*, iv, 114.

dining-room for the servants and the ordinary guests. A comparatively new development, the great chamber was normally situated on the first floor. Here the family dined in private and entertained their special guests. In the larger houses another innovation was the long gallery which might stretch the whole length of the building; this was apparently used for musical gatherings and also for exercise in bad weather. Where the family was reasonably wealthy the principal rooms were often distinguished for their sumptuous decoration, with elaborate plaster ceilings, carved chimneypieces of wood or stone, and fine oak panelling. A splendid example of this is the great chamber at Gilling Castle which Sir William Fairfax is said to have completed in 1585. This has an elegant chimneypiece, richly carved wainscoting, a painted frieze depicting the coats of arms of many Yorkshire families, a ceiling hung with pendants and windows ablaze with heraldry.[1] Of comparable splendour is the Jacobean great hall at Burton Agnes, the work of Sir Henry Griffith. Perhaps the most outstanding feature of this room is the magnificent oak and plaster screen which Celia Fiennes particularly admired on her visit to the house in 1697.[2]

The gentry were not only interested in beautifying their houses, they were also carrying out improvements of a more utilitarian nature. Thus we find them building new stables, barns and dairies, modernising the water supply and installing an efficient drainage system. In 1619 it was stated in the course of a lawsuit that Sir John Bourchier of Hanging Grimston had 'caused a troughe or pipe of woode to be layd ... for conveyeinge the Water' to his house. Similarly, Christopher Wandesford had lead pipes put down to improve the water supply at Kirklington Hall.[3]

Some Elizabethan and Jacobean houses were approached through a gatehouse which had both a functional and an ornamental purpose. More often, however, there was a simple arched gateway. The grounds which immediately enclosed the hall consisted of gardens, orchards and perhaps a bowling green. During the reign of Elizabeth it became fashionable to arrange the gardens in the formal Italian style, with flower beds of intricate design, dwarf hedges and gravel walks. In

[1] See J. Bilson, 'Gilling Castle', *Y.A.J.*, xix, 105.

[2] C. Morris (ed.), *The Journeys of Celia Fiennes*, 90. This screen was apparently brought from Barmston Hall, the seat of the Boynton family until they inherited Burton Agnes in 1654 (L. Ambler, *The Old Halls and Manor Houses of Yorkshire*, 65).

[3] P.R.O., Chancery Proceedings, Series II, C.3/302/5. T. Comber, *Memoirs of the Life and Death of the Lord Deputy Wandesforde*, 67.

addition, the English had a liking (in Francis Bacon's words) for 'fair alleys, ranged on both sides with fruit-trees...and arbours with seats'.[1] A common feature in manor-house gardens at this time was the stone-built summer-house or banqueting chamber. At Weston Hall, built by Sir Mauger Vavasour towards the end of Elizabeth's reign, there still exists a three-storeyed pavilion decorated with heraldic devices which appears to have been erected shortly after the house.

Few contemporary descriptions of Yorkshire manor-houses have survived from this period. In 1618, however, we have the following detailed account of Breckenbrough Hall, the home of Sir Thomas Lascelles:

The house is fayre and very substantiall, consisting of two strong large bricke towers of three stories high, well leaded over, th'one sutable to th'other in proportion and uniformity. Betwene them is onely the hall, which is faire and large, high roofed, well lighted, and a large and good chimney. From each of those towers goes out a wing towards the gate, which makes a handsome four-square courte, wherein is a fayre well, which serveth the house with verie clere and good water. In th'one of those wings there be two kitchins, bakehouse, brewehouse, and other houses of office, with lodging chambers over. In th'other wing there be lodgings and other roomes. There be two large barnes strongly tymbred, dove-cote, stable, oxehouse, kilne and other houses; a very fayre square garden, adjoyning on the south side of the house, with delicate walks, having on both sides thorne hedges finely cutt, arbours, and good store of excellent fruite trees, and a lardg orchard with good fruits besides.[2]

Some families spent a fortune on housebuilding. Howley Hall, the work of Sir Robert Savile and his son Sir John (later Lord Savile), cost them no less than £30,000 and must clearly have been one of the largest houses in Yorkshire, if not in the country. Sir Henry Slingsby the diarist compares it with such houses as Audley End and Temple Newsam: 'we see an emulation in the structure of our houses, if we behold at Tibbalds, and that of my Lord of Suffolk's at Audley End; so, in this country my Lord Everie's at Maulton; my Lord Savil's at Howley; Sir Arthur Ingram's at Temple Newson.'[3] Expenditure of this order was beyond the means of most gentlemen, whether or not they had other sources of income besides their estates. Brian Stapleton's manor-house at Carlton, 'a faire house' completed in the middle of

[1] *The Essayes or Counsels Civill and Morall of Francis Bacon Lord Verulam*, 142.
[2] *Surtees Society*, liii, 269–70.   [3] *Camden Miscellany*, viii, 15. *Slingsby Diary*, 52.

Elizabeth's reign, was said to have cost 'foure or five thousand pounds buildinge'. William Maleverer's house at Ingleby Arncliffe, which was built towards the end of the sixteenth century, cost him £2000. Sir Stephen Proctor spent £3000 on the construction of Fountains Hall which was completed in 1611 and still survives in its original form. In 1644 Christopher Copley, a member of the lesser gentry, rebuilt Wadworth Hall at a cost of 'at least £600'.[1] Even these figures are impressive when translated into current values but it must be borne in mind that expenditure on building might be spread over a considerable period: indeed some of the larger houses took ten, twenty or thirty years to complete. In the accounts of Sir Henry Slingsby (whose diary has just been quoted) we can trace his building expenditure year by year as he carried out alterations and improvements at Red House and Scriven:

	£	s	d
1635–6	186	6	0
1636–7	149	0	0
1637–8	244	14	11
1638–9	242	11	11
1639–40	49	9	1
1640–1	474	6	6
	1346	8	5

Sir Henry's income in this period amounted to between £1500 and £2000 a year.[2]

As a general rule the contents of the house were as clear an indication of the owner's wealth as the house itself. The inventory taken at Walton Hall in April 1624[3] enables us to see in intimate detail how a well-to-do squire furnished his home. At this time the house belonged to Sir Thomas Fairfax who left an estate worth some £2700 a year.[4] In the great chamber there was a substantial quantity of furniture which included the following:

A drawing table, a rownd table, a livery cubberd, and a little table, all having carpetes of greene cloth, a couch chare and 2 other high chares covered with greene cloth, a frame on which stands a paire of virgenalls, a chare with other

---

[1] P.R.O., Court of Wards, Book of Decrees, Wards 9/xcvi/ff.263–5 and Book of Affidavits, Wards 9/dlxxiii/238. *Y.A.J.*, xvi, 124. J. W. Morkill, *Kirkby Malhamdale*, 219. P.R.O., Chancery Proceedings, Six Clerks' Series, C.10/55/32.

[2] See Appendix A, including the explanation of Sir Henry's accounting year.

[3] *Archaeologia*, xlviii, 136–48.   [4] *C.R.S.: Recusant History*, iv, 63.

chares and stooles in it, a paire of white and black checkered tables...two dornix[1] window curtins and an iron rod for them, two formes, 3 irish stitched low stooles, two set work low stooles, an iron chimney, a clock, cushions.

Among the items in the lord's bedchamber were:

A standing bedsteed with tester and head peece wrought with black velvet and yellow silk and five curtins of red cloth, a matt, a feather bed, a fine quilt, 2 paire of blanketes, a boulster, 2 pillowes and a counter pointe...The white damask chare, a little red chare, an orpharion, five pictures, a standing cubberd, a great chest, a cabinet...

In many houses the principal rooms were decorated with hangings of tapestry which usually depicted allegorical or pastoral scenes. The lesser gentry, however, had to be content with painted cloths. Maps (which are frequently mentioned in inventories of the period) represented another type of wall decoration; at Newburgh Priory, for example, a schedule of heirlooms prepared in 1622 includes various maps and pictures which were displayed in the gallery.[2] In the early seventeenth century at least, many gentlemen had pictures on their walls: not only the great squires but also a significant number of middling landowners. Not infrequently a likeness of the sovereign testified to the owner's patriotism; in the main, however, such collections consisted of family portraits which were generally inscribed with coats of arms and sometimes with the age of the sitter. These might include companion portraits like the pictures of Sir Mauger Vavasour of Weston and his wife which were painted in the year of the Armada or group portraits like the picture of Sir Matthew Boynton of Barmston and his family at Burton Agnes. However faithful the representation the figures were often wooden and lifeless and the general standard of portraiture left much to be desired. Some Yorkshire gentlemen, however, employed the services of the best foreign artists: thus Sir Richard Cholmley of Roxby had his portrait executed by Federigo Zuccaro, the celebrated Italian artist who visited England in 1574, while his descendant Sir Hugh Cholmley of Whitby commissioned one of the most fashionable artists of his day, Sir Peter Lely, to paint his picture.[3]

Among the richer gentry no self-respecting squire thought his home complete without a collection of plate, however modest in size. The

---

[1] A corruption of the Flemish name for Tournai in Belgium.
[2] *H.M.C. Various*, ii, 112.   [3] F. O. Morris, *The Ancestral Homes of Britain*, 14.

collection of Sir Timothy Hutton of Marske, which was inventoried in 1629, may be taken as an example[1]:

one guilt bason and ewre, two guilt flagons, one pomegrannett guilt bowle, one great guilt salt, one little guilt salt, nine guilt spoones, one guilt bowle with a cover, six guilt plates, twelve silver plates, two dozen and a halfe of silver spoones, one basen and ewer percell guilt, one silver skinker, one silver crewitt, 3 silver bowles, one silver sugar box and spoone, one silver porringer.

In many cases a collection was worth no more than £30, £40 or £50. In the reign of Elizabeth, however, some of the leading families had plate amounting to £300 or £400 in value while in the early seventeenth century there were collections worth £1000 or more. In contrast, the minor gentry could rarely afford to indulge in this kind of luxury spending yet their houses were often well stocked with brass and pewter, as indeed were the houses of the wealthier families.

Although inventories of the period seldom mention jewellery there are frequent references in wills to necklaces, rings, brooches and gold chains. In 1647 it was alleged that on the death of Francis Burdett of Birthwaite ten years earlier the following items had been omitted from the inventory of his goods: 'one Nuggett and Curkanett of rubies and diamonds, a diamond ring and a ruby ring, one pair of bracelets of pearl, one gould ring, one jewell.'[2] This type of omission must have been relatively common.

One of the clearest indications of status in a class-conscious age was the possession of a coach. Apparently of Hungarian origin this mode of conveyance was introduced into England about the middle of the sixteenth century. Among the first Yorkshiremen to own a coach was Sir Cotton Gargrave of Nostell Priory who was one of the wealthiest landowners in the West Riding with an income of at least £2000 a year. In the inventory taken after his death in 1588 there appears the item 'Coche horses the Coch and a litter', the value being given as £20.[3] Naturally the coach had particular appeal for the womenfolk because of the increased opportunities for travel which it provided. In the diary of Lady Margaret Hoby of Hackness there are numerous references to coach journeys. The first entry occurs on 23 August 1599

[1] *Surtees Society*, xvii, 254.

[2] P.R.O., Chancery Proceedings, Six Clerks' Series, C.10/28/14.

[3] P.R.O., Duchy of Lancaster, Special Commissions, D.L.44/442. B.M., Additional MSS 24470, f.80.

when she notes that 'I took my Coach and went to linton' (her mother's house) while on the following day she records that 'I took the aire in the Coach with Mr Hoby'.[1] By the reign of Charles I a 'gentlemanly equipage'[2] had come to be regarded as a necessity rather than a luxury in the upper circles of the squirearchy.

For probate purposes the term 'personal estate' was taken to include the deceased's clothes and ready money, his stocks and bonds (if he had any), the contents of his house, stables and barns, his farm animals and the crops growing on his demesne lands. If he was a man of substance his household goods alone could amount to £1000 and upwards. In 1636 Sir Arthur Ingram was said to have lost goods to the value of £4000 when his new mansion at Temple Newsam was seriously damaged by fire, while in 1649 Thomas Stringer of Sharlston claimed that parliamentarian soldiers had taken from him ready money, plate and household stuff worth £3500.[3] As in the case of landed incomes there were wide variations in the size and value of personal estates. The following table[4] illustrates the two extremes:

	Date	Total value of personal estate
Henry Beckwith of Clint	1608	£62
Sir Henry Bellasis of Newburgh Priory	1624	£8000
Thomas Ayscough of Lower Newstead	1624	£81
Francis Gatenby of Maunby	1630	£38
Sir John Hotham of Scorborough	1643	£10,000

During the period under consideration the values of personal estates tended to follow an upward trend, certainly among the richer gentry.[5] In the reign of Elizabeth a leading squire might have £2000 or £3000 in personal property, in the reign of Charles I between £5000 and £10,000. Although this trend is partly explained by the falling value of money it also reflected a general improvement in material conditions.

[1] D. M. Meads (ed.)., *The Diary of Lady Margaret Hoby 1599–1605*, 66.

[2] As Sir Hugh Cholmley of Whitby described his coach (*Cholmley Memoirs*, 56).

[3] Knowler, i, 525. P.R.O., S.P.Dom., Committee for Compounding, S.P.23/ccxiv/155, 157.

[4] The round figures are from the records of lawsuits, the remaining figures from inventories. Shillings and pence have been omitted. P.R.O., Chancery Proceedings, Series II, C.3/364/41 and Six Clerks' Series, C.6/191/20. *Surtees Society*, cx, 11–12. Leeds Central Library: Richmondshire Wills and Administrations (Ayscough and Gatenby).

[5] See the list in Appendix C.

For some gentlemen material possessions were not enough: they also needed titles to enhance their position in society. While such ambitions were difficult to fulfil under Queen Elizabeth[1] her Stuart successors actively promoted the sale of honours as a valuable source of revenue. Baronetcies were supposed to be granted only to gentlemen who had £1000 a year or more in land and indeed the price originally fixed — £1095 payable in three annual instalments — put the honour beyond the reach of all but the wealthiest families.[2] The first Yorkshire baronets, six in number, were created on 29 June 1611. These included Sir William Wentworth of Wentworth Woodhouse, who was the richest gentleman in Yorkshire with an income of £6000 a year, and Sir Henry Bellasis of Newburgh Priory who, as the owner of an estate worth nearly £4000 a year, could claim this distinction in the North Riding.[3] It is significant, however, that of the thirty-five Yorkshire landowners who acquired the honour in the period 1611–42 no fewer than twenty-five either had the charges completely remitted or purchased their baronetcies at a time when courtiers were selling them at a price substantially lower than that initially demanded, while the remainder included three recipients of Nova Scotia baronetcies which cost £166. 13s. 4d. (the sterling equivalent of 3000 Scottish merks).[4]

While there was an immediate rush of applicants when the order of baronetcy was instituted it is noteworthy that the sale of peerages at first aroused little interest within the Yorkshire gentry. No doubt the main factor was the high cost: in 1615, for example, baronies were apparently being offered at £6000 each.[5] When, however, the price fell substantially in Charles I's reign several Yorkshire gentlemen bought their way into the nobility. Two cases may be cited: in 1628 Sir Thomas Fairfax of Denton acquired the Scottish barony of Cameron with an immediate down-payment of £1500, while in 1629 his kinsman Sir Thomas Fairfax of Gilling was said to have paid £1300 for an Irish viscounty though his friends put the cost at no more than £900.[6]

Another means of emphasising status was the maintenance of a large

---

[1] See above, 6.
[2] Detailed information about the order of baronetcy is to be found in F. W. Pixley, *A History of the Baronetage*.
[3] G.E.C. (ed.), *Complete Baronetage*, i, 30, 43, 44, 48, 49, 55. Knowler, i, dedication.
[4] For the declining cost of baronetcies see L. Stone, *The Crisis of the Aristocracy, 1558–1641*, 52–5.
[5] *Cal.S.P.Dom. 1611–18*, 269.   [6] *Fairfax Correspondence*, i, 14, 16, 156.

establishment of servants. From the family memoirs we learn that Sir Richard Cholmley, who was one of the greatest squires in Elizabethan Yorkshire, made his chief place of residence at Roxby 'where he lived in great port, having a very great family, at least fifty or sixty men-servants, about his house... He never took a journey to London that he was not attended with less than thirty, sometimes forty men-servants, though he went without his lady'.[1] In August 1609 Sir Henry Bellasis had a total of fifty-one indoor and outdoor servants at Newburgh Priory and Murton Grange. Rather lower down the scale there were gentlemen with incomes of £1000 or £2000 a year who employed twenty or thirty servants.[2] This sort of establishment was far beyond the resources of the small landowner but some of the middling gentry seem to have been well provided: thus in 1640 Thomas Stringer of Sharlston had twenty servants in his employment.[3]

In the larger households the domestic establishment included a steward, a housekeeper, perhaps a chaplain and a schoolmaster, a butler, a cook, serving-men, maidservants and scullery maids. In addition, there were often numerous outdoor servants: bailiffs, farm labourers, gardeners, stablemen and gamekeepers. In the case of the richer families at least the menservants wore a distinctive livery, both for their normal duties and on special occasions such as when Sir Richard Cholmley of Whitby met Lord Scroope, the new lord president of the Council of the North, beyond Doncaster 'attended with twenty of his own servants, all well mounted, and in handsome liveries of grey cloth trimmed with silver lace'.[4]

To facilitate the running of a great house the steward was sometimes given a book of regulations setting down the precise responsibilities of the domestic staff. The following instructions appear in a household book which belonged to the Fairfaxes of Denton, one of the most prominent families in Yorkshire:

all the Servants [must] be ready upon the Terras at such tymes as the Strangers do come, to attend their alightinge...When Prayers shall beginne (or a very little before) the Gates on all sides must be shutt and locked, and the Porter must come into Prayers with all the Keyes...Dinner must be ready by Eleven of the Clock...The Great Chamber being served, the

---

[1] *Cholmley Memoirs*, 7.

[2] Y.A.S. Library: Newburgh Priory MSS, Box 3, Bundle 15, account book (no pagination). See Appendix D.

[3] Y.A.S. Library: MS 311 (no pagination).   [4] *Cholmley Memoirs*, 22.

Steward and Chaplaine must sit down in the Hall, and call unto them the Gentlemen if there be any unplaced above, and then the Servants of the Strangers as their Masters be in Degree...

In the great chamber none of the servants was to 'fill Beere or Wine but the Cup-bord Keeper, who must make choice of his Glasses or Cups for the Company, and not serve them hand over heade. He must also know which be for Beers and which for Wine; for it were a foul thing to mix them together'.[1]

The money wages of servants were usually paid quarterly or every six months. By statute the maximum rates were settled at quarter sessions and any employer who exceeded the current limits was liable to be fined.[2] That the wages were extremely modest may be seen from the following examples[3]:

	Date	Number of servants	Wages per quarter £ s d
Bellasis of Newburgh Priory	1609	51	24 16 8
Ingram of Temple Newsam	1632	21	12 8 4
Stringer of Sharlston	1640	20	10 14 1
Hawksworth of Hawksworth	1658	25	14 18 7

Although the wages bill was seldom a heavy charge on income it represented only a part of the expenditure involved since the servants were normally fed, clothed and accommodated at their master's expense.

In the houses of the richer gentry the squire's family, his guests and his servants could amount to a sizeable community. On one recorded occasion the household of Sir Thomas Wentworth (the future Earl of Strafford) consisted of sixty-four persons, including an establishment of forty-nine servants.[4] In the conditions then prevailing the maintenance of a large household was regarded as a valuable public service. By virtue of their wealth and station the gentry were expected to engage in housekeeping on a lavish scale, providing employment and assisting the local economy, relieving the poor who begged at their

---

[1] Printed in *The Regulations and Establishment of the Houshold of Henry Algernon Percy, the Fifth Earl of Northumberland*, 421–4.

[2] Statute of Artificers: 5 Elizabeth I, c.iv.

[3] Y.A.S. Library: Newburgh Priory MSS, Box 3, Bundle 15, account book of Sir Henry Bellasis (no pagination). Leeds Central Library: Temple Newsam MSS, TN/EA/12/19. Sheffield Central Library: Bright MSS 87. Sir Arthur Ingram had several houses and his total establishment of servants must have been much larger than this.

[4] J. Hunter, *South Yorkshire*, ii, 84.

gates and entertaining travellers as well as relatives and neighbours. All this was comprehended in the term 'good hospitality' which not infrequently appears in the epitaphs of country gentlemen. For a picture of North Country housekeeping of the traditional kind we may turn to the household account books of Sir William Fairfax of Gilling which belong to the period 1571–82. As a general rule there were between thirty and fifty persons dining in the hall and particularly on guest-days great quantities of food were consumed. The entry for 14 May 1579 records a supper given in honour of the Earl of Rutland. On this occasion the guests were named as the Earl of Rutland, Sir Robert Constable, Mr Manners, Sir William Bellasis, Mr Henry Bellasis and his wife, 'with many others', and the food included mutton, beef, lamb, veal, calves feet, chickens, capons, moor-cock, pigeon pie and stewed rabbits.[1] In the memoirs of Sir Hugh Cholmley there is a contemporary description of the hospitality practised in a North Riding manor-house in the reign of Charles I. During the years of prosperity which he enjoyed before the Civil War, he writes,

I had between thirty and forty in my ordinary family, a chaplain who said prayers every morning at six, and again before dinner and supper, a porter who merely attended the gates, which were ever shut up before dinner, when the bell rung to prayers, and not opened till one o'clock, except for strangers who came to dinner, which was ever fit to receive three or four besides my family, without any trouble; whatever their fare was, they were sure to have a hearty welcome. Twice a week, a certain number of old people, widows and indigent persons, were served at my gates with bread and good pottage made of beef, which I mention that those which succeed may follow the example.

The house had been built on a site adjoining Whitby Abbey and it is tempting to think that the monastic tradition of hospitality had been carried on without interruption.[2]

During this period there were many complaints that the traditional style of housekeeping was in decline. As early as 1587 William Harrison referred to 'the decaie of house-keeping whereby the poore have beene relieved' and linked this with 'the inhansing of rents' and 'the dailie oppression of copiholders, whose lords seeke to bring their poore tenants almost into plaine servitude and miserie'.[3] In Yorkshire there were still a considerable number of gentlemen described as great house-

---

[1] *H.M.C. Various*, ii, 67–86.   [2] *Cholmley Memoirs*, 56.
[3] F. J. Furnivall (ed.), *Harrison's Description of England*, i, 241–2.

keepers even in the early seventeenth century: nevertheless it is clear that the benevolent squire who kept open house was no longer the typical figure he had once been. In 1624 a Halifax parson declaimed:

Conscience; Call upon the Gentrie, and feare not their faces. Tell them round-ly that Gentilitie consists not only in cutting of a Card, casting of a Die, throwing of a Bowle, watching of a Cocke, manning of an Hawke, or in hollowing after a deepe-mouth'd Cry of Hounds: but in good Hospitalitie, vertuous actions and generous deeds. Bid them dwell in the Countrey, governe their Tenants, set peace among their neighbours, and maintaine their houses, not contriving into a poor narrow Chamber in a Citie, their whole familie, as too many doe.[1]

For the decay of hospitality there were various factors responsible. In the first place, some gentlemen were deliberately cutting down on their household expenditure either as the result of financial difficulties or simply because they believed in the virtues of economy. Secondly, it was becoming fashionable (certainly from the end of the sixteenth century) for the richer families to sojourn in London, York and other towns, perhaps for several months at a time.[2] In seeking to arrest this trend the authorities were clearly apprehensive about the social and economic consequences: according to a proclamation of 1632 such families were spending 'a great part' of their substance

in excessive Apparel provided from Forreign Parts, to the inriching of other Nations and unnecessary consumption of a great part of the Treasure of this Realm, and in other vain Delights and Expences even to the wasting of their Estates, which is not issued into the Parts from whence it ariseth, nor are the People of them relieved therewith, or by their hospitality, nor yet set on work, as they might and would be, were it not for the absence of the principal Men out of their Countries, and the excessive use of Forreign Commodities.[3]

At the same time, the merchants and professional men who bought themselves country estates were necessarily absentee landlords so long as they engaged in their urban pursuits. Finally, the character of house-hold provisioning was changing. In the past the main emphasis had been on quantity; now there was a desire for greater variety and novelty which was reflected in the growing imports of fruits, spices and wines.

[1] John Barlow, *An Exposition of the Second Epistle of the Apostle Paul to Timothy the First Chapter*, 83.
[2] See above, 20–4.   [3] Rushworth, ii, 288–90.

In 1638 Sir Henry Slingsby related in his diary that there was little use
for the new art of cookery

in our country housekeeping, unless sometimes when we have a meeting of
friends, and then only to comply with the fashions of the times to shew
myself answerable to what is expect'd, and not out of any love unto excessive
feasting; which now a days is very much practis'd. In former times the
fashions were to keep great houses not affecting curiosity as plenty; and
new things, they turn'd the honour of housekeeping into some one single
entertainment for which our own marketts are too mean to afford them that
which their curious appetites would have; but they must send beyond sea to
make the trade of Merchants, only intend'd for publick commodity, now at
last serve for their private ends of vain glory...this abuse and excess is not
receiv'd by great personages of the nobility only, but even others, honoris
gratia, must imitate even beyond their abilities will afford.[1]

At special banquets, when invited guests were entertained, the tables
were often heavily laden with a rich assortment of dishes. In view of the
expenditure which this involved, however, the head of the household
might well feel obliged to exercise a much stricter control over the
amount of food and drink provided for general consumption. In short,
the new fashion in housekeeping was tending to drive out the ancient
open-handed form of hospitality.

Whether the emphasis was on quantity or variety the provisioning
of a large household represented a heavy commitment. At Gilling
Castle the annual charge for provisions amounted to £338. 3s. 9d. in
1579 and £440. os. 2d. in 1580. This was not all cash expenditure since
it apparently included the assessed value of the produce supplied from
the estate.[2] Among the Temple Newsam papers there is a household
account book which cannot be precisely dated but which almost
certainly belonged to Sir Arthur Ingram, the head of the family in the
early seventeenth century. Taking a full year we find that the sum of
£799. 18s. 8d. was spent on provisions which included meat, fish,
poultry, eggs, fruit, vegetables and oysters.[3] Although Sir Henry
Slingsby had no great liking for extravagant banquets he was still put
to great expense in his housekeeping. In 1638 he wrote:

The number we are at this time in houshold is 30 persons whereof 16 are
men servants, and 8 women, besides ourselves. Our charge is much every
year...being well accommodated with good faithfull diligent servants, so that

[1] Slingsby Diary, 24–5.   [2] H.M.C. Various, ii, 85–6.
[3] Leeds Central Library: Temple Newsam MSS, TN/EA/14/2.

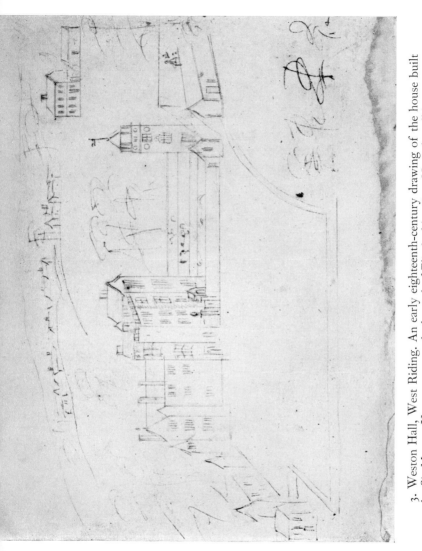

3. Weston Hall, West Riding. An early eighteenth-century drawing of the house built by Sir Mauger Vavasour towards the end of Elizabeth's reign. Note the tall banqueting chamber on the right. *See page* 106.

4. The hall screen at Burton Agnes Hall, East Riding. *See page* 105.

at least I spend every year in housekeeping £500, if the demesne grounds which I keep in my own hands be reckon'd according to the Rent it would give, and the charges in getting it; which yet serves not the house with corn, but [I] am fain to buy.

In Sir Henry's accounts the item shown as 'house provision' averaged £300 a year in the period 1635–6 to 1640–1; the lowest amount was £210. 5s. od. in 1635–6 and the highest £372. 19s. 4d. in 1638–9.[1]

New houses which were stylish and commodious, luxury items such as plate, tapestry and jewellery, peerages and baronetcies, large establishments, lavish housekeeping, all these were tokens of prosperity. As we shall see later, they could also signify improvidence: the prodigality of the gentry, declared Fynes Moryson in 1617, is 'greater then in any other Nation or age'.[2] Even when this reservation has been made, however, it is clear that the upper and middling gentry had considerable purchasing power at their disposal whether or not they possessed additional sources of income. Among the lesser gentry the standard of living was also improving although to a far more limited extent. If we take land-buying as a criterion of affluence, however, any preconception about a uniformly prosperous class must be discarded. The total holdings of the gentry might be increasing to some extent but a great deal of property was changing hands within their ranks and the rising families were in a clear minority. On the whole, the most striking gains were being made by the lawyers, merchants and royal officials who were drawing a significant amount of liquid wealth into the gentry: indeed they alone had the means of building up a major estate from modest beginnings in the course of a single generation. This does not necessarily mean, however, that the profit margins of landownership were too negligible to permit expansion: on the contrary, many families with large or medium estates were buying property out of their estate revenue. At the same time it seems likely that some wealthy landowners had no particular desire to increase their landholdings, preferring to use their surplus money in other fields of expenditure. In this connection it is noteworthy that over a six-year period Sir Henry Slingsby spent over £1600 on housebuilding and household goods but only £80 on land purchase.[3] In the final analysis the real gulf was between the minor gentry on the one hand and the

---

[1] *Slingsby Diary*, 26–7. See Appendix A, including the explanation of Sir Henry's accounting year.

[2] Fynes Moryson, *Itinerary*, iii, 149.   [3] See Appendix A.

9—Y.G.

richer gentry on the other. Although the theory that the 'mere land-owner' rarely prospered cannot be sustained as a general proposition it undoubtedly has some validity when applied to the small landed families with no other form of income. For them there was little prospect of economic advancement.

CHAPTER VI

The Seeds of Decay

IF ONE section of the Yorkshire gentry was becoming increasingly wealthy another section was clearly in financial difficulties. In part this was the result of poor estate management, for some men of property lacked either the capacity or the application to make successful land-owners. According to a lawsuit heard in the Court of Wards Brian Franke of Alwoodley was a weak, imperfect and inexperienced gentleman who was 'not sufficientlie able to Manage his Estate': because of this his elder brother, who was childless, had hesitated before settling the family estate on him in 1619.[1] Similarly it was said of Sir Francis Foljambe of Aldwark, who inherited property worth £3000 a year from his elder brother, that at the time of his succession he was 'a man of no estate or fortune, and of small understandinge by reason of his education to manage so great an estate... and the rather because the estate was so much troubled and Incumbred with statutes and divers other Charges, which did occasion many and great suites'. Faced with this situation Sir Francis brought in his relative Ambrose Wortley, a counsellor at law, to take care of his legal business and help him run the estate. In spite of this assistance, however, he found himself in severe financial straits as the result of a mixture of bad fortune, mis-management and extravagance and at his death in 1640 he left property worth only £1000 a year.[2]

Knowledge of the law was generally regarded as an important, if not an essential, requirement for a man of broad acres and indeed many gentlemen sent their sons to the inns of court. The landlord who had no legal background might find himself at a serious disadvantage in his business dealings. In a Chancery suit brought in 1625 Thomas Worsley of Hovingham claimed that Sir John Wood of Beeston, who was well versed in the law, had taken advantage of his ignorance of legal matters and cheated him over a marriage settlement. Sir John (he alleged) had

[1] P.R.O., Court of Wards, Pleadings, Wards 13/120.
[2] P.R.O., Chancery Proceedings, Series II, C.3/425/20. N. Johnston, 'History of the Family of Foljambe', *Collectanea Topographica et Genealogica*, ii, 80–1.

not only neglected to pay much of the £1000 which he had promised as his daughter's marriage portion but had also sought to exclude him from any benefit out of his estate by purchasing an extent on the property.[1]

In addition, there was the problem of the corrupt steward, who was a stock figure in contemporary literature. The Danbys of Masham, a North Riding family, were particularly unfortunate in this respect. For a considerable period Elizabeth Danby and her son Christopher, who inherited the family estate as a minor in 1590, entrusted the management of their affairs to an attorney who was both a kinsman and namesake of the young heir. At the beginning of his stewardship he persuaded them to go and live in Oxford and other places outside the county 'for their easier charge in howsekeepinge' although his real motive was to enrich himself at their expense. During their absence (which lasted six years) he played havoc with the estate: no records of income and expenditure were maintained, property was sold at ridiculously low prices and leases were renewed at the old rent for cash payments which he converted to his own use. At this time the rents and profits of the estate amounted to some £1500 a year but he allowed them only a small proportion and kept the rest for himself, pretending that he would spend the residue on repairing the houses and stocking the grounds; in practice, however, he permitted the houses 'to decaie and to fall to utter ruin' and wasted and consumed all the stock and household goods. Altogether he was alleged to have defrauded his employers of £7000. As a result of his activities the fortunes of the Danby family sharply declined but it took them some time to realise what was happening and he was not finally dismissed until 1608.[2]

Some landowners not only failed to develop their estates but allowed farm-houses, cottages and fences to fall into a state of disrepair. In 1619 there were said to be many tenements in the manor of Ryther 'in so great decay by reason of the long leases that have beenne made of them for lives, that no tenents can be procured to inhabite them unlesse there be great costs and charges furst bestowed on them to make them tenentable'.[3] In some cases an improvident squire kept too much land

---

[1] P.R.O., Chancery Proceedings, Series II, C.3/390/10. For extents see below 146–7.
[2] P.R.O., Star Chamber Proceedings, Star Chamber 8/120/2. C. Whone, 'Christopher Danby of Masham and Farnley' (*Thoresby Society*, xxxvii, 1). See also below, 370.
[3] P.R.O., Court of Wards, Feodaries' Surveys, Wards 5/49 (estate of John Robinson of Ryther).

in his own possession for unproductive, or relatively unproductive, purposes. Great parks were created to provide facilities for hawking and hunting: Sir Richard Gargrave of Nostell Priory, for instance, set aside some 1200 acres of his estate for parkland. Of Sir George Reresby of Thrybergh we are told: 'His diversion was sometimes haukes, but his chiefest was his breed of horses in which he was very exact: but his breed was not in that reputation to gett any profit thereby, and the keeping of much ground in his handes both at Thriberge and Ickles for the running of his horses, which he might have lett at good rates, made it the more expense.' Another gentleman who went in for horse-breeding was Sir Richard Cholmley of Whitby: his horses ran over most of his demesnes and according to his son the business was altogether 'vain and unprofitable'.[1]

On some estates the rent yield was well below the potential value, sometimes over a lengthy period. Apart from the problems of copyhold tenure which have already been discussed[2] this might be due to the landlord's ignorance as to the real value of his property, to his reluctance to put up the rents of his tenants or to the type of leasing policy which involved heavy entry fines and small rents. Sir Hugh Cholmley of Whitby relates in his memoirs that the property which his father settled on him, though yielding only £1500–£1600 a year, was really worth £2700 a year, yet 'no friend I had, but my father himself, did believe it of that value, so much of it was in lease for fourteen or fifteen years at low rents, and neither the tenants, nor my father's officers, for their own interests, would admit of his valuation'.[3] Another North Riding squire, Sir George Wandesford of Kirklington, owed his financial difficulties largely to his poor business sense. The rents at which he granted leases were generally uneconomical while parts of his estate were leased out to old servants and retainers at bare acknowledgments to the lord. In 1602 (to quote a specific case) he let some land in Kirklington for twenty-one years to one James Milner in consideration of good and faithful services done and to be done and for a rent of 6s. 8d. to be paid for the use of the church of Kirklington every Easter.[4]

Not a few landowners who were heavily in debt and in urgent need

[1] J. Hunter, *South Yorkshire*, ii, 219. B.M., Additional MSS 29443, f.3. *Cholmley Memoirs*, 25.
[2] See above, 39–43.   [3] *Cholmley Memoirs*, 23, 44.
[4] T. Comber, *Memoirs of the Life and Death of the Lord Deputy Wandesforde*, 20. H. B. McCall, *Family of Wandesforde of Kirklington and Castlecomer*, 59, 63, 248.

of money raised large sums by granting leases of thirty years or more in return for substantial fines. By this means the long-term interests of the estate were sacrificed to their immediate financial needs. One Yorkshire squire who resorted to this type of leasing practice was William Middleton of Stockeld: in 1583, for example, he leased two messuages in Askwith for a term of 141 years, the tenant paying £240 as an entry fine and a rent of £2. 3s. 4d. a year. In 1612 Middleton told an Exchequer official that because of his great debts he had been obliged to grant long leases of a good part of his lands.[1] In some cases a gentleman did permanent injury to his estate in this way. In 1601 John (later Sir John) Yorke of Gouthwaite made a number of leases of property in Appletreewick for terms of 5000 years, while in the early years of James I's reign other lands of his were let for similar periods. When the Court of Wards feodary surveyed the estate of the Yorke family in 1638 he valued the whole property, consisting of over 16,000 acres, at no more than £350 a year, noting that most of the lands were in lease for 3000 years or more and some part of them for three lives.[2]

In many cases the declining fortunes of a gentle family were attributed simply to extravagance. Within the landed classes there was the constant danger that an estate which had been carefully nurtured for generations might be dissipated within a single lifetime through the excesses of a spendthrift heir. This accounts for the emphasis placed on frugality in the precepts which a father sometimes drew up for the guidance of his son. Writing in 1636 Christopher Wandesford of Kirklington warned his heir: 'Be not excessive in your Expences upon your own Person, upon Building, Gardens, Dogs, Horses and the like. That Humour steals upon many wise Men exceedingly...Avoid the Vanity of great and riotous Feasting; whether it be to entertain great Men for Ostentation and Compliment, or for Popularity among your Neighbours.'[3] The possibility that a wastrel might inherit the family estate was one of the main reasons for the growing practice of entailing property so that each generation had no more than a life-interest.[4] For the same reason an improvident heir was on occasion disinherited in favour of a younger son.

In spite of Puritan attacks on extravagance the prevailing climate of

---

[1] *Y.A.S.R.S.*, lxv, 17. B.M., Lansdowne MSS 153, f.81.
[2] *Calendar of Yorke MSS*, 215, 833. W. Grainge, *Nidderdale*, 47, 135, 136. P.R.O., Court of Wards, Feodaries' Surveys, Wards 5/49.
[3] Christopher Wandesford, *A Book of Instructions*, 81, 83.   [4] But see below, 155–6.

opinion provided little encouragement for the cultivation of thrift. In a society which believed that riches were for spending the nobility and gentry were expected to live in a manner 'answerable to their estates' or, to use another contemporary expression, 'according to their degree and quality'. Men of property who practised frugality were generally unpopular. According to a contemporary account Sir John Hotham, one of the richest squires in Yorkshire, earned the disrespect of 'all sorts of people' because of 'his very narrow living'. Following his arrest for betraying the cause of Parliament he was found to have at least £4800 in money which was an unusually large amount for this period.[1] Often the personal estate of a wealthy gentleman, though rich in plate and furnishings, included no more than £50 in ready money: indeed when Sir John Reresby of Thrybergh related that his grandfather 'was thought to have mony on him when he dyed' he clearly regarded this as worthy of special notice.[2] Needless to say, this tendency to live up to one's income had obvious dangers: with little surplus capital available a new and unforeseen commitment could upset the delicate equilibrium between income and expenditure and occasion heavy borrowing from moneylenders.

Francis Bacon wrote: 'A man had need, if he be plentiful in some kind of expense, to be as saving again in some other. As, if he be plentiful in diet, to be saving in apparel; if he be plentiful in the hall, to be saving in the stable; and the like. For he that is plentiful in expenses of all kinds will hardly be preserved from decay.'[3] In Yorkshire there were many gentlemen who experienced financial difficulties through living beyond their means. Sir William Constable of Flamborough was noted for his profuse extravagance and high living which led to the overthrow of his estate. Sir Thomas Reresby of Thrybergh had 'an humor to live high at the first, which he did not abate as his fortune decreased'. His heavy expenditure was attributable to such items as housebuilding, lavish hospitality and his 'great attendance, seldom going to church or from home without a great many followers in blew coats and badges, and beyond the usuall nomber for men of his quality and fortune'. Sir George Reresby, his

---

[1] B. Whitelock, *Memorials of the English Affairs*, i, 206. T. T. Wildridge, *The Hull Letters*, 161–3. In all, the sum of £6200 was found but part of this was claimed by a relative.
[2] B.M., Additional MSS 29443, f.2.
[3] *The Essayes or Counsels Civill and Morall of Francis Bacon Lord Verulam*, 87.

son, 'was remarkable for being expensive in cloaths and in his journeys'. Sir Thomas Lascelles of Breckenbrough was a spendthrift who
reduced his estate from £1500 to £400 a year and left his heir a heavy
burden of debts. Charles Meynell of Hawnby was said to have run
through a patrimony worth £1000 a year. Sir Henry Cholmley of
Whitby, being related to George Earl of Cumberland, 'frequented
much his company, which drew him to live in a higher port, and to a
greater expence; and, being much addicted to fleet hounds and horses...
did much increase his expences'. Such cases were typical of a considerable section of the gentry.[1]

Another major cause of indebtedness was the financial provision
which a gentleman had to make for his wife, his daughters and his
younger sons. A large jointure out of the estate could be a serious
matter for the heir, particularly when his mother lived to an advanced
age. The financial troubles of Sir John Reresby of Thrybergh were
ascribed by his son partly to the Civil War and partly to 'the narrowness of his then present fortune ther being two great jointures out of
his estate till about three years before he died'.[2] Another gentleman in a
similar plight was Robert Stapleton of Wighill who at his death in 1635
had only £244 a year in land out of an estate valued at £921 a year:
as both the family mansions were included in the jointures he seems to
have lived mainly in London.[3]

The long continuance of a jointure was not the only problem: an
estate could also be seriously burdened with the payment of annuities
to younger sons and the raising of marriage portions for their sisters.
According to Christopher Wandesford, 'the whole clear Estate being
divided into three Parts' one-third should be reserved 'for Provision
for Children's Portions, and the like', and indeed several cases have
been found where this principle was strictly applied.[4] Nevertheless
some gentlemen were remarkably prolific, witness the numerous
progeny of Sir Timothy Hutton depicted or recorded on his memorial
at Richmond. In such cases the family might be faced with a period of
financial stringency or worse. Sir John Mallory of Studley had to make

---

[1] M. Noble, *The Lives of the English Regicides*, i, 146. B.M., Additional MSS 29442
ff.46–7, and 29443, f.2. P.R.O., Chancery Proceedings, Series I, C.2 James I/L3/51.
Foley, vi, 341. *Cholmley Memoirs*, 14. For Sir William Constable see also below, 353.
[2] B.M., Additional MSS 29440, f.3.
[3] H. E. Chetwynd-Stapylton, *The Stapeltons of Yorkshire*, 232, 239. P.R.O., Court of
Wards, Feodaries' Surveys, 5/49 and 50.
[4] Christopher Wandesford, *A Book of Instructions*, 78. *Y.A.J.*, ii, 3.

provision for eighteen children, and his father for sixteen, both exclusive of the heir, so that it is hardly surprising to find him selling off
part of his estate. Sir Guildford Slingsby of Hemlington bequeathed all
his lands, worth £200 a year, first to his wife, then to his eldest son, and
stipulated that after his wife's death their six other sons should each
have £20 a year out of the property.[1] Sometimes money had to be
borrowed for the maintenance and advancement of the children: in
1639, for example, Stephen Jackson of Cowling secured a loan of £850
for the marriage portions of his sisters and in return charged his estate
with a rent of £91 a year so that he was left with a net income of only
£99 a year.[2] In other cases property was sold for the raising of portions.

The various types of charge discussed above could be heavy taken
individually, but when two or more of them ran concurrently the heir
might find himself in an extremely serious position. In 1652 Walter
Calverley of Calverley succeeded to an estate worth £505 a year which
was charged with a jointure of £250, together with annuities and rent-
charges amounting to £162; there were also debts owing to the sum
of £2246. His grandfather, Sir Walter Pye, put the situation to him
bluntly:

Looke uppon your revenew as it is clogged with your Mothers Joynture
which is a full halfe of whatsoever your Estate can be and seriously consider
if by thrift you may pay it out of your rents, if not there are but two wayes,
A good Wyfe or the Sale of lands and the sooner you put either in practise
the more will it be for your advantage: you shall have in both my best helpe.[3]

As we have already seen[4] many Yorkshire gentlemen visited London
either on business or for pleasure. This could involve significant
expenditure: thus when Sir Timothy Hutton of Marske paid a brief
visit in 1605 it cost him nearly £40. Sir Henry Slingsby of Scriven
was a fairly regular visitor to the capital from the days of his youth: in
his diary he writes of his journey up to London in December 1639 and
his residence there during the period 1640–2 when he served as an M.P.
first in the Short Parliament and then in the Long Parliament. For the
year beginning March 1639 his account book reveals that he allocated

---

[1] J. R. Walbran, 'A Genealogical and Biographical Memoir of the Lords of Studley,
in Yorkshire', *Surtees Society*, lxvii, 325, 326. P.R.O., Chancery, *Inquisitions Post Mortem*,
Charles I, C.142/dccxxviii/7 and S.P.Dom., Committee for Compounding, S.P.23.
ccxviii/223.

[2] P.R.O., S.P.Dom., Committee for Compounding, S.P.23/clxxix/368.

[3] B.M., Additional MSS 27411, ff.44, 47, 68, 73, 74, 126, 130, 135.

[4] See above, 21–4.

£200 of his income to meet his expenses in London while in the following year he set aside no less than £731 for this purpose.[1]

Often a journey to London also meant a visit to the court. Some
gentlemen became courtiers in the hope of making a fortune and not
infrequently dissipated their revenue in extravagant living. Sir Thomas
Reresby of Thrybergh, who sold or mortgaged much of the family
property, is said to have fallen into debt partly through his attendance
at court where he gained nothing except a knighthood. In the same
way Sir Philip Fairfax of Steeton, a courtier who was distinguished
only for his reckless spending, left his heir a sadly reduced and embarrassed estate.[2]

Some young men who visited London were in the habit of frequent-
ing gaming-houses. Gambling was in fact a popular diversion among
the gentry and might be associated with various activities, horse-racing,
cock-fighting, bowls, dice, backgammon and cards. An account book
which belonged to Sir Francis Monckton of Cavil contains a number of
entries relating to gambling expenses. In the summer of 1620 he lost
£3 playing cards at a Doncaster race-meeting, 23s. playing cards at
Brantcliffe, 35s. 'at the lottery' on several occasions and more money
in a card game at Sir Ferdinando Leigh's house.[3] Addiction to this
pastime sometimes brought a gentleman into great debt. This happened
to Sir Richard Beaumont of Whitley, an inveterate gambler who kept
fighting-cocks: there is a tradition in the Beaumont family that he had
to sell all his property in Huddersfield to pay off his gambling debts.
In 1692 Sir Thomas Strickland of Thornton Bridge warned his son
against the gambling habits of his grandfather and namesake which had
caused great damage to the family estates in the reign of James I: 'The
First thing I advise thee against is the being a Gamster a crime incident to the Family, and nothing more dangerous to destroy they soul
and they fortune: for our family was reduced from a plentifull fortune
to a weake condition by that failing in they great grandfather who was
otherwise an accomplished person.'[4]

[1] *Surtees Society*, xvii, 197–204. *Slingsby Diary*, introduction vi, 45, 49–53, 64, 69, 71,
75. See Appendix A.
[2] B.M., Additional MSS 29442, f.46. Sir Clements R. Markham, *Admiral Robert
Fairfax*, 8.
[3] Nottingham University Library: Galway of Serlby MSS 12149, seventeenth-century
account book (no pagination).
[4] P. Ahier, *The Legends and Traditions of Huddersfield and its District*, i, 40, 41.
Huddersfield Central Library: Whitley Beaumont MSS, WBC/37 and 40. H. Hornyold,
The Stricklands of Sizergh, 137.

Whether he had been extravagant or otherwise in his lifetime a squire could involve his family in heavy expenditure after his death. In part at least this was due to social convention which decreed that a gentleman should be buried in a style corresponding to his position in society. With this necessity in mind some men of substance left elaborate instructions on the funeral arrangements to be made. In 1568 William Swift of Rotherham stipulated in his will:

And as touchinge my funeralles, I will my executors shall make preparacion for suche necessarye thinges to be used at that tyme as shalbe seamelie and decente for my degree and callinge, and speciallye I will that the daye of my buriall there be provyded a substanciall honest dynner for all my worship-full and honest frendes, which I truste will take paines to come to my funer-alles, upon which daye I will in anye wyse that everye poore man, woman, and childe have his dynner, and a pennye in silver.

In addition, a number of relatives and friends were to have 'blacke gownes and hoodes of...fyne clothe, and my wife and childrenn to be clothed in blacke after the auncyente custome of this realme'.[1] Not all gentlemen wanted or could afford a splendid funeral: in 1642, for instance, Robert Rockley of Rockley instructed his executors that 'it is my mynde and desire to be buried with as little trouble and charge as may be'.[2] Even so, the upper and middling gentry were usually buried with considerable pomp unless they were either staunch Puritans or Catholics who preferred a clandestine funeral.

The expenditure on a gentleman's funeral included such charges as the purchase of mourning clothes, the provision of a dinner and gifts of money to the poor. Generally speaking, the total outlay varied in accordance with the status of the deceased. Among the lesser gentry a funeral might cost no more than £5 or £10 whereas the richer gentry often spent as much as £50, £100 or even £200. When Sir William Ingleby of Ripley was buried in 1579 the total expenditure amounted to £136. 7s. 8d. This included the following items: 'in blackes for murning gownes and cottes' £96, 'to the paynter for armes and other such like' £16, 'charges to the poore in redie money' £8 and 'charges of the funerall dinner' £13. 6s. 8d. At the burial of another wealthy squire, William Middleton of Stockeld (a convicted recusant who was laid to rest in the parish church of Spofforth in 1614), the charges

---

[1] *Surtees Society*, cxxi, 51–2.   [2] *Y.A.S.R.S.*, ix, 23.

included £92. 11s. 8d. spent on mourning clothes for relatives and servants.[1]

Another means of honouring the dead and paying tribute to their wealth and position was the erection of costly monuments in churches and family chapels. In 1579 Sir John Constable of Burton Constable arranged for the sum of 500 marks to be spent on tombs for himself and his son John who had predeceased him, while in 1627 Maximilian Colt, the celebrated sculptor, undertook to provide tombs for Sir George Savile of Thornhill and his wife Lady Elizabeth for the sum of £200.[2] Often the monument had as its centrepiece an effigy which was cut in alabaster, marble or occasionally stone. In many Yorkshire churches the leading gentry can be found depicted in this way: for example, Sir William Bellasis at Coxwold, Sir John Savile and his son Sir Henry at Methley, Sir Marmaduke Wyvill at Masham, Sir Richard Beaumont at Kirkheaton and Sir Thomas Vavasour at Hazlewood.[3]

After the funeral expenses had been met the family had to make various payments to the civil and ecclesiastical authorities. In the first place, there was the cost of proving the will which in the early Stuart period might amount to several pounds. Secondly, the family had to bear the charges involved in carrying out an *inquisition post mortem* (or 'finding the office' as this process was often called) on the landed possessions of the deceased. Here the expenditure could be far from trivial: in 1631 (to quote a specific instance) the cost of finding the office after the death of Anne Middleton of Thrintoft, an heiress, came to a total of £27. 19s. 2d. which included fees paid to the high sheriff, the escheator and other officials.[4] Thirdly, the heir who succeeded to any land held in chief by knight's service was obliged to sue out his livery, in other words, to obtain legal possession from the Crown which had *primer seisin* of such lands. Since the average manor was held under this form of tenure many families had dealings with the Court of Wards and Liveries once every generation. For the purpose of assessing the charges the Court of Wards feodary made a survey of the property; and in such cases the value returned by the feodary was generally more than the value shown in the *inquisition post mortem* but

[1] *Surtees Society*, civ, 135. *Y.A.S.R.S.*, lxv, 162.

[2] Beverley County Record Office: Burton Constable MSS DDCC/134/6. T. D. Whitaker, *Loidis and Elmete*, i, 323.

[3] See the articles by Mrs K. A. Esdaile, the greatest authority on English church monuments, in *Y.A.J.*, xxxv and xxxvi.

[4] *Y.A.S.R.S.*, lxv, 162–3.

still substantially less than the actual value.[1] It was in fact almost a sacred principle that where livery was involved the lands should be valued at moderate (or 'mean') rates. In 1638 Sir Henry Slingsby the diarist secured an order from the Court of Wards 'moderating' a survey which the feodary had made three years before, following his father's death. Sir Henry notes in his diary: 'it was thought so unreasonable a survey, as Mr Moor, to whom the order was made, survey'd it at £311 less than Goodhand had done it.' From the official records we find that on 14 November 1638 Thomas Moore valued the West Riding property at £130. 10s. od. although it was actually worth over £900 a year.[2] Fines for livery might amount to £20 or £30 or even £100 and in addition there were fees to be paid to officials. In 1632, following the death of Marmaduke Constable of Everingham, his steward put the cost of 'sewing out of the Livery primer seisin to the King and charges depending thereupon' at above £200. In the Court of Wards records the fine is shown as £123. 9s. 7d. to be paid as follows: £23. 9s. 7d. on 18 May 1633, £50 on 21 November 1633 and £50 at Michaelmas 1634.[3]

When the *inquisition post mortem* was taken the Court of Wards feodary was in attendance in order to ascertain whether the lands were held in chief by knight's service and whether the heir had been a minor at his father's death. If both these conditions were fulfilled the new owner was declared in ward to the Crown which took custody of his person and his estate. Sometimes the family challenged the legality of these proceedings: in 1629, for example, Frances Baildon claimed that the estate of her late husband, William Baildon of Baildon, was held in free and common socage but this argument proved unavailing.[4] Such was the mortality rate at this time that many families found it necessary, as the result of a minority, to petition the master and council of the Court of Wards for the custody and lands of an heir who had been

---

[1] Surveys of this type are found in P.R.O., Court of Wards, Feodaries' Surveys, Wards 5/48 and 50 (Yorkshire).

[2] *Slingsby Diary*, 15–16. P.R.O., Court of Wards, Feodaries' Surveys, Wards 5/48. Y.A.S. Library: Slingsby MSS, Box D5, account book of Sir Henry Slingsby. For John Goodhand see H. E. Bell, *An Introduction to the History and Records of the Court of Wards and Liveries*, 44 and G. E. Aylmer, *The King's Servants: The Civil Service of Charles I, 1625–1642*, 370.

[3] *C.R.S.*, liii, 435. P.R.O., Court of Wards, Miscellaneous Book, Wards 9/cclxxiii/f.251.

[4] W. P. Baildon, *Baildon and the Baildons*, ii, 281. See J. Hurstfield, *The Queen's Wards*, 34–57.

designated a ward of the Crown. During the years 1558–1642 at least
260 Yorkshire gentle families (out of a total of 963) had first-hand
experience of the system of wardship.[1] Some families indeed sustained
several minorities in this period. In 1612 Christopher Wandesford of
Kirklington was the fifth successive heir who had inherited as a minor
and according to his daughter, Alice Thornton, the financial consequences of wardship had reduced the family estate to one-quarter or
one-fifth of what it had once been. This tradition was maintained when
Wandesford's premature death in 1640 created a new minority.[2]

During the reign of Elizabeth the wardship of a minor was not
infrequently granted to a complete outsider who might be a courtier or
a man of position in the county. So keen was the competition that a
speculator sometimes made his bid in anticipation of a minority: thus
in October 1588, when Sir William Fairfax of Gilling was said to be on
his death-bed, John Alford offered 400 marks for the wardship of his
son but in the event Sir William lived on until 1597.[3] To such men the
wardship was little more than a piece of property to be bought and
sold. As a general rule it was quickly conveyed to the family: in 1565
Thomas Ashley, a courtier, sold the wardship of Edward Barton of
Whenby to the heir for the sum of £200, while in 1571 the father-in-
law of William Maleverer of Ingleby Arncliffe purchased his wardship
from Henry Lord Hunsdon for £100.[4] In the early seventeenth
century the Court of Wards normally granted custody of a ward to the
mother or a close relative: indeed from 1611 onwards the next of kin
had a prior right to the wardship if application was made within the
first month.[5] Even then, there was sometimes a family quarrel over
possession of the wardship. In October 1624 Sir Thomas Wentworth
(the future Earl of Strafford) told Sir Walter Pye, attorney of the Court
of Wards, that there were two great parties which would put in for the
wardship of his cousin Thomas Danby of Masham: the first group
consisted of the ward's mother and her friends, and the second of Lord

---

[1] The main sources are as follows: P.R.O., Court of Wards, Feodaries' Surveys
(Wards 5/48, 49 and 50), Indentures of Wardships and Leases (Wards 6), Entry Books of
Contracts for Marriages and Leases, Entry Books of Petitions and Books of Surveys
(Wards 9).

[2] T. Comber, *Memoirs of the Life and Death of the Lord Deputy Wandesforde*, 3, 19,
23. *Surtees Society*, lxii, 26. See also below, 152.

[3] *Cal.S.P.Dom. 1581–90*, 551.

[4] P.R.O., Chancery Proceedings, Series II, C.3/1/51. *Y.A.J.*, xvi, 198. See also
below, 369.

[5] J. Hurstfield, *op. cit.*, 282.

Darcy of Aston, the grandmother, Wentworth himself and others of the father's kindred. There were so many objections to the mother (she had already remarried within two months of her husband's death) that Sir Thomas was convinced that she could never be thought a person capable of such a trust. The first round appears to have gone to the mother's party: an entry dated 30 May 1625 in a Court of Wards precedent book records that upon the refusal of Lord Darcy and Sir Thomas Wentworth to compound as petitioners for the wardship of Thomas Danby, Sir Henry Anderson (presumably a friend of the mother) was admitted to compound for the same. It was not long, however, before Sir Henry came to terms with the grandmother's party and possession of the body and lands was assigned to Christopher Wandesford of Kirklington who had been prevailed upon by his friend Wentworth to assume the duties of guardian.[1]

The price of a wardship, and the rent at which the estate was leased during the minority, depended to a great extent on the valuation of the ward's property. For this purpose the Court of Wards normally had three main sources of evidence at its disposal: the *inquisition post mortem*, the certificate of its local official — the feodary — and the 'confession' or particular of the estate which the family had to submit when petitioning for the wardship. Since the *inquisition post mortem* threw no light on the true value it is hardly surprising that the Court began to rely more and more on the assessments made by its officials in the counties.

An undated memorandum which has been preserved among the Wentworth Woodhouse muniments provides an interesting record of Wentworth's views on the shortcomings of the Court of Wards and how these could be remedied. In his opinion the main defect from the Crown's viewpoint lay in the abuses of the feodaries who (he alleged) generally certified the lands of wards at much lower rates than they were really worth. The answer to this problem was to give the feodaries strict instructions that they should always view the property themselves and certify the true yearly value of all lands found in the office; in addition, they should be required to show their certificates to some specially nominated gentlemen resident in the county so that the master and

[1] Sheffield Central Library: Strafford Letters, xxi. Wentworth to Pye, 11 October and 2 November 1624. B.M., Lansdowne MSS 608, f.16. P.R.O., Court of Wards, Entry Book of Contracts for Marriages and Leases, Wards 9/ccvii/ff.73, 212. T. Comber, *op. cit.*, 45–6, 59–60.

council of the Court of Wards could be privately advised as to their accuracy or otherwise. In Wentworth's view it was not feasible to bring in higher values in the *inquisition post mortem* because this would result in a 'mighty noise'.[1]

This criticism of the feodaries would have been fully justified in the reign of Elizabeth when property was rarely valued with any pretence at accuracy. Administrative inefficiency was in fact a major characteristic of the system until Sir Robert Cecil became master of the Court of Wards in 1599 and set about the task of increasing the revenue. From the beginning of the seventeenth century there is evidence of a deliberate effort on the part of the Court of Wards to secure more realistic assessments and it is symptomatic of this new policy that the feodary's report was usually entitled 'Certificate of the Improved Value'.[2] The task of the feodary was not an easy one for the ward's family often sought to conceal the true value of the estate. In the case of Walter Vavasour of Hazlewood, who was a few months within age at his father's death in 1632, the certificate shows only one specific item of property, some farm-houses in Bramham valued at £3. 6s. 8d. a year. In explanation the feodary informed the Court of Wards that the ward's father was supposed to have died seized of a number of manors: he had pressed the executors about this but they had denied the allegation. These manors he estimated to be worth £800 a year.[3] Although the feodaries encountered considerable difficulties they seem generally to have done their best to produce accurate valuations. In 1613 the lands of Henry Calverley of Calverley were valued at £350 a year, which corresponded to the true value, while in 1629 the estate descending to John Reresby of Thrybergh was certified to be worth £1155 a year as compared with a rental value of £1228 a year on the eve of the Civil War.[4] Naturally some feodaries were more efficient or more honest than others but on the whole the standard of assessment was substantially higher than in any other field of taxation.

In the reign of Elizabeth the price of a wardship rarely exceeded £100 (certainly in the case of Yorkshire wards) although the family

---

[1] Sheffield Central Library: Strafford Letters, xxi, 50.

[2] J. Hurstfield, *op. cit.*, 314. H. E. Bell, *An Introduction to the History and Records of the Court of Wards and Liveries*, 55–6. See also M. J. Hawkins (ed.), *Sales of Wards in Somerset, 1603–1641*.

[3] P.R.O., Court of Wards, Feodaries' Surveys, Wards 5/49.

[4] P.R.O., Court of Wards, Entry Book of Petitions, Wards 9/ccxvi/f.20, and Feodaries' Surveys, Wards 5/49. Y.A.S. Library: MS 527. B.M., Additional MSS 29443, f.6.

might have to pay a larger sum if there was a middleman to be bought off. This situation changed rapidly in the early seventeenth century when the revenue from wardship fines rose steeply, mainly on account of the improved methods of valuation. In this period the normal price range was as follows: upper gentry £500 to £1000, middling gentry £200 to £500, lesser gentry £30 to £200. These were considerable sums, far exceeding any other type of fiscal imposition; on the other hand, they were usually payable in instalments over a period of up to two years. In contrast, the Court of Wards made little effort to improve the yield from rents. The annual rent was generally a negligible charge on the ward's estate and even then the guardian often fell badly into arrears with his payments. The following examples[1] may be given to illustrate the charges levied by the Court of Wards:

Ward	Date of grant	Fine	Rent	Annual income
Henry Gascoigne of Thorpe on the Hill	1591	£4. 6s. 8d.	£3. 9s. 1d.	£360
Sir Thomas Bamburgh of Howsham	1623	£600	£100	£1340
Francis Swale of South Stainley	1630	40 marks	£4. 18s.	£140
Francis Burdett of Birthwaite	1637	£500	100 marks	£800

In addition, the relatives could be put to a good deal of expense in securing a grant of the ward's body and lands. In 1629 Francis Monckton of Cavil laid out £52. 19s. od. in negotiating for the wardship of his nephew William Savile of Wakefield; besides legal and travelling expenses this sum included £11. 7s. 6d. for fees paid to officials, of which the feodary received £6. 16s. od.[2]

In his memorandum on the Court of Wards Wentworth argued that the worst aspects of the system from the subject's point of view were

[1] Gascoigne: P.R.O., Court of Wards, Miscellaneous Books, Wards 9/cxviii/f.307, and cccxlviii (no pagination), and Chancery Proceedings, Series I, C.2/G 14/2. Bamburgh: Court of Wards, Entry Book of Contracts for Marriages and Leases, Wards 9/ccvii/ff.20 and 159. Y.A.S. Library, MD 237 (c). Swale: Court of Wards, Entry Books of Contracts for Marriages and Leases, Wards 9/ccviii/f.76 and ccix/f.87, and Chancery Proceedings, Six Clerks' Series, C.9/10/115. Burdett: Court of Wards, Feodaries' Surveys, Wards 5/50 and Chancery Proceedings, Six Clerks' Series, C.10/28/14. For other examples see Appendix B.

[2] Nottingham University Library: Galway of Serlby MSS 12149: seventeenth-century account book (no pagination). See also below, 377.

the great fines which were demanded for the custody of the ward and the excessive fees which had to be paid to officials upon the grant of a wardship or the suing out of a livery. These charges (he claimed) had been the undoing of many families in the kingdom.[1] Undoubtedly the exactions of the Court of Wards were a real source of grievance, particularly in the early seventeenth century. Charles I recognised this fact when, on 24 August 1640, he promised the Yorkshire gentry 'that the wardshipps of such as miscarried should be free' if they continued to support him in his war with the Scots.[2] Not surprisingly it was the minor gentry who found the charges most burdensome. In 1624 Richard Langley of Ousethorpe left his infant son, Christopher, an estate worth £130 a year which was subject to a mortgage revocable on payment of £500; of this the ward's grandmother had one-third and his mother was to have another third as dower. In making a grant of the wardship and lands the Court of Wards required a fine of £70 and a rent of £10 a year. Another Yorkshire ward, Robert Greene of Thundercliffe Grange, was faced with an equally difficult situation. When compounding for his delinquency in 1646 he testified that he had been in ward for above twenty years; that he had been forced in consequence to make a conveyance of his lands (worth £50 a year) for a term of eight years, and that he was still indebted in the sum of £300.[3] Nevertheless, in spite of the potential dangers, the casualty rate among families which had to bear the charges of wardship was comparatively low. Of the 260 families which underwent this experience in the period 1558–1642 only forty found themselves in financial difficulties that could reasonably be attributed, either wholly or in part, to the system of wardship. Most families managed to avoid the sale of property and indeed a significant number of former wards went in for housebuilding or land purchase.

The succession of a minor might involve other hazards besides the impositions of the Court of Wards. Even when custody of the ward and his lands was granted to the next of kin the estate was not necessarily managed in his best interests and indeed in some cases where the mother remarried there were complaints that the stepfather had exploited the property for his own ends. In 1605, following the execution

[1] Sheffield Central Library: Strafford Letters, xxi, 50.
[2] P.R.O., S.P.Dom., Charles I, S.P.16/cdlxiv/82.
[3] P.R.O., Court of Wards, Feodaries' Surveys, Wards 5/49 and Entry Book of Contracts for Marriages and Leases, Wards 9/ccvii/ff.68, 200, and S.P.Dom., Committee for Compounding, S.P.23/lviii/ff.102–5, and clxxxii/111.

of Walter Calverley of Calverley for the murder of two of his children, Henry Calverley (the only surviving son) became a ward of the Crown.[1] During the period 1614–25 control of his estate was in the hands of Sir Thomas Burton, his guardian and stepfather. In 1626 Calverley made formal complaint to the Court of Wards about Sir Thomas's proceedings with him, alleging in effect that he had abused his trust in order to enrich himself at the heir's expense. According to this petition Sir Thomas had often said that out of his love for Henry and respect for his deceased mother he would give to the ward the last two years' profits arising out of a lease of two-thirds of the estate but in the event this promise had not been fulfilled. The guardian had also pretended that he had authority from the Court of Wards to fell timber to the value of £200 to £300 and had refrained from acting on this fictitious licence in the hope that his stepson would not call him to account when he came of age. In addition to all this Sir Thomas had refused to reveal to the ward any information about his estate: he had kept from him all the deeds and writings and had forbidden him to have any intercourse with his friends.[2]

Similar allegations were made in a Chancery bill of 1648 which was presented on behalf of Nicholas Conyers of Boulby. His mother and her friends (it was claimed) had taken possession of all the deeds concerning the estate and pretended title to the property, sometimes by reason of a limitation supposed to have been made by his grandfather and sometimes by reason of the grant of wardship. Although he was the legal heir they would not provide an account of the profits which had been received from the estate since his father's death nor would they allow him anything for his maintenance. Moreover, they had felled all the timber and sold or converted the same to their own use.[3]

2

In this period a substantial amount of money was spent on litigation, a favourite pursuit of the upper classes. Many Yorkshire gentry went to law or had proceedings brought against them over such matters as

---

[1] This episode, which features in the play *A Yorkshire Tragedy* (sometimes ascribed to Shakespeare), is described in T. D. Whitaker, *Loidis and Elmete*, 219–29.

[2] B.M., Additional MSS 27411, ff.14, 19, 22, 23, 26–8.

[3] P.R.O., Chancery Proceedings, Series II, C.3/439/11.

title to land, the provisions of a will or a marriage settlement and the repayment of a loan. Sometimes a bitter feud produced a whole string of lawsuits. During the early years of the seventeenth century Sir Stephen Proctor of Fountains Abbey had a long and hard-fought contest with some of his wealthy neighbours, including Sir William Ingleby of Ripley, Sir John Mallory of Studley and Sir John Yorke of Gouthwaite. In this quarrel religion was clearly a major factor: Sir Stephen was a Puritan magistrate who displayed great energy in apprehending seminary priests and seizing the goods of recusants while his adversaries were 'men backwarde in Religion' who sought to protect their Catholic tenants. In 1611 it was alleged that Sir William Ingleby, out of his 'great hatred and mallice', had attempted to impoverish his Protestant neighbour through ruinous litigation. As a result of this enmity Sir Stephen had been involved in forty separate lawsuits over the previous twelve years and had spent between £2000 and £3000 in legal expenses and damages.[1] In the North Riding there was a similar feud between Sir Thomas Hoby of Hackness, another arch-Puritan, and the Cholmleys of Whitby who for many years had supported the Catholic cause. Sir Hugh Cholmley relates how his father had become engaged in a legal battle with his troublesome neighbour: Sir Thomas Hoby (he recalls)

having a full purse, no children (and as it was thought not able to get one), delighted to spend his money and time in suits. This Sir Thomas exhibited four several bills in the Star Chamber against Sir Richard; had him also in suit in the Exchequer, where he endeavoured to overthrow all the Royalties and Liberties belonging to the manor of Whitby; which suits were not only chargeable in themselves, but drew Sir Richard from his affaires to London, and there occasioned many expences and increase of debts.

When Sir Hugh was put on the commission of the peace the quarrel flared up once more: Sir Thomas (he tells us) 'began a suit against me in the Star Chamber, and I one against him in the Court of York; but finding himself to have the worst end of the staff, procured the lord Coventry, the lord keeper, to send for me to compose both'.[2]

Some country gentlemen had little knowledge of the law but might be compelled to take legal action against their own inclinations. Sir Robert Dyneley of Bramhope, who was 'a playne and symple gentleman

---

[1] P.R.O., Star Chamber Proceedings, Star Chamber 8/227/1, 2, 4–7, 35–7.
[2] *Cholmley Memoirs*, 20–1, 55.

ignorant and without any experience what belonged to suits in lawe', became an unwilling litigant when challenged in the courts at Westminster. The expenditure which this entailed must have confirmed his worst fears: according to his friends who had some experience of the law his attorney's charges amounted to 'deepe and Covetous extorcion'.[1] In contrast, there were many gentry who would willingly resort to litigation on any pretext. One such was Sir Richard Hawksworth of Hawksworth who, like his father before him, had a quarrelsome disposition and an income capable of supporting a prolonged series of lawsuits. Around the beginning of 1623 he brought a Chancery bill against a neighbour, William Baildon of Baildon, alleging that the latter had refused to pay a free rent of 5s. a year. In his reply the defendant claimed that Sir Richard and his father had threatened that they would make him spend £500 in legal costs. In 1627 Lady Hawksworth left her husband and went to live with her parents, Sir Henry and Lady Goodricke, at Ribston Hall; as a result there was extensive litigation over the custody and maintenance of their young son and in 1632 Sir Richard estimated that this had so far cost him £500. Between 1632 and his death in 1658 Sir Richard was involved in at least fifteen separate cases in the law-courts. These included suits with his son-in-law William Lister of Thornton over the marriage portion of his daughter Katherine and with another son-in-law Francis Baildon over their coalmines on Baildon common.[2]

Litigation weakened many an estate. In the middle years of Elizabeth's reign Richard Goldsborough of Goldsborough spent £900 in legal proceedings arising from a property dispute and this was undoubtedly a major factor in the decline of the family. In 1609 Sir Thomas Metcalfe of Nappa had an action brought against him over the tithes of the rectory of Aysgarth, of which he had a lease from Trinity College Cambridge. According to his own testimony the litigation which followed cost him £2000 and resulted in the overthrow of his estate.[3]

Some of the gentry who actively opposed the Crown during the

[1] P.R.O., Chancery Proceedings, Series II, C.3/306/92.
[2] W. P. Baildon, *Baildon and the Baildons*, ii, 256–7. H. Speight, 'Hawksworth Hall and its Associations', *Bradford Antiquary*, New Series, ii, 279–83. P.R.O., Chancery Depositions, C.22/638/39. Sheffield Central Library: Bright MSS, papers of Sir Richard Hawksworth.
[3] W. P. Baildon, *op. cit.*, iii, 13. W. C. and G. Metcalfe, *Records of the Family of Metcalfe* (in particular pp. 135–202 for Sir Thomas Metcalfe's litigation and financial difficulties.)

reign of Charles I suffered considerable financial losses in consequence. In 1633 Sir David Foulis of Ingleby, who had attempted to stir up resistance to the scheme for knighthood compositions, was sentenced to imprisonment and fined £8000, including damages to Lord Wentworth. His eldest son Henry was also committed to prison (but soon released) and fined £500. Although the son produced a deed purporting to show that in 1632 his father had conveyed to him all his property, subject to certain annuities, this expedient proved unsuccessful: the deed was declared to be fraudulent and Sir David's lands (worth over £1000 a year) were put into Wentworth's possession at a rent of £660 a year to the Crown. As a result the family became heavily indebted to moneylenders and had to sell part of the estate.[1] Another gentleman who opposed the knighthood scheme was James Maleverer of Ingleby Arncliffe, a neighbour of Sir David Foulis: his estate was distrained in the sum of around £2000, most of which he was compelled to pay. His wife told her brother that

in the beginning of these troubles which befell his estate for his knighthood money, he was in very little debt, and within two years he was forced to borrow considerable sums of money upon hard terms, and felled much wood to his great prejudice. Besides he was forced (the better to follow this business) wholly to neglect his affairs at home and in other parts of his estates, which consisted much upon his own manning.

In 1639 Maleverer borrowed £6000 from the Earl of Kingston, mortgaging his whole estate as security, but twelve years later none of the principal money had been repaid. In 1646 he found himself in prison for debt.[2]

Fines imposed in the Star Chamber and other courts might be heavy yet they were not necessarily ruinous in practice. Some fines were subsequently reduced or even remitted altogether, while it was not unusual for payment to be made by means of agreed instalments. In 1614 Sir John Yorke of Gouthwaite and other members of his family were heavily fined in the Star Chamber for putting on a Catholic play. Three years later Sir John was arrested for not paying his fine and as a

---

[1] Rushworth, ii, 215–20. Sheffield Central Library: Strafford Letters, xiv. John Morley to Lord Wentworth, 24 April 1634, xx. Richard Marris to Lord Wentworth, 19 and 20 April, and 10 November 1634. P.R.O., Chancery Proceedings, Series II, C.3/451/74 and C.3/453/99. *V.C.H.*, *N.R.*, ii, 227.

[2] Rushworth, ii, 71, 135–6. *Y.A.J.*, xvi, 176–7, 179. B. M., Egerton MSS 3562, ff.13–17, and 3568. *Cal. Committee for Compounding*, 2243. W. Notestein (ed.), *The Journal of Sir Simonds D'Ewes*, 152.

result he contracted to pay the sum of £1200 in half-yearly instalments of £30. 13s. 4d. The payment of these instalments apparently ceased in 1631 while the respective fines of £1000 and £500 imposed on Lady Yorke and Richard Yorke (her brother-in-law) were still wholly unpaid in 1640.[1]

Gentlemen who held administrative offices in the county were for all practical purposes unpaid yet they could be put to substantial expense in carrying out their duties. The charges were particularly heavy in the case of the shrievalty: numerous fees had to be paid to government officials, hospitality had to be dispensed and uncollected fines or taxes might be levied out of the sheriff's own estate. On occasion a gentleman who was extravagant by nature spent far more than was strictly necessary in executing the office of sheriff.[2]

Finally, the question arises as to how far taxation was a cause of indebtedness. In normal circumstances the principal tax which fell on the landed classes was the subsidy which was levied at the rate of 4s. in the pound on the annual value of land or alternatively at 2s. 8d. in the pound on the value of goods. Since Parliament often granted two or three subsidies in a single act (at least from 1589 onwards) this might appear to represent a heavy fiscal burden but nothing could be further from the truth. In the first place, the assessed values of land recorded in the subsidy rolls were a small fraction of the true values, as was generally accepted: indeed few gentlemen in Yorkshire were rated at more than £20 a year. From a detailed examination of the subsidy rolls[3] a rough correlation has been found between the assessments and the real values of the estates taxed in this way: that is to say, landowners assessed at £20 almost invariably had £1000 a year or more (and few persons of this standing were put down at less than £20); a rating of £10 usually corresponds to an income of around £500 a year, while few gentlemen whose lands were valued at 20s. or 40s. enjoyed an income of £100 a year. Secondly, the subsidy was in no sense an annual tax. During the period 1603–42, for example, there were seven subsidy acts which provided altogether for the raising of twenty subsidies.[4] Thirdly, it was unusual for the subsidy to be collected in

[1] C. H. D. Howard, *Sir John Yorke of Nidderdale*, 45–6, 67. *Calendar of Yorke MSS*, 188.
[2] See below, 253–4.   [3] P.R.O., Exchequer, Lay Subsidy Rolls (E.179).
[4] 3 James I, c.xxvi. 7 James I, c.xxiii. 18 James I. 21 James I, c.xxxiii. 1 Charles I, c. vi. 3 Charles I, c.viii. 16 Charles I, c.ii.

one payment: normally the act stipulated that the tax should be paid in several instalments which might be spread over two or three years. That the subsidy was a modest tax can be seen from the particular case of Sir Timothy Hutton of Marske who succeeded his father in 1605 and died in 1629. His annual income came to £1077 in 1606 and £1096 in 1625 and his estate was invariably assessed at £20 by the subsidy commissioners. Between 1605 and 1629 sixteen subsidies were levied so that his total payments amounted to no more than £64.[1]

During the reign of Charles I the government resorted to various fiscal expedients in its efforts to produce an adequate revenue. Under the 'forced loan' scheme which, after more than one false start, was effectively launched in October 1626 landowners had to pay a sum equal to the rate at which their lands had been assessed for the last subsidy. Immediate payment was insisted upon, 'the better to accommodate our greate occasions, which are present and pressing', though the commissioners might, at their discretion, accept half the sum demanded as an initial payment, the other half to follow before December 1626. This was a heavier imposition than the average subsidy levy yet so far as the individual taxpayer was concerned it amounted to no more than the five subsidies which Parliament voted in 1628.[2]

Knighthood compositions, for which the authorities issued a commission in January 1630, were in effect, if not in theory, a form of taxation falling on the landowning classes. All men who had lands or rents worth £40 a year or more were required to compound for failing to take upon themselves the order of knighthood at the coronation of Charles I. For this purpose the commissioners were instructed to examine the subsidy books, the book of the freeholders of the county, and other records of the same kind. Anyone whose land was rated at £3 or under in the subsidy books had to pay £10 (the minimum limit) while for a richer landowner the charge was to be at least three and a half times his rating. Special provision was made for justices of the peace: no one serving on the commission was permitted to compound at less than £25.[3] Knighthood compositions seem to have been a more serious matter than any other general tax levied under the early Stuart

[1] Northallerton County Record Office: Hutton MSS, estate papers. P.R.O., Exchequer, Lay Subsidy Rolls, E.179/214/337, 343, 359 and 583A, and 215/432.

[2] P.R.O., S.P.Dom., Charles I, S.P.16/xxxvi/43. Statute 3 Charles I, c.viii. For examples of individual assessments see Appendix B.

[3] P.R.O., S.P.Dom., Charles I, S.P.16/clix/32 and Exchequer, Special Commissions, E.178/7154.

monarchs: indeed a number of Yorkshire squires had to pay £50, £60 or, exceptionally, even more.[1]

In 1635 the government issued a writ of ship money extending to the whole country a tax which had previously been confined to a number of coastal towns. Similar writs followed in 1636, 1637, 1638 and 1639. The instructions from the Privy Council to the high sheriff and from the sheriff to the high constables provided little specific guidance as to how individual contributions were to be assessed, at least in the case of the Yorkshire ship money levies[2]. In practice the method of assessment seems to have varied from shire to shire: in some counties landowners were charged at so much an acre while in Durham (at least on one occasion) the tax was levied at the rate of 3s. 6d. for every pound which a subsidyman was credited with in the book of rates.[3] Little information is available about the procedure followed in Yorkshire or about the amounts which individual landowners were required to pay. The evidence which has survived consists mainly of scattered references. In 1636 Sir Charles Egerton of Newborough, Staffordshire, was charged £7 for his Yorkshire property while in the following year he had to pay £6; this prompted him to complain to the sheriff that many Yorkshiremen paid only £2 for estates thrice as large as his.[4] One of the rentals preserved among the estate papers of Thomas Beaumont of Whitley bears the annotation: 'The whole lay [sic] for the Towneshipp of Whitley for ship Moneyes comes to £1.11s. od. whereof I was assessed 9s. the 11th of december 1638.' At this time Beaumont's property in Whitley appears to have been worth about £212 a year. In December 1638 Mauger Norton of Richmond paid 10s. in respect of his property in that town which was valued at £180 a year when he compounded for delinquency.[5] To judge from these isolated cases and from the evidence available for other counties[6] we must conclude that

[1] P.R.O., Exchequer of Receipt, Miscellanea, E.407/35, ff.56–68 (printed in *Y.A.S.R.S.*, lxi, 89–107). For examples see Appendix B.

[2] See, for example, P.R.O., S.P.Dom., Charles I, S.P.16/cdi/48, and the instructions to the high constable of Staincross in Spencer Stanhope MSS 60232 (Sheffield Central Library).

[3] P.R.O., S.P.Dom., Charles I, S.P.16/ccclxxvi, *passim*. R. Surtees, *History and Antiquities of the County Palatine of Durham*, i, xciv. See also C. G. Bonsey and J. G. Jenkins (ed.), *Ship Money Papers, and Richard Grenville's Note-book*.

[4] B.M., Additional MSS 6672, 222, 237.

[5] Huddersfield Central Library: Whitley–Beaumont MSS, WBE/I/1. *Calendar of Yorke MSS*, 186. P.R.O., S.P.Dom., Committee for Compounding, S.P.23/clxxxvii/185.

[6] See, for example, P.R.O., S.P.Dom., Charles I, S.P.16/ccclxxvi, *passim*.

ship money was far from being a heavy tax on the landed classes.[1] Apart from the constitutional issues the most disturbing feature in the taxpayer's eyes was the likelihood that it would become a regular annual levy.

The landowning classes were also obliged to contribute to the military expenses of the county.[2] In 1583 instructions were issued that for the keeping of cavalry horses the inhabitants of the various shires should be rated according to the actual value of their property and not according to the subsidy assessments. In 1638, when the government was anxious to increase the number of horsemen in the county militia, it was decided that all who had lands of inheritance worth £200 a year clear should henceforth be charged with a light horse and men of £300 a year with a horse and rider. (Some of the richer gentry had to provide two or three horses.)[3] In 1640, when the trained bands were in the field for a lengthy period, it cost 2s. 6d. a day to maintain a horse and rider.[4]

On the whole, the general taxes levied on the gentry, whether sanctioned by Parliament or otherwise, represented a negligible charge on income. Even then, a hard landlord might recover the money from his tenantry. During the reign of Elizabeth a tenant of Sir Robert Constable on the manor of Holme on Spalding Moor was usually required to pay 'halfe one yeres rent over and above his accustomed yerely rente' whenever the landlord was charged with a subsidy or with the provision of horsemen or footmen. Similarly, when George Anne of Frickley granted a lease in 1594 he included a covenant that the tenant should contribute £3. 6s. 8d. towards 'the charges and setting forth of every hableman with horse and harness' whom the landlord, his wife or heirs might be called upon to provide during the term of the lease.[5] More serious than the general impositions were the discriminatory taxes: the exactions of the Court of Wards and the annual rents

---

[1] By the ship money writ of 1635 a total sum of £217,500 was charged on the kingdom and it has been calculated that this was equivalent to between two and three subsidies (M. D. Gordon, 'The Collection of Ship-Money in the Reign of Charles I', *Transactions of the Royal Historical Society*, Third Series, iv, 150).

[2] For a general discussion of military expenditure see L. Boynton, *The Elizabethan Militia*.

[3] *Cal.S.P.Dom. 1581–90*, 118. Rushworth, ii, 726. B.M., Additional MSS 40132, ff.53, 65.

[4] *Slingsby Diary*, 60. For coat and conduct money see below, 315–7.

[5] B.M., Additional MSS 41168, f.18. A. G. Ruston and D. Witney, *Hooton Pagnell*, 291.

payable out of the estates of recusant landowners. As we have already
seen, the charges of wardship could be heavy, at least in the seventeenth
century, although they rarely had fatal consequences. Recusancy fines
will be considered in a later chapter.[1]

[1] See Chapter X

CHAPTER VII

The Declining Gentry

WRITING in the middle of the seventeenth century Thomas Fuller noted that in the counties around London the gentry 'quickly strip and disrobe themselves of their estates and inheritance'. In Berkshire, he observed, estates 'are very skittish, and often cast their owners...I desire that hereafter the Berkshire gentry may be better settled in their saddles'. On the other hand, he believed that there was much greater stability in such counties as Northumberland and Cumberland:

Sure I am that northern gentry transplanted into the south, by marriage, purchase or otherwise, do languish and fade away within few generations; whereas southern men on the like occasions removing northward acquire a settlement in their estates with long continuance. Some peevish natures... impute this to the position of their country, as secured from sale by their distance from London (the staple place of pleasure); whilst I would willingly behold it as the effect and reward of their discreet thrift and moderate expense.[1]

Apart from references to the rise or decline of individual families contemporary comment on the financial position of the Yorkshire gentry is strangely lacking: there is, however, a wealth of raw material available for statistical purposes. Particulars of loans appear on the close rolls and in the books of recognizances which were kept in a special registry.[2] In addition, a great deal of evidence about the indebtedness of the gentry can be found in the estate papers of county families, the Court of Wards records, the compounding papers of royalist families and the records of lawsuits in the Courts of Chancery, Requests and Exchequer.[3] Finally, there are the two main sources of

---

[1] *The History of the Worthies of England*, i, 162, 350 and ii, 554.

[2] P.R.O., Chancery, Close Rolls (C.54) and Lord Chamberlain's Office, Entry Books of Recognizances (L.C.4). See also P.R.O., Chancery, Crown Office, Miscellaneous Books, C.193/xli.

[3] P.R.O., Court of Wards, Feodaries' Surveys (Wards 5) and Entry Books of Petitions (Wards 9); State Papers Domestic, Committee for the Advance of Money (S.P.19) and Committee for Compounding (S.P.23); Chancery Proceedings (C.2, C.3 and C.5–10)

information on property transactions: the feet of fines[1] and the close rolls.

From this evidence it is clear that a high proportion of families within the Yorkshire gentry experienced financial difficulties in the period 1558–1642:

number of families which sold all their landed property	87
number of families which sold most of their property	78
number of families which sold considerable property	164
number of families which were heavily indebted at one time or another but which avoided any significant sale of land	68
total number of families in financial difficulties	397
total number of families in the period 1558–1642	963

Gentlemen who were short of money often secured loans from members of the mercantile community in such towns as York, Hull and Wakefield. In addition, there was a considerable amount of borrowing and lending within the gentry, not only for reasons of kinship but also on a strictly commercial basis. So heavy was the demand for loans, however, that it could be met only in part from local resources and many a Yorkshire squire was obliged to supply his occasions in the London money market. In London money could be borrowed from merchants, tradesmen, lawyers, courtiers and royal officials, either directly or through the agency of scriveners who worked on a commission basis. Provided his credit was good a landowner who was financially embarrassed usually had little difficulty in negotiating a loan; if on the other hand his estate was heavily encumbered it might well be necessary for some of his relatives or friends to join with him in order to provide additional security.

Between 1552 and 1571 the lending of money at interest was a statutory offence. That the law was often circumvented may be judged by the amount of borrowing that went on: in the period 1560–71, for example, some eighty Yorkshire gentlemen appear as borrowers in the entry books of recognizances.[2] By a statute of 1571[3] moneylenders

and Chancery, Entry Books of Decrees and Orders (C.33); Court of Requests, Proceedings (Requests 2); and Exchequer, Bills and Answers (E.112), Depositions (E.134) and Special Commissions (E.178). For family papers see the Bibliography.

[1] P.R.O., Common Pleas, Feet of Fines (C.P.25(2)). The Yorkshire fines for the period 1558–1625 are printed in *Y.A.S.R.S.*, ii, v, vii, viii, liii and lviii.

[2] Statute 5 & 6 Edward VI, c.xx. P.R.O., Lord Chamberlain's Office: Entry Books of Recognizances, L.C.4/clxxxix, cxc, cxci, *passim*.

[3] 13 Elizabeth I, c.viii.

were permitted to charge interest up to a maximum of ten per cent. In practice ten per cent became established as the norm and this high rate of interest continued to have legal force until the end of James I's reign. For the gentry who were forced to borrow heavily an interest rate of this order was clearly a serious matter: writing of his father's great indebtedness Sir Hugh Cholmley of Whitby states that 'one of the greatest cankerworms was use-money, being then at £10 in the £100; and he borrowing most at scriveners, as the custom then was, given them 20s. for every £100 which amounted that money to £11 in the £100'.[1] In 1624, as the result of 'a very great abatement in the value of Land', new legislation was brought in limiting the rate of interest to a maximum of eight per cent and prohibiting scriveners from charging more than 5s. for every £100 borrowed.[2]

Money lent at interest was frequently secured either on a bond or a recognizance 'in the nature of Statute Staple' (sometimes known as a statute).[3] In such cases the loan was usually repayable within one or two years: thus, the bond or recognizance was essentially a short-term borrowing device. At the same time the lender was often prepared to grant a limited extension beyond the original date for repayment if he was satisfied as to the debtor's good faith. In 1629 a London money-lender wrote to Sir Richard Beaumont of Whitley:

I cannot but certifie you that I have received the twentie pounds which you lately sent unto mee and that I am most willinge to fullfil that, which you request by your letter, for six Mounths longer, and bee still assured, that I am soe confident of your good and honest performance, that had I any occasion for Monies I had rather make use of any other, then that which is in your handes.[4]

If the borrower defaulted he was normally liable to forfeit a penal sum equal to twice the amount of the loan. In the case of a recognizance the creditor could then obtain from the clerk of recognizances a certificate authorising the issue of a Chancery writ of extent. By this writ the sheriff of the county was required to extend the borrower's estate, that is, to seize his lands, have them valued by a jury and deliver

[1] *Cholmley Memoirs*, 25.
[2] 21 James I, c.xvii. This rate of interest was to continue for seven years and then to the end of the first session of the next parliament. In the event it remained the legal maximum until 1651.
[3] For bonds and recognizances see L. Stone, *The Crisis of the Aristocracy, 1558–1641*, 517–24.
[4] Huddersfield Town Hall: Whitley-Beaumont MSS, WBC/34.

possession, at least in theory, to the creditor. As a general rule, however, the estate was charged with an annual rent for the purpose of repaying the debt. This rent was based on the jury's valuation and since the latter was usually well below the true value the debtor continued to take most of the revenue to his own use. In the case of a bond it was also possible to have the borrower's lands extended but this required a judgment in a court of law and the writ of *elegit* which was issued in such circumstances only entitled the creditor to possession of half the estate.

There were two kinds of mortgage in this period. In the one case the property intended as security was conveyed to the lender in fee simple but with the proviso that it should revert to the borrower when the loan had been repaid. Generally the mortgagor was allowed to remain in possession and enjoy the profits so long as he observed the conditions of the loan. In the other main type of mortgage the lender received a long lease of the property and in a separate indenture granted the mortgagor a sub-lease at a rent normally corresponding to the statutory rate of interest. To illustrate this kind of transaction we may take an actual example. On 19 January 1631 Marmaduke Franke of Kneeton borrowed the sum of £1000 from Robert, Earl of Kingston and as security demised to him the manor of Kneeton for a period of 500 years. Later, on 30 January, the Earl leased back the manor to the borrower who undertook to pay him a rent of £80 a year until such time as the debt was discharged.[1]

The main attraction of a mortgage loan was the fact that, with the security which it provided, money could be borrowed for considerably longer periods than was possible with a loan which was secured on a recognizance. Often a mortgagor was allowed five to ten years in which to repay (and indeed in some cases the period of the loan was as much as twenty years). Until the seventeenth century, however, there was a serious drawback in this type of loan arrangement: at common law the borrower who defaulted over payment of either the principal or the interest forfeited the whole of his mortgaged property, even though it might be worth far more than the amount of the debt. In the reign of Elizabeth the practice developed in Chancery of relieving a mortgagor in special cases of hardship, for example, when he was unable to make payment on the appointed day because of illness or theft. During the

---

[1] P.R.O., S.P.Dom., Committee for Compounding, S.P.23/lxxxi/139, 140, 146, 147. See below, 371.

course of the early seventeenth century the exceptional became the general. By a series of judgments the principle was established that any defaulting borrower could redeem his property in Chancery provided he paid the principal, together with interest and costs, within a reasonable time after the forfeiture. This principle, which apparently took shape in the period 1615–30, gave rise in turn to the right of fore-closure: that is to say, the mortgagee could secure a Chancery decree requiring the borrower to pay the money owing by a specified date, failing which the premises passed into the mortgagee's absolute owner-ship.[1]

One of the earliest references to the equity of redemption appears in the memoirs of Sir John Reresby of Thrybergh. According to this account his great-grandfather Sir Thomas Reresby mortgaged his Derbyshire lands for £800 'and charged them besides with £3000 for portions to two of his daughters, and soon after dyed'. His son Sir George succeeded in 1619 and we are told:

Sir George Reresby, that had the Equity of Redemption in him, neglected to look after it till the Creditours and thos that married the two daughters gott a decree in Chancery to sell the estate, soe that it was aliened and never reguarded in his time. Sir George, dying, left my father Sir John under age and ward to his mother, who had more care of her own land...then of that of the family. Soon after my said father was married he began to look into the state of the Saile, and commenced suit against the Purchassours. But the Contest being likely to be tedious and chargeable,...he closed with some offers of small summs of Mony for accommodation, and confirmed the Purchassours Estates.[2]

It has been argued that the development of the equity of redemption did much to promote greater stability within the landed interest; that once the severity of the common law had been moderated the land-owner under financial pressure felt able to make use of the long-term borrowing facilities which the mortgage loan arrangements provided and so gained a reasonable breathing-space in which to put his affairs in order.[3] While such evidence is not conclusive in itself it is significant that members of the Yorkshire gentry increasingly resorted to mort-gage borrowing during the early seventeenth century. The figures in

[1] See R. W. Turner, *The Equity of Redemption*.
[2] B.M., Additional MSS 29440, f.35.
[3] M. E. Finch, *The Wealth of Five Northamptonshire Families 1540–1640*, 32–3, 168–9.

the following table, though not exhaustive, serve to illustrate the general trend:

Number of mortgage loans
secured by members of the
Yorkshire gentry in

1600–9	5
1610–19	21
1620–9	30
1630–9	55

Notwithstanding the general power of redemption, however, the borrowing of money on mortgage terms was not without its risks. If there was a delay in payment of the principal or interest the mortgagee still had the right to enter into the mortgaged premises and remain in effective possession until the property was redeemed. Although the creditor was expected to account for the profits he had received when the final reckoning was made, this could mean that the mortgagor was denied a substantial, and sometimes a major, part of his estate revenue over an extensive period. In this vulnerable position, with little money to spare for litigation, the mortgagor would have difficulty in preventing a wealthy and ruthless moneylender from exploiting the situation to his maximum advantage. In a Chancery bill of 1654 Sutton Ogle-thorpe described how, some years before, he had been deprived of the greater part of his patrimony through the misapplication of a mortgage lease. In August 1627 his grandfather William Oglethorpe of Ogle-thorpe and his father, who was also called William, had borrowed the sum of £1000 from Robert Viscount Newark (later Earl of Kingston) and as security had mortgaged the manors of Bramham and Clifford which were then worth £400 a year. The eight per cent interest charge, which took the form of a half-yearly rent of £40, was duly paid for the space of three years when the complainant's father, who was in prison for debt, unhappily defaulted. As a result Viscount Newark, it was alleged in the bill, not only entered into possession of the mortgaged property (as he was entitled to do) but also took the profits of the manor of Oglethorpe, worth £200 a year, over a three-year period. In 1634 the estate descended to Sutton Oglethorpe and according to his own testimony he 'made many iourneys to his great Charge to the said Viscount', who lived at Holbeck Woodhouse in Nottinghamshire,

attendeing many tymes att his gates and desired of him to knowe what his demaunds were touching the said Rent And the Arrearages thereof. And offered to give him full satisfaction therein. And your Orator also to his great Charge sent divers of his ffreinds to the said Viscount for the said purpose. But the said Viscount would not give to your Orator or his said friends any Reasonable Answer therein but said hee would lye in the ffleete before he Assigned his Lease unto your Orator.

Subsequently the mortgagee sold his interest in the premises to Sir Thomas Gascoigne of Barnbow, a recusant neighbour of the Ogle-thorpes, who in turn disposed of most of the property in small parcels, in some cases to sitting tenants. In all (Oglethorpe claimed) Sir Thomas had made a net profit of £4000 out of the transaction and still retained in his possession the profits of the manorial courts and certain land worth altogether £170 a year.[1]

Another Yorkshire squire who had a bitter experience of mortgage borrowing was William Scudamore of Overton. After inheriting the family estate in 1621 he was soon resorting to the sale of property but even then he still remained heavily indebted to moneylenders. In this situation Sir Thomas Wentworth (the future Earl of Strafford) saw an opportunity for making substantial profits at his expense. First he purchased a recognizance in which Scudamore had bound himself for the payment of £400 and immediately took steps to have the manor of Overton extended; then he persuaded a mortgagee to sell him his interest in the manor and in 1627 entered into possession of the premises. According to his own account Scudamore offered to sell the manor to Wentworth but they were unable to agree on a price and the transaction fell through. After this Wentworth continued to take the whole revenue of the manor until his death in 1641 when the property passed into the hands of his trustees. While he was in possession (Scudamore alleged) he disposed of the timber and destroyed all the underwoods to the value of at least £2000; ploughed up the ancient pasture grounds; let the premises at uneconomic rents and refused to accept the mortgagor as under-tenant at a much higher rent; and en-closed within the royal park of Galtres some 400 acres of moorland belonging to the manor. By 1650 Wentworth and his trustees had received, at least according to Scudamore's calculations, £10,000 over and above the money owing on the mortgage and recognizance.[2]

Faced with the problem of growing indebtedness the prudent land-

---

[1] P.R.O., Chancery Proceedings, Six Clerks' Series, C.5/402/106.
[2] P.R.O., Chancery Proceedings, Six Clerks' Series, C.9/5/189. Sheffield Central Library: Strafford Letters, xxi, 37, 46. *N.R. Records*, iv, 157–8. *V.C.H., N.R.*, i, 179.

owner took steps to bring his expenditure under control. On the whole, frugality did not come easily to the squirearchy: nevertheless it was not unusual for a gentleman in financial straits to turn over the bulk of his property to trustees or to his heir for the specific purpose of discharging his debts while he and his wife lived modestly on the small sum which had been reserved for their maintenance. One obvious source of economy was housekeeping expenditure which might account for at least one-third of a family's total outgoings. Sometimes a hard-pressed squire gave up housekeeping altogether and took up residence in York or some other large town where he was under no necessity to live in a style 'answerable to his estate'. This practice aroused the disapproval of the Privy Council who in October 1614 informed the attorney general that 'his Majestie hath taken notice of a great resort of gentlemen of quality and livelyhood, together with their wives and families, into the citty of London, and other principall citties and townes of this realme, with a purpose (as it appeareth) to settle their habitacion there, for saving of charges and other private respectes'. As a result, it was feared, there would be a great decay of hospitality.[1]

In his memoirs Sir Hugh Cholmley of Whitby describes how his father and grandfather responded to their financial difficulties. Of his grandfather he relates:

After much land sold, and debts still increasing, and having a numerous issue, he confined himself to a proportion; and turned the land into the hand of his eldest son (then married) for the payment of debt, and increase of his children's portions; and about the 58th year of his age retired with his wife and family into the city of York, where he continued to his death.

Subsequently the eldest son, Sir Richard Cholmley, himself became indebted and 'made over to [Sir Hugh] the whole estate for ten years, for payment of the said debts, reserving only £400 per annum for himself for that time, and then lived retired at Whitby'.[2]

As the result of vigorous remedial action involving substantial retrenchment and improved methods of estate management not a few gentlemen who had been faced with the prospect of bankruptcy and ruin were able to weather the crisis with at least the bulk of their estates still intact. When Sir George Wandesford of Kirklington, an improvident squire, died in 1612 he left behind him a heavily burdened estate which had been seriously neglected and mismanaged. The heir,

[1] *Acts of the Privy Council 1613–14*, 596–7.　　[2] *Cholmley Memoirs*, 15, 26, 42.

Christopher Wandesford, later described the situation to his son: 'My Father (as you will find by your Rentalls) left me not in present Revenue above £560 per annum, and that charged with three Brothers and two Sisters unprovided for. The Debts which he did owe, were near £800, no furniture at all to the Value of a Stooll at either of my Houses; my self left in Minority, which cost me near a £1000 for my Wardship.' Out of his estate the young heir had to pay £100 a year for his stepmother's jointure and annuities amounting to £60 a year. According to his daughter Alice these charges and the interest payable on his father's debts left him with a clear income of no more than £300 a year. In these difficult circumstances his first concern was to secure a grant of his wardship and lands. On 10 November 1612 he and his grandfather, Ralph Hansby of Bishop Burton, made their appearance in the Court of Wards and offered the sum of £500 for the wardship and marriage. At this stage of the negotiations, however, the Court of Wards officials demanded £1150. Three days later Christopher Wandesford raised his offer to £600 but on the same day his uncle William Wandesford and his stepmother made a rival bid which was substantially higher: £1000 for the wardship and a rent of £94 a year for the estate. Finally, on 4 December 1612, Ralph Hansby was granted custody of the body and lands of his grandson for a fine of £900, payable over four years, and a rent of £97. 6s. 8d. a year.[1]

Christopher Wandesford now had possession of his own wardship (since his grandfather was merely the nominal grantee) but the price exacted was clearly more than he had anticipated. In September 1614, however, he married Alice Osborne, sister to Sir Edward Osborne of Kiveton, and through her secured a portion of £2000, half of which he used to discharge his wardship. After completing his negotiations with the Court of Wards he immediately set about the task of restoring the family fortunes. In the first place, he took over part of the demesne for crop cultivation and the rearing of livestock, his primary object being to supply the needs of his household. Secondly, he embarked on a new leasing policy, substituting economic rents for entry fines, and in the period 1612–40 virtually doubled the rental income of the estate which he had inherited. Thirdly, he took effective steps to limit

[1] Christopher Wandesford, *A Book of Instructions*, 89. T. Comber, *Memoirs of the Life and Death of the Lord Deputy Wandesforde*, 3, 15, 19, 23, 65. P.R.O., Court of Wards, Entry Book of Contracts for Marriages and Leases, Wards 9/cciv/ff.9, 107, and Entry Book of Petitions, Wards 9/ccxv/ff.40, 41.

his expenditure: thus his household was run on the principle of 'frugal hospitality' and, he told his son, 'I was moderate in my personall Expences'. Even then he found it necessary to resort to short-term borrowing on the security of bonds 'which', he relates, 'I was forced to do continually, rather than by the Sale of some Part of my Lands, by Mortgages or some more disadvantageous Bargains, to weaken my Estate and lessen my Revenues'. Eventually, as a result of his sound business methods, he repaid his father's debts to the last penny and proceeded to carry out improvements at Kirklington Hall.[1]

About the time that Christopher Wandesford was looking forward to a period of relative prosperity Sir Hugh Cholmley of Whitby was just beginning a similar recovery operation. When he took over his father's estate in 1626 the revenue amounted to £1500 or £1600 a year out of which the sum of £400 a year was reserved for the maintenance of Sir Richard and his wife. His father's debts were at that time above £11,000 while his own came to £600 or £700 and (he writes) 'money being now at £10 in the hundred, the very interest and what my father was to have, amounted to as much as the revenue of all the land was at present'. One of Sir Hugh's first actions was to buy in two recognizances of £500 each which represented the greatest encumbrance on the estate. He then concentrated his energies on improving the yield from the estate which he appears to have managed on an extremely tight rein, shortening leases and bringing the rents more into line with the actual values of holdings. His father had kept substantial property in his own hands but this had proved to be an unprofitable enterprise in view of the general depression of the early 1620's and 'the fall of prices of all goods at that time': Sir Hugh therefore endeavoured to let as much as possible of this land to tenants. Largely through his own efforts but partly no doubt through a gradual improvement in the economic situation the estate revenue followed a marked upward trend: his Fyling Hall property, for example, increased in value from £160 to £240 a year in a comparatively short period. At his father's death in 1632 he was left with debts of £4000 to pay. Some of the debts had been discharged through the sale of land but the estate as a whole had survived the crisis and as early as 1633 he was purchasing new property. In 1636 he was at the peak of his prosperity: 'having

---

[1] T. Comber, *op. cit.*, 20, 21, 23, 28, 29. Christopher Wandesford, *op. cit.*, 81, 89–92. See above, 44.

mastered my debts', he writes, 'I lived in as handsome and plentiful fashion at home as any gentleman in all the country, of my
rank.'[1]

While some gentry retrieved their fortunes through good management others seemed incapable of meeting the challenge. As the situation
went from bad to worse their only response was to go on borrowing
until their credit (or the patience of their friends who were engaged
with them) was completely exhausted. If he possessed extensive
property an improvident landowner might run up a formidable collection of debts before the moment of reckoning came, in some cases
as much as £10,000 or even £20,000. Gentlemen of more modest
estate were naturally unable to borrow on this scale but it was by no
means unusual for the eldest son to inherit debts considerably in excess
of the value of his father's personal estate. As the declining gentry
defaulted over loan repayments their creditors quickly moved in,
bringing actions for debt in the law-courts, securing writs of extent,
entering into mortgaged premises and taking possession of goods
and chattels. On occasion a defaulter either refused to appear in
court or defied a judgment which had been obtained against him
and as a result found himself outlawed for debt and threatened with
arrest.

If he had influence at court a gentleman who was being harassed by
his creditors might be able to secure an official letter of protection
which gave him temporary immunity from their attentions. Such a
dispensation, however, was beyond the reach of the average country
squire.[2] Compelled to fend for themselves, some men took flight or
went into hiding (sometimes after concealing the title to their estates
under complicated trusteeship arrangements) and not infrequently they
managed to evade their creditors for months or even years. In 1618
Sir Thomas Metcalfe of Nappa, who had inherited a sadly diminished
estate and was heavily indebted to moneylenders, was said to be living
in obscure places or 'places of privelege'. Similarly, the Privy Council
were informed in 1634 that John Carvile of Milford had been owing
£2000 for the last ten years and for most of that time had 'obscured
himselfe, and lived in privileged places, where' John Culpeper, one of
his creditors, 'cannot procure him to be arrested, and hath lately bene

---

[1] *Cholmley Memoirs*, 23–6, 34, 42–6, 49, 53–4, 56.
[2] For letters of protection see *Acts of the Privy Council* and the *Calendar of State Papers Domestic*.

in Ireland and purposeth to goe thither againe, standing outlawed, having land worth above five thousands which hee hath secretly conveyed to his friends in trust, thereby to defraude the petitioner of his debt'.[1] Not all debtors, however, were so successful in avoiding arrest. During this period a number of Yorkshire gentlemen (some of them men of high rank) were committed to prison for failing or refusing to settle their debts. Sir Arthur Pilkington of Stanley, the first baronet of that family, was imprisoned on at least two occasions: in his youth, shortly after inheriting the family estate, he was consigned to York Castle at the suit of one of his father's creditors, while in 1649, not long before his death, he was said to have been in prison for four years on account of unpaid debts.[2]

In the last resort the struggling landowner embarked on the sale of land. Among the more substantial gentry an estate was often wholly or largely entailed but until the classical strict settlement was perfected in the latter part of the seventeenth century it was usually possible to overcome this restriction. From about the middle of the fifteenth century a tenant in tail who wished to sell some of his property could break the entail by means of a legal device known as a common recovery. If, however, the terms of the family settlement were such that the hard-pressed landlord merely had a life estate the problem was more difficult but not necessarily insuperable. Provided the heir had been granted the remainder in tail his father might persuade him, if he was out of his minority, to join with him in suffering a common recovery in order to free the premises which were intended to be sold. If the heir was only a child the life tenant might still be able to find a purchaser who was willing to buy the property subject to the son's willingness to confirm the grant when he came of age. To overcome the purchaser's misgivings it was usual for further land which had not been included in the entail to be conveyed to him as collateral security in case the heir sought to evict him from the premises which he had acquired. Thus when Sir John Reresby of Thrybergh sold entailed property in Woodlaithes shortly before the Civil War he found it necessary not only to enter into a recognizance but also to make a conveyance of his reversionary interest in the manor of Ickles as security, with the proviso that if the

---

[1] W. C. and G. Metcalfe, *Records of the Family of Metcalfe*, 183. P.R.O., Privy Council Registers, P.C.2/xliv/ff.105, 114.

[2] P.R.O., Chancery Proceedings, Series II, C.3/284/69 and S.P.Dom., Committee for Compounding, S.P.23/ccxi/25.

heir should confirm the sale within six months after attaining his majority then the conveyance should be void.[1]

Although most families which sold land managed to escape total disaster the fatality rate among the Yorkshire gentry was by no means insignificant: in all, eighty-seven families were forced to dispose of the whole of their landed property in the period 1558–1642. Sometimes an estate was sold subject to the payment of a life annuity, as may be seen from a Chancery case of 1642 between Thomas Lord Fauconberg and Thomas Lepton, formerly squire of Kepwick. The latter had inherited property worth some £300 a year but he had been obliged to sell his whole patrimony to satisfy his father's debts. Lord Fauconberg, the purchaser, complained in his bill that Lepton had concealed from him certain encumbrances and extents on the premises. In reply Lepton and his wife denied this charge and put in a counter-accusation. Shortly after the deed of bargain and sale had been sealed (they claimed) Lord Fauconberg had granted them annuities of £50 each for their lives, in consideration of £750 deducted from the purchase price. These annuities represented their sole means of support yet after the first year Fauconberg had withheld payment. Altogether he owed them arrears of £1000.[2]

Some gentry who sold out continued to live in the same region where they had been landed proprietors. The more resilient sought to make a living in commerce or industry or by working the land as tenant farmers: William Jackson of Cadeby, for example, appears to have become a tenant of the family which purchased his father's estate while his younger brother Thomas described himself in 1657 as a cutler.[3] In contrast, there were other ruined gentlemen who had serious difficulty in making the necessary adjustment. From an Exchequer lawsuit we learn that John Pudsey, who had once owned the manor of Arnforth in Craven, had subsequently fallen into very great poverty and had been maintained at the charge, and as one of the poor, of the parish of Horton in Ribblesdale.[4]

Not a few landless gentry had to depend entirely on the goodwill of

[1] Leeds Central Library: MSS of Lord Mexborough, Reresby papers, letter of Sherland Adams, 12 July 1654. B.M., Additional MSS 29443, f.8.

[2] P.R.O., Chancery Proceedings, Series II, C.3/425/7.

[3] P.R.O., Chancery Proceedings, Six Clerks' Series, C.5/29/124 and S.P.Dom., Committee for Compounding, S.P.23/cxci/703.

[4] P.R.O., Exchequer Depositions, E.134, 32–3 Charles II, Hilary 10, and Chancery, *Inquisitions Post Mortem*, Charles I. C.142/dxxxi/174. T. D. Whitaker, *Craven*, 156.

relatives or friends for their sustenance. Needless to say this type of charity could often be humiliating for the recipients, a point which is well illustrated in Roger Dodsworth's account of the last days of Robert Roos of Ingmanthorpe. This gentleman, he tells us,

having had suites all his lief for landes that were Strangeweys at Upsal Castle, Kilvinton, &c, and being tyred with them, did resign all his lands into the hands of th'Erle of Rutland in that tyme when he was lord president of the North, to the end his debts should be paid and he have some exhibition during lief, which seameth was not much, for he had a chamber wherin he lay in South Dighton, and had his dyet sent every meale tyme from Mr Manners's table, who then lyved att the parsonage house ther.[1]

If London was something of a magnet for the well-to-do gentry it also had its attractions for impoverished members of the class who were seeking opportunities to start a new life. Richard Aske, formerly of Aughton, whose father had dissipated a large inheritance, became a barrister of the Inner Temple and was destined to serve as one of the parliamentary counsel at the trial of Charles I. Similarly, the gentlemen who registered their arms at the London visitation of 1633–4 included several merchants or tradesmen who had once owned, or been heirs to, landed property in Yorkshire: for example, William Newby, formerly of North Fenton, who described himself simply as a merchant, and Ralph Rasing, formerly of Broughton, who was then a goldsmith.[2] On the other hand, some men who took shelter in London spent their last days there in pitiful circumstances. Perhaps the most tragic story of all, because of the extremes of wealth and poverty which it embraces, is the downfall of Sir Richard Gargrave of Nostell Priory. Although he had been born a younger son Sir Richard eventually inherited an estate which was so large that he could ride on his own land from Wakefield to Doncaster. He was, however, a man of great improvidence and he soon found himself in financial difficulties. In 1634 he was said to be living in the Temple for sanctuary, 'having consumed his estate to the value of £3500 per annum att the least, and hath not a penny to maintain himself but what the purchasers of some part of his lands in reversion after his mother's death allow him, in hope that he will survive his mother, who hath not consented to the sale'. Subsequently,

---

[1] *Y.A.S.R.S.*, xxxiv, 32.
[2] *Masters of the Bench of the Honourable Society of the Inner Temple and Masters of the Temple*, 30. *Harleian Society*, xvii, 124, 186.

in order to make a living, Sir Richard was reduced to travelling with pack-horses and according to tradition he died at an old hostelry with his head resting on a pack-saddle.[1]

On occasion a ruined squire left the country after disposing of his estate. Francis Holmes, formerly of Hampole, went to Ireland where he served as an attendant to the Earl of Devonshire and later entered the household of the Marquis of Huntly in Scotland. Sir William Babthorpe, formerly of Osgodby, fought with the Spanish army in the Netherlands. Ralph Hungate, formerly of North Dalton, took part in an expedition to the New World and, according to a Court of Wards decree, he perished 'in the River Wyapeco above the Falls in Guiana and was buried next unto captaine Harcourt' in May 1630.[2]

Several of the families which went under in this period had at one time been leading gentry with landed incomes of £1000 a year and upwards. If, however, the upper gentry were not invulnerable they were undoubtedly in a much better position to weather a financial crisis than the middling or lesser gentry. In the first place, their capital resources were substantial enough to enable them to go on borrowing over an extensive period: consequently they would normally have ample opportunity to improve their estates and bring their expenditure under strict control before their creditors began to take action. Secondly, if the worst came to the worst, they had the choice of selling off outlying property in order to settle their debts and clear the main estates of encumbrances. Where a major landed family passed from wealth to poverty in the course of one or two generations this was usually because of gross mismanagement or reckless extravagance or perhaps a combination of both.

Lower down the economic scale it was correspondingly more difficult for a struggling landowner to extricate himself from his predicament and families with no more than £50, £100 or £200 a year were particularly vulnerable. At his death in 1629 Francis Swale of South Stainley left an estate worth £140 a year, together with goods and chattels valued at £102. 8s. 4d. On the other side of the balance sheet there were debts to the sum of £322. 16s. 0d. and children's portions amounting to £500 which had still to be raised. Solomon, the heir, was then nineteen and his wardship and lands were granted to his uncle

---

[1] J. Hunter, *South Yorkshire*, ii, 213–14. B.M., Additional MSS 24470, ff.37, 38, 80.
[2] P.R.O., Transcripts, Gunpowder Plot Papers, P.R.O. 31/6/1. Foley, iii, 200. Beverley County Record Office: Langdale MSS, DDLA/19/81.

William Ingleby of Ripley for a fine of forty marks and a rent of £4. 18s. od. a year. Besides the heavy burden of debts, portions and wardship charges there was also the considerable expenditure involved in providing the heir with a legal education at Gray's Inn and in maintaining the brothers and sisters (of whom there were eight). That the estate was preserved in these circumstances was due to a combination of factors. In the first place, the guardian (who was one of the richest landowners in the West Riding) used his own money to supplement the income from his nephew's property. During the fifteen months which preceded the ward's coming of age Ingleby received £166. 19s. od. from the estate while his disbursements came to £308. 6s. 8d. Secondly, Solomon's first wife was said to have had a 'very considerable' fortune. Finally, the young squire was called to the bar in 1634 and proceeded to take up a legal career as a counsellor at law.[1]

Another minor landowner who faced serious difficulties was Robert Savile of Marley in the parish of Bingley. When his father, John Savile, died in 1634 he left a personal estate to the value of £800 and a real estate which consisted of Marley Hall and some eighty acres of land worth about £60 a year. His debts, however, amounted to over £1000 while a further £600 had to be found for marriage portions. Following the *inquisition post mortem* Robert Savile was declared in ward to the Crown and his wardship and lands were granted to three trustees for a fine of 100 marks and a rent of £20 a year. According to John Binns, one of the trustees, the estate revenue was insufficient to meet all items of expenditure which included the maintenance of the ward and his sisters, the charges of the Court of Wards and the legal costs involved in clearing the young man's title to his estate. In August 1640, when he was on the point of joining the king's expedition against the Scots, Savile granted a twenty-one-year lease of the property to John Binns and Christopher Armitstead with the proviso that he would be able to re-enter into possession if he returned safely from the war. These men, who were acting as feoffees, undertook first of all to pay off his debts (including the money borrowed for his maintenance and education) and then to raise the marriage portions due to his sisters.

[1] P.R.O., Chancery Proceedings, Six Clerks' Series, C.9/10/115, and Court of Wards, Entry Books of Contracts for Marriages and Leases, Wards 9/ccviii/f.76 and ccix/f.87. Leeds Central Library: Richmondshire Wills and Administrations, inventory of Francis Swale, 2 January 1629(-30). R. J. Fletcher (ed.), *The Pension Book of Gray's Inn 1569–1669*, 323.

A decade later he was again borrowing heavily and before his death he had disposed of his whole patrimony.[1]

Small or medium-sized estates which went on the market were often acquired by neighbouring landowners who merged the property with their existing holdings. In 1638 Sir Arthur Ingram the younger bought out Mauger Clough of Thorpe Stapleton, whose lands adjoined his main estate at Temple Newsam, for the sum of £4500. After entering into possession the Ingrams had the manor-house demolished because of its proximity to their own mansion.[2] This process of absorption was a characteristic feature of the period but it would be wrong to assume from this that the general tendency was for landed property to be concentrated more and more in the hands of the great squires. In fact the situation was considerably more complex. Although comparatively few of the major gentry were completely uprooted many families at this level can be found selling manors and other property. The Stapletons of Carlton, for example, still possessed a substantial (if seriously encumbered) estate on the eve of the Civil War but it was far smaller than the estate which they owned in the middle years of Elizabeth's reign. Between 1590 and 1598 Brian Stapleton and his eldest son had been obliged, as a result of heavy debts, to dispose of a major part of their landed possessions: the manors of Bingham and Burton Joyce in Nottinghamshire (worth £1400 a year) and the manors of Kirkby Overblow, Walkingham and Kearby in their native West Riding.[3] Basically, the position was that great quantities of land were being thrown up from all sections of the gentry and were passing into the hands of a variety of purchasers: peers and other leading squires, enterprising gentry of medium income, merchants, lawyers, civil servants and well-to-do yeomen. Most of the purchasers with a professional or commercial background were becoming landowners for the first time. Some were buying property on such a scale that they quickly reached the upper stratum of the squirearchy; more often, however, they helped to replenish the ranks of the middling gentry.

To judge from the relative movement of rents and prices the economic position of the country gentry was becoming progressively

[1] P.R.O., Chancery Proceedings, Six Clerks' Series, C.9/6/16 and C.10/37/184; Court of Wards, Feodaries' Surveys, Wards 5/49 and 50. *Bradford Antiquary*, ii, 168.

[2] Leeds Central Library: Temple Newsam MSS, TN/TS/12. B.M., Harleian MSS 4630 98.

[3] Beverley County Record Office: Beaumont of Carlton Towers MSS, DDCA/1/5 and 6, 32/1 and 4. Y.A.S. Library: MD 218. *Y.A.S.R.S.*, vii, 152 and viii, 34.

stronger between the accession of Elizabeth and the outbreak of the
Civil War. By the end of the sixteenth century most landlords should
have been able to improve their estate revenue sufficiently to counter-
act the effects of the Price Revolution: indeed the weight of evidence
suggests that in the early seventeenth century many landowners were
not simply combating inflation but were actually gaining ground in
terms of net profitability.[1] In addition, the development of satisfactory
long-term borrowing facilities under the early Stuarts enabled a
country squire to deal more effectively with the problem of meeting
a new and heavy demand on income.[2] As the following table reveals,
however, a high proportion of families were in financial straits in the
period 1600–42, even discounting those families whose difficulties had
begun in the previous century:

number of families in financial difficulties, 1558–99	208
total number of families within the gentry, 1558–99	709
number of families in financial difficulties, 1600–42:	
(a) continuation of difficulties originating in 1558–99	102
(b) difficulties due to new factors	208[3]
total number of families within the gentry, 1600–42	854

In seeking to explain this situation it is possible to identify a number of
factors on the other side of the balance sheet. In the first place, the
Court of Wards began to exact much higher charges for wardship from
the beginning of the seventeenth century.[4] Secondly, recusancy fines,
in the form of annual rents, had a greater impact on the Catholic
gentry in the early Stuart period than in the reign of Elizabeth (and not
least since there was no statutory provision for the sequestration of
papist estates until 1587). In 1642 there were fifty-six recusant heads
of families paying rents to the Crown as compared with sixteen in 1592;
moreover, the rents were on average considerably heavier in the reign
of Charles I than at any time previously.[5] Thirdly, litigation appears to
have been on the increase. Fourthly, the size of marriage portions was
much greater in the early seventeenth century than in the reign of
Elizabeth, even allowing for the decline in the value of money. During
the Elizabethan period £500 or £600 was regarded as a sizeable
portion, even among the richer gentry, and marriage settlements

[1] Above, 45–8.   [2] Above, 147–8.
[3] This includes some families which had recovered from earlier difficulties by 1600.
[4] Above, 133.   [5] Below, 220.

involving larger sums appear to have been comparatively rare. In contrast, a wealthy Stuart landowner would often feel obliged to give his daughters individual portions of £2000, £3000 or even £4000.[1] Finally, various social trends in the early seventeenth century helped to stimulate expenditure among the propertied classes: in particular, the heavy demand for titles which the Stuart monarchs were only too willing to satisfy; the practice of taking the whole family to London on a protracted visit; the growing competition in housebuilding; and the increase in foreign travel, both for educational and other purposes.[2]

2

Although general economic factors could be important the financial success or failure of a landed family depended in the last resort on individual character. Whatever the prevailing conditions an estate could be seriously, even disastrously, impaired if the owner was an incompetent or negligent landlord, a lunatic or a spendthrift. In his family history Sir John Reresby of Thrybergh mainly attributes the fluctuations in his family's economic fortunes to the personal character-istics of his predecessors. Thomas Reresby (c. 1540–87) was an efficient landlord who increased the family property by several pur-chases and made additions to Thrybergh Hall. So successful was he that his son Sir Thomas (1557–1619) inherited the 'greatest and freest Estate both reall and personal of any heir of the familie to that day'. Like his father the new squire engaged in land-buying but, largely as the result of his own and his wife's extravagance, 'he lived to sell more then he bought'. Although his landed possessions were still sub-stantial in 1619 Sir Thomas left them heavily encumbered, having mortgaged the whole of his Derbyshire property and settled on his wife a jointure to the value of £500 a year. His son Sir George (1586–1628) was 'a great manager at home' whose account books revealed close attention to detail; on the other hand, he had expensive tastes and his horse-breeding activities proved financially unsound. On the whole 'he sould more than he bought to the familie' but, what was more serious, he failed to redeem the Derbyshire property which had been mortgaged. Sir John Reresby (1611–46), the father of the family historian, also resorted to the sale of land and at his death left debts

[1] See also above, 124–5.   [2] Above, 21–4, 76–80, 102–7, 111, 125–6.

amounting to £1200. In his case, however, the difficulties were not self-created: as his son explains, these had arisen 'not thorow ill Husbandry, but by reason of the warr, and the Narrowness of his then present fortune, ther being two great jointures out of his Estate till about three years before he dyed'.[1]

Personal characteristics could be of particular significance in circumstances where the estate of a lawyer, merchant or royal official passed at his death into the hands of a son who had no other source of income besides his inheritance. If the new owner had a good head for business the transition might be achieved without difficulty (and indeed he sometimes went on to increase his landed possessions). In other cases, however, the son quickly found himself in financial difficulties, either because he attempted to maintain his father's standard of living on a reduced income or simply because he had inherited none of his father's ability. In his book of evidences, begun in the reign of James I, Thomas Meynell of North Kilvington makes a passing reference to the rise and decline of the senior branch of his family, the Meynells of Hawnby. Robert Meynell, who died in 1563, was 'one of the Councell at Yorke, and Chancellour of Durham a longe tyme, seriant at lawe, a purchacer and a great getter. He bought in his tyme Hawnby, Normanby, Heslerton, Bawke, and many other lands: as much as wold now yeild 2000 pownds by the yeare. But his sonne, shortly after, sould a great deale of it'. Although Roger Meynell, the son, disposed of a substantial quantity of land he was still in possession of a competent estate at the time of his death and it was left to his grandson Charles to dissipate the remainder of the family property in the reign of James I.[2] More spectacularly, the Herberts of York (a family which had originally come from Monmouthshire) had hardly entered the ranks of the country gentry before they met with financial disaster. Thomas Herbert, who was a successful merchant, built up a sizeable estate in the North Riding and elsewhere and in 1614, shortly before his death, secured the grant of a coat of arms. Unfortunately his son Christopher, who set himself up as a country squire at North Otterington, was a wastrel with little business sense and he quickly drifted into debt. According to Christopher's eldest son 'he sold away his lands att Stamford, Ottrington, Askham

---

[1] B.M., Additional MSS 29442, ff.42–7 and 29443, ff.1–3, 6, 8. P.R.O., Chancery, Entry Book of Decrees and Orders, C.33/cxxxix/f.47. For other family case histories of this kind see Appendix B.
[2] C.R.S., lvi, 3. Foley, vi, 341. V.C.H., N.R., i, 542 and ii, 33, 48, 238.

Richard, Yorke, Heslington, Bishopthorp, St. Lawrence, St. Gervaise, Sheriffhutton, Fulforth, Dringhouses, Skipwith and other places, which in very short time and obscurely were consumed'. By the time of his death in 1625 Christopher Herbert had lost the whole of his inheritance and he was so poverty-stricken that his personal effects were valued at under £40.[1]

Such examples can be multiplied but at the same time it is important to recognise that not a few gentlemen who had been pursuing lucrative careers left their estates seriously encumbered. In a Chancery bill of 1638 Richard Bourchier of Newton upon Ouse was said to have sold his patrimony and taken refuge in privileged places in the hope of evading his creditors. On the face of it, this was a straightforward case of a declining landowner failing to master his difficulties but in fact he had largely inherited his financial problems from his father, Sir John Bourchier, a merchant and projector who had died heavily indebted in 1626.[2] Gentlemen who held offices of profit, whether in the county or in Whitehall, also had their share of casualties. Sir Thomas Chaloner of Guisborough, who was in charge of the household of Prince Henry, James I's eldest son, instructed his executors to sell part of his estate towards the payment of debts and legacies and most of his goods and chattels were used for the same purpose.[3] Sir Richard Etherington of Ebberston, a lawyer who had obtained a grant of various offices within the honor of Pickering, found himself outlawed for debt in 1621 and eight years later disposed of his manor of Ebberston.[4] Sir Guildford Slingsby of Hemlington, who had a long career as a civil servant in the field of naval administration, claimed in 1624 that he was £1000 in debt to his utter undoing.[5] In such cases the primary cause of indebtedness might be extravagance, lavish hospitality (which was almost obligatory among central government and household officials), extensive litigation or simply a numerous progeny. In addition, some nouveaux riches tried to build up their estates too quickly (perhaps in a spirit of competition) and overstrained their resources in the process.

---

[1] Y.A.J., i, 183, 186–8. N. Mackenzie, 'Sir Thomas Herbert of Tintern: A Parliamentary "Royalist" ', Bulletin of the Institute of Historical Research, xxix, 38–9. V.C.H., N.R., i, 441. Harleian Society, lxvi, 122.

[2] P.R.O., Chancery Proceedings, Series II, C.3/396/138. H.M.C. Coke MSS, i, 72–3. Y.A.S.R.S., lviii, 228.

[3] P.R.O., Chancery Proceedings, Series I, C.2/F.11/44.

[4] V.C.H., N.R., ii, 436, 450.   [5] H.M.C. Coke MSS, i, 176.

Great squires and smaller landowners who had no other source of income besides their estates, courtiers, Crown officials, lawyers, merchants,—no section of the Yorkshire gentry was entirely immune from the economic ailments of the period. Even if a gentleman had both the capacity and the determination to surmount financial hazards he still needed a reasonable share of good fortune. According to his son Sir Richard Cholmley of Whitby, a man of 'great insight and judgement', would have overcome his debts

by his frugality and private living, if that the Lord Scroope had not...come to be Lord President of his Majesty's Council in the North, and Lord Lieutenant of Yorkshire, which happened in the year 1619; and Sir Richard being cousin-german to him half removed, held himself obliged, not only to wait upon him, but to appear in such a posture as was suitable to their relation, and the quality of Sir Richard's person...and now friendship and kindness increasing between the said Lord Scroope and Sir Richard, it drew him much to York, and thereby put him not only out of his retired way of living, and neglect of his private affairs, but occasioned great expence.[1]

[1] *Cholmley Memoirs*, 21–2.

CHAPTER VIII

Catholicism and Persecution

IN THE sixteenth century Europe was a battleground in which Catholicism and Protestantism fought for supremacy. No country remained entirely immune from the new doctrines of the Reformation and for a time it looked as though Protestantism might triumph everywhere except in Italy and Spain. North of the Alps a number of territories broke free from the Church of Rome: Sweden, Denmark, Norway, Switzerland, England, Scotland and Holland. In England the Reformation, as a manifestation of government policy, followed an erratic course. Henry VIII repudiated the authority of the Pope over the English Church and dissolved the monasteries but in his reign Protestants were put to death for the denial of Catholic doctrine. During the reign of his son Edward VI, a minor, Protestantism had powerful support in governing circles. So long as Protector Somerset was in control moderation was the keynote of the reform programme but after his downfall the official policy on religion assumed a more radical character which was reflected in the Prayer Book of 1552. When Mary, a devout Catholic, came to the throne this trend was sharply reversed: Catholicism was restored as the national religion, the links with Rome were re-established and the Mass supplanted the Protestant form of communion. After a period of retreat the forces of conservatism had apparently emerged victorious, but events were soon to prove otherwise. In 1558 Mary died after a brief reign of five years and her sister Elizabeth, who succeeded, had little affection for the Old Religion. Within six months of Elizabeth's accession two parliamentary statutes — the Acts of Supremacy and Uniformity — were passed which established a national church independent of papal authority and with the Prayer Book of 1552, modified to some extent, as the authorised liturgy. The Protestant cause had finally prevailed.

The Elizabethan religious settlement was enshrined in the statute book but it had still to be enforced. The greatest opposition was expected in the counties north of the Trent where the dissolution of the monasteries had already led to one major uprising, the Pilgrimage of Grace. In the centres of industry and commerce Protestantism had been steadily gathering strength since the early years of the century[1] but the northern population as a whole was still predominantly conservative in religion. Nevertheless, in spite of the prevalence of Catholic beliefs and customs, the Old Religion inspired little popular enthusiasm at this time. The breathtaking series of changes over the previous generation had given rise to a mood of bewilderment and apathy which existed at all levels of society. In these circumstances the Elizabethan settlement, a compromise designed to have the widest possible appeal, at first encountered little resistance in the province of York. A large majority of the parish clergy submitted and kept their benefices, even if their sympathies lay with the traditional faith, while the Catholic population as a whole, in the absence of guidance from the Holy See, saw nothing wrong in outwardly conforming to the law. In the early years of Elizabeth's reign there is no evidence of any significant decline in church attendance, which under the Act of Uniformity was compulsory: recusancy, or the deliberate refusal to attend Protestant worship, varied in strength from region to region but it did not become a general problem until the arrival of the missionary priests. At this time, therefore, religious conservatism is mainly to be found in a substantial body of laity who had residual Catholic sympathies but who nevertheless conformed to the new order, though in some cases refusing to take the holy sacrament. To convinced Protestants such men were known as 'Church Papists', to the seminary priests and Jesuits as 'schismatics'. How long they would maintain their neutrality was a matter for conjecture.

What caused the authorities most concern was the attitude of the propertied classes to the new religious settlement. In June 1564 the archbishop of York told the queen that his province was 'in good quiettenes, the comen people beinge rightelie handled both tractable and corrigible touching religion...as for the staie againste religion in these parts it was onelie the nobilitie, gentlemen and clergie. And although the nobilitie remayne in their wonted blyndnes yet the gentlemen begynne to reforme themselves and the clergie allso'.[2] That the Old Religion still commanded widespread sympathy among the

---

[1] For illuminating studies on the growth of Protestantism see A. G. Dickens, *Lollards and Protestants in the Diocese of York 1509–1558* and *The English Reformation*.
[2] P.R.O., S.P. Borders, S.P.59/viii/450.

ruling classes may be seen from the episcopal reports on the magistracy which were submitted to the Privy Council in the autumn of 1564. The reports from the northern bishops show that there were many Catholic-minded justices on the commission of the peace: in some counties, and in particular Lancashire, they heavily outnumbered the magistrates who were listed (not always correctly) as supporters of the Elizabethan settlement.[1] In general, however, the conservative gentry displayed great caution in these early years. A Catholic squire might give shelter to a clergyman deprived of his living and even hear Mass in his private chapel but usually he took care to attend his parish church on Sundays. Open defiance was rare and when it occurred the authorities sought to enforce obedience. In 1565 proceedings were taken against Sir William Babthorpe, one of the leading East Riding Catholics, for his 'open unsemelie doinge and sainge'; as a result Archbishop Young told Sir William Cecil in April 1565 that Babthorpe and the other malcontents were 'nowe in greate awe and obedience whearein it is meet they be kepte'.[2]

In Yorkshire the religious loyalties of the gentry aroused considerable speculation in official circles. Writing from York in December 1569, while the Northern Rebellion was still at its height, Sir Ralph Sadler roundly declared that there were not ten gentlemen 'in all this countrey that do favor and allowe of her Majesties proceedings in the cause of religion'. In 1572 Sir Thomas Gargrave, vice-president of the Council of the North and himself a Yorkshireman, attempted a more dispassionate analysis of the Yorkshire gentry — or rather a selected minority — with the following results: Protestants 43, Catholics 40, 'doutfull or newtor' 38. These figures illustrate the difficulty of 'making windows into men's souls' which the queen insisted was not her intention. Most of the gentlemen shown as 'doutfull or newtor' were in fact crypto-Catholics and so indeed were a number of Gargrave's Protestants, in particular Sir William Bellasis of Newburgh Priory, Thomas Waterton of Walton, Edward Ellerker of Risby and Roger Radcliffe of Mulgrave.[3] The prevalence of outward conformity

[1] *Camden Miscellany*, ix: 'A Collection of Original Letters from the Bishops to the Privy Council, 1564.'

[2] P.R.O., S.P.Dom., Elizabeth Addenda, S.P.15/xii/58. Sir William Babthorpe and his wife finally submitted in September 1565 (P. Tyler, *The Ecclesiastical Commission and Catholicism in the North, 1562–1577*, 75).

[3] P.R.O., S.P.Dom., Elizabeth Addenda, S.P.15/xv/77 and xxi/86. (Gargrave's list is printed in J. J. Cartwright (ed.), *Chapters in the History of Yorkshire*, 64–72.)

at this time makes it difficult to estimate the strength of the Catholic gentry with any degree of precision but there is sufficient material available to make the attempt worth while. The main sources of information consist of the archiepiscopal visitation books, the records of the Northern High Commission, the archbishop of York's list of recusants compiled in 1577 and two lists of Catholic provenance dating from 1574 and 1582.[1] If we take the year 1570 for the purposes of this analysis the following pattern emerges:

	Catholic families	Total number of families
North Riding	122	154
East Riding	92	126
West Riding	152	279
City of York	2	8
	368	567

The actual number of Catholic families may well have been higher: nevertheless it is clear that, viewing the Yorkshire gentry as a whole, the majority of families were still well disposed towards the Old Religion even if the incidence of recusancy was low. This was the general picture, but there were important regional variations. In the West Riding Protestantism had already made considerable headway, particularly in the neighbourhood of the industrial towns such as Leeds, Halifax, Bradford, Huddersfield, Wakefield and Sheffield. In the East Riding, on the other hand, the Protestant gentry were still a comparatively insignificant minority. In the final analysis, however, the real stronghold of Catholicism was the North Riding, a wild and inaccessible country which offered little encouragement to disciples of the reformed faith. The Richmondshire gentry were particularly noted for their attachment to the Old Religion: in 1570, for example, Sir Thomas Gargrave claimed, with only a little exaggeration, that all the gentlemen in this part of the North Riding were (as he put it) 'evil in religion'.[2]

When the Earls of Northumberland and Westmorland took up arms in November 1569 the conservative gentry were faced with a dilemma. Hitherto, in spite of their affection for the Catholic faith, they had

[1] Borthwick Institute of Historical Research: Visitation Court Books and High Commission Act Books. P.R.O., S.P.Dom., Elizabeth, S.P.12/cxvii/23 (printed in C.R.S., xxii). C.R.S., xiii, 86.
[2] Cal.S.P.Dom., Elizabeth Addenda 1566–79, 222.

regarded themselves as loyal subjects of the queen but now the opportunity had arisen to join in an armed insurrection which had as one of its principal aims the overthrow of the Elizabethan settlement. In the early stages of the revolt the authorities were seriously alarmed at the conduct of the northern gentry. On 26 November Lord Hunsdon informed Cecil that 'all the gentylmen savyng a few of thys est rydynge themselves remayn yn theyr howses as newtars but eyther theyr suns and ayers or second suns be with the rebels'. On 30 November Sir Ralph Sadler reported that the gentry were now showing themselves 'very willing and forwarde' in the queen's service 'but for all that I cannot assure my self of such of them as be papists for if the father com to us with ten men his soon goeth to the Rebells with twenty'.[1] In Yorkshire, from the evidence of the official records, some eighty gentlemen were involved in the rebellion.[2] These came, without exception, from traditionally Catholic families and consisted in the main of heirs and younger sons, some of them household servants of the Earl of Northumberland. Only a few gentlemen of substance took an active part in the rebellion: Sir John Nevile of Liversedge, Richard Norton of Norton Conyers, Thomas Markenfield of Markenfield and Thomas Hussey of Topcliffe. The great bulk of the Catholic gentry either supported the Crown or maintained a strict neutrality which in some cases entailed a hurried flight from the county. This reluctance to join the rebel cause is not difficult to understand. In the first place, the chances of a decisive victory were hardly strong enough to impress a Catholic squire who had been content to hide his religion: after all, England had not experienced a successful rebellion since the foundation of the Tudor dynasty in 1485. Secondly, some Catholics had a vested interest in the maintenance of the existing régime, either because they had acquired monastic property or because they held offices of profit under the Crown. Finally, we must not underestimate the degree of loyalty which the queen inspired even in the ranks of the conservative gentry.

In the savage retribution which followed the collapse of the Northern Rebellion the Catholic gentry escaped relatively lightly. Only five Yorkshire gentlemen were executed for their part in the rising: John Fulthorpe, Robert Pennyman, Thomas Bishop the younger, Thomas

---

[1] P.R.O., S.P.Dom., Elizabeth Addenda, S.P.15/xv/49 and 54.
[2] P.R.O., Exchequer, Estreats, E.137/133/1. *Cal. Patent Rolls, Elizabeth, 1569–72, passim.* Sir Cuthbert Sharp, *Memorials of the Rebellion of 1569.*

Norton and Christopher Norton. Some of the rebels, among them the Earl of Westmorland, fled abroad and forfeited their estates to the Crown. In the autumn of 1571 we find Sir John Nevile and Christopher Danby at Louvain, Richard Norton and his sons Francis and Sampson at Mechlin and Thomas Markenfield at Rome. On the whole, however, there was little expropriation within the landed classes: most persons of quality were pardoned and allowed to compound for their lands at an extremely moderate rate.[1]

The Northern Rebellion was finally crushed in February 1570. In the same month a papal bull was published in Rome excommunicating and deposing the queen. Apart from its political implications the bull put an end to the uncertainty about the attitude of the Holy See to the Elizabethan church settlement. For the true Catholic there could be no more outward conformity: it was now incumbent on him to defy the law and stay away from church. In Lancashire the news of this pronouncement appears to have had a marked impact on the Catholic population: in October 1570, for example, it was reported that in most places the people had fallen from their obedience and refused to attend divine service in the English tongue.[2] In Yorkshire, and indeed in other counties, the increase in recusancy was at first comparatively modest. A handful of Yorkshire gentry, including Thomas Leeds of North Milford and Thomas Pudsey of Barforth, were imprisoned as obstinate recusants but most of their fellow Catholics continued to attend Protestant services.[3]

It is a matter of conjecture whether English Catholicism could have long survived if outside intervention had been limited to the papal bull of 1570. Undoubtedly there were conservative gentry who were determined at all costs to maintain the Catholic tradition in their families. Typical of this group was Sir Thomas Metham, a wealthy East Riding squire. In the opening years of Elizabeth's reign he employed Philip Sherwood, an unbeneficed clergyman of Catholic sympathies, as a private tutor for his children. Subsequently, in February 1570, Sir William Cecil was informed:

We have heare one Sir Thomas Metham, a knighte, a moste wilfull and

---

[1] Sir Cuthbert Sharp, *Memorials of the Rebellion of 1569*. P.R.O., S.P.Dom., Elizabeth Addenda, S.P.15/xx/75 and Exchequer, Estreats, E.137/133/1.

[2] *Cal.S.P.Dom., Elizabeth Addenda, 1566–79*, 321.

[3] Borthwick Institute of Historical Research: High Commission Act Books, 1569–70 (R VII/AB 10), 1571–2 (R VII/AB 16), 1572–4 (R VII/AB 4). A. G. Dickens, 'The First Stages of Romanist Recusancy in Yorkshire, 1560–90', *Y.A.J.*, xxxv, 165–8, 182.

obstinate Papiste, he utterly refusethe to come to the divine service or here
yt said; to receave the Communion, to come to anie sermons, or to rede anie
bokes excepte they be approved (as he saithe) by the churche of Rome, or
to be conferred with all. He refuseth to answere and stand and to be tried
before the Quenes Majesties Commissioners for causes ecclesiastical. He
usethe the corrupte Lovaine bokes. And at Lovayne mainteinethe amongst
those Rebells two of his sonnes, to whom he bothe writethe often, and
from them receaveth letters agayne.[1]

A gentleman of substance might be in a position to educate his sons at
a continental university but the primary requirement was a priesthood
capable of ministering to the spiritual needs of the Catholic population.
At this time there were a number of unbeneficed clergymen in the
northern counties: the so-called 'Queen Mary' priests who had been
ejected for refusing to accept the new religious settlement, and the
Scottish priests who had fled from their native land after the Protestant
Reformation of 1560. These 'old' priests helped to keep the faith alive
in the early part of Elizabeth's reign but their teaching was not always
in strict accordance with the official policy of the Holy See. More
important, their numbers were steadily declining as death and imprisonment took their toll and once this process had advanced far enough it
is difficult to see how the Old Religion could have maintained its
position without external assistance.

If Elizabeth and Cecil thought that the English Catholics would be
left to their own devices they reckoned without the crusading spirit of
the Counter-Reformation which was already at work in France,
Germany and Poland. In 1568 a Catholic refugee, William Allen,
founded an English seminary at Douai which quickly became a centre
for the training of missionary priests. So began the foundation movement which resulted in the establishment of further English seminaries
at Rome, Valladolid, Seville, Madrid and Lisbon as well as monasteries,
convents and schools in the Spanish Netherlands and elsewhere. In
1574 the first missionaries from Douai arrived in England and before
the end of 1580 no fewer than a hundred seminary priests had entered
the kingdom.[2] In the summer of 1580 there was another important
development: the arrival of a Jesuit mission under the leadership of
Edmund Campion and Robert Parsons. On the Continent the Jesuits

[1] P. Tyler, *The Ecclesiastical Commission and Catholicism in the North 1562–1577*, 39.
P.R.O., S.P.Dom., Elizabeth Addenda, S.P.15/xvii/72.

[2] T. F. Knox, *The First and Second Diaries of the English College Douay*, Introduction,
lxii.

had already proved their worth as a spearhead of the Counter-Reformation: now, for the first time, they were working in defiance of a government which regarded their activities as a treasonable conspiracy.

In Yorkshire the Catholic gentry soon felt the influence of these events. In the first place, they began to send their sons to the continental seminaries, either to be trained as missionaries or simply to receive a Catholic education. From the evidence available the first student at Douai who came from a Yorkshire manor-house was Robert Morton of Bawtry, whose entry was recorded in 1573. He was followed in 1576 by two youths who may be identified as sons of Dr Thomas Vavasour of York and Thomas Pudsey of Barforth.[1] Not surprisingly it was the recusant gentry who showed most enthusiasm in the early years, though later on many children from 'schismatic' families would be sent to continental seminaries and convents. Secondly, the missionaries who entered the northern counties soon found their way to the houses of Catholic gentlemen who could be expected to offer them shelter and hospitality. In the early months of 1581 Edmund Campion visited a number of Yorkshire gentry, including Sir William Babthorpe of Osgodby and Dr Thomas Vavasour of York, an episode which led the Privy Council to issue orders for their arrest.[2]

As the work of the Catholic missionaries proceeded a growing number of 'Church Papists' began to reject conformity and stay away from Protestant services. In Yorkshire there was a striking increase in recusancy between 1578 and 1582. The conservative gentry were particularly affected and in these years over a hundred families were involved in recusancy cases. With similar developments in other counties there could no longer be any doubt that a major Catholic revival was in progress.[3]

Such events naturally invited counter-measures and between 1581 and 1593 a whole series of penal laws was enacted. The severity of these laws is a measure of the anxiety which the Catholic reaction inspired. Seminary priests and Jesuits who attempted to reconcile the queen's subjects to the Church of Rome or otherwise withdraw them from their natural obedience to the Crown could be put to death for

---

[1] T. F. Knox, *op. cit.*, 5, 105.

[2] B.M., Lansdowne MSS 30, f. 78. *Acts of the Privy Council 1581–2*, 152.

[3] A. G. Dickens, 'The First Stages of Romanist Recusancy in Yorkshire, 1560–90', *Y.A.J.*, xxxv, 169–70, 182. Borthwick Institute of Historical Research: High Commission Act Books, 1576–80 (R VII/AB6) and 1580–5 (R VII/AB17).

the crime of high treason. Laymen who were converted through their efforts or who gave them assistance were likewise threatened with the death penalty. Anyone hearing Mass could be fined 100 marks and sentenced to a year's imprisonment. For convicted recusants the penalty was a fine of £20 a month or, if they defaulted, seizure of all their goods and two-thirds of their landed property; in addition, they were forbidden to travel outside a five-mile compass of their homes without special licence.[1] These were the main provisions of the Elizabethan penal code. In the reign of James I, following the discovery of the Gunpowder Plot, the recusancy laws were further strengthened. Convicted recusants were no longer permitted to enter the professions or hold offices of profit; special provision was made for persons who sought to escape the penalties of recusancy through occasional conformity, and a new oath of allegiance was introduced with the aim of splitting the ranks of the Catholic party.[2]

For Catholics the period 1570–1620, taken as a whole, was an era of suffering and hardship unparalleled in the history of English Catholicism. This does not mean that the pressure was consistently maintained: in some years a vigorous campaign was mounted, frequently on instructions from the Privy Council, while at other times the recusant minority was left in comparative peace. In the northern counties the energy with which the penal laws were enforced depended to a considerable extent on the character of the lord president of the Council of the North. The most savage waves of persecution occurred under the Earl of Huntingdon, lord president from 1572 to 1595, whose hostility to the Old Religion owed much to the strength of his Puritan convictions.[3] After his death the impetus slackened for a time but under the second Lord Burghley, who held office between 1599 and 1603, the attack on Catholicism was once more resumed. The next incumbent, Lord Sheffield, was also in favour of coercion and after the failure of the Gunpowder Plot there was a further outbreak of persecution which was particularly strong in the years 1606–12. In 1619, however, the appointment of Lord Scroope, reputed to be a secret papist, was a clear indication that the Crown had decided to follow a more conciliatory policy.

[1] 23 Elizabeth I, c.i. 27 Elizabeth I, c.ii. 29 Elizabeth I, c.vi. 35 Elizabeth I, c.i and ii.
[2] 3 James I, c.iv and c.v. 7 James I, c.vi.
[3] For Huntingdon see M. C. Cross, *The Puritan Earl: the Life of Henry Hastings third Earl of Huntingdon*, 226–47, 268–9.

As members of a ruling class the Catholic gentry no doubt expected to be treated leniently when the authorities first began their offensive. In the penal statutes no distinction was made between squire and peasant but in practice wealth, position and influence in high places undoubtedly had their advantages. By this means Catholic landlords could obtain valuable concessions: reductions in the financial penalties for recusancy,[1] special privileges while in prison, remission of the death penalty for harbouring priests. The fact remains, however, that the recusant gentry were in no sense immune from the persecution which marked the period 1570–1620: on the contrary, the Northern High Commission deliberately concentrated its attention on this class of recusant in view of the dependence of the Catholic laity on the leadership and patronage of the country gentry. In the final reckoning, therefore, religious antagonism weighed more heavily than class loyalty.

After the Rebellion of 1569 the Northern High Commission became a major weapon in the suppression of recusancy and from this time forward Catholic gentlemen and their wives were frequently summoned before the commissioners to answer for their disobedience in religion. On making his appearance a recusant who seemed willing to conform was usually required to enter into a bond stipulating that he and his family would dutifully attend their parish church and receive communion. In addition, he was often required to give an undertaking that he would confer with learned ministers, read the scriptures and avoid all contact with Jesuits and seminary priests. An obstinate recusant who utterly refused to conform was generally imprisoned or confined to the house of a staunch Protestant or official of the High Commission. In 1591 the Earl of Huntingdon launched a systematic campaign against the recusant wives of 'schismatic' gentlemen. In the words of Father Richard Holtby, these gentlemen were compelled 'to bring in their own wives, present them to the magistrates, vex them by threats, persuasions, and otherwise, both in prison and at liberty, to procure thereby their fall. Of this number there were and are a great sort of gentlemen, of the best wealth and worship, that delivered their wives to the will of the tyrant'. Eventually, after many entreaties, their womenfolk were released on bond. For this purpose a new type of bond was devised which contained special provisions: in particular,

[1] See Chapter X.

the husband undertook to have divine service three times a week in his house and to keep no servants who were disobedient in religion.[1] In the years 1570–1620 many Catholic gentry endured some form of imprisonment in the cause of religion. Generally the period of confinement was relatively short though some recusants like William Stillington of Kelfield[2] spent much of their adult life in custody at York or Hull. In prison a Catholic gentleman could rent his own private cell, purchase his own food and have his own servants to attend him. Now and again he might be released on parole for health or business reasons: thus in 1575 Dr Thomas Vavasour (a prisoner in Hull Castle) was permitted, on account of ill health, to retire to his brother's house at Duncotes for a period of six weeks.[3] In spite of these privileges, however, prison life under Elizabeth and James I was hardly a salubrious experience and the threat of incarceration frequently led to a hasty submission.

To avoid imprisonment many recusant gentry ignored the summons to appear before the ecclesiastical commissioners. Some feigned sickness, others went to live for a time in London or in another county outside the jurisdiction of the Northern High Commission. This practice was particularly common in the reign of James I: in 1607, for example, several Yorkshire families — the Babthorpes of Osgodby, the Dolmans of Millington, the Babthorpes of Menthorpe and the Constables of Caythorpe — were residing in Lincolnshire in an attempt to escape persecution. In retaliation the ecclesiastical commissioners began to impose fines, usually of £50 or £100, on Catholics who wilfully disobeyed the summons. Father James Sharpe, a Jesuit missionary, describes the procedure in a report written in 1610:

The messenger, if he cannot find the party, doth either fix the process upon the gentleman's door, or give it to the curate to be read against the party publicly, upon the Sunday, in the church. If the party do appear, it is rare if he do escape the tendering of the oath [i.e. the oath of allegiance]: if he do not appear, they set a fine upon his head of some fifty pounds, to some a hundred pounds, for every time they do not appear.

---

[1] Borthwick Institute of Historical Research: High Commission Act Books. M. A. Tierney (ed.), *Dodd's Church History of England*, iii, 121–6.

[2] There are numerous references to William Stillington in the High Commission Act Books from 1578 onwards.

[3] Borthwick Institute of Historical Research: High Commission Act Book, 1574–6, R VII/AB5, f.124.

Father Sharpe then records the tribulations which beset the Babthorpes of Osgodby, with whom he had served as chaplain:

First, the son, Sir William Babthorpe, was fined some four or five hundred pounds for not appearing...The father, Sir Ralph...was so sore pursued by the base ministers of this high commission (who, every month, sent out process in most disgraceful and odious terms against him, to be publicly read in his own parish church, and, after reading, to be fixed upon the church doors) that, after he had, for the space of a twelvemonth, escaped the fines by this art, to wit, by flying out of the country [i.e. Yorkshire], from the day of the writ read in the church (of which by friends he got notice before), until the court-day was past...being at the length wearied with it, he was forced to remove his whole family into Lincolnshire, and there to live.

His son-in-law Sir George Palmes 'did at first lie in prison, and, after being upon bond released, and afterwards urged to return again to prison, was forced to forfeit and pay his bond, and, to keep himself from them, to live privately, so that, for the space of three years he durst not be seen in his father's house, or to be known to be there'. Eventually, as the result of a general summons to Catholics to appear and take the oath of allegiance, Sir Ralph Babthorpe resolved to go abroad and managed to secure a licence enabling him, on grounds of health, to visit the Belgian resort of Spa. In 1612 he and his wife crossed to the Continent and finally settled at Louvain, the principal centre for English Catholic exiles.[1]

One of the most formidable weapons which the Crown possessed in the early seventeenth century was the oath of allegiance. Introduced in 1606 as a test of civil allegiance, the oath denounced 'as impious and hereticall this damnable Doctrine and Position, that Princes which be excommunicated or deprived by the Pope may be deposed or murthered by theire Subjects'. For a Catholic who refused to make this denial the penalty was imprisonment for life and forfeiture of all property. In 1606 bishops and magistrates were empowered to offer the oath to recusants, suspected recusants and noncommunicants, in 1610 to anyone who was aged eighteen or over.[2] Catholic opinion was divided over the legality of the oath: although the Pope condemned it as early as 1607 the controversy went on for some years.

---

[1] *Lincoln Record Society*, xxiii, pp. xciv and xcv. J. Morris (ed.), *The Troubles of Our Catholic Forefathers*, Series i, 235, 246 and Series iii, 456–8.
[2] 3 James I, c.iv and 7 James I, c.vi.

In the reign of James I a number of Yorkshire Catholics were imprisoned for refusing the oath but few representatives of the landed classes suffered this fate. For this various factors were responsible. In the first place, it is clear from the official records that some Catholic gentry, when the choice was forced upon them, were willing to signify their loyalty to the Crown. In 1607, for example, several determined recusants (including George Anne of Frickley, John Gascoigne of Barnbow and Thomas Meynell of North Kilvington) appeared and took the oath before the Northern High Commission.[1] Secondly, a Catholic squire was sometimes able to avoid the dilemma by simply failing to appear on the prescribed day; alternatively, he might have a relative or friend on the commission of the peace who was prepared to certify, without justification, that he had willingly subscribed to the oath.

Early in 1612 the government decided to summon the leading Catholics in each shire to take the oath of allegiance before the Privy Council. A list which was drawn up for this purpose includes the names of eleven Yorkshire squires, all prominent recusants. Subsequently the name of Sir Ralph Babthorpe was crossed out and annotated 'at the Spawe'. William Vavasour of Hazlewood, one of the very first to appear before the Council, refused to take the oath and was sentenced to life imprisonment with forfeiture of all his lands and goods. After spending several weeks in Newgate he offered to pay £700 for his pardon and release but at this stage the offer was declined. Another Yorkshire gentleman to be summoned was William Middleton of Stockeld who had been imprisoned for recusancy in Elizabeth's reign. On 24 June 1612 he wrote to Henry Spiller, an Exchequer official who was probably himself a secret Catholic,[2] explaining that while he was ready to make acknowledgement in all matters of temporal allegiance, 'there be some matters conteyned in the said oath which to my weak understanding (being altogether unlearned) seeme something obscure'. His estate was heavily overburdened and a good part of it had been allotted to his eldest son; nevertheless he was willing to pay a composition of £400 (subsequently raised to £500) to be freed from the oath. If this offer was unacceptable he would endeavour not to be singular in

---

[1] Borthwick Institute of Historical Research: High Commission Act Book, 1607–12, R VII/AB12, ff.84, 89.

[2] For Henry Spiller see E. R. Foster (ed.), *Proceedings in Parliament, 1610* and particularly ii, 128–31.

his opinion, 'but seeke to satisfie the scruples of my conscience rather then to hazard utter overthrow of me and myne'. In August 1612 Sir Julius Caesar, chancellor of the Exchequer, told the king that some recusants of name and quality such as Middleton of Yorkshire, finding that neither Vavasour nor the rest were admitted to composition, 'have lately withdrawen themselves, and secretely keape in obscure places, where neither messengers nor other officers can yet discover them'. Many other recusants in the North and elsewhere had lately fled from their homes and were lurking in secret places. In conclusion, the chancellor suggested that the refusers should be allowed to compound for good sums of money which would weaken their estates. From the evidence available it seems probable that this special drive petered out: in January 1613 William Middleton obtained a pardon and release from the oath, while in the following month William Vavasour received a similar grant, though in his case several years of house imprisonment were to follow.[1] Whether any action was taken against the other Yorkshiremen on the list may be doubted: in any case some of them had already subscribed to the oath on a previous occasion. After this episode William Stillington of Kelfield, an obstinate recusant, was virtually the only Yorkshire gentleman to follow the orthodox Catholic line when put to the test. In January 1614 he declined the oath at the East Riding general sessions and was committed to prison. At the same time, his estates passed into the hands of the Crown and in August 1614 were granted to a courtier, Henry Gibb of the Bedchamber. He in turn sold them back to the Stillington family for the sum of £600.[2]

If the Catholic gentry had ever felt compelled to present a general petition of grievances the activities of the pursuivants would have appeared high on their list. The term 'pursuivant' was applied to a variety of men employed, in an official or semi-official capacity, in searching for priests and Catholic relics, arresting wanted recusants and levying recusancy fines. They included messengers of the Privy Council, officers of the Council of the North and the Northern High Commission, sheriff's officers and private individuals armed with special commissions. On the whole, their notoriety appears to have been well

[1] B.M., Lansdowne MSS 153, ff.44, 46, 52–3, 81, 87. *C.R.S.*, xxxiv, 71–2. P.R.O., Signet Office Docquets, Index 6804, January and February 1612(–13) (no pagination). *Acts of the Privy Council 1615–16*, 583.
[2] P.R.O., Exchequer, Special Commissions, E.178/4864, and Chancery Proceedings, Series II, C.3/380/3. *Cal.S.P.Dom. 1611–18*, 251.

deserved. In 1609, for example, Thomas Marr and Richard Braithwaite were accused of ill-treating an aged gentlewoman, Mrs Dorothy Scroope of Spennithorne, 'since which tyme the said Mrs Scroope hath byn very sicklye and much Compleanethe of hurte and bruising'. From the evidence of reliable witnesses it was further established that Marr, Braithwaite and other pursuivants, pretending to execute certain processes of outlawry, had extorted bribes from a number of recusants. Marr, with his associates, was continually molesting Catholics 'and where he can gett brybes he takethe and when he can not he bringeth the pore parties to prisone. He tooke Mr Christofer Coniers and gott a good bribe on him, Mr George Tockette, Mr Jhon Ingilbie, Mr James Tankerd and many others who all gott dismist for Bribes. He had about Hawvingam of Mris. Houltbie and others x li.' Although the authorities took action on this occasion, the abuses continued.[1]

In making their searches of Catholic manor-houses the pursuivants often came in the dead of night or early in the morning or at dinner-time with a view to catching the household unawares. Even if nothing incriminating was discovered they frequently plundered the house and took away jewels, money and plate. In his account of the persecution Father Richard Holtby describes a search made at Mrs Katherine Arthington's house in Nidderdale on Easter Tuesday 1594:

coming near the house, they drew their swords, bent their pistols, and buckled themselves for battle, as though they would have made an assault to the gentlewoman's house; but perceiving, by one of the house, that there was no fear of fighting, the greatest resistance consisting only in a company of women, they put up their weapons, entered in, the door being open, searched, rifled, turned and tossed all things upside down but found nothing greatly for their purpose. Yet, fearing to be disappointed of their journey, they determined not to depart with speed, but seated themselves in the house, and, as though all were their own made provision for themselves, at the gentlewoman's cost, until Thursday or Friday following.

From time to time the searching of Catholic houses was organised on an extensive scale. Father Holtby writes:

This year, being the year of our Lord 1593, upon the first of February, at night, until the next day at 9 o'clock, being Candlemas-day, there was a general search made for Catholics, all over Yorkshire, Richmondshire,

---

[1] *C.R.S.*, liii, 279–83. See also G. E. Aylmer, 'Attempts at Administrative Reform, 1625–40', *English Historical Review*, lxxii, 229.

Cleveland, the Bishopric of Durham, and Northumberland, wherein all justices of the peace and others of authority, with such as favoured the heretics' cause, together with the ministers themselves, did flock together, entering the houses of the catholics, and all such as were suspected to favour their cause, in great numbers, that it is hard to say how many were abroad that night, in searching: for there came to some houses above a hundred, or seven score persons to search...They got beads and books in divers places, and many [were] forced to forsake their houses, to escape the danger.[1]

The financial consequences of recusancy (which are considered in a later chapter[2]) were more formidable in theory than in practice. Nevertheless the potential dangers could not be lightly ignored and many Catholic landowners preferred to attend Protestant services rather than hazard their estates. In 1607 a list was compiled of Yorkshire Catholics who were said to have submitted as the result of commissions which had been issued for valuing the lands and goods of recusants. In all, the list contains the names of forty-two gentry, some of whom were heavily indebted.[3] Undoubtedly the financial penalties were a major deterrent and, in addition, the Crown offered certain material inducements to Catholic heirs to encourage them to remain conformable. An act of 1604[4] provided that after the death of a recusant the heir, if he was not himself a recusant or if he subsequently conformed, could be released from any arrears or encumbrances on the estate resulting from his predecessor's recusancy. In the early Stuart period a number of Yorkshire gentlemen benefited from this concession.

As a result of the persecution many Catholics were driven into conformity. In Yorkshire over 200 recusant gentry, men and women, yielded under pressure in the years 1570–1620, though in some cases this was only a temporary lapse. In conforming a Catholic gentleman first attended church on a Sunday or holy day and received a certificate of conformity from his parish priest. After this he made a formal submission, perhaps taking the oath of allegiance, before the bishop of the diocese, the assize judges or the justices of the peace at their quarter sessions.[5] Sometimes, as further evidence of his conformity, he might hear divine service in the presence of the archbishop of York, either in York Minster or in the chapel at Bishopthorpe. One Catholic squire, Thomas Barnby of Barnby Hall, felt obliged to make this gesture even

---

[1] M. A. Tierney (ed.), *Dodd's Church History of England*, iii, 114–18.
[2] See Chapter X.   [3] B.M., Lansdowne MSS 153, ff.264–5.
[4] 1 James I, c.iv.   [5] 23 Elizabeth I, c.i.

though he had been a 'Church Papist' for some years. On 25 October 1624 he visited Bishopthorpe bringing with him a written testimony from two neighbouring magistrates, the vicar of Silkstone and other persons of standing. According to this testimony he had frequented his parish church for the space of twenty years or so, 'being in all thinges concerning matters of Religion Conformable to the Laudable Custome of our Church of England'. The archbishop duly gave him a certificate relating that Barnby had been present at evening prayer with himself and his family and had very decently and religiously behaved himself.[1]

It is significant that many who capitulated were new recusants: an even greater number of Catholics who might have emerged as recusants must have been deterred when they saw the treatment meted out to friends and relatives. During the years of persecution there was always a substantial group of 'schismatics' outwardly conforming to the established religion: in 1617, for example, the Spanish ambassador estimated that there were 300,000 recusants in England and 600,000 Catholics attending Protestant worship.[2] Within the Catholic gentry the practice of satisfying the minimum requirements for church attendance was so widespread that the efforts of the missionary priests were mainly directed towards the conversion of 'Church Papists'. The following table shows that even in 1604, when the prospect of greater toleration was encouraging the growth of recusancy, there were many landed families in Yorkshire which, in spite of residual Catholic sympathies, were either fully conformable or guilty only of noncommunicancy:

recusant families	112
noncommunicant families	32
Catholic families which were fully conformable	110
total number of Catholic families within the Yorkshire gentry	254

Even these figures do not reveal the whole picture since most of the recusant families had a 'schismatic' element.[3]

Some 'schismatic' gentry maintained chaplains and sent their children abroad to be educated or trained as missionaries. In the main, however, a long period of conformity tended to breed indifference in matters of religion and particularly where the upbringing of the

[1] Sheffield Central Library: Spencer Stanhope MSS 60255.
[2] G. Albion, *Charles I and the Court of Rome*, 13.
[3] The main sources include E. Peacock (ed.), *A List of the Roman Catholics in the County of York in 1604* and P.R.O., Exchequer, Recusant Rolls, E.377/13.

children was concerned. This process may be seen in the case of the Forsters of Earswick, a North Riding family which remained largely conformist while the persecution continued. On entering the English College at Rome in 1618 John Forster stated that he had been a heretic when he lived in England: he had not been acquainted with any Catholics nor had he any real conception of religion. While away from home he had attended Protestant services but when at home he had taken no part in any kind of worship, nor had he said his prayers like the Catholics.[1] In other 'schismatic' families there was a similar lack of interest in the spiritual welfare of the children. Michael Oglethorpe of Thorner, having conformed to save his estate, took his children with him to church and in 1613 his eldest son was described as a Protestant. James Dalton of Swine was placed under the care of some Protestant friends and attended services and sermons in Anglican churches. Robert Dolman of Pocklington 'was altogether infected by that wicked poison of the heretics' until the age of sixteen, while William Percehay of Ryton lived as a Protestant until he took up residence with a Catholic relative, Sir Richard Fermour, in Oxfordshire.[2] In some cases a conforming squire gave his children a Protestant education. Sir Philip Constable of Everingham, for example, sent two of his sons to Cambridge University, one to Peterhouse and the other to Trinity College, while Michael Warton of Beverley studied first at Beverley Free School (which at that time had a Puritan master) and subsequently at Cambridge.[3]

With 'schismatics' there was always the possibility that regular attendance at church would eventually lead to a wholehearted acceptance of Protestant doctrine. To speed the work of evangelisation the ecclesiastical authorities sought to improve the quality of the northern clergy and from the middle years of Elizabeth's reign a growing number of 'preaching ministers' (often men of Puritan sympathies) were appointed to benefices in the province of York.[4] At the same time, Catholic gentry were frequently obliged to have conference with learned clergy, though rarely with any lasting results: probably a more important factor was the spread of Protestant literature. Apart from this, the authorities made some effort to prevent the growth of Catholi-

[1] Foley, iii, 16, 188. [2] Foley, iii, 148–50, 184, 186 and iv, 545.
[3] Al.Cant., i, 380–1, iv, 378.
[4] See M. C. Cross, The Puritan Earl: the Life of Henry Hastings third Earl of Huntingdon, 248, 253–7, 263–5.

cism among the young. The importance of the mother's role in the upbringing of her children did not escape them and this partly explains the frequency with which recusant wives were imprisoned. In 1619 the Privy Council, hearing that the wife of Thomas Waterton of Walton had been 'seduced and drawne away from the religion established in this realme to reccusancie, to the dainger of the rest of her household', gave order that she should be required to conform herself; if she remained obstinate then she was to be taken to some place 'where she may be kept from any ill affected that doe resorte unto her'.[1] Naturally the Crown was anxious to remove any possibility of receiving a Catholic education. Under the penal statutes it was illegal for a recusant to employ a private tutor, for a schoolmaster to open his own school without a licence from the bishop or for children to be sent abroad to Catholic seminaries. Yet in practice (as we shall see later) the measures taken to enforce this policy never proved really effective.[2] While these legal provisions were essentially restrictive a parliamentary bill drafted in March 1593 attempted a more positive approach:

That the children of recusants...after they be 7 yeres of age shalbe brought upp at the chardgs of their parents to be taken out of that porcion of landes which shall remaine or be to their saide parents, in such places and under the government of such loyall and discreete persons, as shalbe thereunto assigned by anie six of the privye cowncell or by the Busshop of the Diocese or Justice of Assise of the circuite etc.[3]

This radical measure never became law but occasionally the Northern High Commission made stipulations as to how a Catholic gentleman's children should be educated. Thus in October 1592 Leonard Calvert of Kiplin entered into a bond which required him to place his sons George (the future Lord Baltimore) and Christopher under the tuition of a Mr Fowberry, then schoolmaster at Bilton, and to bring them before the commissioners once a quarter if necessary so that their progress could be checked.[4] Such cases, however, occur too rarely to suggest any kind of systematic policy.

On the face of it, the system of wardship represented a considerable threat to the survival of Catholicism within the landed interest. Under a statute of 1606 no ward of the Crown could be granted to a convicted

---

[1] *Acts of the Privy Council 1617–19*, 432.   [2] Below, 194–9.
[3] *C.R.S.*, liii, 117–18.
[4] Borthwick Institute of Historical Research: High Commission Act Book, 1591–5, R VII/AB3, ff.84, 112.

recusant; in the case of Catholic families, the nearest Protestant relative was to have the custody and be responsible for the education of the ward.[1] On the first point the law was scrupulously observed but this apart the Court of Wards appears to have paid little attention to the religious sympathies of the prospective guardian. Usually where a Catholic family was concerned the wardship was assigned to the mother or, if she was a convicted recusant, to a relative who either shared her beliefs or was nevertheless willing to hand over responsibility for the upbringing of the children. In February 1639, for example, the guardianship of John Yorke of Gouthwaite, whose father had been a convicted recusant, was vested in his grandfather Sir Ingleby Daniell of Beswick, a suspected papist who had a recusant wife.[2] Where the wardship of a Catholic heir was granted to a complete outsider this did not necessarily have any religious significance: usually the Crown was simply rewarding a courtier or royal official, a practice not unknown in the case of Protestant wards.

Although the Court of Wards sometimes made special arrangements for the education of Catholic wards[3] there is no evidence that this was a general practice. In the case of Yorkshire families at least the relatives seem to have enjoyed virtually a free hand in the upbringing of the children. Where a family was already drifting into Protestantism it was not unusual for the ward to be educated at a grammar school and subsequently at a university. Occasionally this might happen in a predominantly Catholic family if the relative who had acquired the wardship was a determined Protestant. In the reign of Charles I, Sir George Wentworth of Woolley (who in spite of a Catholic upbringing appears to have had Puritan sympathies) sent his nephew Richard Langley of Ousethorpe to Bradford Grammar School and later paid for his education at Cambridge and Gray's Inn. Even so, Richard Langley was destined to become a Catholic.[4] Although the evidence is not exhaustive it seems probable that in most recusant families the ward and his brothers received a Catholic education. The children of Sir Francis Ireland of Crofton were taught by a seminary priest who later admitted this under examination, while two of the sons of Sir Thomas Strickland

---

[1] 3 James I, c.v.
[2] P.R.O., Court of Wards, Entry Book of Contracts for Marriages and Leases, Wards 9/ccviii/f.248.
[3] H. E. Bell, *An Introduction to the History and Records of the Court of Wards and Liveries*, 125.
[4] *Al.Cant.*, iii, 44. *C.R.S.*, vi, 258.

of Thornton Bridge were sent to the English College at Douai, though only after the heir had come of age.[1]

In one or two isolated cases there is evidence that a religious transformation took place as the direct result of a minority. When Thomas Danby of Masham was left a minor on his father's death in 1624 it seemed inevitable that he would be brought up as a Catholic since both his mother and his grandmother were strongly attached to the Old Religion. At this point, however, fate intervened. There was a fierce dispute between the mother and the grandmother over the custody of the ward and in the end the guardianship was assigned to Christopher Wandesford of Kirklington, representing the grandmother's party. As a result Thomas Danby grew up in the Protestant, almost Puritan, atmosphere of Kirklington Hall, studied at Cambridge and eventually married his guardian's daughter. The Catholic tradition in the Danby family had been broken.[2]

Such cases might occur from time to time but they were hardly typical. In the period 1603–42 thirty-three Catholic families within the Yorkshire gentry sustained a minority. By 1642 six of these families had completely severed their connection with the Old Religion, three were largely Protestant and the remainder were still firmly adhering to the Catholic cause. Furthermore, in most cases where a family went over to Protestantism the process was already well in train when the minority occurred. On the whole, therefore, it is clear that the system of wardship had little impact on the traditional loyalties of Catholic families.

Between the Northern Rebellion and the Civil War there was a striking reduction in Catholicism (using the term in its widest sense) within the ranks of the Yorkshire gentry. This may be seen from the following table:

	Catholic families	Total number of families
1570	368	567
1604	254	641
1642	163	679

Some Catholic families died out, others (usually decaying gentry) went

---

[1] *Surtees Society*, xl, 48. *C.R.S.*, x, 211, 230.
[2] C. Whone, 'Christopher Danby of Masham and Farnley', *Thoresby Society*, xxxvii, 1. T. Comber, *Memoirs of the Life and Death of the Lord Deputy Wandesforde*, 45–6, 59–60. *Al.Cant.*, ii, 7. See also above, 130–1.

to live outside the county. On the other hand, there were forces at work which helped to counterbalance these losses, in particular the emergence of cadet branches within the Catholic circle. In the final analysis, therefore, the main factor responsible for the decline in strength was a large-scale defection to Protestantism.

The transition from Catholicism to Protestantism was often a lengthy process. The Reresbys of Thrybergh represent an interesting example of a family slowly drifting away from the Old Religion, with the womenfolk seeking to arrest this trend. Successive heads of the family, at first 'schismatic' and later Protestant, appear to have tolerated rather than actively encouraged the Catholic practices of their wives and daughters. Like his father, Sir Thomas Reresby (1557–1619) was a man 'popishly affected' but unwilling to take a firm stand on religion. In 1604 he and his wife were reported to be noncommunicants and his children were being educated at home under a recusant schoolmaster. Later, in 1606, he was indicted at the Middlesex quarter sessions for absenting himself from church but he quickly resumed his church-going. His son Sir George (1586–1628) apparently had little affection for the Old Religion in spite of his education and the influence of a Catholic mother. According to his grandson's account of the family, his wife became a papist after her marriage, 'though I have heard it from thos that were servants in the familie that Sir George did both live and die a firm Protestant'. Sir George's eldest son John (1611–46) was educated at a grammar school and subsequently at Cambridge, and when the time came for him to marry he chose a wife with a solid Protestant background. This represents a turning-point in the religious history of the family: the Catholic strain began to lose its power and in another generation or so had vanished without trace. The transformation occurred in spite of the vigorous rearguard action of Sir George Reresby's widow who survived till 1665 and who, in the words of her grandson, was 'much led and persuaded by her confessor and preists'. The grandson himself was entreated to turn Catholic. 'At my going to travell', he relates, 'she recommended to me the Roman religion... truly I doe believe it was the greatest reason that she disposed of her own land away from me, that I could not be persuaded to change my religion.'[1] Sometimes a family went from one extreme to another in

---

[1] B.M., Additional MSS 29443, ff.2–3, 6. E. Peacock (ed.), *A List of the Roman Catholics in the County of York in 1604*, 6. *Middlesex County Records*, ii, 18. P.R.O., S.P.Dom., James I, S.P.14/lxxiv/31.

religion: between 1604 and 1642, for example, at least fourteen Catholic families were won over to Puritanism while in 1642 another six families had mixed Catholic and Puritan sympathies. The Worsleys of Hovingham provide an illustration of this. For many years they were favourably disposed towards the Old Religion and in the reign of Charles I Thomas Worsley paid recusancy fines on his estate. About the time of the Civil War, however, the Worsleys began to turn towards Puritanism and in her will Elizabeth Worsley, once a convicted recusant, could refer to the 'elect children of God' and stipulate that there should be no ringing of bells or other popish custom at her funeral. In a petition to the House of Lords in 1648 Thomas Worsley and his family claimed that although they had always detested Catholicism they had been great sufferers under the prelates for their nonconformity to the Book of Common Prayer. This was special pleading with a vengeance.[1]

[1] P.R.O., Exchequer, Recusant Rolls, E.377/59. Somerset House: Register Brent, f.91 (will 9 September 1652). *H.M.C. Seventh Report*, Appendix, 59–60.

CHAPTER IX

The Recusant Core

WHILE the Catholic gentry as a whole were declining in strength there was an impressive growth in recusancy at this level of society. In 1570 at least 368 families were still sympathetically inclined towards the Old Religion but few stayed away from church on principle. From the latter part of Elizabeth's reign, however, the recusant element tended to go on increasing, in spite of temporary setbacks, until a stage was reached where the terms 'Catholic gentry' and 'recusant gentry' were virtually interchangeable. This general trend is illustrated in the following table:

	1604	1642
total number of gentle families	641	679
total number of Catholic families	254	163
number of families which were at least partly recusant	112	138

Even these figures do not tell the whole story for many families which in the past had been only marginally represented in the lists of presentments were now becoming solidly recusant and often to a point where the head of the family was himself a regular absentee from church.

If the number of recusant families was growing this does not mean that there had been any significant gains from Protestantism. What we are witnessing is a polarisation process within the Catholic gentry: one section was going over completely to Anglicanism while another section was becoming fully and irrevocably committed to the Old Religion. In many cases the transformation of a conservative family from timid conformity to wholesale recusancy went on over several generations. As an example we may trace the religious history of a leading Craven family, the Tempests of Broughton. Henry Tempest, the head of the family in Elizabeth's reign, was described in 1570 as a Catholic and in 1572 as 'doutfull or newtor' in religion. From the evidence available he remained conformable throughout his lifetime. As was often the case it was the womenfolk who first defied the penal laws; in the recusant roll of 1592 there are entries relating to Isabel Tempest (the wife of Henry Tempest) and Katherine Tempest (his daughter-in-law). In 1604 three members of the family were presented for noncommunicancy: Sir Stephen Tempest (who was the eldest son and had recently been knighted), his wife Lady Katherine and his brother Henry. Sir Stephen quickly took steps to demonstrate his conformity and after this temporary lapse the authorities appear to have had no cause to suspect him of strong Catholic sympathies: indeed he was subsequently appointed to the West Riding commission of the peace. After his death in 1625 he was succeeded by his eldest son, also called Stephen, who was the first head of the family to be convicted of recusancy. During the reign of Charles I virtually all the adult members of the family were indicted at one time or another for absenting themselves from church: Stephen Tempest, his wife Frances, his mother Lady Katherine (who had been a recusant for some years), his brothers Richard, George and John Tempest, and his sisters-in-law Elizabeth and Frances Tempest. In addition, we find his sister Mary entering the Benedictine convent at Cambrai.[1]

The increase in recusancy among the Yorkshire gentry may be attributed to several factors: the work of the missionary priests who were flocking into the country in ever-increasing numbers; the greater opportunities available for the 'popishly affected' to have their children educated under Catholic auspices; and lastly the milder policy towards the Catholic community which was inaugurated in the latter part of James I's reign. Naturally it was upon the 'schismatic' families which had not lost contact entirely with the main stream of Catholicism that such factors as these had the greatest influence.

With the growth of the foundation movement on the Continent more and more Jesuits and seminary priests were sent on the English mission. At the time of the Gunpowder Plot there were said to be 300 or 400 missioners working in England while in 1634 the number was estimated at 900.[2] According to one of the annual reports submitted to the English College at Rome some of the Jesuit missioners in Yorkshire had no fixed place of habitation but as necessity required lived

[1] P.R.O., S.P.Dom., Elizabeth Addenda, S.P.15/xviii/39 and xxi, 86. E. Peacock (ed.), *A List of the Roman Catholics in the County of York in 1604*, 19. C.R.S., xviii, 75, 92, 98, 109. Y.A.S.R.S., liv, 20, 215. Borthwick Institute of Historical Research: Court Books for Diocese of York, 1637, R VI/A24, f.60 and 1640, R VI/A25, f.62.

[2] M. A. Tierney (ed.), *Dodd's Church History of England*, iv, 63. C. Butler, *Historical Memoirs of the English, Irish and Scottish Catholics Since the Reformation*, ii, 323.

with various families of the nobility and gentry. Others, however, had a permanent residence where they served and instructed both the household and neighbouring Catholics who attended Mass.[1] Between 1580 and the outbreak of the Civil War at least thirty gentle families in Yorkshire maintained Catholic chaplains at one time or another. In addition, many families were regularly visited by missionary priests or gave them shelter in time of need. Occasionally we learn something of these pastoral activities from the confession of a captured priest: thus in January 1593 Thomas Clarke admitted under examination that he had

said masse at one Mr Tockett in Gisburrowe parish in Cleveland...The said Tockett doth goe to the Churche but his wife when she lyved was a Catholick and therby dyvers of the servants...he hath also byne in the house of one Mrs Katherine Ratclyfe Called Ogthorp by Lith...and there hath said masse divers tymes, and at Mrs Chamblies of Whatbe in her husbands absence, and once or twice at the Ladie Constables, wife to Sir Henrie Constable at Upsall in Richmans sheire.[2]

Often it was the wife who took the initiative in the harbouring of priests while the husband (usually a 'schismatic') merely acquiesced in this breach of the penal laws. According to a contemporary account Dorothy Lawson, the wife of Roger Lawson of Brough,

had every month a priest secretly, though to cloak the matter for her husband's satisfaction, who comply'd with the times, shee went monthly abroad, as if shee had wanted the conveniencys at home...she was forced to convey the priest into the house by night, and lodged him in a chamber, which, to avoid suspicion, was appointed by grant from her husband only for his children to say their prayers.

When Lawson began to visit London more frequently on legal business she and her children regularly had the company of a priest, and soon after her husband's death a Jesuit chaplain came to reside in the household.[3]

In some Catholic manor-houses it was usual for missionary priests to remain hidden in secret rooms, their presence known only to a few

[1] Foley, vii, 1111.
[2] P.R.O., S.P.Dom., Elizabeth, S.P.12/ccxliv/5. The persons named may be identified as George Tocketts of Tocketts, in the parish of Guisborough, Katherine Radcliffe of Ugthorpe, Margaret Cholmley (wife of Henry Cholmley of Whitby) and Lady Margaret Constable (wife of Sir Henry Constable of Burton Constable who owned Upsall Castle).
[3] Father William Palmes, *Life of Mrs Dorothy Lawson of St Anthony's*, 17–18, 21.

trusted servants. This was the case at Gouthwaite Hall in the time of Sir John Yorke, a lifelong 'schismatic' who had a recusant wife. When the Yorkes were on trial in the Star Chamber it was alleged that a few months before the discovery of the Gunpowder Plot two hiding places had been constructed, one on either side of the bedchamber where Sir John and Lady Yorke slept. Sir John (it was claimed) often entertained visitors in conditions of great secrecy. These mysterious guests (who included both priests and Catholic laymen) took their meals in private and, apart from the family, were normally seen only by Marmaduke Lupton, the steward, and two or three other servants. Occasionally, however, someone outside this privileged circle managed to catch a glimpse of what was going on. Elizabeth Browne testified that while visiting Gouthwaite Hall she went upstairs and looked through a hole or crevice 'where shee espied diverse persons within the Chamber at a Masse as she thought'. According to her deposition Humphrey Bayne, one of the servants, threw her down the stairs. On another occasion Robert Jay, a mason who was 'workeinge by Candlelight, it beinge then about twye light', caught sight of Marmaduke Lupton 'bringinge in a straunger thither, which straunger the Ladie Yorke did meete in the hall, and saluted him...by the name of Mr Jarrett'. (The authorities were trying to establish that Father John Gerard had visited Gouthwaite Hall.) Later he met him on the stairs, 'two houres within night it beinge very darke, and had him in his Armes, who seemed...to be offended, and asked him hastelie who is there, whereto [he] answered a good fellowe, and thereupon without any more words speakinge the said Jarrett went upp the staires'.[1]

In other cases the priest lived as an ordinary member of the household and regularly celebrated Mass for the family and the whole body of servants. According to Gregory Panzani, a papal emissary who visited England in the reign of Charles I, some chaplains went about as laymen, mixing freely in the world. This they did to meet the wishes of their employers who preferred that they should not be known or reputed to be priests.[2] In one recorded case Edmund Catterick, who probably served as chaplain at his brother's house, Carlton Hall, in Richmondshire, apparently felt in no personal danger in visiting relatives whose religious beliefs were at variance with his own. Some

[1] P.R.O., Star Chamber Proceedings, Star Chamber 8/19/10.
[2] W. M. Brady, *Annals of the Catholic Hierarchy in England and Scotland 1585–1876*, 91.

time before his arrest and execution he was invited to the home of John Dodsworth of Thornton Watlass, a Protestant magistrate who had married a kinswoman of his, and there admitted to him in private that he was a missionary priest. Ironically enough, he was brought before his relative, now acting in his official capacity, by the pursuivants who arrested him in 1642.[1]

When a gentleman kept a priest under his roof it was necessary to be constantly on the alert in view of the frequent searches which were made. During this period missionary priests were discovered in a number of Yorkshire manor-houses, including Grimthorpe, Upsall Castle, Osgodby, Willitoft and Hazlewood Castle. More often, the searchers had to be content with the kind of material evidence which justified their suspicions. At Gouthwaite Hall in 1612 a pursuivant found in an outhouse two popish vestments, an altar stone, a pair of beads, 'a long thing of velvett to put about ones necke', a chalice, a picture of Jesus Christ in brass, a girdle of white silk and eighteen books, all or mostly Catholic.[2] By all accounts the quantity of evidence collected in this way was extremely impressive. In September 1599 Thomas Lord Burghley, who had recently taken up office as lord president of the Council of the North, told his brother Sir Robert Cecil that he had filled a study with copes and Mass books.[3]

Among the Yorkshire gentry at least the work of the Jesuits and seminary priests consisted largely of rallying the waverers and winning over the 'Church Papists' to wholehearted Catholicism. Many cases are on record where a person of quality owed his conversion to a missionary priest. Father Richard Huddleston, for example, is said to have reconciled to the Church of Rome a number of 'schismatic' families, including the Irelands of Crofton, the Watertons of Walton, the Middletons of Stockeld, the Trappes of Harrogate and the Thimblebys of Snydal.[4] At the same time there were few converts outside the general circle of Catholic families: indeed it was comparatively rare for the priests to make contact with families which had completely cut adrift from the Old Religion. Nevertheless if the Yorkshire missioners broke little fresh ground they had a major role in the revival of Catholicism within the conservative gentry.

[1] R. Challoner (ed.), *Memoirs of Missionary Priests*, 415.
[2] P.R.O., Star Chamber Proceedings, Star Chamber 8/19/10.
[3] *Cal. S.P. Dom. 1598–1601*, 321.
[4] John Huddleston, *A Short and Plain Way to the Faith and Church*, f.5.

Besides the need for a sustained missionary effort the future of Catholicism in England depended in no small degree on the continued ability of popish families to provide their children with a Catholic education. Under an act of 1581 any schoolmaster who stayed away from Protestant services could be sentenced to a year's imprisonment, besides being disabled from teaching, while his employer was liable to a fine of £10 a month. In 1604 it was further enacted that no one should keep a school or work as a schoolmaster 'excepte it be in some publike or free Grammer Schoole, or in some such Noblemans or Noblewomans or Gentleman or Gentlewomans House as are not Recusants, or where the same Schoole Master shall be speciallie licensed thereunto'. Failure to comply with this law rendered the schoolmaster and his employer liable to a fine of 40s. a day each during the period of the offence.[1] In addition, it was illegal for anyone to receive a Catholic education abroad. By an act of 1585 all English students who were being educated in continental seminaries were ordered to return home within six months: otherwise they would be declared guilty of high treason. Subsequently, in 1604, it was laid down that any person sending a child to a foreign college could be fined £100, while the child faced the prospect of being disabled from inheriting or purchasing land.[2] The fact that many families were prepared to defy these laws and did so successfully must be regarded as one of the major factors in the growth of recusancy.

Often the children of a Catholic gentleman received their schooling at home under a private tutor. An official survey of Yorkshire Catholicism undertaken in 1604 brought to light a number of cases which illustrate this point. At Woolley Michael Wentworth had a schoolmaster who was apparently a recusant. At Thrybergh Hall one of the servants was 'George Egleseme a Scottishe man, a scolemaster wich teacheth the children of Sir Thomas Reresby'. In the parish of Normanton, where John Thimbleby of Snydal was presented as a noncommunicant, the recusants included one Lancaster 'a scholemaster retayned by the said Mr Thimbleby'. In Hornby parish John Girlington of Hackforth employed a tutor called William Mease. At Scargill Hall (the commissioners reported) 'Gerard ffawden, a Recusant...dothe teache Francis Tunstall his children'. Finally, the return for Nunkeeling parish records that 'Cuthbert Belton hath remained in the house of Mr Raphe

---

[1] 23 Elizabeth I, c.i and 1 James I, c. iv.   [2] 27 Elizabeth I, c.ii and 1 James I, c. iv.

Cresswell as a scholemaster to his children about fower monethes last, but came not to the church in that time'.[1] During this period most of the leading recusant families, and indeed a number of 'schismatic' families, employed private schoolmasters at one time or another. In addition, some gentlemen sent their children to Catholic schools which had been established without licence from the church authorities. These were mainly small village schools, often short-lived, but there were also some larger schools which attracted scholars from a considerable area. In 1625 it was alleged in the House of Commons that one popish schoolmaster in York 'had 56 schollers, of which there were 36 papistes'.[2]

From the middle years of Elizabeth's reign it became more and more common for English Catholics, and especially propertied families, to send their children abroad to the continental foundations specifically established to meet their needs. By the time of the Civil War there were many foundations of this sort, in France, Spain, Italy, Portugal and the Spanish Netherlands. These included seminaries at Douai, St Omer, Rome, Madrid, Seville, Valladolid and Lisbon; monasteries at Paris, Douai, St Malo and Dieulouard; and convents at Louvain, Brussels, Paris, Gravelines, Cambrai, Ghent and Bruges. The seminaries performed a vital function. Their work was twofold: they trained priests for the English mission and they helped to preserve the faith among the richer Catholic families through the education of their children. Without this double link English Catholicism would have faced extinction.

As we have seen, the first English seminary was founded at Douai in 1568. Between 1568 and 1642 many sons and daughters of Yorkshire gentlemen entered Catholic foundations on the Continent:

number of youths admitted to seminaries and monasteries	184
number of young women admitted to convents	42
number of families represented above	87

These are necessarily minimum figures because in some cases few, if any, admission records have survived from this period.[3]

---

[1] E. Peacock (ed.), *A List of the Roman Catholics in the County of York in 1604*, 3, 6, 13, 78, 85, 128.

[2] *Camden Society*, New Series, vi, 26.

[3] A considerable amount of material in the archives of the English College Rome has been transcribed. This contains much information about students and priests (P.R.O., Roman Transcripts, P.R.O. 31/9 and 10). The Catholic Record Society has printed the

In some ultra-Catholic families it was usual for several children in each generation to go abroad for their education or to be trained for holy orders. It was not only the recusant gentry, however, who sent their children to continental foundations: not infrequently the father was a 'Church Papist' and occasionally even a Protestant who had a Catholic wife. In such cases the mother was normally the guiding spirit but sometimes a relative's influence was at work. On his entry to the English College Rome in 1613 William Constable (a younger son of Sir Philip Constable of Everingham, who conformed for most of his life) related how he had started out on the road to Catholicism. Five years before, after matriculating at Trinity College Cambridge, he had chanced to meet his great-uncle Sir Ralph Babthorpe who asked him if he was willing to become a Catholic. The young student replied that he was and within three weeks Sir Ralph had arranged for him to go to St Omer.[1]

According to her chaplain Dorothy Lawson 'addressed...her children, a dozen in number (except the heire, in whom was deservedly planted the hope of perpetuating that ancient stock, and two daughters, one by sickness, the other impedimented by immaturity of age), each to colleges and religious houses, appointed for men and women, with sufficient maintenance, according to their several vocations'.[2] Among the Catholic gentry it was rare for the eldest son to be educated at a continental seminary. The risks were too great. A number of students died while at college and not a few had to return to England on account

admission registers, together with ordination records, for the following colleges: Douai 1598–1654 (C.R.S., vols. x and xi), Madrid 1611–1767 (vol. xxix), Valladolid 1589–1862 (vol. xxx) and Rome 1579–1783 (vols. xxxvii and xl). Earlier records of Douai are printed in Records of the English Catholics under the Penal Laws (ed. T. F. Knox). J. Kirk's Historical Account of Lisbon College has a list of students and priests. B. Weldon's A Chronicle of the English Benedictine Monks contains lists of professed monks for a number of Benedictine houses. Supplementary material has been obtained from H. Foley (ed.). Records of the English Province of the Society of Jesus, G. Oliver, Collections Towards Illustrating the Biography of the Scotch, English and Irish Members of the Society of Jesus, H. N. Birt, Obit Book of the English Benedictines, 1600–1912 and C.R.S., xxiv (Franciscana). The Catholic Record Society has published the admission registers and other records of the following convents: Cambrai (C.R.S., vol. xiii), Gravelines (vol. xiv) and the Benedictine nunnery at Brussels (vol. xiv). Material relating to other convents is to be found in B. Weldon, A Chronicle of the English Benedictine Monks and C.R.S., vi, xvii, xxiv and xxix. Mention must also be made of A. Hamilton's Chronicles of the English Augustinian Canonesses of St. Monica's at Louvain, 1548–1644.

[1] P.R.O., Roman Transcripts, P.R.O. 31/9/14: 157. Foley, iii, 206. Al.Cant., i, 381.
[2] Father William Palmes, Life of Mrs Dorothy Lawson of St. Anthony's, 21–2.

of ill health. Furthermore, there was always the possibility that the heir might seek to enter the priesthood. This happened in the case of William Percehay (the son and heir of Thomas Percehay of Ryton) who was converted in 1618 while travelling on the Grand Tour and subsequently gained admission to the English College at Rome. In the event he never achieved his desire to become a priest for in 1620 he died while still under training. Fortunately there was another son ready to succeed to the family estate.[1] In view of these considerations the eldest son of a recusant squire was usually educated at home though where the family was reasonably wealthy he would often be sent to one of the inns of court to acquire a knowledge of the law.

From the end of the sixteenth century many families sent their sons initially to St Omer, the leading English Catholic preparatory school on the Continent. Here the Jesuit plan was to prepare boys from ten to fifteen years of age for the seminaries at Rome and in Spain. Since the majority of students entering these Jesuit seminaries had already spent a number of years at St Omer they were usually at least seventeen or eighteen when embarking on their advanced studies and not infrequently in their twenties. At the secular college of Douai, on the other hand, the age of entry tended to be rather lower and it was not unknown for boys of twelve and thirteen to be admitted.[2]

At these colleges there were two types of student: the convictor, who was maintained by his relatives, and the alumnus, who was supported at the expense of the college and had to take an oath that he would accept holy orders. The great majority of students from Yorkshire manor-houses were admitted as convictors although many of them subsequently became Jesuits and secular priests. The course of instruction which they followed consisted mainly of classical studies and, at the advanced stage, theology and philosophy.

During the early Stuart period the Crown became increasingly concerned at the number of English Catholics who were being admitted to the continental foundations and the large sums of money which were being transported out of the kingdom for their support. In an attempt to halt this movement new legislation was brought in, proclamations were issued and efforts were made to tighten up the arrangements under which licences for foreign travel were granted. In 1627 an act was passed

[1] Foley, iv, 545. C.R.S., xxxvii, 188. Acts of the Privy Council 1616–17, 277.
[2] P. Guilday, The English Colleges and Convents in the Catholic Low Countries 1558–1795, 140. C.R.S., x, xi, xxx, xxxvii and xl, passim.

14—Y.G.

which re-affirmed the provisions of the earlier statute of 1604 and further provided that anyone sending children to foreign seminaries or helping to maintain them there would be liable to forfeit all his lands and goods. The same penalty was prescribed for the children unless they were prepared to conform themselves within six months after their return.[1]

In addition to increasing the statutory penalties the Crown also sought to ensure that passes for foreign travel were neither issued indiscriminately nor misappropriated. During the early seventeenth century it became more and more usual for such licences to contain a proviso that the person concerned was on no account to visit Rome. In 1625 the Privy Council specifically directed that every pass should stipulate that the bearer was not to repair to Rome or any of the king of Spain's dominions without special permission. Subsequently, in 1628, the Council ruled that because of the false attestations which were sometimes made no pass should be presented by the clerk of the Council unless he had particular knowledge of the person for whom it was intended or of those who did 'particularly and familiarly know him'. In addition, the pass was to be signed by one of the secretaries of state before submission to the Council.[2]

These measures were largely unsuccessful: the flow of Catholic children into the continental foundations went on without interruption. Some popish squires seem to have experienced no great difficulty in securing passes for their sons to travel abroad (and this was especially true in the years 1619–25 when Sir George Calvert, a Yorkshireman who eventually revealed himself as a Catholic, was one of the principal secretaries of state). The usual reason given in applying for a pass was the desire to gain experience and knowledge through foreign travel. In 1618, for example, Thomas and John Lascelles of Breckenbrough, grandchildren of a member of the Council of the North, were licensed to travel abroad for three years 'to attaine the languadges'. Both brothers were admitted in that year to the English College at Douai and subsequently returned as priests.[3] In the case of young women destined for Catholic convents it was naturally more difficult to produce a convincing reason for requiring a licence to travel. In 1618 Joyce Langdale (a daughter of William Langdale of Langthorpe, a prominent East Riding recusant) was granted a pass to go to Spa, 'shee

[1] 3 Charles I, c.iii.   [2] *Acts of the Privy Council 1625–6*, 252 and *1628–9*, 224–5.
[3] *Acts of the Privy Council 1617–19*, 207. C.R.S., x, 144, 235, 237.

being advised by learned physitians to drinke of those waters at the fountaine as the most assured meanes to give her ease of greevious langusheing deseases whereof shee can finde no reamydie by any course of phisicke here'. This pass contained the proviso that 'shee make no further use of this lycence then only to go to the Spawe for recovery of her health' but before the end of 1618 Joyce Langdale had been admitted to the English Benedictine nunnery at Brussels.[1]

Most of the children from Yorkshire Catholic families whose names appear in the admission registers of the continental foundations in this period seem to have travelled without an official pass. This practice must have been of long standing for as early as 1580 the bishops had been requested to take bonds 'of the parentes and frindes of suche yong gentlemen and others of her Majesties subjectes as are presentlie beyond the seas with out lycence'.[2] Along the North Sea coastline there were a number of shipowners willing to convey Catholic passengers to the Continent and it is probable that many went by this means. Such journeys were not entirely free from risk. John Crathorne was travelling in this way when his ship was driven by a storm into Orford harbour, Suffolk, where he and three other Catholics were betrayed by the crew and thrown into prison. Eventually, however, he regained his freedom and was admitted to the English College at Valladolid in 1608.[3] Many Catholics, with or without passes, made the crossing from one or other of the Cinque Ports, usually Dover. Port officials had authority to tender the oath of allegiance to persons in transit and sometimes a student on his way to or from a continental seminary was taken into custody for refusing the oath. One notable case occurred in 1626 when Henry Wyvill, brother of Sir Marmaduke Wyvill, a North Riding deputy lieutenant, was arrested and committed to prison at Dover. The young man was returning from the English College at Douai and in 1631 we find him going back there to resume his studies.[4] On the other hand, it was not unusual for a Catholic to take the oath of allegiance when it was offered to him; moreover, the customs officials were not all efficient or incorruptible. In practice, therefore, many unlicensed travellers managed to slip through.

The resurgence of Catholicism among the Yorkshire gentry was undoubtedly encouraged by the greater tolerance shown towards

[1] *Acts of the Privy Council 1617–19*, 185. *C.R.S.*, xiv, 184.
[2] *Acts of the Privy Council 1580–1*, 281.   [3] *C.R.S.*, xxx, 96.
[4] *Cal.S.P.Dom. 1625–6*, 388, 450, 458. *C.R.S.*, x, 153, 230, 237, 296.

recusants from the latter part of James I's reign onwards. In 1625 Sir Thomas Hoby, M.P. for Ripon, told the House of Commons that in Yorkshire the recusants were 'doubled if not trebled, since this connivency. In the North Ridinge there were 1200 convicted five yeares since, now 2400'. Similarly, it was alleged in a Commons petition of 1626 that no fewer than 1670 new recusants had been convicted in the East Riding since the appointment of Lord Scroope as lord president of the Council of the North in 1619.[1] To a large extent this change in attitude was the outcome of a foreign policy which led the king to enter into marriage negotiations first with Spain and then with France. For short periods in the 1620's the penal laws were suspended, all proceedings against recusants were halted and the annual fines were remitted. In 1623 the government went even further and allowed Catholics to worship freely in their own homes. Before the end of 1625, however, special commissioners were appointed to see that all the penal statutes were duly put into execution.[2]

Although the penal laws were never set aside for long — mainly on account of parliamentary opposition — the government nevertheless attempted to make conditions less intolerable for the Catholic community by means of administrative changes. In particular, a deliberate effort was made to get rid of the harsher features of the fining system and to curtail the activities of pursuivants and informers.[3] In 1627 a climax was reached with the introduction of a new system of compositions for recusancy which has been attributed to Sir John Savile, vice-president of the Council of the North. Under this system a recusant landowner undertook to pay a composition rent for his estate which was usually leased to him for a period of forty-one years. If he had been a recusant before 1627 his new rent was generally higher than what he had previously paid but it was still a mere fraction of his total income. In return he was granted a number of privileges: first, the right to enjoy his lands and goods without molestation; secondly, immunity for himself and his wife from any further proceedings or punishment in the ecclesiastical courts on account of their recusancy; and finally,

[1] *Camden Society*, New Series, vi, 25. Rushworth, i, 393.

[2] The effect of the marriage negotiations, and of parliamentary pressure, on the Crown's policy towards the Catholic community is described in detail in M. A. Tierney (ed.), *Dodd's Church History of England*, v, 115–64. See also *Cal.S.P.Dom. 1623–5*, 47, 69, 419, 421 and *Cal.S.P.Dom. 1625–6*, 16, 148.

[3] P.R.O., S.P.Dom., James I, S.P.14/cxv/10, 30, 31 and cxviii/135; S.P.Dom., Warrants, S.P.39/xxvi/57. M. A. Tierney (ed.), *Dodd's Church History of England*, v, 121.

complete freedom from any actions or indictments arising from the same offence.[1]

After the commission of 1627 had been despatched the authorities issued a general proclamation drawing the attention of Catholics to the favourable terms on which they would be allowed to compound.[2] 'Schismatics' were no doubt given further encouragement to emerge from their conformity when they heard of the modest rents at which Sir John Savile and his fellow commissioners were granting leases. In September 1627 Sir Thomas Vavasour of Hazlewood told his kinsman the future Earl of Strafford that their proceedings had been 'fayre and equall dureing the last Session...I suppose it wyll rayse a great somme, for most men resolve to Compounde, thoe at first some dislyked the Course'. When a new commission was issued in 1629 the archbishop of York agreed to a working arrangement whereby Catholics who were slow in coming forward to compound would be summoned before the Northern High Commission and informed that they would be granted freedom from ecclesiastical censures if they were willing to treat with the commissioners for the recusant revenue.[3] Whether as a result of these summonses or on account of the inducements offered, many Yorkshire gentry went to the King's Manor at York to make their compositions. Between 1627 and 1640 the commissioners granted leases to thirty-eight heads of families who had never previously been convicted of recusancy (and in many cases it was the first time that any head of the family had been convicted).[4] Once a new recusant had undergone the formalities of indictment and conviction at quarter sessions the composition was generally settled with the minimum of delay. Sometimes a Catholic might even compound before conviction although there were serious doubts as to the legality of this practice.[5]

In putting into effect its policy of moderation the Crown needed a lord president in the North who was fully in sympathy with its aims. For this reason Lord Sheffield, who was too closely associated with the

---

[1] P.R.O., Chancery, Patent Rolls, C.66/2441 (Commission of 23 June 1627. This was subsequently renewed, in virtually identical form, on several occasions.) C.R.S., i, 103. See below, 219.

[2] Cal.S.P.Dom. 1627–8, 226, 230.

[3] Sheffield Central Library: Strafford Letters, xii, 10 September 1627. C.R.S., liii, 299.

[4] P.R.O., Exchequer, Recusant Rolls, E.377/36 seq. C.R.S., liii, 309–63.

[5] Sheffield Central Library: Strafford Letters, xiii. Sir Edward Osborne to Wentworth, 6 September 1633.

campaign of persecution which had been waged, was relieved of his appointment in 1619. His successor, Lord Scroope, came to be regarded as a protector of the Catholic community north of the Trent. When Sir Thomas Wentworth became lord president in 1628 his friend Christopher Wandesford declared that the Catholics were already hanging down their heads like bulrushes; they were saying plainly that their days of security and quietness, when they had been lulled asleep by Scroope's indulgence, would now be followed by days of anxiety and watchfulness. In the event (he predicted) Wentworth would deal justly with them and file off the rust which was eating into the penal laws.[1]

Although the Catholic Church branded him as a tyrant[2] it is clear that Wentworth's main concern in this sphere was to enlarge the recusant revenue and establish it on a solid foundation. When criticised for being too lenient with Catholics he replied: 'I have done more towards a Reformation, soe farre as a pecuniary Mulct inflicted can affect it, then any that went before me.'[3] Wentworth was anxious to avoid anything which might deter Catholics from compounding for their estates. It was primarily his idea that the High Commission at York should cease its activities against recusants (except where their offences were insolent and public) until such time as the revenue was settled. During his period of office other concessions were made for the same reason: the fine of 12d. a Sunday was remitted and Catholics were no longer presented at quarter sessions for such breaches of the law as keeping a recusant servant.[4]

On the whole, the Catholic party fared reasonably well in the reign of Charles I. Once he had compounded a recusant squire was allowed to manage his estate in comparative peace and, apart from the occasional double subsidy, his absence from church cost him nothing more than his rent. Nor was he under any necessity to appear before the Northern High Commission to answer for his recusancy or, alternatively, to absent himself from home in anticipation of a summons.

[1] R. R. Reid, *The King's Council in the North*, 388. Rushworth, i, 392. Knowler, ii, 49–50.

[2] See, for example, Foley, vii, 1128–9.

[3] Sheffield Central Library: Strafford Letters, vi, 7.

[4] Knowler, ii, 159. Sheffield Central Library: Strafford Letters, xii. Sir Edward Osborne to Wentworth, 1 May 1631, and xiii. Sir William Pennyman to Wentworth, 22 August 1633.

Furthermore, he was in no danger of being committed to prison for his religious beliefs.

In his report on the state of English Catholicism, following the papal mission which he undertook in 1632, Gregory Panzani wrote that there remained two pressing grievances: the activities of the pursuivants, who carried out their searches with great violence, and the oaths of allegiance and supremacy.[1] The abuses associated with the pursuivants were never completely checked, though while Wentworth discharged the office of lord president in person he seems to have ensured that Catholics were troubled as little as possible in this respect. In September 1633, however, shortly after his arrival in Ireland, he was informed by the vice-president that there were 'diverse commissions newly granted by the Archbishop and Bishop of Durham for searchinge Recusants houses for Preists, Reliques and popish ornaments which are daily putt in execution whereby both such as have compounded and are yett to compound are soe molested as I much feare the service [that is, the compositions with recusants] will fall to nothinge, unless some course be taken to stay them for the present'.[2] While the pursuivants were still troublesome the oaths of allegiance and supremacy do not appear to have constituted much of a problem for Yorkshire Catholics, at least in any material sense. For in the reign of Charles I they were generally willing to take these oaths.[3]

While the main question which English Catholics had to face was whether to attend their parish church on Sundays there were also special problems in the case of baptism, marriage and burial. The evidence, both positive and negative, which may be obtained from the parish registers of the period is substantial enough to enable general conclusions to be drawn about their attitude to these problems.[4] At one extreme 'schismatic' families like the Beilbys of Micklethwaite Grange conformed to the established religion in all respects. At the other end of the scale there were ultra-Catholic families like the Annes of Frickley which refused to have anything to do with Anglicanism. During the early seventeenth century the parish registers of Frickley and Burgh-

---

[1] W. M. Brady, *Annals of the Catholic Hierarchy in England and Scotland 1585–1876*, 87–8.

[2] Sheffield Central Library: Strafford Letters, xiii. Sir Edward Osborne to Lord Wentworth, 26 September 1633.

[3] B.M., Thomason Tracts E.150(5). *Cal.S.P.Dom. 1623–5*, 515.

[4] What follows is largely based on the parish register material published by the Yorkshire Parish Register Society.

wallis (where their two main seats were situated) record only one event in the life of the Anne family: the burial of an infant son in 1621.[1] Such single-mindedness was, however, comparatively rare. Catholic gentry, recusants as well as 'Church Papists', often had their dead buried, and not infrequently their children baptised, according to the Protestant form of worship. On the other hand it was unusual for a recusant to marry in church.

Although the children of Catholic parents sometimes received a Protestant baptism there are a number of recorded cases where a recusant squire neglected to have this done within the statutory period of one month from birth. At Stokesley, for example, the parish priest noted on four occasions between 1635 and 1638 that Henry Forster, who was heir to the lord of the manor, had failed to have a child baptised in church.[2] In this period the authorities frequently investigated allegations of secret baptisms. The children of Sir Ralph Babthorpe of Osgodby (we are told) were all, with one exception, given a Catholic baptism but the archbishop of York forced him to have them re-christened by Anglican priests. According to Gregory Panzani the missionary priests were not always as scrupulous as they should have been in the christening of children: some of them were prepared to allow heretical godfathers and profane Christian names.[3]

A Catholic couple who had been secretly married could be faced with the necessity of proving the legitimacy of their marriage in court. Thus in 1604 Sir George Palmes of Naburn and his wife were reported to 'have bene called by waie of sitacons into the Consistorie courte at Yorke to prove there mariage, vehemently suspected to have bene married by some popishe priest'.[4] This was a particularly serious matter for landed families in view of the complications which might arise over the descent of property. Nevertheless many Catholic gentry were married by missionary or Marian priests: indeed if they had gone through a Protestant form of marriage this would virtually have amounted to apostasy in the eyes of the Catholic Church. In such cases the wedding ceremony was performed either in the privacy of their own homes or, if this was considered too dangerous, in some secluded glade or field. A description of one of these clandestine marriages has

[1] Clay, iii, 44–7. *Yorkshire Parish Register Society*, xcv and cxvi.
[2] *Yorkshire Parish Register Society*, vii, 69, 72, 73.
[3] Foley, iii, 199, 203. W. M. Brady, *op. cit.*, 93.
[4] E. Peacock (ed.), *A List of the Roman Catholics in the County of York in 1604*, 141.

survived among the records of a Star Chamber case heard in 1631. In the course of these proceedings Henry Scroope of Danby was alleged to have repudiated his marriage to a daughter of Sir Edward Plumpton (a fellow Catholic) by pretending that he already had a wife. According to one deponent Henry Scroope and Anne Plumpton had been married 'by a popish priest in a chamber of Sir Edward Plumpton's house and at twelve of the clock at night'. Another witness thought that

the minister that married them was inclinable to the Catholic religion, but knew not whether he were a priest or noe, for that they never saw his orders; but...[the marriage] was between twelve and one of the clocke in the night-tyme...the same words were used in the marriage as are ordinarily used in marriages in Protestant Churches; and a ring was used in the marriage and Henry Scroope sayd these words: I, Henry, take thee, Anne, to my wedded wife, etc: and afterwards the priest said some short prayers in Latine, which they understood not.[1]

At this time many Catholic squires (including some of the staunch-est recusants) were buried with their ancestors in the parish church. When Sir John Gascoigne of Barnbow, who had been a recusant for most of his life, directed in his will that his body should be placed in 'my Clossett' within Barwick church, close to his father and mother, there was nothing unusual in such a testamentary provision. Although persons who had been excommunicated by the Anglican Church could not legally be buried in consecrated ground it was the general practice among English Catholics (Gregory Panzani writes) to 'procure by money an absolution from the excommunication, in which absolution is expressed, according to some authorities, that such or such a person having been excommunicate, has obeyed and has been absolved'. According to the episcopal visitation book of 1637 both Sir John Gascoigne and his wife were granted an absolution and buried in the church at Barwick in Elmet.[2] Sometimes a recusant was laid to rest in consecrated ground without the authority or the presence of the Anglican minister. In 1636, for example, the curate of Carlton juxta Snaith noted in his register: 'Gilbart Stapylton Esq Lord of Carlton a recusant buryed the 18th of Aprill buryed by home I know not.'[3] In

---

[1] *Camden Society*, New Series, xxxix, 51–7.

[2] G. D. Lumb (ed.), *Wills, Registers and Monumental Inscriptions of the Parish of Barwick-in-Elmet*, 51, 106, 107. W. M. Brady, *op. cit.*, 95–6. Borthwick Institute of Historical Research: Court Book for Diocese of York, 1637, R VI/A24, f.106.

[3] *Yorkshire Parish Register Society*, xcvi, 24.

the case of many recusant gentry no evidence about their last resting-place is available from any source. They were no doubt buried secretly at night in some place known only to the family.

The contribution made by the Catholic gentry in support of the Old Religion was undoubtedly of great value. Writing in 1610 Father James Sharpe said of the East Riding gentry with whom he was acquainted that their devotion 'in making their houses common to all who come even with the danger of themselves and their whole estate, the relieving both corporally and spiritually the poor Catholics who live among them, the maintaining of priests in their houses, some one, some two, is memorable among them'.[1] The task of the missionary priests would have been considerably more difficult without the shelter and protection afforded them by the Catholic gentry. In various localities they maintained special mission centres which were used for the reception of priests arriving from the Continent or as resting-places for priests who had no fixed residence. One of these centres was at Grosmont Priory, near Whitby, 'to which place [Sir Robert Cecil was informed in 1599] doe resorte most dangerous men, both priests and fugitives'. At this time the property belonged to Henry Cholmley of Whitby, a justice of the peace who was subsequently knighted. His wife (we learn from his grandson's memoirs)

was a Roman Catholic, and he living then at Whitby, it was a receptacle to the seminary priests coming from beyond seas, and landing frequently at that port; insomuch as, I have been told, there have been in his house three or four of them together at a time, and, most coming both bare of cloaths and money, have, at his lady's charge, been sent away with a great supply of both; some in scarlet and sattin, with their men and horses, the better to disguise their professions. All which Sir Henry connived at, being a little then in his heart inclining that way, though he went to church.[2]

In many places a Catholic manor-house with its chaplain or visiting priest was an important centre of religious activity. This may be seen from Father Sharpe's account of the Babthorpe family. At Osgodby Hall, he writes,

we were continually two priests, one to serve and order the house at home, the other to help those who are abroad, who, especially in any sickness or fear of death, would continually send to us for help, that they might die in

---

[1] J. Morris (ed.), *The Troubles of Our Catholic Forefathers*, Series iii, 467.
[2] P.R.O., S.P.Dom., Elizabeth, S.P.12/cclxx/99. *Cholmley Memoirs*, 14.

the estate of God's Church. Our house I might count rather as a religious house than otherwise, for, though there lived together in it three knights [Sir Ralph Babthorpe, Sir William Babthorpe and Sir George Palmes] and their ladies with their families, yet we had all our servants Catholic. On the Sundays we locked up the doors and all came to Mass, had our sermons, catechisms, and spiritual lessons every Sunday and holiday. On the work days we had for the most part two Masses, and of them the one for the servants at six o'clock in the morning, at which the gentlemen, every one of them without fail, and the ladies if they were not sick, would, even in the midst of winter, of their own accord be present; and the other we had at eight o'clock for those who were absent from the first. In the afternoon at four o'clock we had evensong, and after that matins, at which all the knights and their ladies, except extraordinary occasions did hinder them, would be present and stay at their prayers all the time the priests were at evensong and matins.[1]

By helping to meet the spiritual needs of their co-religionists the recusant gentry did much to keep the faith alive in the districts where their main estates were situated. Generally speaking, it was in the parishes which had Catholic manor-houses that the largest concentrations of recusants were to be found. In such parishes a high proportion of the Catholics presented for recusancy were dependent, either directly or indirectly, on the lord of the manor: that is to say, members of his family, household servants, labourers on the home farm and manorial tenants. Not surprisingly a popish squire tended to adopt a paternalistic attitude towards that section of the local populace which shared his religious beliefs. For the Star Chamber trial of Sir John Yorke of Gouthwaite testimony was produced that 'the greatest parte of the Tennants and servants of the said Sir John Yorke are popishelie affected and are in greater favour and more countenanced by the said Sir John Yorke and his said Ladie then they that goe to Church are'. When the new oath of allegiance was introduced the parish priest at Middlesmore was required to collect the names of all his parishioners who favoured the Old Religion. Sir John, who was the principal landowner in the area, saw the list and struck out the names of his own servants and others he was anxious to protect. The minister subsequently rewrote the list but not one of his parishioners offered to take the oath and they apparently escaped unpunished.[2]

---

[1] J. Morris (ed.), *The Troubles of Our Catholic Forefathers*, Series iii, 468.
[2] P.R.O., Star Chamber Proceedings, Star Chamber 8/19/10. C. H. D. Howard, *Sir John Yorke of Nidderdale*, 16–17.

Further afield, the Catholic gentry contributed a substantial proportion of the money which was sent abroad for the support of the English foundations on the Continent. When they educated their sons in foreign seminaries it was usually at their own expense while the convents mainly drew their members from wealthy landed families which could afford to pay the dowries required on entry.[1]

During this period many of the priests who served on the English mission were younger sons of Catholic squires. As might be expected, most of the priests from Yorkshire manor-houses returned to work in the north of England, often in their native county. In some cases as many as three or four brothers took up holy orders. Of the four sons of Sir John Gascoigne of Barnbow two became Benedictine monks and a third entered the priesthood, while the eldest son, Sir Thomas, retired in his old age to the monastery of Lambspring where his brother John was abbot. In addition, two of Sir John's daughters were admitted to the Benedictine convent at Cambrai while another daughter who wished to enter a nunnery died on her way to the Continent.[2]

In practising an outlawed religion, with all that this meant in terms of penalties and disabilities, the recusant gentry inevitably acquired something of the character of a class within a class. This sense of isolation was naturally heightened as the large 'schismatic' element of Elizabeth's reign declined in strength and, as a result, the dividing line between the Catholic and Protestant groupings became more sharply defined. To meet their own special needs the recusant gentry were forced to maintain a high degree of self-sufficiency: they had their own priests, their own system of education, their own lawyers specialising in recusancy work, even their own Catholic physicians. At the same time, their common interests and problems drew them together to form a tightly-knit group of families which were already linked to some extent by ties of kinship and ancient lineage. Within this group there was frequent inter-marriage. Fellow Catholics dined together, hunted together and heard Mass together. They acted as godparents, as executors of wills and as trustees in the settlement of property, all within this circle of families. On occasion they showed themselves capable of working together as one body: thus in 1639 a

---

[1] See below, 222–3.

[2] Clay, iii, 101. H. N. Birt, *Obit Book of the English Benedictines 1600–1912*, 38–9, 55. *C.R.S.*, i, 125, x, 286, xiii, 40, 43. B. Weldon, *A Chronicle of the English Benedictine Monks*, 228 and Appendix, 9 and 15.

number of recusant gentlemen were appointed to collect money from the Catholic community for the support of Charles I's war with the Scots.[1]

Relations between the Catholic gentry and the Protestant gentry varied considerably from one region to another. In some parts of the county there was bitter antagonism: for example, where a Puritan magistrate took a delight in harassing the 'popishly affected' or where recusant landowners sought to take advantage of their numerical strength. In 1611 Sir John Mallory and Sir John Yorke were alleged to have harboured great malice against Sir Stephen Proctor, a West Riding justice of the peace, because of the energy he displayed in 'the fynding out, apprehension and punishment of diverse Semynary preists, Recusants and backward people in the Religion nowe established wherby they and theire freinds allys or such as they have favored or some of them have been brought into question'.[2] On the other hand, some recusant gentry had Protestant relatives who helped them by holding leases of their estates from the Crown or by using their authority or influence to soften the penalties imposed on them. Moreover, they were often on friendly terms with neighbouring landowners, especially if their religion was not too openly flaunted. In September 1637 Thomas Tankard of Boroughbridge, a recusant, petitioned the Crown for a reduction in his composition rent. In support of his petition he submitted a certificate signed by three justices of the peace (all of them strong Protestants) and other persons of standing in the neighbourhood, including ministers and churchwardens. According to this certificate he had always behaved himself like a loving and dutiful subject (his recusancy excepted) and had ever been esteemed an honest neighbour and a good housekeeper, completely free from any disorder or factious disposition. Few gentlemen could have hoped for a finer testimonial.[3]

[1] G. Albion, *Charles I and the Court of Rome*, 335. Rushworth, ii, 826.
[2] P.R.O., Star Chamber Proceedings, Star Chamber 8/227/35. See also above, 136.
[3] P.R.O., S.P.Dom., Charles I, S.P.16/ccclxviii/66.

CHAPTER X

The Cost of Recusancy

THE financial position of the recusant gentry deserves particular attention. For besides the general hazards which threatened the landed interest they had to face the special problems of a religious minority under economic pressure: fines and sequestration of property, discriminatory taxation, exclusion from office and the professions. As a result we have an opportunity to study the fortunes of a distinct group of country gentry whose fiscal burdens were, potentially at least, far heavier than normal and who, at the same time, were disabled from supplementing the income from their estates. Taken at their face value the penal laws represented a grave threat to the material interests of the Catholic landowning families. Yet the gravity of the situation cannot be judged merely on the evidence of the penal laws. In this chapter we shall be considering what impact the economic sanctions had in practice and how the recusant gentry fared in comparison with their Protestant neighbours.

Before 1581 the financial penalties for recusancy can hardly have troubled the Catholic gentry. For each day's absence from church (whether a Sunday or a special day of obligation) the churchwardens were empowered to levy a fine of 12d. for the use of the poor. To a country squire this was a trifling amount, but as the Catholic revival gathered strength so the financial penalties were increased. Under an act of 1581 convicted recusants could be fined £20 for every month they stayed away from church: on the basis of a twenty-eight day month this represented an annual levy of £260, an enormous sum for all but the richest Catholics. In 1587 statutory provision was made for the recusant who failed to pay this monthly fine: in such cases the Crown could in future confiscate two-thirds of the defaulter's lands and all his goods and chattels. Subsequently, in 1606, there was a further legislative change enabling the Crown to refuse the fine of £20 a month in the case of wealthy families and to take possession of two-thirds of their landed property even though there had been no default over payment.[1]

These were the main types of financial penalty which could be levied on persons guilty of recusancy. Considerable fines could also be imposed for noncommunicancy, though not until the reign of James I. Under an act of 1606 Catholics who occasionally attended church to escape the penalties of recusancy were required to take the sacrament at least once a year: refusal to comply rendered them liable to a fine of £20 for the first year, £40 for the second year and £60 in succeeding years.[2] In addition, there were fines for a variety of offences under the penal code, most of them originating in the period 1581–1606. A Catholic squire who gave shelter to a recusant or kept a recusant servant could be fined £10 a month for the period of the offence; if he declined to have his child baptised at the parish church a fine of £100 could be levied and if he sent one of his sons to a continental seminary this could likewise cost him £100.[3] Finally, there were the penalties for refusing to take the oath of allegiance introduced in 1606: forfeiture of all lands and goods as well as imprisonment for life.[4]

So far as the major penalties for recusancy are concerned the period 1581–1642 falls naturally into two parts: 1581–1620, when the Crown generally observed the letter, if not necessarily the spirit, of the law and 1620–42, when the government deliberately mitigated the force of the law by means of specific directions to its commissioners and other officials.

The waves of intense persecution which marked the period 1581–1620 might lead us to suppose that the financial weapons would be ruthlessly employed in the general onslaught on Catholicism. In the main, however, there was a considerable gulf between theory and practice. This was due less to any explicit forbearance on the part of the Crown than to the imperfections of the fining system, the venality of officials and the evasive tactics of recusants. In effect the lack of an efficient and reliable bureaucracy and the profusion of influential connections virtually ruled out any possibility of mulcting the Catholic gentry as heavily as the law permitted.

[1] 1 Elizabeth I c.ii (Act of Uniformity). 23 Elizabeth I, c.i. 29 Elizabeth I, c.vi. 3 James I, c.iv.
[2] 3 James I, c.iv.
[3] 35 Elizabeth I, c.i and 3 James I, c.iv. 3 James I, c.v. 1 James I, c.iv.
[4] 3 James I, c.iv. 7 James I, c.vi.

The first point to be noted is that very few recusants paid the fine of £20 a month as a regular charge. At the end of Elizabeth's reign, for example, the total number for the whole country stood at sixteen and in 1613 had dropped to six. The only Yorkshireman to pay the fine over a substantial period was John Sayer of Great Worsall, a wealthy squire for whom the sum of £260 a year was no great burden.[1] Most recusants were either unable or unwilling to pay this amount and from 1587 onwards their default enabled the sequestration machinery to be set in motion. As time went on the imposition of the monthly fine became largely a formality: although the Exchequer recusant rolls contain many entries of this sort the authorities were, on the whole, simply observing the necessary preliminaries leading to the seizure of property. This might suggest that a greater yield was expected from the confiscated estates of well-to-do Catholics: in Yorkshire, however, only one recusant gentleman, Philip Constable of Everingham, paid more than £260 a year in rent to the Crown during the period 1581–1642.[2]

Faced with the threat of expropriation the recusant gentry naturally took what steps they could to delay or soften the blow. In order to deceive the commissioners and juries appointed to value their property they often resorted to fraudulent conveyances which apparently transferred ownership but in reality left them in effective possession. Even after the valuation had been carried out there was still ample opportunity to alter the course of events through the use of influence, bribery, or legal pleading. Thus in 1606 it was alleged that the greater part of William Middleton's estate, after being found by inquisition and 'returned' into the Exchequer, had been discharged on the instructions of Henry Spiller, one of the Exchequer officials. In many cases a recusant was able to claim successfully that his property was not subject to seizure because of some technical irregularity such as an error of wording in the commission issued out of the Exchequer. As a result the estate remained untouched until a new inquisition could be taken.[3]

Some idea of the lengths to which the more ingenious Catholics were prepared to go may be derived from the Star Chamber proceedings

---

[1] B.M., Lansdowne MSS 153, f.177. P.R.O., S.P.Dom., James I, S.P.14/lxxx/68 and Exchequer, Recusant Rolls, E.377/13 and 32. C.R.S., xviii, 18.

[2] Between 1636 and 1642 Philip Constable paid £263. 6s. 8d. a year for the statutory two-thirds of his estate. His income amounted to some £1300 a year when his rent was originally fixed. (C.R.S., lxxx, 427–36. See below, 222).)

[3] B.M., Lansdowne MSS 153, ff.9, 123, 161, 169, 266, 301. P.R.O., S.P.Dom., James I, S.P.14/cxv/9 and S.P.Dom., Charles I, S.P.16/lxxxviii/21.

5. Monument to Sir Timothy Hutton of Marske (1569–1629), Richmond
Parish Church, North Riding. *See page* 124.

6. Effigy of Sir Marmaduke Wyvill of Constable Burton (1540–1618), Masham Parish Church, North Riding. *See page* 128.

brought against Thomas Pudsey of Hackforth in 1617. A lawyer who acted on behalf of northern recusants, Pudsey was alleged to have resorted to various devices in his efforts to avoid the penalties arising from his own absence from church. When the authorities in Yorkshire began to take notice of his own and his wife's recusancy they moved to Surrey where they were unknown. There (it was claimed) they went under the names of James and Ann (his wife's real name was Philippa). In due course the local magistrates convicted them of recusancy and process was awarded out of the Exchequer, but referring to them under their assumed names. They then went to live in Sussex, often moving around from place to place. Growing rich on the fruits of his legal practice, Pudsey bought the manor of Hackforth in the North Riding and had it conveyed to certain friends of his who lived far away from Yorkshire, allegedly to their own use; in practice, however, he received the profits. When Pudsey and his wife went to live at Hackforth the churchwardens were going to present them both for recusancy but he managed to persuade them to indict only his wife, in the name of Ann Pudsey. Process was eventually issued out of the Exchequer but as the name was incorrectly given no fine could be levied. Philippa Pudsey was subsequently convicted under her real name yet, it was argued, her husband's deception had resulted in a great loss to the Crown. Since Pudsey died in 1620 his religious sympathies must have cost him little financially.[1]

In this period the statutory two-thirds of a recusant's estate were normally leased out at a rent corresponding to the assessed value. Everything therefore depended on the accuracy of the valuation. For this purpose there were two alternative types of commission: a general commission directed to the sheriff and magistrates of the county and a special commission issued at the suit of an influential recusant to persons of his own nomination. Naturally there was little prospect of an objective inquiry when a special commission was involved: the commissioners were often friends of the owner and the returns which they submitted usually valued the property at an extremely low rate. In 1608, for example, it was alleged that the estates of John Gascoigne of Barnbow had, through an agreement between his brother Leonard and one or more of the commissioners, been certified at £50 a year for the Crown's two parts and had since been found at £160 a year. In fact the

---

[1] P.R.O., Star Chamber Proceedings, Star Chamber 8/24/1. B.M., Lansdowne MSS 153, f.286.

15*

whole property appears to have been worth about £1000 a year at this time.[1] Whatever the type of commission the valuation system was hopelessly inadequate: no proper survey was carried out, lands and goods were frequently concealed and jurymen were often reluctant to be too hard on their recusant neighbours. In the circumstances it is hardly surprising that the rent for the statutory two-thirds rarely bore any relation to the true value. A few examples may be quoted:

	Annual rent	Actual yearly value
Everingham Cressy of Birkin	£100	£1000
Sir Ralph Babthorpe of Osgodby	£62. 12s. 0d.	£1380
John Vavasour of Hazlewood and his nephew William Vavasour	£39. 4s. 8d.	over £2000[2]

In the same way, the sums laid on recusants for their goods and chattels were relatively small, and indeed were sometimes remitted altogether.[3]

During the reign of Elizabeth leases of recusant estates were mostly granted to courtiers, royal officials and speculators who foresaw the possibility of easy pickings. In 1605 Sir Robert Cecil told the Venetian ambassador that 'under the late Queen the sequestrated property passed to strangers who, in order to wring as much out of it as possible, ruined the houses and lands of the recusants'.[4] In Yorkshire, however, the Crown lessee rarely entered into possession: usually he sold his interest to the owner or to trustees acting on the owner's behalf, presumably on account of the distance from London. One Catholic squire who secured a lease in this way was John Rokeby of Mortham. In 1590 the statutory two-thirds of his estate were conveyed to Lawrence Dutton, one of the messengers of Her Majesty's Chamber, but he quickly assigned the lease to Ralph Lawson of Brough, a Catholic relative of the owner who was clearly no more than a trustee.[5] In the reign of James I recusant landowners could become tenants of their forfeited estates from the outset although a penal statute of 1606

---

[1] P.R.O., S.P.Dom., James I, S.P.14/cxv/9 and Charles I, S.P.16/lxxxviii/21. B.M., Lansdowne MSS 153, ff.267, 286, 301. Foley, iii, 182.

[2] P.R.O., Exchequer, Recusant Rolls, E.377/21 and Chancery Proceedings, C.7/782/71 and C.8/49/47. B.M., Lansdowne MSS 153, f. 286.

[3] B.M., Lansdowne MSS 153, ff.169, 201, 203, 204, 301.

[4] Cal.S.P.Venetian 1603–7, 229.   [5] C.R.S., liii, 304.

expressly forbade the granting of leases either to convicted recusants or to their representatives. During the period 1603–20 very few leases were granted to Yorkshire recusants in name but in most cases the sequestered property was let to a friend or kinsman, often a man of Catholic sympathies, who was simply the nominal lessee. In 1608 it was asserted that many recusant estates had been so undervalued at the inquisition that few outsiders (and this is probably a reference to London-based speculators) felt it worth their while to seek a lease. Even when an outsider offered to pay a higher rent than the owner his offer was not necessarily accepted. In 1605, we are told, the estates of John Gascoigne of Barnbow were let to his own use (nominally to his kinsman Sir William Gascoigne) at a rent of £60 a year, although there were would-be tenants ready to pay significantly more.[1]

This favourable state of affairs was marred to some extent by the practice, not infrequent in the early part of James I's reign, of making an outright grant of the benefits arising from a person's recusancy to a courtier or royal official. An entry book of grants made between 1606 and 1611 contains the names of thirty-five Yorkshire gentry.[2] A number of these recusants were unconvicted and in such cases the grantee was usually required to secure a conviction within twelve months, otherwise the grant became void. So far as can be seen most of the unconvicted recusants managed to escape formal conviction while several recusants who had already been convicted took refuge in conformity.

In a report on northern Catholicism made in 1607 the bishop of Bristol noted that, when the king was pleased to give the penalty of any recusant, composition was made between the parties for a small sum of money; the recusant's lands were then deliberately valued at a lower rate so that the king was often induced to give again because the grant seemed of little worth.[3] Some convicted recusants in Yorkshire were 'granted' more than once but generally speaking the Crown's two-thirds were soon in lease, often to a relative or friend of the owner. The case of William Middleton of Stockeld may be cited. The benefits of his recusancy were assigned in 1607, and again in 1608, to John Naismith, a royal official, and it cost him £500 to buy out the grantee.

[1] 3 James I, c.iv. B.M., Lansdowne MSS 153, ff.115, 169.
[2] B.M., Additional MSS 34765 (a book of entries of all recusants 'granted' under the Signet, 1606–1611).
[3] B.M., Lansdowne MSS 153, f.266.

In return, Naismith procured for him a lease of two-thirds of his estate, which was made out to Sir William Ingleby of Ripley, a relative of Middleton.[1]

Until the reign of Charles I the collection of rents and fines was primarily the responsibility of the sheriff and his officials. To illustrate the inefficiency of this system we may take the case of a noncommunicant, Thomas Barnby of Barnby Hall in the township of Cawthorne. For neglecting to receive communion between 31 October 1615 and 1 November 1616 he was fined £60, half to the Crown and half to the person bringing the information. Unless there had been some distraint for which the evidence is lacking no attempt was made to collect the money owing to the Exchequer until 1623 when the sheriff extended his lands at the extremely low rate of £20 a year and took £8. 1s. 2d. from the issues. In 1624 the new sheriff secured a further £20 but the debt was not finally settled until 1626.[2] Through the laxity and corruption of the sheriff's officers a recusant squire sometimes avoided payment of his rent. In 1613 a list of recusants was compiled showing their arrears of rent: among the Yorkshire recusants were George Catterick, who had died twenty years before (£700), Anthony Catterick his son (£484), Thomas Meynell (£754), Katherine Radcliffe (£618) and William Middleton (£509).[3] From time to time commissions were issued for the levying of arrears but these were only partially effective. Sometimes a Catholic landowner compounded for his debts or undertook to pay them off in a series of instalments; in other cases the heirs were discharged from payment. If the rents from Catholic estates came in slowly the Crown had even greater cause for dissatisfaction over the modest receipts which found their way into the Exchequer from the forfeited goods of recusants; indeed in 1615, the arrears for the whole country were said to amount to 'many thousands'.[4] There was, however, another side to the picture. The sheriff's officers and the special agents employed in searching for concealed property or levying of arrears were not always averse to extorting money from recusants and taking rents or goods for their own use. One of the most notorious agents was Richard Heaton, who worked mainly in York-

---

[1] B.M., Additional MSS 34765, ff.19, 23, and Lansdowne MSS 153, f.81. P.R.O., Signet Office Docquets, Index 6803, June 1608 (no pagination).

[2] Sheffield Central Library: Spencer Stanhope MSS 60255 and 60278.

[3] P.R.O., S.P.Dom., James I, S.P.14/lxxvii/49.

[4] P.R.O., S.P.Dom., James I, S.P.14/lxxx/67.

shire. His activities caused such an uproar that in 1610 he was tried in the Court of Star Chamber for receiving bribes and fraudulently converting the goods of Catholics and 'conformable Protestants.'[1]

Besides the major penalties the recusant gentry had other financial charges laid on them for their religion. On occasion they were required to contribute to the cost of providing light horse for national defence (though in 1599 some Yorkshire gentlemen declined to pay). In the early years of James I's reign, following the discovery of the Gunpowder Plot, they were regularly summoned before the Northern High Commission and if they failed to appear (as often happened) were fined £50 or £100. According to Father Sharpe, one of the chaplains serving the Babthorpe family, the sheriff's officers were apt in such cases to seize goods worth twice the amount of the fine.[2] There were also fines for other Catholic offences which could be imposed either in the ecclesiastical courts or at the quarter sessions. Of these the commonest type was the levy of £10 a month for keeping a recusant servant: in the case of a strongly Catholic household this might involve sums amounting to hundreds of pounds. In practice, however, such fines had little financial significance for the simple reason that they were rarely collected, or at least not in full. The case of Roger Tocketts, a North Riding gentleman, may well have been typical. At the Thirsk sessions in 1624 he was fined £50 for employing a recusant maidservant over a period of five months. This sum remained unpaid for a number of years but finally in April 1635 he compounded with the commissioners for the recusant revenue who accepted 66s. 8d. in full satisfaction of the debt. The commission of 1627 and subsequent commissions did in fact give specific authority for such compositions where Catholics were in arrears with their fines.[3] From 1606 onwards the Catholic gentry faced the prospect of forfeiting all their material possessions for refusing the oath of allegiance. Many took the oath or managed to avoid taking it without incurring punishment. As a result there were few cases of expropriation: in Yorkshire only two recusant gentlemen (William Vavasour of Hazlewood and William Stillington of Kelfield) appear to

---

[1] P.R.O., Star Chamber Proceedings, Star Chamber 8/11/12.
[2] F. C. Dietz, *English Public Finance 1558–1641*, 54, 87. J. J. Cartwright (ed.), *Chapters in the History of Yorkshire*, 180–1. J. Morris (ed.), *The Troubles of Our Catholic Forefathers*, Series iii, 456.
[3] P.R.O., Exchequer, Recusant Rolls, E.377/38 and Chancery, Patent Rolls, C.66/2441 (commission of 1627).

have had their estates sequestered for declining the oath and they were able to regain possession comparatively quickly.[1]

On the whole, the burdens falling on the recusant gentry in the period 1581–1620, taken in isolation, cannot be regarded as disastrously heavy. In practice such men were usually able to farm their estates from the Crown at low rents (which were not always paid) while in normal circumstances their goods remained largely untouched. On the other hand, a recusant squire could be put to considerable expense in paying fees and bribes to officials, in buying off an outsider who had secured a grant or lease of his property or in challenging the legality of the Exchequer proceedings. In addition, he had good reason to fear the excesses of local officials and the activities of informers who continued to trouble Catholics even after conviction.

If the recusant gentry had their grievances the government for its part was becoming increasingly dissatisfied over the inadequacies of the fining system. The yield was relatively small and, in the words of Sir Edward Osborne, 'the Sherife Levys and Paiements through their under-sherifs negligence or knavery are very slow, if ever made at all'. During the 1620's various schemes were proposed which had the dual aim of eradicating the worst features of the system as seen through Catholic eyes and providing a greater and more settled revenue for the Crown.[2]

The various modifications introduced in these years are summarised in a memorandum, probably dating from 1630, which has survived among the state papers of Charles I's reign.[3] This shows how the Crown, through its commissioners and ministers, had moderated the penal laws in a number of ways:

1. The Crown now aimed to take only one-third of the recusant's estate.

2. In such cases the recusant was allowed to keep all his goods.

3. Where a recusant had compounded for his estate he was not liable to pay anything for his wife's recusancy nor was she to be imprisoned on this account.

---

[1] B.M., Lansdowne MSS 153, f.87. P.R.O., Signet Office Docquets, Index 6804, February 1612(–13) (no pagination), S.P.Dom., James I, S.P.14/lxxx/251 and Chancery Proceedings, C.3/380/3.

[2] Sheffield Central Library: Strafford Letters, xviii. Osborne to Wentworth, 13 May 1638. P.R.O., S.P.Dom., James I, S.P.14/cxv/9 and Charles I, S.P.16/liii/35 and lxxxviii/21.

[3] P.R.O., S.P.Dom., Charles I, S.P.16/clxxviii/45.

4. No informer was permitted to sue a recusant who had compounded either on account of his own or his wife's recusancy.

5. After conviction neither the recusant nor his wife was to be punished in the ecclesiastical courts for recusancy.

6. After compounding a recusant was not subject to any further process, commission or inquisition except for lands omitted or newly purchased or inherited which had not been included in his composition.

7. Recusants could take leases of their own lands or alternatively have them made out to trustees on their behalf.

In 1627, as we have seen, a new fining system was introduced with the appointment of commissioners (including the lord president of the Council of the North) who were empowered to 'treat and make composition with' northern recusants for leases of their estates.[1] For the collection of rents and fines the Crown appointed a receiver-general who took over the responsibilities which the sheriffs had previously discharged. During Wentworth's tenure of this office (1629–40) there was a marked increase in efficiency and the old abuses appear to have been largely checked.

In the reign of Charles I there was hardly a recusant gentleman in Yorkshire who failed to secure a lease of his estates, either in his own name or in the name of a relative or friend. Usually the lease was for forty-one years, the maximum term which could be granted. In assessing the composition to be paid the commissioners were required to take into account all freehold property, all leases and such additional sources of income as coalmines. For valuation purposes it was still the normal procedure to hold an open inquisition with a jury in attendance, though compositions were sometimes passed without any inquisition being taken. In addition, the commissioners employed special agents to seek out the true values of recusant estates.

When he appeared before the commissioners a Catholic landowner often produced evidence of annuities and other recurrent charges on his estate. Not infrequently a composition was abated for this reason, provision being made for increases in the rent as and when such liabilities ceased. Thus in 1630 Thomas Tankard of Boroughbridge submitted that there were rent-charges and annuities amounting in all to £376 a year; the commissioners therefore fixed his composition at £66. 13s. 4d. a year, eventually rising to £192 a year on the expiration of these charges.[2]

[1] See above, 200–1. [2] C.R.S., liii, 346–7.

In some cases the amount of the composition represented one-third of the inquisition value, in other cases two-thirds or more. As a general rule, however, the inquisition value was a mere fraction of the actual value. Even if the commissioners had more reliable information at their disposal they were apparently unwilling to take full advantage of this: in 1637, for example, the estates of Thomas Lord Fairfax of Emley were assessed at £2753. 6s. 6d. a year yet his rent was fixed at only £251. 13s. 4d., subsequently rising to some £306.[1] Sometimes a recusant squire managed to secure an easy composition through the influence of a friend or kinsman in high places. In 1633 Lord Wentworth told Sir John Coke that he had approached the king on behalf of his uncle Sir Francis Trappes of Harrogate, 'that haveing twelve children, and being a Thowsand poundes in debt, his Freehold landes not above seaven-score poundes a yeare, I might be admitted to Compound him and his eldest Sonne their Recusancy for eight poundes a yeare'. This approach was successful and in due course the necessary instructions were issued.[2]

For the most part the composition rents were considerably greater than the rents which were being paid at the time the commission of 1627 was introduced. Even so, few Catholic gentlemen were required to pay as much as one-fifth of their total income and many in fact paid less than one-tenth. The following examples[3] may be given in illustration:

	Annual rent	Actual yearly value
Marmaduke Holtby of Scackleton	£20	£150
Sir Ralph Ellerker of Risby and his son Ralph	£50	£600
Sir John Gascoigne of Barnbow	£60	£1200

On the whole, the Yorkshire compounders paid their rents reasonably promptly. In 1638 Sir Edward Osborne, who served as Wentworth's deputy, could write that 'noe revenue the Kinge hathe comes in soe speedily or certainly as this'. This fact testifies not only to the increased efficiency of the system but also to the continuing ability of Catholic landowners to meet their fiscal obligations. Occasionally a recusant

[1] C.R.S.: Recusant History, iv, 63.
[2] Sheffield Central Library: Strafford Letters, v, 7. P.R.O., Signet Office Docquets, Index 6809, 16 September 1633 (no pagination).
[3] P.R.O., Exchequer, Recusant Rolls, E.377/36, and S.P.Dom., Charles I, S.P.16/ clxxviii/40. Leeds Central Library: Gascoigne of Barnbow MSS, GC/E12/2/2.

squire (Sir Edward Plumpton for example) appears to have had difficulty in paying his rent but there is nothing to suggest that this was a common problem.[1]

Apart from his composition rent a Catholic squire had little to pay on account of his recusancy: no fines in the ecclesiastical courts, no forfeiture of goods, no expensive litigation, no payments to outsiders who had acquired an interest in his estate, no significant outlay on fees and gratuities to royal officials. At the same time, the reign of Charles I saw an increase in discriminatory taxation: under the subsidy acts of 1625, 1627 and 1640 convicted recusants of substance were required to pay twice the normal rate of tax. Even at this double rate, however, the subsidy was a comparatively mild form of taxation and in any case there were ways and means of evading the special levy. In April 1641 a West Riding magistrate wrote that 'the recusants, knowing the burthen by the former double impositions in the same kind, do cunningly avoid it; in some places by procuring others to be named subsidy-men (being conformable, or at least not convict) and they themselves to be contributors or bearers with them underhand. And in other places they get advantage by want of certificate made to the commissioners of their conviction'.[2] Between 1627 and 1642 Catholics were rarely fined for offences other than recusancy. This was largely a matter of policy as the authorities were anxious that nothing should prejudice the success of their new system of compositions.[3]

From this survey of the period 1581–1642 the most striking fact which emerges is the discrepancy between statutory provision and administrative practice. If the financial penalties had been rigorously applied the recusant gentry would have faced disaster: in fact the pressure was not so consistently heavy as to force them inexorably into bankruptcy and ruin. The situation might have become critical had the special circumstances of the period 1606–12 continued indefinitely. In these years, when the Jacobean persecution was at its height, the recusant gentry had to endure a multiplication of exactions and charges: fines for neglecting to appear before the Northern High Commission, payments to the grantees of their estates, rents for the statutory two-thirds, pillaging of goods,

---

[1] Sheffield Central Library: Strafford Letters, xviii. Osborne to Wentworth, 13 May 1638 and xii. Thomas Littell to Wentworth, 4 April 1631.

[2] 1 Charles I, c.vi. 3 Charles I, c.viii. 16 Charles I, c.ii. *Fairfax Correspondence*, ii, 206.

[3] Knowler, ii, 159.

legal expenses and fees. With such pressures it is hardly surprising to find a number of recusant squires in financial difficulties at this time. On the other hand, the impact on the Catholic gentry as a whole must not be exaggerated: in 1612 there were only twenty-six heads of families charged with recusancy payments in the Exchequer records.[1]

The fiscal burden which fell on the recusant gentry cannot be considered entirely in isolation for its impact naturally varied according to the financial circumstances of individual families. We must therefore examine the other main items of expenditure. In the first place, there was the financial provision which a man of property normally made for his wife, his daughters and his younger sons: as we have already seen, this could weigh heavily on the heir when he succeeded to the estate. Under the new system of compositions rent-charges and annuities were taken into account in fixing the rent but, even so, they might absorb a substantial part of the compounder's income, as the following example will show:

Philip Constable of Everingham 1632–3

	per annum		
	£	s	d
net income (after deduction of outgoing rents)	1359	9	4½
annuities	399	13	4
to the king for recusancy	250	0	0
remains clear	970	16	0½

'out of which the house and familye is to be kept/3656 li. debte to be payde and childrens portions to be raised'.

On the face of it, this was a difficult situation and Philip Constable could well have complained at the harshness of his composition which was one of the highest in England. Nevertheless he paid his rent promptly and the Constable estates survived not only the recusancy impositions of Charles I's reign but also the greater vicissitudes of the Civil War period.[2]

Education was another item of expenditure. A well-to-do Catholic squire often employed a private tutor for his children, though the chaplain sometimes undertook this function. Each year large sums of

---

[1] P.R.O., Exchequer, Recusant Rolls, E.377/21 and Abbreviate of Receipts (Pells), E.401/2302.

[2] This table has been compiled from figures given in *C.R.S.*, lii, 433–5. See also below 369, and P. Roebuck, 'The Constables of Everingham. The Fortunes of a Catholic Royalist Family During the Civil War and Interregnum', *C.R.S.: Recusant History*, ix, 75.

money were sent abroad for the maintenance of students and nuns in the English seminaries and convents. During the reign of Charles I the authorities at Douai usually charged 200 or 240 florins a year (broadly speaking, around £50 in sterling) in the case of fee-paying students, although it was claimed in 1641 that no convictor could be educated at less than 300 florins a year, taking all expenses into account. In comparison, a contemporary at Oxford or Cambridge might cost his father £40, £50 or £60 a year if he was a fellow-commoner. At Douai the convictor was supposed to pay his fees monthly, six months in advance, but sometimes it was necessary for a member of the college staff to journey through England on a debt-collecting mission.[1] Families wishing to send a daughter to one of the continental nunneries had to pay a dowry which might vary in amount from £200 to over £500. In 1635 Sir John Coke told Wentworth that 'there is a nunnery now erected at Paris wherein are settled twelve sisters and a ladie Abbesse, whither they labour daily to drawe more from hence of the better qualitie, of whom they require porcions of £400 a peace to make them of the Quire or lesse summes if they be putt to bee laundresses and to doe meaner service'.[2] Naturally only the richer sort could afford to pay dowries of this size, yet they probably cost no more than the marriage portions which would otherwise have been required. In 1636 Henry Lawson of Brough made provision in his will for a portion of £500 for his daughter Mary and £400 each for his daughters Dorothy and Anne. Dorothy eventually married but Mary entered the Benedictine convent at Ghent where the usual charge for a dowry was £400.[3]

At this time litigation was a frequent cause of indebtedness among the landed classes. Before the new system of compositions was introduced a Catholic squire might be put to considerable legal expense in attempting to delay the seizure of his estate. On the other hand, few recusant gentry appear to have become involved in Chancery lawsuits. Under an act of 1606[4] a convicted recusant could not bring an action

[1] *C.R.S.*, x, xi, xxx, xxxvii and xl, *passim*, and in particular x, 315, 322, 324, 360, 394, 409 and xl, 473. I am indebted to Professor Charles Wilson for advice on the sterling equivalent of a Spanish Netherlands florin.

[2] W. M. Brady, *Annals of the Catholic Hierarchy in England and Scotland 1585–1876*, 90. Sheffield Central Library: Strafford Letters, xiv. Coke to Wentworth, 21 January 1634(-5).

[3] P.R.O., Chancery, *Inquisitions Post Mortem*, Charles I, C.142/dxxxv/116. *Surtees Society*, xxxvi, 90.

[4] 3 James I, c.v.

in the courts except over landed property but it is probable that financial caution was the major factor.

On the whole, the recusant gentry did not suffer too badly from the fiscal consequences of wardship. Between the years 1600 and 1642 there were 102 families which at one time or another had their main estates seized for recusancy and of these no more than twenty-two families experienced a minority during this period. Although the exactions of the Court of Wards could be burdensome there are very few cases of a Catholic family becoming seriously indebted on this account.

In the more ancient Catholic families particularly there was often a tradition of liberal hospitality. William Middleton of Stockeld, for example, was esteemed as a man who kept a good house even when he was suffering from the financial penalties of recusancy, while John Vavasour of Hazlewood Castle had such a reputation for hospitality that he was described on one occasion as 'the only great and bountiful housekeeper in the north'.[1] Faced with the problems which recusancy brought in its train some Catholic gentry found it difficult to adjust their standard of living to meet the new circumstances. Others (and these were probably the majority) wisely resorted to a policy of retrenchment. In the reign of Charles I Thomas Tankard of Boroughbridge compounded for an estate which his father had left heavily encumbered with debts and annuities. In 1637 he described in a petition to the king how his financial difficulties had forced him to give up housekeeping (and till then he had been regarded as a 'good housekeeper'). Four years later he conveyed his lands, worth over £700 a year, to trustees for the payment of debts, reserving to himself only £100 a year. In December 1641 he and his family were said to be living in York but as events turned out his efforts to save the estate proved successful.[2]

In the search for economies prudence and necessity demanded a curtailment of luxury spending. From this point of view the restrictions on movement were a blessing in disguise since there was little danger that a recusant squire would be drawn into the extravagant world of London society. One type of expenditure which could easily be avoided was the money spent on titles. In this period a number of Catholic gentry acquired knighthoods or baronetcies but these were

---

[1] C.R.S., lvi, 10. Foley, iv, 692.

[2] P.R.O., S.P.Dom., Charles I, S.P.16/ccclxviii/66 and Committee for Compounding, S.P.23/clxxii/273, 275 and cclviii/60. Fairfax Correspondence, ii, 230.

almost invariably 'schismatics'. Although several recusants were granted baronetcies in the reign of Charles I, only one (John Gascoigne of Barnbow) actually paid for the honour and even then this was a relatively inexpensive Nova Scotia baronetcy.[1] In this period the landed classes engaged in housebuilding on an extensive scale and many Catholic gentry followed the prevailing fashion. It is significant, however, that very few recusant squires indulged in this form of expenditure. Sometimes a new house was built before the head of the family was convicted for recusancy: thus Michael Wentworth of Woolley completed his housebuilding in 1635 and shortly afterwards emerged as a recusant, compounding for his estate in 1637. Even so, the 'old decayed house' of the Thimbleby family may well have been typical of the manor-houses which the ultra-Catholic gentry were inhabiting at the time of the Civil War.[2]

The financial penalties represented the main economic consequence of recusancy but in addition there were the artificial limitations on income. In the reign of Elizabeth open Catholics were normally excluded from offices of profit, though they were not legally debarred until the following reign. By an act of 1606 no one convicted of recusancy or having a recusant wife could hold any public office in the kingdom; at the same time, convicted recusants were forbidden to practise law or medicine or to serve in any military or naval appointment.[3]

Although it is difficult to assess the effect of these restrictive measures on the recusant gentry the immediate impact appears to have been negligible in practice. Men of Catholic sympathies who were holding offices of profit in the early years of Elizabeth's reign usually preferred to hide their religion and the same motive helped to strengthen the loyalty of 'schismatics' like Sir William Ingleby and Sir Nicholas Fairfax when the Northern Rebellion broke out.[4] Moreover, it must be recognised that here again the law was not always observed. Anthony Metcalfe of Aldbrough, for example, was both a convicted recusant and a successful lawyer: in 1607 it was alleged that he travelled up to

---

[1] A Nova Scotia baronetcy cost £166. 13s. 4d.

[2] *H.M.C. Various*, ii, 371. Sheffield Central Library: Strafford Letters, xv. Michael Wentworth to Lord Wentworth, 13 May 1635. P.R.O., Exchequer, Recusant Rolls, E.377/50 and S.P.Dom., Committee for Compounding, S.P.23/lviii/48.

[3] 3 James I, c.v.

[4] *Cal.S.P.Dom., Addenda, 1547–65*, 567. *Cal.S.P.Dom., Elizabeth Addenda, 1566–79*, 91, 181.

London every term on legal business although as a recusant he should not have been allowed within ten miles of the capital.[1]

If the recusant gentry were almost wholly dependent on the rents and profits of their estates this situation probably owed little to the harshness of the penal code. Generally speaking, the Old Religion had few attractions for the lawyers and merchants who were bringing new wealth into the squirearchy: they were more inclined towards Puritanism in religion. For the most part the Catholic gentry consisted of ancient landowning families (in some cases grown rich through the acquisition of monastic property) which were deeply rooted in the soil and had few urban connections. In the final analysis it was probably the exclusion from local offices of profit which represented the worst feature of the penal restrictions.

As we have seen, the fact that a gentleman had no other source of revenue besides his estate did not necessarily mean that he was destined to suffer financial hardship. On the whole (and this is certainly true of the period in which recusant estates were subject to seizure and fining) there were no fundamental weaknesses in the economics of landownership *per se*. Although 'mere landowners' at the bottom of the scale found it difficult to make progress in an economic sense the upper and middling gentry included a significant number of prosperous squires who were enlarging their holdings.

The financial penalties, the artificial limitations on income and the restrictions on freedom of movement gave the recusant gentry a powerful incentive to concentrate on the task of increasing the yield from their estates. Sometimes the persecution of Catholics seriously hampered their efforts. In 1610 Father James Sharpe wrote of the activities of the Northern High Commission: 'Thus they continued, for the last four or five years past, fining monthly for not appearing, and so consequently driving goods for fines. By this, many have been brought to that case, that they neither durst keep stock upon their own ground, nor yet could let it out to others.'[2] In normal circumstances, however, there was much emphasis on good husbandry. Many recusant gentry were actively engaged in demesne farming and many sought to improve their estates. The Middletons of Stockeld and the Meynells of North Kilvington went in for large-scale enclosure while the Tempests of Broughton can be found developing their Roundhay property, con-

---

[1] B.M., Lansdowne MSS 153, f.169.
[2] J. Morris, *The Troubles of Our Catholic Forefathers*, Series iii, 457.

verting woodland into arable and erecting limekilns. Similarly, there was growing interest in the exploitation of minerals. The Wentworths of Woolley and the Irelands of Crofton mined coal and the Pudseys of Bolton lead and silver. The Sayers of Great Worsall, and later their relatives the Bulmers of Marrick, had extensive leadmines which in some years yielded £1000 clear profit. In short, a recusant squire often showed commendable enterprise in managing his estates.[1]

In considering the financial position of the recusant gentry we should not forget that many Catholic squires took refuge in outward conformity to save their estates. Until the reign of Charles I there were comparatively few heads of families paying recusancy fines, as the following examples[2] clearly show:

1592	16
1604	20
1612	26
1620	24
1642	56

In the period 1600–42 there were 271 families with Catholic sympathies but only 102 paid fines in respect of their main estates and many of these benefited from long stretches of conformity.

In 1642 none of the families paying composition rents for their estates had an income of £2000 a year or more. On the other hand, two-thirds of these families may be classed as upper or middling gentry, as may be seen from the following comparative table[3]:

Annual income from land in 1642	Families paying composition rents	Other Catholic families	Protestant families
£1000 and upwards	6	16	51
£250 but below £1000	29	38	177
under £250	21	53	288
Total	56	107	516

Notwithstanding the amount of landed wealth which they possessed,

---

[1] *N.R. Records*, i, 78. Leeds Central Library: Temple Newsam MSS, TN/PO 1/111. Y.A.S. Library: MS 381 (t). *Y.A.J.*, xii, 16. *V.C.H., Yorkshire*, ii 375. P.R.O., S.P.Dom., Committee for Compounding, S.P.23/cxxii/67, Chancery Proceedings, Six Clerks' Series, C.7/457/73, and Commonwealth Exchequer Papers, S.P.28/215, order book 1651 seq., f.102. For the Meynells and the Tempests see also below, 375–7.

[2] *C.R.S.*, xviii, 41–110. P.R.O., Exchequer, Recusant Rolls, E.377/13, 21, 29, 48–50.

[3] For a discussion of sources see above, 27–8.

comparatively few of the recusant gentry increased their holdings. In the years 1600–42 only nineteen families acquired new property and even then their land-buying normally occurred in a period of conformity. Once a Catholic squire had his estate seized for recusancy he could rarely afford to spend money on either land purchase or housebuilding: in putting his religion first, therefore, he virtually forfeited any prospect of material advancement. Undoubtedly there were exceptions to the general rule but these were usually the fruit of special circumstances. The Gascoignes of Barnbow, who paid recusancy fines continuously from 1605 to 1642, provide a good illustration of this. During the reign of Charles I they bought a substantial amount of property which raised their income from £1200 to £1700 a year, and in 1635 John Gascoigne was the first Englishman to purchase a Nova Scotia baronetcy. Their prosperity may be attributed to two principal factors. In the first place, they appear to have avoided any heavy charges for their recusancy, paying only £60 a year for a lease of their estates. Secondly, they were exceptionally resourceful landowners, enclosing and developing their property, engaging in sheep-farming, mining coal extensively and lending money at interest.[1]

In an age when there was invariably a sizeable element of the gentry in economic decline (generally as a result of factors which were not directly related to estate management) the ultra-Catholic families were particularly prone to run into difficulties. The following table covers the period 1600–42:

	Number of families in financial straits	Total number of families in the period
families charged with recusancy payments on their main estates	52	102
other Catholic families	59	169
Protestant families	199	583

Not all the recusant families in difficulties owed their predicament to the impact of the penal laws. In some cases a family was already heavily indebted before the head of the household emerged as an open Catholic while in others the period of recusancy was too short to have had any significant economic consequences. In November 1630 Sir

---

[1] Leeds Central Library: Gascoigne of Barnbow MSS. P.R.O., Chancery Proceedings, Six Clerks' Series, C.5/402/106.

7. Passport granted to Thomas Westropp (Westhorpe) of Cornbrough, 1621. Note the signatures of members of the Privy Council, including Sir George Calvert. *See pages 76–7.*

8. Licence granted in 1595 to William Calverley and his wife, convicted recusants, permitting them to travel beyond a five-mile compass of their home, Calverley Hall, in the West Riding. *See page* 174.

John Hotham told Wentworth that Jocelyn Percy of Beverley, who had been summoned to compound for his recusancy, 'hath that which Sir Edwin Sands wisheth as the greatest mischiefe to his Eanemie: highe birth good mynde, and a poore Purse and a hard father alive, a wife and 5 children: debts to my knowledge of some lenthe unpayd'.[1] Another recusant squire, William Bulmer of Marrick, seems to have inherited his financial problems from his father, Sir Bertram, whose improvidence is commemorated in the lines of an old song:

> With new titles bought with his father's
> old gold,
> For which many of his father's old Manors
> were sold,
> Like a new Courtier of the King's and
> the King's new Courtier.[2]

When due allowance has been made for other causes of indebtedness, however, we are still left with the fact that the financial penalties for Catholic offences could have serious implications. For the most notable case of a recusant family struggling under the weight of such penalties we may turn to the Babthorpes of Osgodby. The Babthorpes had considerably increased their estates as a result of the dissolution of the monasteries[3] but between 1604 and 1633 they steadily disposed of all their landed property and Sir William Babthorpe, the last of the family to reside at Osgodby Hall, went to serve as a common soldier in the Spanish army. For a short time Sir Ralph Babthorpe paid the monthly fine of £20 and then in 1607 the benefits of his recusancy were granted to Lord Colville who had to be bought off. Subsequently, in 1609, he managed to secure a lease of his estates (worth about £1380 a year) at the modest rent of £62. 12s. od. Had this been all, the Babthorpes would probably have avoided financial disaster, but their devotion to the Old Religion involved them in other expenditure. Sir Ralph Babthorpe was fined for neglecting to appear before the Northern High Commission to answer for his recusancy while Sir William his son had to pay fines amounting to £400 or £500 for this offence and according to his mother 'was fined to pay such a sum of money' for harbouring priests 'as brought him to great poverty'. There can be little doubt,

---

[1] C.R.S., liii, 377.
[2] W. D. Hoyle, *Historical Notes of the Baronial House of Bulmer and Its Descendants*, 38–42, 53.
[3] See above, 15.

therefore, that the downfall of this family was primarily due to a succession of financial penalties. Yet when we consider that Sir Ralph Babthorpe was noted for his bountiful disposition, that he had several mansions adapted to the various seasons of the year and that he maintained a splendid establishment of more than thirty servants the question inevitably arises whether the Babthorpes ever seriously attempted to master their difficulties.[1]

The Babthorpes of Osgodby were no more typical of the recusant gentry than the Gascoignes of Barnbow. If the landed possessions of this group of families were tending, on the whole, to diminish, the fatality rate was extremely low: thus in the period 1600–42 only four of these families had to sell up all their property. Bad management or extravagance could soon breed insolvency, but the recusant squire who applied himself to good husbandry and eschewed luxury had a good prospect of saving his estate. There were two main dangers: first of all, a multiplication of fines and exactions, as happened in the early years of James I's reign and, secondly, the existence of other factors which were outside the individual's control. In the main, however, the ultra-Catholic gentry held out remarkably well. In the present century we find among the Yorkshire landowning classes a number of families which were noted for their recusancy in the early seventeenth century: these include the Annes of Frickley, the Gascoignes of Barnbow, the Vavasours of Hazlewood, the Lawsons of Brough, the Meynells of North Kilvington, the Cholmleys of Brandsby and the Tempests of Broughton. Calamitous in theory, the financial problems associated with recusancy were not necessarily insoluble. Austerity, not bankruptcy, was the keynote.

---

[1] T. Burton, *History and Antiquities of Hemingborough*, 246, 316–17, 319–21, 361. J. Morris (ed.), *The Troubles of Our Catholic Forefathers*, Series i, 237 and Series iii, 456–7. B.M., Additional MSS 34765, f.13. P.R.O., Exchequer, Recusant Rolls, E.377/29 and Chancery Proceedings, Six Clerks' Series, C.8/49/47. Foley, iii, 199–200. For case histories of other recusant families see Appendix B.

CHAPTER XI

The Government of the County

IN October 1614 the attorney general was informed that the king had taken notice of 'a great resort of gentlemen of quality and livelyhood... into the citty of London, and other principall citties and townes of this realme, with a purpose (as it appeareth) to settle their habitacion there'. This was likely to be of great prejudice to 'the generall gouverment of the kingdome when the country shalbe deprived of the assistance and presence of so many gentlemen, who for the most part beare office or authority in the counties where they dwell'.[1] Without a professional bureaucracy in the shires the Crown was heavily dependent on the country gentry in the field of local administration. It was the gentry who were largely responsible for the maintenance of law and order, the collection of taxes, the implementation of the Crown's social legislation and the organisation and training of the county militia. Together with members of the nobility they served as deputy lieutenants and justices of the peace while in most counties the sheriff was invariably drawn from this class of landed proprietors. In addition, they were employed as sewers commissioners, subsidy commissioners, colonels and captains of the trained bands, coroners and high constables of hundreds or wapentakes. Indeed, there were comparatively few gentlemen who did not serve in some public capacity or another during their lifetime.

In Yorkshire there were various enclaves which, to some extent at least, remained outside the general system of administration. These consisted of the towns of York and Hull which enjoyed county status and had their own sheriffs, and the palatine liberties such as Beverley and Ripon which had their own justices of the peace. Leaving these special cases aside there were three main administrative units: the county as a whole, the riding and the wapentake. At the county level the principal figures were the lord lieutenant and the sheriff. Each riding had its own commission of the peace which functioned as a separate body although a few men with wide territorial interests

[1] *Acts of the Privy Council 1613–14*, 596.

appeared on more than one commission. While, however, the justices were appointed to serve the riding as a whole it became the practice to allocate to them particular wapentakes for their day-to-day responsibilities, a procedure which was also followed in the case of deputy lieutenants and colonels of the trained bands. Superimposed on this basic structure was the authority of the Council of the North whose area of jurisdiction covered not only Yorkshire but also Durham, Cumberland, Westmorland and Northumberland. Besides the small cadre of professional members the Council included a number of leading squires, most of them drawn from the ranks of the Yorkshire gentry. While the number of lay councillors continued to increase, however, the judicial role of the Council tended more and more to overshadow its administrative functions and in the early seventeenth century the laymen usually attended the lord president only on the opening day of the general sessions.[1]

This chapter is primarily concerned with the major officials of the county other than the lord lieutenant: the sheriffs, the deputy lieutenants and the justices of the peace for the ridings.[2] The sheriff presided over the county court, superintended the election of knights of the shire, executed writs and collected fines and other debts owing to the Crown. Deputy lieutenants were responsible, under the general direction of the lord lieutenant, for the military preparedness of the county. Their duties consisted of mustering the able men of the shire, maintaining the efficiency of the trained bands and charging their fellow gentry with men and horses. Justices of the peace dealt with criminal offences, both individually and collectively at petty and quarter sessions: in the words of a seventeenth-century writer, they 'are dayly to administer Justice, and to execute their Office at home, and

---

[1] For the Council of the North see R. R. Reid, *The King's Council in the North* and F. W. Brooks, *The Council of the North* (Historical Association pamphlet G25).

[2] The names of sheriffs can be found in *P.R.O., Lists and Indexes*, ix: 'List of Sheriffs for England and Wales'. Deputy lieutenants are sometimes named in the commissions issued to lord lieutenants and recorded in the Patent Rolls (Chancery, Series C.66). During the reign of Charles I there are references to deputy lieutenants in the papers of Thomas Lord Wentworth (Sheffield Central Library) and in the State Papers Domestic. Lists of justices of the peace appear in the State Papers Domestic and the Patent Rolls. For a detailed account of sources see T. G. Barnes and A. Hassall Smith, 'Justices of the Peace from 1558 to 1688—a Revised List of Sources', *Bulletin of the Institute of Historical Research*, xxxii, 221. Other studies on local administration include T. G. Barnes, *Somerset, 1625–1640: a County's Government during the 'Personal Rule'* and A. Hassall Smith, 'The Elizabethan Gentry of Norfolk' (London Ph.D. thesis, 1959).

out of their sessions'.[1] In addition, they had a considerable range of administrative duties which tended to go on increasing. In the reign of Charles I we find them submitting reports on such matters as the binding of poor children as apprentices, the relief of the aged and impotent poor, and the regulation of the grain trade.[2]

As the duties of magistrates increased so did their numbers. In the early part of Elizabeth's reign there were usually between fifty and sixty men on the three Yorkshire commissions who were intended to be working justices, while in the reign of Charles I the figure ranged between eighty and a hundred. This in turn meant that a large number of gentry were to be found in the higher levels of local administration; in the period 1625–40, for example, a total of 161 Yorkshire gentlemen served as sheriffs, deputy lieutenants or justices of the peace. In detail:

sheriffs	16
deputy lieutenants	37
justices of the peace	157

These represented 136 families out of a total of some 750 families which appeared in the ranks of the Yorkshire gentry in this period.[3]

In the selection of men for the higher offices in the county the two key figures were the lord chancellor (or, if there was no lord chancellor, the lord keeper) and the lord president of the Council of the North who also, at least from the middle of Elizabeth's reign, served as lord lieutenant of Yorkshire. Other members of the Privy Council besides the lord chancellor might exercise influence in this field but his power was the greatest in the sense that he alone controlled appointments to the commission of the peace. This fact was well understood. In his book of precepts Christopher Wandesford warned his son against too frequent attendance at court but at the same time pointed out that

to have some Dependance there upon some Person of Honour and Power, who may give you Countenance, will be needfull...And above all others, whilst you live in the Countrey, your application to the Lord Chancellor will be of most Advantage for you in many Respects; as well to bring you into the more creditable Commissions, if you desire it, as to free you from them in Case you dispose otherwise of yourself.

[1] Michael Dalton, *The Countrey Justice*, 19.
[2] See for example, P.R.O., S.P.Dom., Charles I, S.P.16/ccxciii/11, 83, 106, 120, 129, 130.
[3] Three sheriffs (one of them also a deputy lieutenant) and one other deputy lieutenant were never appointed to the commission of the peace.

Wandesford also advised his son to cultivate the lord president of the Council of the North: 'And seeing your Patrimony is left under a provincial Government, it will be good Discretion to observe and gain the Favour of the Lord President by all the Application you can make unto him. Upon his first Entrance into his Government or your first Knowledge of him, endeavour to put some Obligation upon him more than by ordinary Attendance.' Christopher Wandesford had himself been fortunate in this respect because he and Wentworth were already close friends when the latter was made lord president.[1] As the Crown's principal representative north of the Trent the lord president was able, if he so wished, to bring considerable influence to bear to secure the appointment or dismissal of senior officials in the counties under his jurisdiction. In addition, he was involved in the process of selecting members of the Council of the North and deputy lieutenants who served under him when he was also lord lieutenant of Yorkshire.

Sheriffs were chosen by the monarch from a list of names (usually three for each county) which had been specially drawn up for this purpose. The procedure is described in a note preserved among the state papers which appears to have been written in 1638 and is entitled 'The order of making the bill for sheriffs in the Exchequer in *Crastino Animarum*'. The roll of nominees was prepared at a meeting of Privy Councillors and judges in the Exchequer. After certain preliminaries had been completed it was usual for the lord treasurer's remembrancer to read out, one shire at a time, the names of those who had appeared on the sheriffs' roll for the previous year but who had not been pricked. Next the judges 'in whose circuit the shire is will beginne to nominate to the Lords parsons fitt to fill up the bill to the number of three'. Then the Privy Councillors

either add to the parsons list in the last bill, or strike out some one and sometimes all of them, filling the bill with new names as their pleasure is. They never sett him before that was behind nor sitt any newe parson before one that remained in the old bill. The clarke of the Crowne attendeth with the booke of the peace, and there is ready a booke of all such as have beene sheriffes for these many yeares. It is comonly a good cause to be spared out of the bill, if one have beene sheriff within seven yeares last, except in Rutlandshire where the choice is small.

The account continues: 'When the Lords have gone thorough all the

---

[1] Christopher Wandesford, *A Book of Instructions*, 60–3. Knowler, i, 49–50.

shires they heare the whole bill reade over, which is the time to alter any thing att their pleasures.' After the meeting the lord treasurer's remembrancer brought the lord keeper and the lord treasurer a fair copy of the roll in its final form and this they took in to the king.[1]

As the time drew near for the appointment of new sheriffs it was not unusual for members of the Privy Council to be approached, either directly or indirectly, by gentlemen who feared that their names would be pricked. In the autumn of 1582 Lord Burghley received letters from two Yorkshire magistrates who were anxious to secure exemption: Sir William Mallory of Studley, who claimed that he was entirely unfitted for the shrievalty, and Cotton Gargrave of Nostell Priory, who pleaded that he was greatly overburdened with his late father's debts. Both supplicants were spared on this occasion but Gargrave was appointed the following year and Mallory in 1592.[2] Further cases of this sort are to be found in the private papers of Sir John Coke, who was one of the principal secretaries of state between 1625 and 1640. In November 1626 Thomas Alured, a royal official who acted as Coke's agent, asked him if Sir Matthew Boynton of Barmston, a fellow Yorkshireman, could be excused from the shrievalty on account of his youth. Sir Matthew was then thirty-five and had been short-listed on three previous occasions: in 1618, 1619 and 1625. Although he managed to escape once again his luck ran out in 1628 when he was finally pricked as sheriff.[3] Robert Rockley of Rockley, a deputy lieutenant and justice of the peace, was more fortunate, perhaps because of the backing of his friend the lord deputy. In October 1638 William Raylton, Wentworth's agent in London, wrote to Sir John Coke asking him as a favour to the lord deputy to ensure that Rockley was not chosen as sheriff of Yorkshire. The request was made on the grounds that Rockley had a number of children who would be impoverished by the heavy charge and that, furthermore, he was responsible for managing Wentworth's Yorkshire estates. In the event he was not called upon to act as sheriff.[4]

One of Wentworth's friends actually sought appointment as sheriff but in his case there were special circumstances. In September 1633,

[1] P.R.O., S.P.Dom., Charles I, S.P.16/dci/9.
[2] H.M.C. Salisbury MSS, ii, 524, 530.
[3] H.M.C. Coke MSS, i, 286. P.R.O., Chancery, Petty Bag Office, Sheriffs' Rolls, C.227/27A, 28A and S.P.Dom., Charles I, S.P.16/ix/43.
[4] H.M.C. Coke MSS, ii, 197.

shortly after he had assumed office as vice-president of the Council of the North, Sir Edward Osborne wrote to the lord deputy:

I am advised by many of my good freinds to gett to be sherife this next yeare, having now such an opportunity for the easy discharge of the place as will never fall outt againe after I leave this imploiment, which I conceave to be true, and therefore am very desirous to follow their advise, butt nott withoutt your Lordships good leave and approbation, which I humbly desire, being assured the two offices may well stand togeather withoutt any disparagement to mine...All attendance that is required may be done by the under-sherife which will be a great ease, besides the same charge I am now att both in house and apparell with some addition in the assize weekes will serve...I beseech you be pleased to write to my Lord Treasurer, Lord of Carlile, or Lord Cottington to gett me prickt.

No trace has been found of Wentworth's reply (Sir Edward was still waiting to hear from him on 7 November) but it seems likely that he dismissed the idea as impracticable; at all events the vice-president never achieved his wish.[1]

Before the reign of Charles I deputy lieutenants exercised office by direct appointment of the monarch. As a general rule the selection appears to have been made from a list based on the recommendations of the lord lieutenant but often including additions requested by members of the Privy Council. That the procedure was by no means rigid may be seen from a collection of documents which has survived among the state papers for the year 1623. In a letter to Sir Edward Conway, his fellow secretary of state, written on 4 July 1623, Sir George Calvert expressed the hope that his cousin Sir Thomas Wentworth of Wentworth Woodhouse would not be forgotten when the deputy lieutenants for Yorkshire were chosen. The following day Conway replied that the king was ready to select the deputy lieutenants and had not passed by Wentworth without a word of praise. The Earl of Middlesex, the lord treasurer, also had an interest in this matter for on 7 July he sent a message to Conway asking him to request the king to stay the appointment of deputy lieutenants for Yorkshire until he could wait on his majesty. In a further letter dated 27 August Calvert told his colleague that, for the deputy lieutenants, 'I can say nothing to them, unless my lord President have left a List with you, of thos whom he recommends, in which number though he should forgitt Sir

[1] Sheffield Central Library: Strafford Letters, xiii. Sir Edward Osborne to Wentworth, 26 September and 7 November 1633.

Thomas Wentworth, I hope you will not'. Finally, there is a schedule (possibly made up on 27 August) of the names of the principal gentry within the three ridings 'conceived meetest' to be deputy lieutenants. This must have been the list which was finally submitted to the king because the last two names for the West Riding are annotated 'which of these two, His majestie will allowe'. It is interesting to note that for the North Riding a sixth name has been added in different handwriting, that of Sir Richard Cholmley of Whitby who, according to his son, owed his appointment to his kinsman Lord Scroope, the lord president of the Council of the North and lord lieutenant of Yorkshire. Sir Thomas Wentworth's name, however, was not included in the list.[1]

From the accession of Charles I the lord lieutenant of a county was allowed to choose his own deputies. Under the terms of his commission as lord lieutenant of Yorkshire Wentworth had full power to appoint by letters of deputation such sufficient and meet persons as he thought fit to assist him.[2] He continued to exercise this power after he took up office as lord deputy of Ireland and indeed there was no provision for any delegation of authority in this respect. Consequently whenever the need arose for a new deputy lieutenant or colonel, Sir Edward Osborne, the vice-president of the Council of the North, was obliged to write off to the lord deputy. Although his recommendations were generally accepted this procedure was clearly irksome to him: in 1638 he complained to Secretary Coke that it was impossible to appoint even a lieutenant-colonel except under Wentworth's own hand and he suggested that in the absence of the lord lieutenant his authority should be vested in the vice-president and Council of the North. In February 1639 Sir Edward was granted, at Wentworth's request, the office of deputy-lieutenant-general: this gave him absolute power in the military sphere as though the lord deputy had been present in person.[3]

Wentworth was naturally acquainted with many of the principal gentry in his native West Riding so that the selection of deputy lieutenants for this part of the county presented no real problem; in the case of the other ridings, however, his personal knowledge was less extensive. Shortly after assuming office as lord lieutenant he asked Sir

[1] P.R.O., S.P.Dom., James I, S.P.14/cxlviii/26, 34, 44, 55 and cli/69, 71. *Cholmley Memoirs*, 22.
[2] P.R.O., Chancery, Crown Office, Docquet Books, Index 4211, 373, and Patent Rolls, C.66/2464 (Commission of 15 December 1628).
[3] *H.M.C. Coke MSS*, ii, 204. Knowler, ii, 282, 285. See also below, 312.

John Hotham of Scorborough for his opinion on the men whom he proposed to appoint as his deputies in the East Riding. Sir John considered them to be acceptable:

for the first man all I will say is that I wish he may deserve in anie service within his power these and the other manie noble favors whiche he hathe received from you, I am sure he will Ever Endeavor it. For the tow next I thinke without Exception they are the ablest and best affected to doe his maiestie's service in respect of their undoubted affection to religion whiche... in these partes is not Easie to finde in gentlemen of prime ranke and you know against some of them that theire were Complaintes from the Parlemente to his maiestie...Theire remaine the last, wherein you have not done Amisse. Give me leave to deliver my reason...tis true he is somewhat lesse than nothinge yet he hath always made one as a Cypher to ad to the number and he wilbe sure to be of the safer side. He dwels nere the Sea Coast in the End of a Countrey, where is none Else neere him. Besides he hath beene longe one of your Councell and wilbe like hearbe John in the pot, noe good, small harme...Sir Henrie Griffith [not apparently on Wentworth's list] is a baronet made a yeare agoe and was a Deputie leiutenante.[1]

Wentworth's choice of deputies is interesting in that the majority (twenty-two out of thirty-one) were relatives or close friends of his. These included his nephew Sir William Savile of Thornhill, his brother-in-law Sir Edward Rodes of Great Houghton and his cousin Sir Thomas Danby of Masham. As we shall see later, such personal ties were not necessarily a guarantee of unquestioning loyalty to higher authority.

As has been said the appointment of justices of the peace was the responsibility of the lord chancellor or lord keeper. Some idea of his special position may be gained from the fact that in 1639 the king gave order that the lord keeper should write to the prime gentlemen of each county, inviting them to be 'hearty' in the ship money business, which 'considering his power and authoritie with the Justices of Peace, is lykelie to advance it muche'.[2] Although the lord chancellor was personally acquainted with many of the leading gentry he had to rely heavily on the local knowledge of the circuit judges in compiling a new

[1] Sheffield Central Library: Strafford Letters, xii. Sir John Hotham to Wentworth, 7 January 1628(-9). The men on Wentworth's list may be identified as Sir John Hotham, Sir Matthew Boynton of Barmston, Sir William Constable of Flamborough and Sir Christopher Hildyard of Winestead.

[2] P.R.O., S.P.Dom., Charles I, S.P.16/cdxviii/45.

book of the peace or in replacing magistrates who had died or been dismissed. In addition, he might on occasion take advice from such men as the lord president of the Council of the North or the archbishop of York besides consulting his colleagues on the Privy Council.

Often the selection of magistrates was a matter of pure routine. In some cases a barrister might be appointed because of his professional knowledge of the law, in others a son might succeed his father on the commission after the latter's death or retirement. Sometimes there were so few gentry of any standing in a particular district that the choice was virtually automatic. Sir Hugh Cholmley of Whitby relates in his memoirs that in 1631, the neighbourhood 'suffering much for want of a Justice of Peace, there not being any within twelve miles of Whitby, I condescended to be put into the commission'. Sir Hugh's father was still on the commission but some five years before had decided to live in retired fashion, settling most of the family estate on his son. The only other gentleman in the whole liberty of Whitby Strand who had an estate of any size was Sir Thomas Hoby of Hackness, a magistrate of long standing. Sir Hugh's appointment was, therefore, almost in the natural order of things.[1]

If Sir Hugh Cholmley 'condescended to be put into the commission' there were other gentlemen who secured appointment through the influence of friends or relatives. In June 1637 Lord Fairfax of Denton wrote to his eldest son Ferdinando: 'I would have Tom [his grandson] put into the commission of the peace, because you know I am not able to do anything and I would have my name left out...I have written to my Lord Chamberlain, who, I hope, will effect that which is required.' Within a matter of weeks Thomas Fairfax had his name added to the commission of the peace. In July 1641 Sir William Fairfax of Steeton, who had been living away from Yorkshire for some years, wrote to his kinsman Ferdinando Lord Fairfax accepting the command of a company in the latter's regiment of trained bands. This, however, was by no means the limit of his ambitions: 'since I am resolved to settle myself in this county', he wrote, 'I cannot but think it is my duty to do it the best service I can, and therefore, if your lordship think fit to get me put in commission for the West Riding, I shall endeavour to perform what I am able and acknowledge your lordship's favour.' In

---

[1] *Cholmley Memoirs*, 26, 42, 55. P.R.O., S.P.Dom., Charles I, S.P.16/ccxii, and Chancery, Crown Office, Docquet Books, Index 4212, 64.

August 1641 Sir William was appointed to the West Riding commission.[1]

In recommending his friend Sir William Pennyman for the place of *custos rotulorum* in the North Riding (an appointment which would have made him head of the commission of the peace) Wentworth told the lord keeper that he conceived him to be the fittest man he could choose in those parts, considering his quality (a baronet), his sufficiency, his integrity and his good affection to the king's service.[2] These were some of the main factors which might be taken into account in selecting men for important local offices and we must now consider them in detail.

If the laws governing religion were to be properly enforced it was clearly important that local administration should be in the hands of men who were in favour of, or at least not antagonistic towards, the Elizabethan church settlement. Until 1606 there was no specific provision in the penal code for the exclusion of recusants from public employment: it was, however, a statutory requirement that persons appointed to offices under the Crown should take the oath of supremacy acknowledging the monarch to be supreme governor of England in all spiritual and temporal matters. In practice the oath appears to have caused little embarrassment to the average Catholic squire who conformed to the extent of attending Protestant services; moreover, there were reports that some magistrates had taken up their appointments without submitting to this test of loyalty.[3] During the reign of Elizabeth many popish gentry can be found occupying positions of responsibility in Yorkshire as members of the Council of the North, sheriffs, commissioners for musters, deputy lieutenants and justices of the peace. These were mainly 'schismatics' but they also included such men as Sir William Babthorpe of Osgodby and Sir Thomas Danby of Masham who were occasionally presented for recusancy or noncommunicancy[4]; in short, it was only the hardened recusants who were automatically excluded from consideration. The primary factor in this situation was the relative scarcity of well-to-do landowners whose religious views

[1] *Fairfax Correspondence*, i, 305, ii, 252–3. P.R.O., Chancery, Crown Office, Docquet Books, Index 4212, 251 and 475.

[2] Knowler, ii, 70.

[3] 1 Elizabeth I, c.i (Act of Supremacy). *Acts of the Privy Council 1592*, 253.

[4] P.R.O., S.P.Dom., Elizabeth, S.P.12/cxxi. Borthwick Institute of Historical Research: High Commission Act Books 1564–8 (R VII/A4) f.33, 1569–70 (R VII/AB10) f.139, 1572–4 (R VII/AB4) ff.42, 43, and 1580–5 (R VII/AB17) f.10.

were above suspicion. The problem was particularly acute in the early years of Elizabeth's reign when the Crown was forced to rely for the purposes of local administration on a small core of Protestant gentry and a considerably larger group of conservative gentry. In the first decade of the Elizabethan church settlement the religious sympathies of the propertied classes were in an extremely fluid state and the queen's advisers no doubt hoped to win over many of the half-hearted Catholics by admitting them to offices of trust and authority. In the final analysis, however, they really had no choice.

Since the Earl of Huntingdon, who served as lord president of the Council of the North from 1572 to 1595, pursued a harsh policy towards the Catholic community we might expect to find him paying special attention to the religious opinions of potential candidates for high office. There is in fact some evidence that he attempted to exercise a tighter control. In a letter to Sir Francis Walsingham in July 1577 he commented on the doubts which had been expressed about the suitability of Francis Wortley for appointment to the Council of the North. The Earl of Leicester (he wrote) had told him that 'theare was som suspicion of hym for religion...I have had som tawlke with hym of those matters wherin he hathe usyd to me bothe good and earenest speache and for action I knowe he geavyth good testimonye...yf I have any cause to suspecte hym for religion, surelye I wolde not for any thynge have namyd hym'.[1] Even in Huntingdon's time, however, the 'Church Papist' in public office was a common figure. In September 1587, for example, the archbishop of York named several Yorkshire magistrates who were sympathetic towards the Old Religion. James Ryther of Harewood (he told Burghley) was 'a soure, subtil papist, and brought into commission in respect thereof. Ready to hinder any matter that shall touch any papist. He dependeth upon Sir Thomas Farefax to make good his evil causes'. George Woodruffe of Woolley had a wife who was 'an obstinate recusant; and of long time hath been. One that doth very much hurt. An argument that he is not well affected himself. Such men as have such wives are thought very unfit to serve in these our times'. Brian Stapleton of Carlton 'is noted to be a great papist. And so is his eldest son'. Finally, there was Sir Henry Constable of Burton Constable: 'He is sheriff of this shire this year; but was in commission before, and looketh for to be in again. His wife is a most

---

[1] P.R.O., S.P.Dom., Elizabeth, Addenda, S.P.15/xxv/27.

obstinate recusant.'[1] In fact the lord president and his leading officials appear to have been well aware that there was a crypto-Catholic element within the magistracy. In December 1572, after William Tankard had been removed from the commission of the peace on account of his great age, Huntingdon suggested to the lord treasurer that it was better to displace more of the papists on the commission than to re-admit him. One of the lord president's main sources of information would have been the list of Yorkshire gentry which Sir Thomas Gargrave, the vice-president, had compiled in September 1572. A number of gentlemen who are shown in this list as Catholics or suspected Catholics held office while Huntingdon was in the seat of power.[2]

Towards the end of Elizabeth's reign the authorities began to make greater efforts to prevent the infiltration of Catholics into important local offices. In 1592 the Privy Council issued directions aimed at purging the commission of the peace. In the first place, all the justices then in office were required to take the oath of supremacy in public fashion and anyone refusing was to be removed from the commission. Secondly, it was stipulated that such magistrates as were 'themselves Recusantes or husbandes or fathers of such Recusantes' would no longer be permitted to hold office.[3]

As a result of the legislation which followed the discovery of the Gunpowder Plot it became a statutory offence for a recusant or the husband of a recusant to hold any kind of public office.[4] During Lord Sheffield's term of office as lord president of the Council of the North (1603–19) it was rare even for a 'Church Papist' to hold a responsible position in the county. In his account of the Yorkshire mission written in 1610 Father James Sharpe relates that in the East Riding, which had many recusant or 'schismatic' gentry, there were 'scarce 3 or 4 Justices of Peace or men of authority in the Commonwealth who are men of ancient families and of great estate; for all such who are suspected to be backward in religion are barred from such offices and dignities'[5] On occasion, however, the lord president was prepared to disregard the letter of the law. In February 1609 he informed Sir Thomas Fairfax of

---

[1] John Strype, *Annals of the Reformation*, iii, part ii, 465.
[2] *Cal.S.P.Dom., Addenda, 1566–79*, 426–7, 435. P.R.O., S.P.Dom., Elizabeth Addenda, S.P.15/xxi/86. See M. C. Cross, *The Puritan Earl: the Life of Henry Hastings third Earl of Huntingdon*, 163, 166.
[3] *Acts of the Privy Council 1592*, 253–61. [4] 3 James I, c.v.
[5] J. Morris, *The Troubles of Our Catholic Forefathers*, Series iii, 466. Cf. P.R.O. S.P.Dom., James I, S.P.14/xiv/25.

Gilling that he proposed to make him his vice-president during his absence from York, adding in a postscript to his letter: 'Although it is not usuall for any to supply this place whose wyves are Recusants, yet my good opinion of your selfe and the hope that I have of your own freedom from that secte will not suffer me to admit of that barr to your imployment.'[1]

Lord Scroope, who served as lord president of the Council of the North from 1619 to 1628, was well disposed towards the Old Religion and during his régime it was not unusual for Catholics to be appointed to local offices. The House of Commons complained on several occasions about this trend which was in evidence not only in Yorkshire but in other counties. Thus in 1626 the king was presented with a petition which contained a comprehensive list of recusants and suspected papists who were exercising office in the shires. In the case of Yorkshire three noblemen were cited: Lord Scroope, Lord Dunbar and Lord Eure. In addition, there were a number of gentlemen, most of them seated in the East Riding. These included Sir Thomas Metham of North Cave, who (it was alleged) had never been known to receive communion, Sir Marmaduke Wyvill of Constable Burton, who was married to a convicted recusant, and Nicholas Girlington of South Cave, whose wife seldom attended church.[2]

The extent of this Catholic infiltration under Lord Scroope must not be overestimated: it had, for example, hardly any impact on the commission of the peace. Moreover, even Lord Wentworth, who was lord president from 1628 to 1641, sometimes found it necessary to appoint a man with Catholic connections if he was otherwise well qualified (and indeed both Sir Thomas Metham and Sir Marmaduke Wyvill served under him as deputy lieutenants[3]). In some parts of the county the incidence of Catholicism among the propertied classes was still so high that the authorities had great difficulty in choosing men for the public service. In August 1629 Christopher Wandesford of Kirklington wrote in a letter to his friend the lord president:

I have severall tymes moved you concerning Sir William Gascoyne...when I consyder howe confydently my Lord Moulgrave (to omitt Sunderland) did imploye him as captayne, his former services abroad, his justification for his ladyes living apart from him, her recusancye (albeit his privy self is knowne

[1] C.R.S.: Biographical Studies, iii, 89.   [2] Rushworth, i, 391–6.
[3] Sheffield Central Library: Strafford Letters, xviii. Sir Edward Osborne to Lord Wentworth, 5 December 1638.

to his neybors), together with his constant repayre to our Church and performance of all service therin required I fynd him distinguished with very remarkable notes from the Common case of justly suspected, besydes that which is most trewe upon my own knowledge of 27 families in Ritchmondshyre of knights and esquires fit to serve as captaynes he is but one of the 11 that are Protestants, all the rest being recusants and justly suspected; and of those 11 divers for adge or otherwise unfit for personall service.[1]

Although no particular social qualifications were laid down, the choice of sheriffs and deputy lieutenants was confined almost exclusively to the prime gentry of the county, that is to say, the squires who headed their class by reason of wealth and social rank. In the early Stuart period these officials were normally possessed of titles before they entered office: indeed all but two of the men appointed to the shrievalty of Yorkshire in the years 1603–42 were knights or baronets and one of the two esquires was knighted before rendering his account.[2] In contrast there was a much lower percentage of knights among the sheriffs and deputy lieutenants of Elizabeth's reign, primarily because knighthoods were more difficult to obtain in that period than under the Stuart monarchs.

According to Thomas Wilson, writing in 1600, it was usual for all knights to be placed on the commission of the peace 'unless they be putt by for religion or some particular disfavor'.[3] In Yorkshire most knights (and, from 1611 onwards, baronets) were appointed to the magistracy if they normally resided in the county. The main exceptions were Catholic or at least recusant landowners and city merchants (whether or not they had country estates). Some knights, like Sir Edward Waterhouse and Sir Arthur Dakins, were admitted to, or retained on, the commission of the peace even though a financial crisis had seriously weakened their estates.

During this period most gentlemen who held major offices were recruited from the ancient families of the county. Some of these families had a long tradition of public service: the Saviles of Thornhill, for example, provided seven sheriffs of Yorkshire between 1380 and 1613. On the other hand, it was not unusual for representatives of the newer gentry to be appointed, particularly if they were men of sub-

---

[1] Sheffield Central Library: Strafford Letters, xvi. Christopher Wandesford to Lord Wentworth, 5 August 1629. Lord Sheffield was created Earl of Mulgrave in 1626 while Lord Scroope became Earl of Sunderland in 1627.

[2] This was Michael Warton of Beverley who was appointed sheriff in 1616 and knighted in 1617.   [3] *Camden Miscellany*, xvi, 23.

stance. In December 1638 the Yorkshire commissions of the peace contained eighty-seven gentlemen who were intended to be working magistrates; of these twenty-seven were from families which had either been granted arms or had entered the county since the accession of Elizabeth.[1] In the early seventeenth century the authorities would have found it difficult to restrict their choice to families which had long held sway in the county for a considerable number of ancient families had either died out, suffered a financial disaster or declared their support for the Catholic cause. The effects of this process may be illustrated by reference to the Yorkshire commissions of 1564. In November 1564 there were fifty-three working justices but in only nineteen cases were their families still represented in the magistracy during the reign of Charles I.[2]

Generally speaking, the leading officials in the county were drawn from the wealthier sections of the gentry. The following table details the landed income of the gentlemen who served as sheriffs, deputy lieutenants or justices of the peace in the period 1625–40[3]:

Income £ a year	All gentlemen in these offices	Sheriffs	Deputy lieutenants	J.P.s
2000 and over	16	4	8	16
1000	44	9	19	41
750	13	2	4	12
500	38	1	5	38
250	37		1	37
100	9			9
under 100	4			4
Total	161	16	37	157

Under a statute of Henry VI[4] justices of the peace were required to have lands or tenements to the value of £20 a year or more. With the passage of time this requirement had long since become meaningless: 'I do not doubt', wrote William Lambard in his *Eirenarcha* (first published around 1581), 'but as the rate of all things is greatly growne

[1] P.R.O., S.P.Dom., Charles I, S.P.16/cdviii.
[2] *Camden Miscellany*, ix: 'A Collection of Original Letters from the Bishops to the Privy Council, 1564', 70–2, 79.
[3] For an account of the sources used in producing statistics of yearly incomes see above, 27–8. This table shows the income which an individual enjoyed for at least the major part of his term of office.
[4] 8 Henry VI, c.xi.

17—Y.G.

since that time, so also there is good care taken that none be now placed in the Commission, whose livings be not answerable to the same proportion.'[1] It is significant that the instructions issued to the commissioners for knighthood compositions in Charles I's reign stipulated that no justice of the peace was to pay less than £25 'it beinge presumed that they are all of good estates'.[2] As will be seen from the above table the gentlemen who sat on the commission of the peace were for the most part upper or middling gentry: indeed if recusants had not been disqualified the magistracy could have been recruited entirely from this source.

Although there was no legal requirement, deputy lieutenants were almost invariably men of great wealth. Sheriffs, for their part, were to have 'lands sufficient in the county to answer the king and his people'. In 1636 the circuit judges were told that when submitting their list of nominees for the office of sheriff they should select men who were the wealthiest in the county.[3] In practice the expenses of the office were so great that only the more substantial gentry could afford to serve as sheriff.[4]

Justices of the peace were supposed to be 'good men and lawful', 'men of the best reputation'.[5] In September 1587 the archbishop of York gave the lord treasurer his views on the character of certain magistrates in his diocese. First he explained: 'I deal with no knights... but I assure you some of them be of the baddest sort; unworthy to govern, being so far out of order themselves... And to speak the truth, although there be many gentlemen in Yorkshire, yet very hard choise of fit men for that purpose.' The archbishop then proceeded to comment on the shortcomings of individual justices. Robert Lee of Hatfield was 'a notable open adulterer. One that giveth great offence, and will not be reformed. He useth his authority to work private displesure as to serve other mens tournes. A very bad man, and one that doth no good'. Peter Stanley of Womersley was 'noted to be a great fornicator. Of small wisdome and less skill... A man of none account'. Thomas Wentworth of North Elmsall was a 'very senseless blockhead; ever wronging, and wronging his poor neighbours: being a great graine-

---

[1] William Lambard, *Eirenarcha*, 31.
[2] P.R.O., Exchequer, Special Commissions, E.178/7154.
[3] 9 Edward II, Stat. 2 and 2 Edward III, c.iv. P.R.O., Privy Council Office Registers, P.C.2/xlvi/347.
[4] See below, 250-5.   [5] W. Lambard, *Eirenarcha*, 30. 18 Edward III, Stat.2, c.ii.

man of himself. He bought in the beginning of last year, in every market, so much as he could, and heaped it up in his houses to set against the dearest'.[1]

During the early seventeenth century several wealthy landowners appear to have been excluded from high office because of the scandal which marked their private lives. Both Sir John Vavasour of Spaldington and Sir Richard Hawksworth served as captains of militia but neither of them was appointed to the commission of the peace. Although Sir John had Catholic connections the authorities had no cause to suspect him of 'backwardness in religion' and he was never legally disqualified from holding office on religious grounds. In 1617, however, his wife asked the Northern High Commission to intervene in a matrimonial quarrel which had led to their separation. Seven years later she was still refusing to go back to her husband.[2] In Sir Richard Hawksworth's case the details of his marital difficulties were as well known in London as in York. In 1628 his wife submitted a petition to the Privy Council in which she complained that he had ill-treated her and that as a result she had been forced to leave home with her child and return to her parents. Subsequently the Privy Council besought the archbishop of York to use his good offices to bring about a settlement of the dispute but there was never any hope of a reconciliation. As his neighbours could have testified Sir Richard was a man of violent temper; in 1638 he was presented at the Pontefract quarter sessions for insulting one William Taylor and 'speaking openly and publicly these contemptuous words, viz. "he cared not for anie Justice of Peace in Yorkshire" '.[3]

According to his grandson, Sir George Reresby of Thrybergh, whose education had been of the most rudimentary kind, 'never took any publique imployment upon him in his country, as being discouraged from it by being noe scholler and his wife being a papist'.[4] On the whole, the men who occupied the principal offices in the county were a well-educated group, as may be seen from the following table[5]:

---

[1] John Strype, *Annals of the Reformation*, iii, part ii, 463–4.
[2] Borthwick Institute of Historical Research: High Commission Act Book 1612–25, R VII/AB9, ff.174, 343, 352, 376.
[3] H. Speight, 'Hawksworth Hall and its Associations', *Bradford Antiquary*, New Series, ii, 279–83. *Acts of the Privy Council 1628–9*, 263, 334. *Y.A.S.R.S.*, liv, 64. Cf. above, 137.
[4] B.M., Additional MSS 29443, ff.2, 3. Cf. above, 72.
[5] For sources see above, 73 *n* 3.

(a) total number of gentlemen who served as sheriffs, deputy lieuten-
    ants or justices of the peace in the period 1625–40   161
(b) number educated at both a university and one of the inns of court   60
(c) number educated at a university only   30
(d) number who received a legal but not a university education   32
(e) total of (b), (c) and (d)   122

A good knowledge of the law was a valuable asset in local administration, particularly in the case of a justice of the peace. Sir Hugh Cholmley of Whitby wrote in his memoirs that he remained at Gray's Inn for
three years

and totally misspent my time, to my great regret since I came to be of riper
judgement, and saw what advantage the study thereof might have been to
me, in conducting and managing of affairs in the country, as well as concerning my own private as the public, where every man that hath but a
smattering of the law, though of no fortune or quality, shall be a leader and
director for the greatest and best gentlemen on the bench[1].

Some of the men who held offices of a military nature had gained
first-hand experience in the Irish wars or on the Continent. In the reign
of Charles I, for example, the Yorkshire deputy lieutenants included
Thomas Lord Fairfax of Denton, who had fought in France, Germany
and the Low Countries, and Sir John Hotham of Scorborough, who
had served under Count Mansfeld during the Thirty Years War.[2]
Most deputy lieutenants, colonels and captains, however, appear to have
had little practical knowledge of military affairs: in July 1638 the vice-
president of the Council of the North told Secretary Coke that the
commanders of the Yorkshire militia were all so ignorant in the use of
arms that unless the king sent down eight or ten expert men the trained
bands could not be brought into any useful order for many months.[3]

Apart from anything else the government needed local officials
who could be relied upon to carry out its directions. This factor
assumed particular importance in the reign of Charles I when the
Crown's efforts to govern without Parliament led to the progressive
alienation of the propertied classes. Having made the sheriff responsible
for the levying of ship money the authorities took special care in the
selection of men for the shrievalty. In September 1636 the lord keeper

---

[1] Cholmley Memoirs, 38.
[2] Fairfax Correspondence, i, introduction xx and 12–14. Knowler, ii, 288.
[3] H.M.C. Coke MSS, ii, 189.

wrote to the circuit judges: 'Whereas his Majestie for some speciall reasons is pleased to have a List of the names of fower or more of the ablest [that is, the wealthiest] most serviceable and welaffected persons in each severall County within your Circuite fit to bee high Sherrifes in every County. These are therefore to require you forthwith to send me the Lord Keeper for his Majestie such a List, and that you prepare and make up the same presently.'[1] In Yorkshire several prominent gentlemen who attempted to stir up resistance to arbitrary taxation were stripped of all their offices. Refusal to pay taxes, however, did not necessarily mean automatic dismissal or permanent exclusion from the magistracy. It was easy enough to dismiss a few ringleaders whose actions could not be overlooked but the Crown was virtually powerless when faced with widespread opposition among the ruling families of the shires.

During this period the average well-to-do squire could reasonably expect to become at least a justice of the peace provided his religious sympathies were above suspicion. This is not to say that all members of the squirearchy were anxious to exercise public office. In his book of precepts Christopher Wandesford told his son that he left it to him to decide what part he wanted to play in the government of the county. 'Only let me tell you, I have heard, it was the Observation of a very wise Man...that "the happiest Condition of Life in the Kingdom was to be under the Degree of a Justice of Peace, and above the Quality of a High Constable'."[2] This was broadly the view of Sir Henry Slingsby the diarist who warned his son: 'In the carriage of publick affairs, my advice is that you appear cautious; Many by putting themselves upon numerous imploiments have lost themselves; though in neighbourly Offices to be modestly active manifests signal arguments of Piety.' Sir Henry appears to have been a man of scholarly tastes with little interest in local administration: although he was the head of one of the leading families in the West Riding he never served on the commission of the peace. In 1638 he noted in his diary:

My Lord Deputy of Ireland sent his letters unto my Lord Mayor of York and to my self as Deputy Lieuetenants. My Lord Mayor had a commission, but I had no other but his Lordship's letters; by which I sat to assist my Lord Mayor in the taking the view of arms, the which I did perform most diligently, a thing not usual with me who does little affect business...after

[1] P.R.O., Privy Council Office Registers, P.C.2/xlvi/347.
[2] *A Book of Instructions*, 61–2.

2 months service I gave it over, being left out by the Vice-President in a general Summons to all the Deputy Leiftenants.[1]

Although some gentlemen had little taste for public administration the average squire clearly regarded it as a privilege to serve his county in some office of distinction, the shrievalty only excepted. Service as a deputy lieutenant or justice of the peace was particularly attractive because of the prestige which such appointments conferred; thus in September 1633 we find Sir William Savile of Thornhill, the wealthiest baronet in Yorkshire, writing to thank his uncle, Lord Wentworth, for his kindness in making him a deputy lieutenant and colonel.[2] Not surprisingly there were some men who liked the trappings of power but were less enthusiastic about the duties that went with it. In 1635 Sir John Gibson told the lord deputy that when the deputy lieutenants met together at York, 'ther beinge some speach of Colonells [deputy lieutenants normally served as colonels of the trained bands] Sir Edward Stanhope beinge asked if he were one blushed, but answered not. Me thought he was out of Countenance'.[3] Similarly, some justices of the peace were rarely present at quarter sessions even though they were clearly intended to be working magistrates.

There was one county office to which few men aspired: the shrievalty. This was no longer the great office it had once been and it is some measure of the decline which had occurred in relative status that sheriffs were on occasion fined at the quarter sessions. The sheriff was also subject to certain disabilities which must have proved irksome: he could not, for example, leave his county without special licence.[4] During the reign of Charles I the office no doubt held even less attraction for the average squire in view of the unpopularity incurred in executing the ship money writs.

In the final analysis, however, it was financial considerations which mainly accounted for the general reluctance to serve as sheriff of the county. As many gentlemen knew to their cost the expenditure associated with the office could be extremely heavy. In the first place, there

---

[1] *Slingsby Diary*, 14, 215.

[2] Sheffield Central Library: Strafford Letters, xiii. Sir William Savile to Lord Wentworth, 21 September 1633.

[3] Sheffield Central Library: Strafford Letters, xv. Sir John Gibson to Lord Wentworth, 9 August 1635.

[4] 4 Henry IV, c.v. John Wilkinson, *A Treatise... Concerning the Office and Authorities of Coroners and Sherifes*, f.44. See also G. E. Aylmer, *The King's Servants: The Civil Service of Charles I, 1625–1642*, 184, 188–92, 194–5.

were the fees which the sheriff had to pay to Exchequer and other
government officials on his entry into office and in settling his account:
according to John Wilkinson's treatise on the sheriff, first published in
1628, these could amount to well over £100.[1] Secondly, he had to meet
the salary of his under-sheriff besides maintaining a considerable body
of attendants. Thirdly, he was liable to be fined if he failed to perform
his duties efficiently. In 1606 fines totalling £230 were imposed on Sir
Timothy Hutton of Marske, mainly on account of his negligence in
carrying out the instructions of the Court of Wards, while in 1613 Sir
Henry Slingsby of Scriven paid a fine of £200 for absenting himself
from the York assizes during his shrievalty[2]. Fourthly, the sheriff had
to provide hospitality for the judges and other men of standing who
attended the half-yearly assizes. In 1600 the Privy Council attempted
to limit the scale of hospitality because the 'excessive and extraordinary
expences' which some sheriffs had incurred often discouraged 'men of
good abillyty and service' from undertaking the office. The judges
were therefore directed to give order to the sheriffs that 'from henceforth no table be kept by any of them at any Assizes or Sessions, but
that they take order to rayse some ordinary in some convenyent place...
where the Sherive and the Justices of Peace together may have such
competent provision made for them and at such rate for the ordinary as
shalbe fytte'.[3]

These were not necessarily the only items of expenditure. Perhaps
the worst feature of the system, potentially at least, was the fact that
the sheriff was held personally responsible for the money which he was
required to collect. For this reason several years might elapse before he
was able to settle his account and even then he might be obliged to make
up the whole or part of any deficit out of his own resources. In practice
much depended on the character of the under-sheriff: if the under-
sheriff is lewd or ignorant, John Wilkinson relates, he 'may both undoe
his high Sherife, and himselfe ... by totting and nichiling, that is, in
charging or discharging ... unorderly, unhonestly, or ignorantly'.[4] To
illustrate this point he might well have referred to the case of Sir
William Wentworth of Wentworth Woodhouse who had been sheriff

[1] J. Wilkinson, *op. cit.*, ff.77–80.
[2] P.R.O., Court of Wards, Book of Extents, Wards 9/dclxxvii/f.3. *Slingsby Diary*,
267–8, 408.
[3] *Acts of the Privy Council 1599–1600*, 783–5. An 'ordinary' was a public eating house
or a public meal.
[4] John Wilkinson, *Office and Authorities of Coroners and Sherifes*, f.75.

of Yorkshire in 1601–2. In an Exchequer suit begun in 1608 Sir William claimed that John Wormall, his under-sheriff, had failed to deliver in great sums of money which had either not been levied or were still in his possession. Since Wormall had refused to submit proper returns he had found it necessary to send out divers persons to make inquiries among Yorkshire recusants as to the exact amounts which had been collected from them. As the result of his under-sheriff's negligence or corruption Sir William had been arrested by a serjeant-at-arms and required to enter into a bond for the payment of £400 into the Exchequer; had been sent for by a pursuivant, at the direction of the lord treasurer, for failing to settle his account; had spent over £300 in legal costs and associated expenditure; and was liable to be charged with a substantial sum which Wormall had levied but not paid in.[1] Another Elizabethan sheriff, Sir Marmaduke Grimston of Grimston Garth, found himself in a similar predicament but for rather different reasons. In his case the under-sheriff died during the course of his shrievalty and as a result of the break in continuity Sir Marmaduke was faced with a large shortfall in his account. In a subsequent Chancery suit one of the participants claimed, rather surprisingly, that he had been £10,000 in arrear when he completed his term of office in 1599 and that at his death in 1604 he still owed £8000. From the evidence of Exchequer records, however, it appears that the sum which was charged on his estate and recoverable in annual instalments did not in fact exceed £700; even so, there was a lengthy dispute between Sir Marmaduke's widow and her new husband on the one hand and Thomas Grimston, his brother and heir, on the other about their respective liabilities and some years were to elapse before the Exchequer finally granted a *Quietus est*.[2]

During the reign of Charles I the collection of ship money meant an additional financial burden for the sheriff. In 1637 Edward Nicholas, secretary of the navy, recommended that sheriffs who were remiss or negligent in levying arrears or who returned false accounts should be made to pay 'a good part of the said Arere'.[3] Over the next few years a number of sheriffs who failed to collect the full amount specified in

---

[1] P.R.O., Exchequer Depositions, E.134, 6 James I, Hilary No. 16 and 10 James I, Trinity No. 8.

[2] P.R.O., Chancery Proceedings, Six Clerks' Series, C.8/19/6 and Exchequer, Sheriffs' Accounts of Seizures, E.379/167.

[3] P.R.O., S.P.Dom., Charles I, S.P.16/ccclxxvi/96.

their writs were required to pay the residue themselves. One sheriff who suffered in this way was Sir Thomas Danby of Masham. Following his appointment in 1637 his account book contains various items of expenditure relating to his fiscal responsibilities. In the period 28 November 1637 to 2 January 1638 he spent £100 'about ship money besides other charges towards the assize week' while on 10 January 1638 he took £60 with him for his charge in London 'about ship money'. Sir Thomas appears to have displayed no lack of zeal in the service yet he was unable to collect the whole of the £12,000 charged on the county in 1637. In October 1639 he received a peremptory letter from the Privy Council requiring him to pay in the arrears which (in their view) had been largely occasioned by his negligence in executing the writ; if he failed to bring in the money to the treasurer of the navy by 24 November he was to appear before the Council to answer for the same. On 30 November the Council sent out a further letter addressed to both Danby and his immediate successor, Sir William Robinson of Newby. After relating that there remained an arrear upon the writ issued in 1637 of £1237. 15s. 6d. and upon the writ issued in 1638 of £510 they commanded the two former sheriffs to pay to Sir William Russell as much of the arrear as they had already collected and not paid in, and to assess and collect the residue. There is a note on the back of this letter (which has been preserved among Sir Thomas Danby's private papers) to the effect that it had been received on 15 January 1640 and that the two Yorkshiremen had met on 22 January, no doubt to agree on a common line. In a rough draft which has also survived Sir Thomas claimed that while he had done everything possible to levy the sum outstanding several attempted distresses had met with violent resistance and the collectors and assessors had refused to come in and complete their accounts. However justified his defence may have been he was forced, according to his grandson, to pay the arrear of £1237 himself, 'to his great damage.'[1]

Once they had been appointed to the shrievalty some gentlemen were determined to exercise the office with as much ostentation as possible. Sir Robert Stapleton of Wighill, whose name was pricked in 1581, is said to have entertained the judges with great magnificence, meeting them with 'seven-score men in suitable Liveries'.[2] Sir Richard

[1] Cartwright Memorial Hall, Bradford: Cunliffe–Lister MSS, Bundles 11 and 25. See also below, 309.
[2] William Camden, *Britannia*, 731.

Gargrave of Nostell Priory, an improvident squire who was sheriff in 1605–6, rode through the streets of Wakefield bestowing 'great largesses upon the common people, in congratulation for so wise, peaceful and religious a king as England then enjoyed'.[1] Sir Thomas Reresby of Thrybergh (relates his great-grandson)

was Sherif of Darbyshire, which office he is reported to have performed at too prodigall a rate, in the year 1613. I find amongst old papers a bill of fair for provisions the Lent assizes with the superinscription upon it with Sir Thomas his own hand — the Stuarts [that is, the steward's] appointment for Lent assizes at Derby when I was sherif for that county — wherin I find 15 severall sorts of foule, amongst others young swanns, knots, bitters, &c., three venaison pastys appointed for every meale, 13 severall sorts of sea fish, 14 severall sorts of freshwater fish, each appointed to be ordered a different way, &c.[2]

This was one reason for Sir Thomas's great expenses and debts.

If some sheriffs chose to serve their term in great splendour others were equally determined to restrict their expenses to the minimum. When Sir Thomas Wentworth (the future Earl of Strafford) was appointed in 1625 his friend Sir John Jackson of Hickleton advised him to follow that 'private and husbandly' course which his immediate predecessors had commended to him. Shortly afterwards Sir Thomas informed Christopher Wandesford that he intended to execute the office in such a fashion that moderation and sobriety would be the hall-marks of his expenditure: he would be betraying his fellow gentry if he sought to revive the former licentious custom which was so much to their prejudice. Accordingly he would keep within the articles made when Sir Guy Palmes was sheriff (1622–3). The office of under-sheriff would be executed by his own servants and, in short, he would closely and quietly attend his own private fortune.[3] When Sir William Penny-man was appointed sheriff in 1635 he similarly decided to employ one of his servants as under-sheriff: 'I have rather intrusted him with the office', he told Wentworth, 'then an ordinary undertaker, because I presume it wilbe safer both for my self and the Countrey, to suffer by an Undersheriffe's ignorance rather then his subtilty.'[4] This was the advice which John Wilkinson gave in his treatise: it was better that the

---

[1] J. Hunter, *South Yorkshire*, ii, 213.   [2] B.M., Additional MSS 29442, f.47.
[3] Knowler, i, 30, 32.
[4] Sheffield Central Library: Strafford Letters, xvi. Sir William Pennyman to Lord Wentworth, 9 March 1635(–6).

sheriff should keep the office in his own house 'so that hee may take a continuall survey of it himselfe'; by this means he could give his servant 'good allowance and yet have sufficient out of the honest gaines of the office, to passe his accounts, and to defray part of his other charge'.[1] Although it was illegal some sheriffs farmed out the office of under-sheriff for a consideration, allowing the incumbent to make what profit he could through fees and perquisites. In 1635 commissioners were appointed to treat and compound with those who had broken the law in this way and were liable to be tried for the offence. One Yorkshire sheriff who leased out the office of under-sheriff was Sir John Hotham: in 1635 he was indicted in the Star Chamber on account of this and other irregularities which had been uncovered. Fortunately for him the king quashed the proceedings at Wentworth's instigation.[2]

The sheriff who preferred economy to ostentation might strive to keep his expenditure to the absolute minimum yet it could still make heavy demands on his private income. The shrievalty of Sir Richard Cholmley of Whitby, who was appointed in 1624, is said to have cost him no less than £1000, and he was already over £12,000 in debt.[3] This was in spite of the fact that in 1622 a new policy of retrenchment had been inaugurated and the collection of ship money as a general tax still lay in the future. It is not surprising, therefore, that in contrast with the other major offices of local administration the shrievalty was regarded as an honour to be avoided at all costs.

[1] John Wilkinson, *Office and Authorities of Coroners and Sherifes*, f.49.
[2] P.R.O., Chancery, Crown Office, Docquet Books, Index 4212, 179. P. Saltmarshe, *History and Chartulary of the Hothams* 111. Sheffield Central Library: Strafford Letters, xv. Sir John Hotham to Lord Wentworth, 17 November 1635.
[3] *Cholmley Memoirs*, 24, 25.

CHAPTER XII

The Growth of Puritanism

On 20 January 1600 Lady Margaret Hoby of Hackness noted in her diary that after dining 'I reed in perkins tell I went againe to the Church ...after, tell night, I kept Companie with Mr Hoby who reed a whill of Cartwrights book to me'.[1] William Perkins and Thomas Cartwright, two of the leading figures in the Elizabethan Puritan movement, were among the first English theologians to propagate the religious concepts and doctrines of John Calvin whose adopted city of Geneva had become under his influence the spiritual capital of European Protestantism. Dr Cartwright, a Cambridge professor of divinity, had his university career abruptly terminated as a result of his campaign in favour of a church organisation based on the Geneva model. In 1574 he felt obliged to seek refuge abroad. Dr Perkins, another Cambridge don, was perhaps the most influential of all Puritan scholars. While Cartwright was primarily interested in the establishment of a Presbyterian form of church government Perkins made his reputation by expounding and elaborating the basic doctrines of Calvinism and applying them to contemporary social problems.[2]

One of the cardinal features of the Calvinist theology which gave special flavour to English Puritanism (at least in the extent of its application) was the doctrine of predestination. 'Predestination', wrote Calvin, 'we call the eternal decree of God, by which he has determined in himself, what he would have to become of every individual of mankind. For they are not all created with a similar destiny; but eternal life is foreordained for some, and eternal damnation for others.'[3] However devout he might be the individual was powerless to shape his own destiny: salvation could not be attained through personal merit but

[1] D. M. Meads (ed.), *The Diary of Lady Margaret Hoby 1599–1605*, 97. In this period dinner was a midday meal.

[2] See A. F. Scott Pearson, *Thomas Cartwright and Elizabethan Puritanism*, W. Haller, *The Rise of Puritanism*, M. M. Knappen, *Tudor Puritanism*, P. Collinson, *The Elizabethan Puritan Movement* and C. Hill, *Society and Puritanism in Pre-Revolutionary England*.

[3] J. Allen (ed.), *Institutes of the Christian Religion by John Calvin*, ii, 145.

only through God's free grace. How then could the fortunate minority be sure that they were saved? In answer to this question William Perkins and his disciples emphasised the paramount importance of faith: if a man truly believed in Christ's power of redemption this was the surest guarantee that he was one of God's elect.

Generations of English Puritans took great comfort from the doctrine of predestination as taught by such men as William Perkins. Frequently their wills reflect not only the hope but the conviction that God had singled them out for eternal salvation. In August 1646 William West of Firbeck, a West Riding squire, began his will with a particularly lengthy Calvinist preamble. After commending his soul to the Lord he stipulated that his body should be buried in Firbeck church

being in hope and confidence that by the only merritts of my only Lord and Saviour Jesus Christ all my Sinnes are forgiven And that my body att the last day (though now corrupt and mortall) shall att his glorious comeing to Judge both the quick and the dead rise a glorious incorrupt and immortall body And that my soule and body shalbee then reunited and clothed with the pure robe of the righteousnes of Christ Jesus and purified in his imaculate blood and sanctification of his spiritt and received into the kingdome of heaven there to injoy the glorious presence of the Godhead and the everlasting unspeakable and unconceaveable happines prepared for the Saints and blessed Angells of God according to the good pleasure of his will before the foundation of the world.[1]

The name 'Puritan' was frequently employed as a term of abuse. At the parliamentary by-election held at Knaresborough in November 1641 Thomas Stockdale of Bilton Park professed to be shocked when Sir William Constable, a fellow Puritan whose candidature he supported, was described as such by the opposing faction.[2] In the normal contemporary sense the term denoted that section of the Protestant clergy and laity which believed that reforms were necessary within the Church of England. To the Puritan party the Elizabethan religious settlement was too much of a compromise between the old and the new: in its organisation, discipline and worship the Church still retained Catholic features which, they claimed, were incompatible with the true Protestant religion.

Although they shared a common theology the Puritans were far

---

[1] Somerset House: Register Grey, f.104 (will dated 8 August 1646).
[2] *Fairfax Correspondence*, ii, 266.

from unanimous over the precise nature of the reforms that were required. At one extreme there were some who favoured the abolition of bishops, deans and chapters and the establishment of a full Presbyterian system of church government consisting of ministers, elders and deacons. Under this system ministers would no longer be appointed by the church authorities or the owners of lay impropriations: instead, as in Calvin's Geneva, they would be elected by the congregations of the faithful. While the extremists advocated radical changes in the structure of the Church most Puritans would probably have been content with a modest degree of reform. Sir Henry Slingsby of Scriven was in favour of depriving the bishops of their secular powers but he feared that the abolition of episcopacy would have far-reaching consequences. As a member of the Long Parliament he supported the bill for 'taking of their votes in the house of Peers, and for medling with temporal affairs, but I was against the bill for taking away the function and calling of Bishops; this is a business chiefly aim'd at by the Parliament and solicit'd by our countrimen that live beyond the seas in Holland hoping that if episcopy were abolish'd they might peacably live at home and enjoy their consciences'.[1] Although he did not consider episcopal government of absolute necessity,

I am of opinion that the taking of [bishops] out of the church as the government is now establist and so long continu'd, may be of dangerous consequence to the peace of the Church; for admitting that government of Bishops be not of divine right, nor in every point, as it is now exercis'd, of Apostolical right, yet we find some foundation thereof in the wrighting of the Apostles... The comon people judges not with things, as they are with reason or against; but long usage with them is instead of all, so that they would think themselves loose and absolved from all government when they should see that which they so much venerat'd so easily subverted.[2]

The fear that a major alteration in church government might lead to social and political anarchy must have acted as a powerful moderating influence within the Puritan squirearchy. In addition, many Puritan gentlemen owned impropriate rectories and tithes and they were naturally apprehensive about the possibility of losing part of their revenue as the result of a radical overhaul of the Church's finances. In May 1641 Thomas Stockdale of Bilton Park expressed the view that all tithes should be restored to the Church but hastened to add that lay

[1] See below, 308.   [2] *Slingsby Diary*, 67–8.

impropriators should be compensated from the lands belonging to the bishops, deans and chapters. Since he held the rectory of Farnham in freehold possession his insistence on compensation is not altogether surprising.[1]

For the majority of Puritans liturgical reform was probably more important than alterations in church organisation and discipline, although the uncompromising attitude of the prelates, particularly in the reign of Charles I, tended to emphasise the close relationship between these two aspects of the reform programme. On 6 April 1571 William Strickland of Boynton, M.P. for Scarborough, launched the parliamentary campaign for reforming the Book of Common Prayer: 'althoughe', he declared,

the booke of Common praier is (god be praysed) drawne very neere to the sinceritie of the truth, yet are there som things inserted more supersticious or erronious then in soe high matters be tollerable. As namely in the administracion of the Sacrament of Baptisme, the sign of the Crosse to be made with some Ceremonies: and the ministracion of that Sacrament by woemen in tyme of extremetye and some such other errors...

And he emphasised that it was essential 'to have all things brought to the puritie of the Primitive church and institucion of Christ'.[2] Other features of church worship which aroused Puritan criticism included the ringing of bells, the playing of organs, the use of a ring in the marriage ceremony and the wearing of priestly vestments. Although opinion might vary as to whether a particular item merited censure as a Catholic survival there was a general desire for a plainer form of worship with the sermon as an integral part of the service.

Since the Bible was in their eyes the sole authority on matters of religion the Puritans attached great importance to the sermon as a means of expounding the scriptures. Not infrequently a Calvinist squire made special provision in his will for a sermon to be preached at his funeral or, if he had the spiritual welfare of his fellow parishioners at heart, for a specified number of sermons to be given at his expense in the parish church. In 1613 Richard Thornton of Tyersall, in the township of Pudsey, bequeathed the sum of 10s. each to Mr Saxton, late minister of Pudsey, and Mr Toller, minister at Sheffield, on con-

---

[1] *Fairfax Correspondence*, ii, 107. Leeds Central Library: Bilton Park MSS, BL 257.
[2] B.M., Cotton MSS, Titus F.1, ff.135–6. Extracts are printed in Sir John Neale, *Elizabeth I and Her Parliaments, 1559–1581*, 193–4.

dition that they would each deliver a sermon at Calverley church within one year after his death; in addition, he left the sum of 12s. 4d. to Mr Richard Rothwell, another minister, entreating him also to preach a sermon at Calverley.[1] Some idea of the enthusiasm for godly preaching which existed in the main Puritan areas may be gained from the autobiography of Joseph Lister, a Bradford clothier. In his account of Bradford Puritanism in the years immediately preceding the Civil War he refers to the sermons of Elkanah Wales who had served as minister at Pudsey chapel since 1615: 'I have known that holy Mr Wales spend six or seven hours in prayer and preaching, and rarely go out of the pulpit; but sometimes he would intermit for one quarter of an hour, while a few verses of a psalm were sung, and then pray and preach again.'[2]

During the reign of Charles I Archbishop Laud and his nominee Archbishop Neile of York not only refused to countenance Puritan ideas on the form of public worship but actually pressed ahead with their own High Church reform programme. The essence of this programme was a greater emphasis on outward display. Among the Laudian innovations were the introduction of elaborate church furnishings, the provision of altar rails, the requirement to take communion in a kneeling position and the practice of bowing to the altar. Some ministers refused to conform and were deprived of their livings while others, despairing of any change in the situation, emigrated to New England; the great majority, however, submitted to the will of the ecclesiastical authorities. This trend of events, coupled with the greater tolerance shown towards the Catholic party,[3] was naturally repugnant to men of Calvinist opinion who feared, or at least contended, that popery was being restored. In 1638 Sir Henry Slingsby the diarist wrote of the Reverend Timothy Thurscross, a prebendary of York, that he was 'a man of most holy life, only he is conformable to the church discipline that now is used and to those late impos'd ceremonies of bowing and adoring towards the altar'. Subsequently he told Thurscross: 'I thought it came too near idolatry to adore a place with rich cloaths and other furniture and to command to use towards it bodily

---

[1] *Bradford Antiquary*, New Series, iii, 28–9. Saxton and Toller may be identified as Peter Saxton, rector of Edlington 1614–40, and Thomas Toller, vicar of Sheffield 1588–1635. Both were Puritans.
[2] T. Wright (ed.), *Autobiography of Joseph Lister of Bradford, 1627–1709*, 7.
[3] See above, 199–202.

worship.'[1] In February 1642 a petition was sent up from Yorkshire entreating the king, among other things, to purge the Church of Laudianism. After calling for sterner measures against the Catholic party the petitioners prayed that scandalous ministers (that is, the ritualist element of the clergy) should be dismissed and that 'ceremonial burdens may be removed, and religion settled in such a way, that such as make all conscience obediently to submit to magistracy and civil authority in every degree and latitude of it, both supreme and subordinate, may not suffer under any penalty merely only for conscience sake'. This petition was signed by fourteen knights and baronets, fifty esquires and 'divers gentlemen'.[2]

For various reasons it is difficult to make a precise assessment of the strength of the Puritan gentry. In the first place, there is no equivalent in this context of the official lists of Catholics presented for recusancy and other breaches of the penal laws. Although the records of the ecclesiastical authorities at York contain frequent references to Protestant nonconformists — at least in the seventeenth century — these are, for the most part, clerical offenders. Secondly, just as the Catholic party consisted of recusants and 'Church Papists' so there were avowed Puritans and men of Puritan inclination who felt obliged to keep their religious opinions to themselves. Thirdly, there were some gentlemen who were considered to be sympathetic to the Puritan cause but through political or personal motives rather than from genuine religious conviction. According to a seventeenth-century antiquary, Sir Hugh Cholmley of Whitby, one of the Crown's leading opponents in 1640, was not himself a Puritan in religion: nevertheless he was 'kind and friendly to the Puritans or Professors of Religion'.[3] Clearly it would not be appropriate to include such men in a muster of the Puritan gentry.

In spite of the difficulties there is sufficient evidence to provide the basis for a broad assessment. Some gentlemen were described as Puritans by their contemporaries; others can be identified as such through the religious opinions revealed in their wills, correspondence and parliamentary speeches or through the support which they gave to the Puritan cause. In addition, the Yorkshire petitions of 1642 which called for church reform are a useful supplementary source in

[1] *Slingsby Diary*, 8.   [2] *Fairfax Correspondence*, ii, 367–72.
[3] Dr Williams's Library: Morrice MSS, 'A Chronological Account of Eminent Persons, &c', vol. iii (no consistent pagination).

view of the fact that many of the signatories were members of the gentry.[1]

From this body of evidence it can be said that in 1642 there were at least 138 Puritan families within the Yorkshire gentry (including six families which also had a Catholic element). Geographically, they were distributed broadly as follows:

	Total number of gentry families	Number of Puritan families
North Riding	195	22
East Riding	142	34
West Riding	320	74
York	22	8
	679	138

In view of its strong Catholic tradition[2] it is not surprising to find that the North Riding had the smallest percentage of Calvinist gentry. The West Riding, on the other hand, was noted for the extent of its attachment to the Puritan cause. In his autobiography Adam Martindale, a Puritan minister, wrote that at the time of the Civil War he was invited to serve five different congregations in Cheshire but 'I had much more inclination to goe into the West-riding of Yorkshire. The noble spirit of the gentrie and others in those parts was very attractive'.[3] In this part of the county Puritanism was mainly concentrated in the town and neighbourhood of Sheffield and the clothing region around Halifax, Bradford, Leeds and Wakefield. Within the East Riding it was strongly entrenched in Hull and Beverley and also in a chain of parishes along the northern fringe of the riding. In 1642 there were thirty gentle families seated in Dickering and Buckrose, the two northernmost wapentakes, and of these no fewer than fourteen can be described as Puritan in religion. No other wapentake in Yorkshire appears to have had such a high percentage.

The influence of Calvinism was by no means confined to the minor gentry: on the contrary, it had made striking inroads at the higher levels of landed society. In 1642 the Puritan party included nine baronets and twenty-five knights. Equally impressive are the figures of landed income[4]:

[1] B.M., Egerton MSS 2546, ff.23–4. *Fairfax Correspondence*, ii, 367–72. See also the Cleveland petition of 10 February 1642 (House of Lords MSS: calendared in *H.M.C. Fifth Report*, Appendix, 7).   [2] See above, 169.
[3] *Chetham Society*, iv, 76.   [4] For a discussion of sources see above, 27–8.

Annual income from land in 1642	Total number of gentle families	Number of Puritan families
£1000 and upwards	73	23
£250 but below £1000	244	75
under £250	362	40
Total	679	138

The Puritan gentry of 1642 consisted to a large extent of ancient families which were well established in county society; nevertheless, as the following table shows, the newer families were far from being an insignificant minority:

(a) families represented in the Yorkshire gentry of 1558	90
(b) Yorkshire families granted arms after 1558	31
(c) families which entered the county after 1558	17
Total	138

In contrast, new gentility is rarely found within the ranks of the Catholic squirearchy of this period.

As we have seen, the Yorkshire gentry of 1570 included a majority of families with residual Catholic sympathies: more specifically, 368 out of a total of 567 families.[1] Of the Protestant families it is possible to identify only 25 as Puritan in 1570: it is clear, therefore, that in the period 1570–1642 there was a striking increase in the number of Puritan families. To some extent this was due to the entry of new families, either from other social classes or from other counties, but the primary cause was the spread of Puritan beliefs within the ranks of the gentry.

In some cases a family came under the influence of Calvinist doctrines through intermarriage or the particular circumstances of a minority. The Thorntons of East Newton, for example, had remained sympathetic to the Old Religion throughout the reign of Elizabeth but the turning point probably came when Robert Thornton married Elizabeth Darley, the daughter of a staunch Puritan, Sir Richard Darley of Buttercrambe. In 1641 their eldest son William, who had been left a minor four years earlier, was sent to Emmanuel College, one of the main centres of Cambridge radicalism. According to his wife he was 'a very godly, sober and discreet person' whose attitude to the Church of England was that of a moderate Puritan.[2]

[1] See above, 169.
[2] N.R. Records, iii, 76. Clay, ii, 17–18. Al.Cant., iv, 223. Surtees Society, lxii, introduction x, and 77–9.

One factor which must have played a significant part in the growth of Puritanism, at least among the educated classes, was the profusion of religious works written by Calvinist theologians; these included such men as Thomas Cartwright, William Perkins, John Preston and Richard Sibbes.[1] Even more important perhaps was the evangelical zeal of the Puritan clergy in the parishes who had a key role as field commanders in the struggle for men's souls. During the reign of Elizabeth the ecclesiastical authorities at York sought to increase the number of able preaching ministers as a means of destroying the influence of Catholicism, and some of the best preachers who were recruited for this purpose were thoroughgoing Calvinists. According to a detailed study which has been undertaken there were approximately 180 Puritan clergy in Yorkshire between 1603 and 1640. In these years their numbers went on increasing until the time of Archbishop Neile when, as a result of the Laudian reaction, they declined sharply. In 1603 there were around 38; in 1633, the peak year, 96 and in 1640, 65.[2] In some parishes such as Halifax and Leeds there had been a succession of Puritan ministers for fifty years or more before the outbreak of the Civil War.[3]

During this period there were strong Puritan influences at work in the field of education. Wakefield Grammar School, which was established by royal charter in 1591, came into existence largely through the beneficence of George Savile, a gentleman who had grown rich in the wool trade, and his son George who were both men of Calvinist sympathies. Similarly, Dr John Favour, the celebrated Puritan vicar of Halifax, was instrumental in founding Heath Grammar School which was opened in 1600.[4] These were two particularly noteworthy cases but in addition many benefactions which were provided for the support of Yorkshire schools came from members of the gentry or the urban middle class who favoured the Puritan cause. As a general rule the master of a public grammar school was nominated by the school governors or the leading citizens of the town. In the large towns especially these were often Calvinist merchants and tradesmen who tended to select a schoolmaster whose views on religion coincided

---

[1] See W. Haller, *The Rise of Puritanism*.

[2] J. A. Newton, 'Puritanism in the Diocese of York (excluding Nottinghamshire) 1603–1640' (unpublished London Ph.D. thesis, 1956), 450.

[3] R. A. Marchant, *The Puritans and the Church Courts*, 321, 322.

[4] W. K. Jordan, *The Charities of Rural England, 1480–1660*, 320, 323–6.

with their own. In the early seventeenth century there were a considerable number of Puritan masters (usually ordained ministers) in charge of public grammar schools; these included Anthony Stephenson at Hull, John Garthwaite and John Pomeroy at Beverley, Christopher Shute at Giggleswick and Thomas Rawson at Sheffield.[1]

The first statutes of Wakefield Grammar School, which were drawn up by the governors in 1607, reflect the Puritan emphasis on the importance of religion in a child's education:

For as much as this schole is principallie ordained a seminarie for bringinge up of christian children, to become in time ambassidours of reconciliation from God to his Church: and generally is intended a schole of christian instruction for vertue and maners

the schoolmaster must therefore be

an enemie to popish superstition, a lover and forward imbracer of Gods truth...given to the diligent readinge of God's worde...we will have none to be elect Scholemaster but such a one as is able to teache his scollers the truthe of religion, out of Gods booke, and who also is as it were a minister and preacher of the same truthe to his schollers under him...The scholemaisters office and charge is diligently to instruct and informe his schollers in the groundes of religion, for which purpose we will that upon the Saturdaies from one of the clocke till two in the afternoone, he shall teache and examine his schollers in the principles of christian religion. Upon the Sabbaoth daies he shall cause them diligently to repaire to churche where his carefull eye shall overview their cariadge and behaviour, their attention also and diligence in notinge the heads of instruction delyvered by the preacher: for we will have him to geve order to all his schollers (which by theire capacitie and skill in writinge are able) in writinge to note the sermons for the helpe of their memories and theire more profitable learninge.[2]

According to Charles Hoole, who became master of Rotherham Grammar School about 1633, the curriculum in use under his predecessors included a special period of religious instruction. 'A part of Thursday in the afternoon', he writes, 'was spent in getting the Church catechisme and the six principles of Christianity made by Mr Perkins.'[3] This was a popular tract written by William Perkins and first published

[1] A. G. Matthews, *Calamy Revised*, 394, 463. R. A. Marchant, *op. cit.*, 248, 269, 270, 278. *Y.A.S.R.S.*, xxvii, 130.
[2] M. H. Peacock, *History of the Free Grammar School of Queen Elizabeth at Wakefield* 62–3, 65.
[3] *Y.A.S.R.S.*, xxxiii, 208.

in 1592 under the title *The foundation of Xtian Religion: gathered into six principles to be learned of ignorant people that they may be fit to heare Sermons with profit*. In 1613 the commissioners of charitable uses reported that John Rayney, a London draper who was a generous benefactor to Worsborough Grammar School, had given 'the whole workes of Mr William Perkins in three bookes to bee and remaine in the chappell of Worsbrough for ever for the use of the preacher Schoolemaister and other well disposed Christians'.[1]

Some Calvinist gentlemen sent their sons to public grammar schools such as Beverley, Hull and Wakefield. Others entrusted their children's education either to a resident tutor or, more often, to a clergyman who kept a private school. Sir Thomas Norcliffe of Langton, a strong Puritan, was brought up under Thomas Sugden, the minister at Hayton. Luke Robinson, the son and heir of Sir Arthur Robinson of Deighton, received part of his education under William Alder, rector of Aughton, who was eventually deprived of his living for nonconformity. Subsequently he entered the school of John Garthwaite who, after leaving Beverley Free School, had apparently established himself as a private schoolmaster in York.[2] Another Puritan gentleman, Thomas Bosvile of Braithwell, received his schooling under two masters whom he described as Mr Jackson and Mr Saxton. The latter may be identified as Peter Saxton, the Puritan rector of Edlington, a neighbouring parish. In 1638 Bosvile was inducted as vicar of Braithwell.[3]

The influence of Puritanism was felt not only in the grammar schools but also at Cambridge University and the inns of court where there was a strong Protestant tradition. Some of the Cambridge colleges were particularly noted for their radicalism, among them Emmanuel, Sidney Sussex, Queens' and Christ's College. Not a few Yorkshire schoolmasters had been educated at Cambridge and in addition a number of grammar schools had special ties with the university. At Christ's College there were scholarships reserved for pupils of Giggleswick School while Coxwold Free School had as its visitors the master and fellows of Sidney Sussex.[4] In the charter establishing Wakefield Grammar School the master and fellows of Emmanuel College were

---

[1] *Y.A.J.*, xxxix, 150.

[2] J. Peile (ed.), *Biographical Register of Christ's College*, i, 384, 430. R. A. Marchant, *op. cit.*, 224–5, 248.

[3] J. Venn (ed.), *Biographical History of Gonville and Caius College*, i, 291.

[4] *Y.A.S.R.S.*, xxxiii, 271–7. T. Whellan, *History and Topography of the City of York and the North Riding of Yorkshire*, ii, 652.

authorised 'to nomynate chuse and electe a fytte master of arte to be Scoolemaster' if the governors failed to appoint a new master within sixty days. Two of the first five masters were in fact nominated by the College.[1]

One of the most renowned Puritan teachers at Cambridge was John Preston who became a fellow of Queens' College in 1609 and master of Emmanuel College in 1622. In choosing his pupils he showed a marked preference for the heirs to men of substance, hoping in this way to promote the growth of Puritanism among the rich and influential.[2] These pupils included Sir Henry Slingsby of Scriven who was admitted to Queens' College in 1619 and remained there until 1621. From the diary which he began in 1638 it is clear that he had given a great deal of thought to religion and was in favour of some degree of church reform, although not to the extent of supporting the establishment of a Presbyterian system. Among Sir Henry's contemporaries or near-contemporaries at Queens' College there were a number of Yorkshire gentlemen who either came from Puritan families or subsequently emerged as Puritans: Sir William Strickland of Boynton and his brothers Walter and Thomas, Sir Hugh Bethell of Alne, Robert Stapleton of Wighill and his brother Sir Philip Stapleton of Warter Priory.[3]

Most Puritan gentlemen who received a university education went to Cambridge, as may be seen in the following table:

heads of Puritan families in 1642	138
number who were educated at	
(a) Cambridge	43
(b) Aberdeen and Cambridge	1
(c) Leiden and Cambridge	1
(d) Oxford	9
Total	54

At Cambridge (which had far stronger links with Yorkshire than Oxford) the most popular colleges were Sidney Sussex, Emmanuel, St John's and Christ's. In addition, over one-third of the 138 heads of families had studied at one of the inns of court.[4]

Since Calvinist influences had penetrated deeply into the urban middle class, the Puritan party was not so heavily dependent on the

[1] M. H. Peacock, *op. cit.*, 13, 116–17, 121–2.
[2] *Slingsby Diary*, 318. I. Morgan, *Prince Charles's Puritan Chaplain*, 33.
[3] *Al. Cant.*, i, 145 and iv, 90, 151, 174, 175.
[4] For sources see above, 73 n 3.

support of the gentry as the Catholic element of the community which in the main had its roots in the countryside. Nevertheless the growth of Puritanism in the rural areas owed much to that section of the squire-archy which desired a more thoroughly Protestant form of worship and church organisation. Many of these families were the owners of lay impropriations and as such were in a position to make a significant contribution to the Puritan cause by appointing ministers of the Calvinist persuasion. During the reign of Charles I, when the church authorities were markedly hostile to any form of Protestant noncon-formity, there were no fewer than eighty Yorkshire benefices under the control of Puritan lords and gentlemen.[1]

In some cases a Calvinist squire owned several rectories which (although this is difficult to substantiate) may have been acquired more from religious than economic motives. The Stricklands of Boynton in particular were great patrons. In the inquisition taken after Walter Strickland's death in 1636 we find six benefices listed: Auburn with Fraisthorpe, Carnaby, Hessle and Appleton le Street in possession and Boynton and Wintringham in reversion. In addition, Strickland presented to the rectory of Sherburn during the reign of James I. Sir William, the eldest son, was a Puritan like his father: he is described as 'a publick Professor of Religion, and one that openly owned it, and that to the uttermost of his power Sheltered and Protected the strictest professors thereof'. Among the ministers who enjoyed the patronage of the Strickland family during the early seventeenth century there are a number who can be identified as men of Puritan sympathies: these include Peter Clark at Carnaby, Thomas Clark and Enoch Sinclair at Auburn with Fraisthorpe and William Chapman at Sherburn.[2]

When the ecclesiastical authorities granted leases of impropriations the right of presentation was not always reserved to the archbishop of York: in 1637, for example, Brian Stapleton of Myton, a Calvinist squire, was required under the terms of his lease 'to procure some godly and lawfully allowed Minister to preach fower sermons a yeare in Myton Church'.[3] It is conceivable, therefore, that some at least of the

---

[1] Apart from estate papers the main sources are Lambeth Palace MSS 918 and 919 (no consistent pagination) and P.R.O., Chancery, Surveys of Church Livings, C.94/iii.

[2] P.R.O., Chancery, *Inquisitions Post Mortem*, Charles I, C.142/dliii/45. Dr Williams's Library: Morrice MSS, 'A Chronological Account of Eminent Persons, &c', vol. iii (no consistent pagination). R. A. Marchant, *The Puritans and the Church Courts*, 319, 320, 323.

[3] Lambeth Palace MSS 919.

Puritan gentlemen who obtained leases were primarily interested in the prospect of nominating ministers of their own choice. This was no doubt a major, if not the principal, motive of Thomas Westby of Ravenfield when in 1638 he persuaded the farmer of the tithes of Mexborough and Ravenfield to assign the lease to him, covenanting in the deed of assignment to find a minister at his own cost to officiate at Ravenfield.[1]

Although the Puritan gentry were strongly in favour of the principle that the parish clergy should have adequate maintenance[2] they did not necessarily feel obliged to set a good example to their neighbours even when they owned church property of considerable value. Some Calvinist patrons treated their ministers generously while others were close-fisted. In December 1633 John Alured of Sculcoates executed a deed whereby John Spofforth, a Puritan curate whom he had appointed, was put in possession of all the tithes in the parish of Sculcoates for so long as he remained there as 'preacher of the Word of God'. In contrast, Sir Arthur Ingram of Temple Newsam allowed the minister at Birdsall the modest salary of £10 a year out of an impropriate rectory worth £168 a year.[3]

If they were sometimes parsimonious as patrons of livings, the Puritan gentry nevertheless extended financial assistance on a significant scale in their efforts to foster the growth of a preaching ministry which, they confidently expected, would help to spread the gospel of Calvinism. In 1611 Sir William Gee of Bishop Burton left a rent-charge of £26. 13s. od. a year for the maintenance of a preaching minister at Bishop Burton. According to his epitaph he was 'a man illustrious for piety, integrity and charity, especially to the ministers of God's Word'.[4] In 1622 Thomas Cutler of Stainborough provided for an endowment of £300 to be paid out of his estate towards the maintenance of 'a zealous preacher of God's Word for ever at Staynburgh-chapel, or some time at Barnsley, as my son Gervase Cutler shall think fit'. Fourteen years later his widow, Ellen Cutler, added a further £320.[5] In 1624

---

[1] Lambeth Palace MSS 919.

[2] See, for example, the Yorkshire petition of February 1642 which called for church reform (*Fairfax Correspondence*, ii, 369).

[3] L. M. Stanewell (ed.), *Kingston upon Hull: Calendar of the Ancient Deeds, Letters and Miscellaneous Documents 1300–1800*, 126. Lambeth Palace MSS 918. P.R.O., Chancery Surveys of Church, Livings, C.94/iii/ff.52, 64. For Birdsall rectory see also A. F. Upton, *Sir Arthur Ingram*, 239.

[4] W. K. Jordan, *The Charities of Rural England, 1480–1660*, 377.

[5] J. Hunter, *South Yorkshire*, ii, 268. W. K. Jordan, *op. cit.*, 384.

Thomas Moseley of York, a wealthy merchant, arranged for an annuity of £4 to be paid to the minister of St Michael's church in York towards the furtherance of holy and sacramental sermons and religious exercises. This augmentation was to remain in force so long 'as he contineweth preaching minister'. Subsequently his daughter-in-law, Elizabeth Moseley, gave an annuity of £40 to St John's church in York towards the maintenance of a preaching minister.[1] In 1628 Sir Timothy Hutton of Marske directed in his will: 'I doe give unto a preachinge minister' at Marrick, 'soe longe as it shall continue in my poore posterity, twenty pounds per annum, soe he doe continue and lie there, and that he be of honest conversacion.' In addition, he granted an annuity of £10 to 'that sanctifyed man, Mr Danyell Sherrard', the preacher at Poppleton, 'untill he gett a liveinge worth forty pounds per annum'.[2]

During the early seventeenth century an impressive number of chapels were built in the West Riding to meet the spiritual needs of outlying communities which were poorly served by the existing parish system. Invariably the product of local initiative, these were mainly situated either in the clothing region or in the general vicinity of Sheffield, that is to say, in areas where Puritan influences were particularly strong.[3] Although the establishment of a chapel was usually a community effort the Puritan gentry of the neighbourhood often made an important contribution. In 1619 Sir John Savile of Howley and his son Sir Thomas gave a parcel of ground at Headingley, near Leeds, as the site for a large chapel on condition that the feoffees would maintain a 'good learned and Sufficient Minister or Clergyman'. Among the feoffees were Alexander Cooke, the Puritan vicar of Leeds, and two other neighbouring gentlemen, Ralph Hopton of Armley and Seth Skelton of Osmondthorpe.[4] The building of a chapel at Denby, in the parish of Penistone, in 1627 was largely due to the enthusiasm of Godfrey Bosvile of Gunthwaite, the principal landowner in the area. He chose as minister Charles Broxholme, a zealous Puritan who had enjoyed the patronage of Mary Lady Brooke (whose husband was related to Godfrey Bosvile) and other members of the Greville family. Broxholme was soon in trouble with the church authorities for his nonconformity and in 1632 was suspended and fined. He was succeeded by another Puritan, Daniel Clark, who married a daughter of Godfrey

---

[1] W. K. Jordan, *op. cit.*, 378, 384.   [2] *Surtees Society*, xvii, 249, 251.
[3] See W. K. Jordan, *op. cit.*, 395–8.
[4] *The First and Second Decree of the Committee of Pious Uses in Leedes*, 13–14.

Bosvile.[1] In 1629 work was started on a new chapel at Attercliffe, near Sheffield. The following year divine service was performed there for the first time, the vicar of Sheffield preaching two godly sermons, and on 27 October 1636 the chapel was formally consecrated. From as early as 1630 a curate from Sheffield parish church also served as minister at Attercliffe and it was agreed that he should receive an allowance of £10 a year in addition to his curate's stipend. Most of this sum was provided by Stephen Bright of Carbrook Hall and William Spenser of Attercliffe Hall who were the two wealthiest inhabitants of the district. The first minister to officiate at the chapel was Stanley Gower, a man of strong Puritan views. One of his successors, William Bagshaw, also served as domestic chaplain to Colonel John Bright whose father had been a leading spirit in the project.[2] Some time before the Civil War Ralph Hopton of Armley (who, as we have seen, was one of the original trustees of Headingley chapel) gave a piece of land in Armley for the building of a chapel there. When he died in 1642 the work was still in progress but the chapel was finally completed with the help and encouragement of his successors.[3]

Like the Catholic gentry the richer Puritan squires often employed household chaplains. Sir Timothy Hutton of Marske regarded this as so important that he stipulated in his will that his eldest son should 'alwaies keepe a Levite in his house... and give a competente and sufficiente allowance unto him'. It is possible that one of Sir Timothy's chaplains was John Jackson, 'a good old Puritan' whom he had presented to the living of Marske in 1620: at least this appears to be the implication of the reference to 'Mr Jackson's chamber' in the inventory taken at Marske Hall in 1629.[4] Sometimes a minister might serve as a domestic chaplain while he was waiting for a suitable living. In October 1603 Lady Margaret Hoby of Hackness recorded in her diary that her husband Sir Thomas had 'made Mr Staneford (who was without a place) an offer to Come and winter with us, wher he shoul have all thinges needfull touching his diat and Lodginge, without monie'.[5]

[1] J. Hunter, op. cit., ii, 352–3. R. A. Marchant, The Puritans and the Church Courts, 235, 238.

[2] J. Hunter, Hallamshire, 406–7, 409, 412. B. Dale, Yorkshire Puritanism and Early Nonconformity, 246.

[3] R. Thoresby, Ducatus Leodiensis, 193. The First and Second Decree of the Committee of Pious Uses in Leedes, 22.

[4] J. Peile (ed.), Biographical Register of Christ's College, i, 292. Y.A.J., vi, 245, 248.

[5] D. M. Meads (ed.), The Diary of Lady Margaret Hoby 1599–1605, 207.

Chaplaincies also represented a means of providing shelter and employment for ministers who had been silenced by the church authorities because of their nonconformist opinions. In 1630 Thomas Shepard, then a preacher at Earls Colne in Essex, was forbidden to exercise his ministry in the diocese of London. With the bishop's officers threatening to arrest him, he received a letter from Ezekiel Rogers, the Puritan vicar of Rowley in Holderness, inviting him 'to come to the knight's house, called Sir Richard Darley, dwelling at a town called Buttercrambe, and the knight's two sons, viz. Mr Henry and Mr Richard Darley, promising me £20 a year for their part, and the knight promising me my table...I resolved to follow the Lord to so remote and strange a place'. The Darleys of Buttercrambe were one of the leading Puritan families in Yorkshire but the new chaplain was far from impressed by the moral standards of the household. At his arrival, he relates, 'I found divers of them at dice and tables...I was, I saw, in a profane house, not any sincerely good...Yet the Lord did not leave me comfortless; for though the lady was churlish, yet Sir Richard was ingenious'. The reformation began when Shepard preached a sermon at the marriage between John Alured of Sculcoates, 'a most profane young gentleman', and one of Sir Richard's daughters. During this sermon 'the Lord first touched the heart of Mistress Margaret', a serving gentlewoman, 'with very great terrors for sin and her Christless estate. Whereupon others began to look about them, especially the gentlewoman lately married, Mrs Allured; and the Lord brake both their hearts very kindly. Then others in the family, viz. Mr Allured, he fell to fasting and prayer and great reformation...Others also were reformed, and their hearts changed; the whole family brought to external duties'.[1]

Chaplains in Puritan households sometimes had an additional function as lecturers: indeed a chaplaincy could simply be a disguised lectureship. A key figure in the Puritan movement, the lecturer was a minister without a cure of souls who supplemented the work of the parochial clergy by giving sermons or lectures in the parish church. At the ecclesiastical visitation of 1632 Thomas Shepard was said to have preached without licence at Buttercrambe: according to his own testimony, however, his words had fallen on stony ground because he

---

[1] A. Young, *Chronicles of the First Planters of the Colony of Massachusetts Bay, 1623–1636*, 522–6.

writes that 'I remember none in the town or about it brought home'.[1]
Shepard left Buttercrambe Hall in 1632 and was succeeded as chaplain
by another Puritan minister, Francis Peck. In January 1635 the churchwardens of Barmston admitted that Peck had preached in their church
without showing his licence, 'being brought in by Sir Matthew
Boynton knighte'. Sir Matthew Boynton of Barmston, a strong
Calvinist who later settled with his family in the Low Countries, owned
three impropriate rectories in this area: Barmston, Rudston and
Bridlington. In 1634 he took into his household an ejected minister,
Henry Jessey, who had been deprived of the living of Aughton for
rejecting the Laudian innovations and removing the crucifix. While in
Sir Matthew's employment Jessey regularly preached at Barmston
(which already had a Puritan incumbent, Martin Briggs) and at Roxby,
a North Riding village where the Boyntons had manorial rights.[2]

Life in a strict Puritan household was characterised by a daily round
of prayers, bible-reading and religious instruction. This absorption
with spiritual matters is perhaps nowhere better conveyed than in the
repetitive entries which appear in the diary of Lady Margaret Hoby of
Hackness. Here, for example, is the entry for Friday, 21 December
1599: 'After privat praier I ded a litle, and so went to church: after the
sermon I praied, then dined, and, in the after none, was busie tell 5 a
clock: then I returned to privat praier and examenation: after supped,
then hard publeck praers and, after that, praied privatly, havinge reed
a Chapter of the bible, and so went to bed.' For such a family church-
going was not simply a matter of Sunday observance: on the contrary,
they often attended church several times a week. When visiting Linton
Grange (the home first of her mother and then her cousin Robert
Dakins) Lady Margaret and her husband went to church either at
Wintringham or Thorpe Bassett and we can see from the evidence of
her diary how thoroughly Puritan was the form of worship practised in
these East Riding parishes. At this time church services appear in the
main to have consisted of sermons and exercises. The religious exercise
was essentially a Puritan institution which was designed to improve
morals and scriptural knowledge. One of its basic features was a form

---

[1] R. A. Marchant, *The Puritans and the Church Courts*, 123. A. Young, *op. cit.*, 526.
[2] R. A. Marchant, *The Puritans and the Church Courts*, 122–3. Lambeth Palace MSS 918
(Barmston and Rudston). P.R.O., Common Pleas, Feet of Fines, C.P.25(2)/523 (Bridlington). Edmund Calamy, *A Continuation of the Account of The Ministers...who were
Ejected and Silenced after the Restoration in 1660*, i, 46. See below, 308, for Sir Matthew's
sojourn in the Low Countries.

of catechism but it could also include preaching, psalm-singing and fasting. Among the ministers who preached or conducted exercises were a number of known Puritans: John Philips, rector of Thorpe Bassett, William Langdale, vicar of Ganton, William Ward, vicar of Scarborough, and Richard Rhodes, chaplain to Sir Thomas Hoby. On 18 September 1603 Lady Margaret noted in her diary: 'Mr Hoby, my mother, and my selfe, with our sarvants, went to Thorpbasitt wher we hard Mr phileps preach: in the after none we hard him at winteringame, wher he continewde his exercise untill 5 a cloke att night.' Three days later she was writing: 'This day... Mr philipes Came and preached at winteringame: we were accompaned with him and his wiffe, Mr Strickland and his wiffe, my Cossine Dakins and his wiffe, with divers others.' On 2 October there is the entry, 'Mr Langdall Came to winteringe, and preached...verie profetable', while on 25 October it is recorded that 'the exercise of fastinge and preaching was Continewed by Mr ward and Mr Rhodes Untill 2 or 3 A Clocke at night'.[1]

In parishes like Wintringham and Thorpe Bassett Calvinist families were able to attend services which basically conformed to their own ideas on church worship: or rather they could do so for as long as the archbishop of York was a man like Matthew Hutton who had Puritan sympathies. During the early seventeenth century, however, there is growing evidence that in some areas Puritan ministers and laymen were going further and holding conventicles: that is, secret and unlawful prayer-meetings 'outside the worship of the Church'. John Birchall, who became rector of St Martin's York in 1633, presided at conventicles which were held in the house of Dr Scott, dean of York, without his knowledge. Timothy Thurscross, a prebendary, 'afterwards so well knowne being then a Puritan... joyned with them in their Meeting, as did the Lady Bethell, widow of Sir Walter Bethell, or Sir Hugh Bethell, and divers other Ladyes and some people of Quality as well as others of meane condition'.[2] In July 1636 Sir Matthew Boynton of Barmston and Martin Briggs, rector of Barmston, were summoned before the Northern High Commission to give evidence about a conventicle which they had attended at Colton, near York, in 1634. Sir Matthew, who was then in London, never answered the summons.[3]

---

[1] D. M. Meads (ed.), *The Diary of Lady Margaret Hoby 1599–1605*, 91, 205, 207. R. A. Marchant, *The Puritans and the Church Courts*, 259, 269, 271–2, 290.

[2] Dr Williams's Library: Morrice MSS, 'A Chronological Account of Eminent Persons, &c', vol. iii (no consistent pagination).

[3] R. A. Marchant, *The Puritans and the Church Courts*, 88. See below, 306–7.

The growth of the conventicle movement was, in part at least, a direct response to the Laudian policy of Archbishop Neile with its emphasis on external ceremony and clerical uniformity. Archbishop Neile, for his part, was determined to stamp out this manifestation of Puritan discontent. In 1639 Sir Henry Slingsby of Scriven noted in his diary that from time to time a sermon was delivered in the family chapel at Red House, 'altho' we incur some danger if it were complain'd off, it being contrary to the orders of the Church. I once assay'd to get it consecrat'd by our Bishop which is Bishop Neale, but he refus'd, having as he saith express command not to consecrate any, least it may be occasion of conventicles, and so I think it may be abus'd.'[1]

Since the wholehearted Calvinist regarded himself as a member of God's elect and his religion as an all-pervading force which touched every part of his daily life, the legions of the godly might be expected to display a certain degree of uniformity in terms of personal character and behaviour. In the strict code of moral principles to which the Puritan faithful were required to conform there was great emphasis on the virtue of diligence, both as a social necessity and a religious obligation. Conversely, idleness was adjudged a sin whether it was found in the low-born or the privileged who enjoyed inherited wealth: as William Perkins put it, 'Every person of every degree, state, sexe or condition without exception, must have some personal or particular calling to walke in'.[2] Whatever his field of activity the true Christian had a duty 'to scorn delights and live laborious days', to occupy his waking hours with work and prayers to the exclusion of vain pastimes such as hunting, hawking and gaming.[3] In Yorkshire the Puritan magistrate was often one of the most energetic and conscientious members of the bench, and not least in matters of religion. In 1611 Sir Stephen Proctor of Fountains, a West Riding justice of the peace, was said to have done good service in a commission for seizing the goods of recusants, in which task he was 'more diligent, with charge and travile, then any other Justice or Knight or Esquire named in that commission'.[4] Sir Thomas Hoby of Hackness, for many years a deputy lieutenant and a magistrate in both the North and East Ridings, received an even

---

[1] *Slingsby Diary*, 19.   [2] William Perkins, *Works*, 909.
[3] See L. B. Wright, *Middle Class Culture in Elizabethan England*, 170–85.
[4] P.R.O., Star Chamber Proceedings, Star Chamber 8/227/35.

greater tribute in 1635 when a Cheshire squire, Sir William Brereton, wrote of him in his journal:

This man the most understanding, able and industrious justice of peace in this kingdome. Noe warrant graunted out butt he takes notice thereof in a booke: and att sessions an account demaunded of all those warrants sent out: which if the constables to whom they are delivered, doe not exequute nor returne, and give an account: they are called uppon att the sessions: or if those that require and procure the warrants keepe them in their hands, and make use of them for their owne ends and do nott deliver them to bee served they are bound over to the sessions.[1]

A similar degree of application and attention to detail was often in evidence when the Puritan gentry were handling their personal affairs. Not infrequently their wills are of exceptional length because of the elaborate arrangements which were made for the financial support of the heir during his minority (sometimes involving a sliding scale) or the payment of annuities and portions to the younger sons and daughters. Detailed accounts which have survived among their family muniments[2] provide further evidence of the businesslike spirit in which the Puritan gentry conducted their affairs. In such cases it is clear that the head of the family was in the habit of keeping a close watch on his income and expenditure.

Some of the most efficient and enterprising landowners in Yorkshire at this time were men with a Puritan outlook on religion. Sir Stephen Proctor of Fountains mined coal and lead on an extensive scale and, in the teeth of bitter opposition from his Catholic neighbours, made enclosures on various parts of his estate; in 1611 he was said to have enclosed 3000 acres of land in Kirkbyshire and Nidderdale.[3] Sir John Savile of Howley had a great ironworks at Kirkstall which appears to have been worth over £2000 a year at the time of his death.[4] In 1621 Sir Henry Anderson, a Newcastle businessman, bought the estate of Long Cowton and began to carry out enclosures which (it was alleged) also took in the lands belonging to the rectory. At the time of the purchase the manor was valued at £292 a

---

[1] *Surtees Society*, cxxiv, 6. See Sir Thomas Hoby's letter printed in *C.R.S.*, liii, 374–5.
[2] Such collections include the Temple Newsam MSS (Leeds Central Library), the Bright MSS (Sheffield Central Library) and the Slingsby MSS (Y.A.S. Library).
[3] P.R.O., Star Chamber Proceedings, Star Chamber 8/16/20 and 227/1, 3, 4, and 35.
[4] See above, 64.

year but on the eve of the Civil War it was yielding a revenue of
£1000 a year.[1]

Lower down the economic scale there were Puritan gentlemen with
few social pretensions who threw their energies wholeheartedly into
the business of managing and developing their estates. In the reign of
Charles I William Copley of Wadworth undertook the cultivation of
an extensive demesne which he held on lease, having turned over his
own estate to his son Christopher. After entering into possession
Christopher Copley planted orchards, hopyards and timber trees,
carried out enclosures and made other improvements to the property.[2]
From the evidence of their estate papers the Bosviles of Warmsworth,
who were relatives and neighbours of the Copley family, had a similar
passion for good husbandry: in the reign of James I, for example, we
find Gervase Bosvile farming a considerable acreage in Warmsworth,
Thorne and Alverley and improving the yield from his estate by means
of enclosures and the redistribution of strips.[3]

The Puritan gentry were not only energetic landowners: they also
included a substantial number of professional and commercial families.
The following table shows how they compared in this respect with the
Yorkshire gentry as a whole:

	Puritan gentry	Yorkshire gentry as a whole
number of families in the period 1558–1642	147	963
number of families which at one time or another were represented in the professional or commercial gentry[4]	68	265
number of heads of families in 1642	138	679
number engaged at one time or another in a professional or commercial career	35	108

Many of the merchants and lawyers who appear in the ranks of the
Yorkshire gentry had either been born into Calvinist families or had
come under the influence of Calvinism while they were learning their

---

[1] P.R.O., Chancery Proceedings, Series II, C.2 James I/A1/13, and Chancery Decrees
and Orders, C.33/ccvii/f.236. *Cal. Committee for Compounding*, 2337.

[2] P.R.O., Chancery Proceedings, Six Clerks' Series, C.7/418/25 and C.10/55/32. See
above, 53.

[3] Leeds Central Library: Battie Wrightson MSS, and in particular BW/R/4. See
above, 33.

[4] For the various types of activity included see the table on 85, above.

19—Y.G.

trade or profession. The Puritan gentry had particularly close links with the world of commerce: they can be found lending money at interest, buying stock in trading companies[1] and apprenticing their sons to city merchants.

If the Puritan theologians proclaimed the glory of work with evangelical fervour they were equally insistent about the importance and necessity of thrift. Ostentation and self-indulgence (factors responsible for the decline of many gentle families) were anathema to them: the sincere Christian, they held, must be sober in his attire, frugal in his diet and generally restrained in his expenditure on worldly goods.[2] Whatever its impact on the solid burgesses of the towns the gospel of thrift appears, on the whole, to have had only a moderate influence on the Calvinist gentry, or at least those families which could afford to engage in luxury spending. A Puritan squire might bewail 'the vanity of all worldly things'[3] but the tokens of affluence often had a magnetic attraction for him. This conflict between moral precept and personal inclination is reflected in the memorandum of advice which Henry Tempest of Tong prepared for his son in 1648. Having been left a good inheritance (he relates) he had delighted in building and whatever took his fancy. Gold and silver he had in plenty but on seriously contemplating such things he had found them to be 'vanity and vexation of spirit': they were 'excellent servants but bad masters'. And he told his son: 'Seek thou first the Kingdom of God and the righteousness thereof and all these things shall be added unto thee.'[4]

During this period many Puritan gentlemen, in accordance with contemporary fashion, built themselves fine new houses. These included two of the largest mansions in Yorkshire: Temple Newsam, the work of Sir Arthur Ingram, and Howley Hall, which was completed by Sir John Savile after his father's death.[5] In addition, the more substantial Puritan families were generally well endowed with the sort of material possessions which advertised wealth and status: collections of plate, hangings of tapestry, high-quality furniture, pictures, jewellery and coaches. In 1634 a party of travellers from Norwich were shown

---

[1] See below, 310.
[2] See L. B. Wright, *Middle Class Culture in Elizabethan England*, 185–200.
[3] See above, 104.
[4] Cartwright Memorial Hall, Bradford: Tempest MSS, Henry Tempest's advice to his son, 16 February 1647(–8).
[5] See above, 103, 106.

round Sir Arthur Ingram's house in York and gazed with admiration at his 'store of massie Plate, rich Hangings, lively Pictures and Statues, rich £150 pearle Glasses, fayre stately £500 Organ, and other rich Furniture in every Roome'.[1] In 1643 it was reported that goods worth over £4000 had been taken from Boynton Hall, the seat of Sir William Strickland, by royalist troops.[2] Another Puritan squire, Sir Gervase Cutler of Stainborough, had a personal estate to the value of £4000 plundered by both sides; in addition, he made a gift of family plate worth £1000 in support of the royalist cause.[3]

Although they felt assured of the supreme distinction, membership of God's elect, the Puritan gentry did not necessarily disdain earthly titles. In 1626 Thomas Alured, a royal official, sought a knighthood for his brother, Henry Alured of Sculcoates. In a letter to Sir John Coke, one of the principal secretaries of state, he wrote: 'If you would bespeak, against the coronation, two or three knights that you may have in your power...I should acknowledge it a favour if you would vouchsafe my elder brother that honour.'[4] During the early Stuart period several Calvinist squires purchased baronetcies. Sir William Constable of Flamborough bought the honour in June 1611, shortly after the order was instituted and while he was still a minor. Similarly Sir Matthew Boynton of Barmston acquired a baronetcy in 1618 with an immediate down-payment of £1100, but the money was subsequently refunded.[5] Most of the wealthy Puritan gentry, however, appear to have been unwilling to spend so heavily on the purchase of titles. Although there were nine baronets within their ranks in 1642 five of these had been granted the honour free of charge as the Crown sought to gather support on the eve of the Civil War.[6]

In one respect at least the Puritan gentry were completely out of sympathy with the social values of their class. This was their dislike of elaborate and pretentious funerals, an attitude which was based on a mixture of religious and financial considerations. When George Trotter of Skelton Castle drew up his will in March 1647 he inserted

---

[1] L. G. Wickham Legg (ed.), *A Relation of a Short Survey of 26 Counties*, 21.

[2] *H.M.C. Thirteenth Report*, Appendix i, 102.

[3] P.R.O., S.P.Dom., Committee for Compounding, S.P.23/clxxx/574, 582. J. Hunter, *South Yorkshire*, ii, 267.

[4] *H.M.C. Coke MSS*, i, 248.

[5] G.E.C. (ed.), *Complete Baronetage*, i, 44, 114. *Cal.S.P.Dom. 1611–18*, 599.

[6] A number of free grants are recorded in P.R.O., Signet Office Docquets, Index 6811 under the years 1641 and 1642.

what had become a virtually standard clause in Puritan wills: 'I be-
queath my body to be buried wheresoever it shall please the Lord to
make a separacion betwixt it and my soule, avoidinge all pompe and
unnecessarie and superflous expence of monies.'[1] Thomas Stockdale of
Bilton Park, who made his will in 1651, went even further and stipulated
that the cost of his funeral should not exceed £10.[2] To the strict
Calvinist church monuments with effigies smacked too much of idolatry. In March 1639 Sir Gervase Cutler gave direction that at his
death there should be no tomb erected to his memory 'but a plaine
stone, with this worde onely uppon it, *Christo Resurgam*';[3] and such
leading families as the Stricklands of Boynton and the Hobys of
Hackness commemorated their dead with simple wall tablets on which
the inscriptions were the dominant feature. In some cases, however,
family pride overcame religious scruples and a number of wealthy
Puritans, among them Sir John Savile of Methley and Sir William
Gee of Bishop Burton, have their likenesses preserved in tomb effigies.

If the Puritan gentry showed a tendency to conform to the standards
of a society which believed in conspicuous consumption they were
rarely guilty of living beyond their means. During this period Sir
William Constable of Flamborough was virtually the only Calvinist
squire to find himself in financial difficulties as the result of personal
extravagance.[4] More typical is the kind of Puritan gentleman who,
while maintaining a good standard of living, normally had a healthy
reserve of ready money at his disposal. In this category was Sir
Matthew Boynton of Barmston who in April 1642 was able to invest
the sum of £1000 in a scheme (or 'adventure' as it was called) for the
recovery of Ireland from the Catholic rebels. When he drew up his will
in October 1645 his personal estate included at least £2600 in money
and bonds.[5] Another Puritan squire who had a considerable amount of
liquid wealth available was Sir Richard Hawksworth of Hawksworth:
in May 1652 he noted on one of his accounts that he had £709. 9s. 9d.
'all in gold' stored in trunks while in February 1658 an inventory of his
goods and chattels revealed that he had left £860. 16s. 9d. in gold and
silver.[6] Although the Puritan gentry were generally careful in their

[1] Borthwick Institute of Historical Research: York Wills, will dated 5 March 1646(-7).
[2] Y.A.S. Library: Bilton Park MSS, BL 240.
[3] Borthwick Institute of Historical Research: York Wills, will dated 23 March 1638(-9).
[4] For Sir William Constable see above, 123 and below, 351.
[5] Somerset House: Register Fines, f.75 (will dated 1 October 1645).
[6] Sheffield Central Library: Bright MSS 89a and 182.

spending this does not necessarily mean that they were lacking in charitable instincts: on the contrary, they were often generous benefactors, not only in the sphere of religion but also in such fields as education and poor relief.[1]

In view of their industry, their attention to detail and their general dislike of reckless extravagance the Puritan families should, in theory at least, have been one of the most prosperous groups within the Yorkshire gentry. On the whole, the figures[2] bear out this inference:

total number of Puritan families in the period 1600–42	145
families which added considerably to their estates and avoided heavy debt	69
families which sold all or most of their property	8
families which sold considerable property	14
families which were heavily indebted but avoided any significant sale of land	11
total number of families in financial difficulties	33

The difficulties experienced by a section of the Puritan gentry were due to a number of factors (not all within the control of the individual) but probably the most important was expenditure on litigation. Self-righteous and self-assertive, the more extreme Puritans quarrelled with their neighbours, their fellow magistrates, even with their own relatives, and this often led to proceedings in the law-courts. As the country moved towards Civil War this factious spirit was to take on new significance.

[1] For the Puritan attitude to charity see W. K. Jordan, *Philanthropy in England, 1480–1660* and *The Charities of Rural England, 1480–1660*.
[2] For a discussion of sources, see above, 93, 144–5.

CHAPTER XIII

The Disaffected Gentry

In February 1614 the lord president of the Council of the North informed the lord chancellor that there had been numerous complaints about the evil carriage of Sir John Savile of Howley, *custos rotulorum* for the West Riding, who 'maketh Use of his Authority to satisfy his own Ends'. One of the wealthiest landowners in Yorkshire, Sir John was extremely ambitious, arrogant, hot-tempered and unscrupulous. By December 1615 his conduct as a magistrate had caused such a scandal that he had little choice but to resign the post of *custos rotulorum* (a highly coveted appointment of great prestige value) which was then assigned, at his suggestion, to Sir Thomas Wentworth of Wentworth Woodhouse, the future Earl of Strafford. Following his resignation Savile resolved to seek a patron at court and managed to ingratiate himself with the king's new favourite, Sir George Villiers, who became Earl and later Duke of Buckingham. In September 1617 Buckingham wrote to Wentworth requesting him to surrender the office of *custos rotulorum* in favour of Savile. Sir Thomas, however, refused to comply with this request, pointing out that he was under no obligation to his predecessor: if Sir John (he wrote) 'should supply the roome in my place, the worlde conceaving generally and I having felt experiencedly to be very little frendly towards me, itt might justly be taken as the greatest disgrace that could be done unto me'. Sir John never forgave Wentworth for crossing him in this way and since the young squire of Wentworth Woodhouse was no less proud and ambitious this incident marked the beginning of a ruthless struggle for power which was to be a dominant factor in Yorkshire politics for more than a decade.[1]

The rivalry between Savile and Wentworth was brought into sharp focus during a parliamentary election. In this period the county election was regarded as of great importance not merely because of the

---

[1] Knowler, i, 2–4. J. J. Cartwright (ed.), *Chapters in the History of Yorkshire*, 184–91. See also C. V. Wedgwood, *Thomas Wentworth, First Earl of Strafford, 1593–1641: A Revaluation*.

social prestige which a knight of the shire enjoyed but because it provided an opportunity to test the strength of the opposing groups within the shire. In standing for the county Sir Thomas was usually able to count on the backing of a large section of the Yorkshire squirearchy who in turn rallied their freehold tenants on his behalf. In June 1625, when Savile was disputing his election as knight of the shire, he told the House of Commons that he had been supported by the greatest number of men of quality who had appeared at such a poll at any time during the last twenty years.[1] Among the principal landowners who sided with Wentworth were the following:

North Riding. Sir Henry Bellasis of Newburgh Priory, Sir Richard Cholmley of Whitby, Sir Thomas Dawney of Sessay, Sir Thomas Fairfax of Gilling (also of Walton, W.R.), Sir Thomas Hoby of Hackness, Christopher Wandesford of Kirklington.
East Riding. Sir Matthew Boynton of Barmston, Sir William Constable of Flamborough, Sir John Hotham of Scorborough.
West Riding. Henry Lord Clifford, John Lord Darcy of Aston, Sir Richard Beaumont of Whitley, Sir Thomas Fairfax of Denton, Sir Arthur Ingram of Temple Newsam, Sir John Jackson of Hickleton, Sir Peter Middleton of Stockeld, Sir Edward Osborne of Kiveton, Sir Henry Savile of Methley, Sir Henry Slingsby of Scriven, Thomas Wentworth of North Elmsall, Sir Francis Wortley of Wortley.

This list includes virtually every Yorkshireman who was granted a baronetcy between 1611 and Charles I's accession in 1625 and virtually every Protestant squire of real substance in Wentworth's native West Riding. The most notable exception under both heads is his relative Sir George Savile of Thornhill with whom he was engaged in protracted litigation.[2] By virtue of their social and financial status Wentworth's chief supporters played a leading part in the administration of the county: the great majority sat on the commission of the peace and many of them also served at one time or another as members of the Council of the North, sheriffs and deputy lieutenants.

If Wentworth's party was essentially the party of the well-to-do country gentry Sir John Savile, for his part, appears to have been in the habit of making direct appeals to the small freeholders who constituted a majority of the county electorate. In December 1620 Wentworth told

---

[1] J. J. Cartwright (ed.), *op. cit.*, 223–4.
[2] H. C. Foxcroft, *Life and Letters of Sir George Savile*, i, 5, 7.

Sir George Calvert, who was running in harness with him at the election: 'I find the Gentlemen of these Parts generally ready to do you Service...but Sir John Savile by his Instruments exceeding busy, intimating to the common Sort under Hand, that Yourself', not being resident in Yorkshire, 'cannot by Law be chosen.'[1] Sir John's principal stronghold was the clothing region around Leeds, Wakefield and Halifax. Here his estates were situated but, more important, he had set himself up as a patron of the West Riding clothiers and earned their loyalty by zealously watching over their interests in the House of Commons.[2]

For some time observers of the Westminster scene had been able to discern two opposing parties in the political field: the Court Party which consisted of men with court connections who actively supported the Crown, and the Country Party which represented, through the medium of the House of Commons, the interests of the country at large or at least of the propertied classes in the counties. Since Sir John Savile enjoyed the patronage of the reigning favourite his fortunes were inevitably bound up with the Court Party. During Buckingham's régime he displayed great diligence in the service of the Crown and in return for his loyalty, both in county affairs and in the House of Commons, he was made a member of the Privy Council and vice-president of the Council of the North.[3] Wentworth also had influential friends in Whitehall, in particular, Sir George Calvert, one of the secretaries of state, and Bishop Williams, the lord keeper. His motives in maintaining links with the court were twofold: in the first place, he was seeking to counter Savile's intrigues against him and, secondly, he was anxious to secure a major appointment commensurate with his talents. In January 1626 he even had the temerity to solicit the office of lord president of the Council of the North[4] but so long as Buckingham was in power he had little hope of furthering his political ambitions.

During the period of Buckingham's ascendancy Wentworth came to be regarded as one of the leaders of the popular party in the House of Commons although there was little radicalism in his political views. Most of his principal supporters in Yorkshire also served as Members of Parliament and in the main they represented the type of gentry (wealthy squires with no court loyalties) who formed the backbone of

---

[1] Knowler, i, 10.
[2] Knowler, i, 11. R. R. Reid, *The King's Council in the North*, 394–5.
[3] R. R. Reid, *op. cit.*, 398. [4] *Cal.S.P.Dom., 1625–6*, 228.

the Country Party. Although there was nothing resembling a party organisation or a political programme in the modern sense the Country Party members in the House of Commons were in general agreement on certain issues. In the first place, they attached great importance to the liberties and privileges of Parliament. When James I argued in 1621 that these privileges were enjoyed only through the favour of the Crown Wentworth declared in the subsequent debate that 'The common Lawes are but custome, and wee claime our liberties by the same title as wee doe our estates, by custome'.[1] Secondly, as landowners the Country Party representatives had strong convictions about the sanctity of property. Arbitrary taxation was regarded as a direct threat to what they termed 'the propriety of our goods': if the king had the power to impose taxes without parliamentary consent the possessions of his subjects were, in theory at least, entirely at his disposal. Since the country gentry were primarily responsible for the collection of taxes the compulsory loan schemes to which Charles I resorted in the early years of his reign inevitably produced a conflict of loyalties. In these circumstances some Yorkshire squires like Sir Thomas Wentworth were prepared to face imprisonment rather than contribute, while others like his friend Sir Thomas Fairfax of Denton faithfully carried out their duties as commissioners.[2] Another cause which always met with an enthusiastic response within the Country Party was the preservation of religion. During Buckingham's régime there were a number of developments which aroused misgivings in Protestant minds: the infiltration of Catholics into major offices, both in Whitehall and in the counties; the relaxation of the penal laws; the growth of High Church influences; and the marriage negotiations first with Spain and then with France. Anti-Catholic feeling was at its strongest among the Puritans who made up the radical wing of the Country Party. Of the Yorkshire Puritan members the most prominent, certainly in debates on religious affairs, was Sir Thomas Hoby, who was virtually an automatic choice for the type of committee which inquired into the working of the penal laws. While Sir Thomas saw Catholicism as a national problem he was particularly concerned about the state of religion in Yorkshire. In 1620 he was admonished for behaving disrespectfully towards Lord Scroope, the Catholic-minded lord president of the Council of the North, whose

---

[1] W. Notestein, F. H. Relf and H. Simpson (ed.), *Commons Debates, 1621*, v, 239.
[2] See below, 292, 293.

appointment in 1619 had marked the beginning of a more tolerant era for northern Catholics.[1]

At the Christmas election of 1620 Sir Thomas Wentworth and Sir George Calvert were returned as knights of the shire. Following his defeat Sir John Savile claimed that Wentworth had attempted to intimidate the freeholders, and the sheriff, Sir Thomas Gower of Stittenham, was accused of deliberately excluding many of Savile's supporters from the poll. Although Savile produced a number of witnesses in his favour the House of Commons eventually ruled that the election was valid.[2] At the next election (which was for the Parliament of 1624) Savile managed to gain his revenge: he and his son Sir Thomas were elected as county representatives and Wentworth had to take up one of the Pontefract seats which had been kept in reserve for him.[3] In June 1625 Wentworth stood with Sir Thomas Fairfax of Denton in the county election. The Saviles attempted to win the day by bringing in troops of apprentices so that one of Wentworth's correspondents was prompted to say that it was more like a rebellion than an election; in spite of this stratagem, however, the two Country Party candidates were declared successful. Characteristically Savile took steps to challenge the return and again the sheriff (this time Sir Richard Cholmley of Whitby) was alleged to have acted unfairly on Wentworth's behalf. After considering the arguments of the rival parties the Commons decided in Savile's favour and a new election was ordered for 1 August. On 16 July Sir Thomas wrote to his colleague Fairfax: 'It should be handsomely infused into the gentry how much it concerns them to maintain their own act, and that the whole kingdom looks not only whether Sir John be able to carry it against you and me, but indeed against all the gentlemen too besides.' When the day of the election came Wentworth and Fairfax were again returned but on 12 August the king dissolved Parliament.[4]

In the following November seven of the parliamentary leaders, among them Sir Thomas Wentworth, were appointed sheriffs of their respective counties. This was the outcome of a deliberate plan conceived by the Duke of Buckingham with the intention of disqualifying

---

[1] *Commons Debates, 1621, passim. Camden Society*, New Series, vi, 25. W. Notestein and F. H. Relf (ed.), *Commons Debates for 1629*, 72, 114, 234. *Cal.S.P.Dom 1619–23*, 168.

[2] J. J. Cartwright (ed.), *Chapters in the History of Yorkshire*, 208–12.

[3] J. J. Cartwright (ed.), *op. cit.*, 214. Knowler, i, 27.

[4] Knowler, i, 27. *Fairfax Correspondence*, i, 8–10. J. J. Cartwright (ed.), *op. cit.*, 215–26.

them from standing at the new election which would shortly be announced. Following the pricking of sheriffs Sir Arthur Ingram wrote to Wentworth: 'God give you Joy, you are now the great Officer of Yorkshire; but you had the Endeavours of your poor Friend to have prevented it. But I think, if all the Council that were at Court had joined together in Request for you, it would not have prevailed.' With Wentworth disqualified two other major squires, Sir William Constable and Sir Francis Wortley, decided to take on the Saviles in the county election. In December Wentworth told his friend Christopher Wandesford: 'Now, as that noble Baronet of the East hath declared himself to you, so hath Sir Francis Wortley to me, that he intends to stand. From which good purpose I did not study his Conversion; for, I foresaw if he gained it, Savile were lost for ever.' In the event Wentworth's hopes were not fulfilled: when the election took place Sir William Constable was returned for one of the county seats but Sir John Savile managed to win the other.[1]

The new Parliament which was due to meet on 6 February 1626 had been called with the express purpose of seeking financial support for the Spanish war which represented the latest phase of Buckingham's erratic foreign policy. In the meantime preparations were being made for the raising of what amounted to a compulsory loan from the gentry and other wealthy subjects of the Crown. The borrowing of money on privy seals was far from being a new expedient: Queen Elizabeth, for example, had made use of this device on several occasions. The privy seal in this context was a printed letter from the sovereign to a named individual exhorting him to lend a certain sum of money for a specified period. One such letter has survived among the papers of Godfrey Copley of Sprotborough: issued in April 1626, this is a request for the loan of £15 which would be repaid within eighteen months.[2]

In March 1626 letters of appointment were despatched to the men who had been selected for the task of superintending the loan scheme in Yorkshire. Sir Conyers Darcy was made responsible for the North Riding, Sir Henry Savile and Sir Henry Goodricke for the West Riding and Sir Matthew Boynton for the East Riding.[3] The size of the proposed contribution (reported to have been of the order of £5000) caused great discontent in the county and there was a general reluctance to pay.

[1] Knowler, i, 29, 32–3, 35. J. J. Cartwright (ed.), op. cit., 226–8, 362.
[2] Y.A.S. Library: Copley of Sprotborough MSS, DD38.
[3] Acts of the Privy Council 1625–6, 288–9, 369–70.

Some of the Yorkshire M.P.s complained to the Privy Council that the sum demanded was higher than any previous assessment and exceeded the charge laid on any other county. In the light of these representations the Council consented to a reduction and the M.P.s for Yorkshire constituencies met together and agreed on a new division of cost among the ridings and towns, the whole amounting to £4100. Following this meeting Sir John Savile undertook to do everything in his power to ensure the speedy payment of the sum allocated to the West Riding which was still above the usual rate.[1]

On 14 April letters were sent to the West Riding collectors discharging them from office and instructing them to repay any money which they had received and return the old privy seals to London. At the same time their successors were issued with new lists of individual assessments which amounted to about £2000, as compared with the sum of £1800 which had been allotted to the West Riding at the meeting of Yorkshire M.P.s. In the case of the East Riding Sir Matthew Boynton was retained as collector and directed to refund the difference between the old and new rates to persons who had already contributed to the loan.[2]

For reasons which remain obscure the former collectors for the West Riding took their time over repaying the loan money in their hands and this led to further trouble. On 3 May Sir Gervase Cutler, one of the new collectors, reported to the Privy Council that he had delivered the fifty-five privy seals which had been sent to him but that a number of gentlemen had refused payment on the grounds that they had received similar privy seals from Sir Henry Savile and assumed that it was not the intention to charge them double. Some of these refusers, including Sir Francis Wortley and Sir John Jackson, had said that they would give their answer in London. Others had treated the privy seals with contempt: when, for example, a servant of Sir Gervase Cutler attempted to deliver such a letter at the house of Philip Anne of Frickley, a recusant squire, two of the latter's retainers 'threwe the privy Seale out of the dores after him'. Presumably as a result of this report Sir Henry Savile and Sir Henry Goodricke were reprimanded for their negligence and ordered to pay back the money without further delay.[3]

On 7 July the justices of the peace throughout England were

[1] *Fairfax Correspondence*, i, 61. *Acts of the Privy Council 1625–6*, 421–2.
[2] *Acts of the Privy Council 1625–6*, 423–32.
[3] P.R.O., S.P.Dom., Charles I, S.P.16/xxvi/32. *Acts of the Privy Council 1626*, 10.

instructed to call together the subsidymen and exhort them to furnish a free gift or benevolence. Since, it was explained, the late House of Commons had been prepared to grant four subsidies (though in fact this was conditional on a redress of grievances) the king expected his subjects out of their loyalty to supply him with an equivalent sum as though the proposed subsidy act had been passed.[1] A fortnight later the lord lieutenant of Yorkshire was informed that it had been decided to make the county responsible for half the cost of three men-of-war which the town of Hull was required to provide for coastal defence. The levying of ship money in wartime was not without precedent: nevertheless there were complaints about the heavy burden and it was eventually agreed that the assessment should be reduced to two ships, that the county should bear one-third of the cost, and that Hull should have assistance from Halifax, Leeds and Wakefield with the remaining two-thirds.[2]

Between August and October the Yorkshire justices of the peace submitted their returns, wapentake by wapentake, on the response of the subsidymen to the 'free gift' scheme. The subsidymen (they reported) were generally unwilling to contribute and even where an offer had been made it was too negligible to merit serious consideration: in Holderness, for instance, four subsidies usually amounted to £800 but the justices doubted whether it would be possible to raise as much as £30. Although poverty was often pleaded as an excuse the propertied classes were in effect refusing to pay subsidies for which there was no parliamentary authority.[3]

In the autumn of 1626 there was an incident in the East Riding which sheds some light on the divisions within the squirearchy of that region. On 5 October Henry Viscount Dunbar, writing from his country seat at Burton Constable, informed the Duke of Buckingham, in his capacity as lord high admiral, that three ships had run aground at Barmston and that Sir Matthew Boynton had taken possession of many of their goods which he was holding at his house, Barmston Hall. At Dunbar's suggestion the Duke commissioned Sir Thomas Metham of North Cave and Sir William Alford of Meaux Abbey to investigate the matter but as late as 7 November they were reporting that Sir Matthew's absence had prevented them from coming to a knowledge of the goods in

---

[1] *Cal.S.P.Dom. 1625–6*, 369. *Acts of the Privy Council 1626*, 133–4.
[2] *Acts of the Privy Council 1626*, 108–9, 146, 243, 244–5.
[3] *Cal.S.P.Dom.1625–6*, 410, 425, 428, 440, 465. *Fairfax Correspondence*, i, 72–4.

question.[1] In part Dunbar's attitude appears to have been conditioned by a private quarrel with Boynton over their respective manorial rights: thus in Easter term 1627 he was to bring two actions of trespass against Boynton and his servants for taking away ship timber from the sands of Barmston.[2] This, however, was not the only factor involved. While Sir Matthew had pronounced Puritan sympathies Dunbar was the most substantial Catholic layman in the East Riding (and indeed in 1630 he was to compound for his recusancy). In June 1626 the House of Commons had submitted a petition to the king complaining of the number of Catholics who held important offices in the counties and among the men whom they listed were two East Riding deputy lieutenants, Lord Dunbar and Sir Thomas Metham.[3] Last but not least there were political differences. Lord Dunbar had court connections and was clearly on good terms with the Duke of Buckingham while Sir Matthew (as Dunbar took care to warn his patron) wholly sided with Sir John Hotham and Sir William Constable who in all things were opposed to the Duke.[4] About the beginning of November Boynton's name was put forward for the shrievalty of Yorkshire, no doubt as a punishment for his association with the popular party. Fortunately for him Thomas Alured, a royal official who was brother to Henry Alured of Sculcoates, another Puritan squire, interceded on his behalf with Sir John Coke, one of the secretaries of state, and as a result Sir Matthew was reprieved, though only until 1628.[5]

Faced with a nation-wide resistance to the 'free gift' scheme the Privy Council decided to abandon it in favour of a general loan equivalent to five subsidies. Whereas the previous loan on privy seals had involved perhaps 350 wealthy individuals in Yorkshire the new loan was to be raised from the whole body of subsidymen, that is to say, virtually all the gentry and many yeomen and merchants. As in the case of parliamentary subsidies a number of commissioners (subsequently increased to include all justices of the peace) were appointed in each county to superintend the collection of the loan.[6] Among them was Sir Thomas Wentworth who was no doubt still smarting from the insult administered to him in July 1626 when he had been replaced as

[1] Cal.S.P.Dom. 1625–6, 447, 461, 471.
[2] G. Poulson, The History and Antiquities of the Seigniory of Holderness, i, 201–2.
[3] C.R.S., liii, 321. Rushworth, i, 392–3.   [4] Cal.S.P.Dom. 1625–6, 447.
[5] H.M.C. Coke MSS, i, 286. See above, 235.
[6] Acts of the Privy Council 1626, 353. P.R.O., S.P.Dom., Charles I, S.P.16/xliv/4.

custos rotulorum for the West Riding by his arch-enemy Sir John Savile. Sir Thomas, however, was not the only Yorkshireman to be made aware of the Crown's disfavour. During the course of this year three of his associates in the Country Party (all of whom had sat in the Parliament of 1626) were removed from the commission of the peace: Sir Thomas Hoby, Sir William Constable, who was replaced as *custos rotulorum* for the East Riding by Sir William Alford, and Sir John Hotham.[1]

In spite of the wording of the proclamation which announced it[2] the new loan scheme was clearly nothing more than a compulsory levy undertaken without parliamentary authority and offering little prospect of repayment. On 20 February 1627, however, Lord Scroope reported to Buckingham that the Yorkshire commissioners had signified their willingness to contribute to the loan and that in his view there was every hope of a successful outcome. Of more immediate concern to him was the stalemate which had been reached over the provision of warships. At a general meeting of the loan commissioners he reminded them that the county was under an obligation to assist the town of Hull in meeting this requirement, but his exhortations fell on deaf ears: 'he perceived by the gentlemen that the county would not be drawne to contribute to that charge, but do absolutely denie it'.[3]

During the early months of 1627 the collection of the loan money appears to have proceeded satisfactorily: indeed on 4 April Sir John Savile was writing to Buckingham to tell him that he had 'procured all this Countrie to subscribe'.[4] Shortly afterwards, however, the Privy Council began to receive reports of sporadic resistance. On 18 April some of the East Riding commissioners informed the Council that while the subsidymen as a whole were willing to lend there was a hard core of loan refusers among the gentry. Sir William Constable, who had been summoned first by a general and then by a special writ, had sent answer that 'he was not at leisure, or had other business or words to that effect'. Sir John Hotham, for his part, had deliberately absented himself from home before the constable arrived with a summons and had subsequently ignored a second warrant which had been left at his house. Others who had stayed away included Sir William Hildyard of Bishop

---

[1] Knowler, i, 35–6. P.R.O., Chancery, Crown Office, Docquet Books, Index 4211, ff.206, 207, 209, 262.
[2] Rushworth, i, 418.   [3] P.R.O., S.P.Dom., Charles I, S.P.16/lv/9, 11.
[4] P.R.O., S.P.Dom., Charles I, S.P.16/lix/35.

Wilton (a commissioner), Sir William Acclom of Moreby and Walter Strickland of Boynton.[1] Later in the month the principal Yorkshire commissioners received from the Privy Council a list of twenty-five subsidymen in the West Riding (most of them gentry) who had so far neglected to pay their contributions. In due course the persons named were summoned to appear before the commissioners and on 29 May Sir Thomas Fairfax of Denton, Sir Henry Savile of Methley and two legal members of the Council of the North held a special sitting at York for this purpose. Under the threat of more drastic action a number of defaulters submitted. Others failed to answer the summons, in some cases (but not invariably) because they were in London or abroad. In a letter to the commissioners Sir Thomas Wentworth, who had been assessed at £40, claimed that he was unfit to travel and told them that he intended, with their permission, to give his answer in person before the Privy Council.[2]

Meanwhile, the ship money controversy was still continuing. In March the county had been asked to contribute one-third of the cost of three ships which had been charged on the town of Hull. On 10 May, however, a number of deputy lieutenants and justices of the peace wrote to the Privy Council explaining why they had failed to collect any of the money. Although they were willing to undertake the commission (they informed the Council), 'yett haveing noe legall power to Levie the same upon the subiect wee dare not presume to doe itt'. Furthermore, the county had already been put to great expense in providing the late unusual loan which had been 'soe readilie furnished... att one speedie and entyre payment'. In conclusion they begged to be relieved of the charge: 'wee are rather to become humble Suitors to his Majestie for a good deale of ease then that his Majestie or your Lordships will Accumulate any maritime charge upon us besides the Continuall Charge of the Countie in watching Beacons and Trayninge soe great a proporcion of men, and other burthens.'[3]

In June three of the East Riding loan commissioners complained to the Privy Council that the other members of the commission, being many, had left the business to a very few. The signatories of this letter, it is worth noting, were Sir Thomas Metham and Sir William Alford, both of whom were identified with the interests of the Court

[1] P.R.O., S.P.Dom., Charles I, S.P.16/lx/52.
[2] J. J. Cartwright (ed.), *Chapters in the History of Yorkshire*, 233–9.
[3] *Acts of the Privy Council 1627*, 161. Y.A.S. Library: Fairfax MSS, MS 38, ff.94–5.

Party, and Nicholas Girlington of South Cave, a magistrate with Catholic connections[1]. With their letter they enclosed the names of forty-five persons, virtually all inhabitants of the wapentake of Hart-hill, who had either delayed or refused payment of the second instalment of their loan money. These included some of the principal landowners in the area, men such as Sir John Hotham (who was probably the ringleader), Marmaduke Langdale of Cherry Burton (his brother-in-law), Henry Alured of Sculcoates and John Stillington of Kelfield.[2]

In the North Riding there appears to have been scarcely any opposition to the forced loan except in the wapentake of Bulmer. On 21 July the loan commissioners submitted the names of several landowners in that division who for one reason or another had declined to contribute. Of these the most prominent was Sir John Bourchier of Beningbrough, a Puritan squire, who had sent answer that he was not prepared either to subscribe his name or to pay his assessment.[3]

From the spring of 1627 onwards many gentlemen from all over England were imprisoned for refusing to pay their loan contributions. In spite of the entreaties of his friends Wentworth remained obdurate and early in July the Privy Council ordered him to be committed to the Marshalsea prison. Three months later Sir John Hotham and Sir William Constable were also taken into custody.[4]

On 2 January 1628 order was given for the release of seventy-six loan refusers[5] and with public sympathy solidly in their favour a considerable number of these gentlemen secured election to the Parliament which had been called for 17 March. In Yorkshire Sir Thomas Wentworth was returned for the county, defeating Sir John Savile in the process, while Hotham and Constable were elected for Beverley and Scarborough respectively. In the Commons Wentworth attacked the evils of arbitrary taxation and arbitrary imprisonment but was careful to absolve the king from all responsibility. 'This hath not been done by the King', he argued, 'but by Projectors, who have extended the Prerogative of the King, beyond the just Symetry, which maketh a sweet harmony of the whole.'[6]

During the summer of 1628 Wentworth made great efforts to

---

[1] Rushworth, i, 393.   [2] P.R.O., S.P.Dom., Charles I, S.P.16/lxviii/51.
[3] P.R.O., S.P.Dom., Charles I, S.P.16/lxxi/64.
[4] *Acts of the Privy Council 1627*, 352, 382, 402, 418, 449 and *1627–8*, 17,75.
[5] *Acts of the Privy Council 1627–8*, 217.   [6] Rushworth, i, 500.

establish himself in favour at court. The first indication that he was succeeding came on 21 July when he was created Baron Wentworth (the same day as Sir John Savile's elevation to the peerage). On 5 August it was reported from London that Wentworth and his kinsman Christopher Wandesford 'are grown great Courtiers lately, and come from Westminster-Hall to White-Hall...The Lord Weston tamper'd with the one, and my Lord Cottington took pains with the other, to bring them about from their violence against the Prerogative'.[1] Following the murder of his patron the Duke of Buckingham on 23 August Savile's position at court was seriously weakened and Wentworth sought to press home his advantage by accusing him of taking bribes from Catholics who had compounded for their recusancy; as a result he was forced to relinquish his office of vice-president of the Council of the North together with the receivership for the northern recusant revenue. That Savile's power was not completely destroyed may be judged from the fact that he remained comptroller of the king's household; nevertheless in December Wentworth achieved a great personal triumph over his ancient rival when he succeeded the ailing Lord Scroope (now Earl of Sunderland) as lord president of the Council of the North.[2]

Within a year after his release from custody Wentworth had become the Crown's chief representative in northern England and his friends hastened to congratulate him on his sudden turn of fortune. On 29 December Christopher Wandesford sent a message that he would come to him 'when and whither you please to appoint me. For, now the Case is altered, you know your own Rule, what is to be done by them who live under a Monarchy'.[3] On securing the lord presidency Wentworth did not forget his friends and associates in the Country Party. In the first place, a number of Yorkshiremen who had been removed from the commission of the peace for political reasons were reinstated within a few days of his appointment. These included Sir John Hotham, Sir William Constable, Sir Thomas Hoby and Christopher Wandesford.[4] Secondly, Wentworth took immediate steps to increase the number of his supporters in the Council of the North and offered Sir Thomas (now Lord) Fairfax of Denton, who was already

---

[1] James Howell, *Epistolae Ho-Elianae*, 216.
[2] R. R. Reid, *The King's Council in the North*, 402–3.   [3] Knowler, i, 48–50.
[4] P.R.O., Chancery, Crown Office, Docquet Books, Index 4211, ff.260, 261, 262.

a member, the office of vice-president.[1] Thirdly, his preference for gentlemen who had assisted him in his struggle with Savile was particularly in evidence in his choice of deputy lieutenants. In the East Riding, for example, he selected Sir John Hotham, Sir Matthew Boynton and Sir William Constable, together with Sir Christopher Hildyard of Winestead who was regarded as a neutral, and passed over such men as Viscount Dunbar, Sir Thomas Metham and Sir William Alford who had served under the Earl of Sunderland.[2] It would be wrong to infer from this that Wentworth was engaged in a full-scale purge of leading officials since some of his closest friends had held important offices under the previous régime and all existing members of the Council of the North retained their places.[3] Nevertheless the fact remains that as a result of Wentworth's accession to power a considerable number of gentry were given senior appointments for the first time and these included men who had been in active opposition to the Crown.

Wentworth's action in deserting the Country Party must be judged in the light of his political opinions. Although he had been opposed to arbitrary acts of power he believed in a strong and authoritarian system of government based on the royal prerogative. Under this concept Parliament had a role to play in the body politic but it was essentially a subordinate role which involved no interference with the Crown's executive functions. To Wentworth, however, authoritarian government also meant responsible and beneficent government distinguished for its efficient administration and its care and protection of the poorer members of society. 'Princes', he declared in his opening speech as lord president, 'are to be indulgent, nursing fathers to their people, their modest liberties, their sober rights ought to be precious in their eyes', and he emphasised that one of his primary aims would be to 'shelter the poor and innocent from the proud and insolent'.[4]

The policy of 'Thorough' with which Wentworth's name is associated involved a greater emphasis on state intervention in the social and economic fields, determined efforts to re-assert the authority of the Council of the North and closer supervision of the work of justices of the peace. Inevitably it aroused resentment and not least among the country gentry whose interests Wentworth had once espoused. The first real signs of opposition, however, came in direct response to the

---

[1] R. R. Reid, *op. cit.*, 498. Sheffield Central Library: Strafford Letters, xii. Lord Fairfax to Wentworth, 22 January 1628(–9).
[2] See above, 238.   [3] R. R. Reid, *op. cit.*, 496–8.   [4] *The Academy*, vii, 582–3.

Crown's attempts to achieve financial self-sufficiency. From 1629 to 1640 the king ruled without Parliament and he was therefore obliged to seek ways and means of supplying his occasions without the aid of parliamentary subsidies. In January 1630 a number of commissioners were appointed for the purpose of compounding with the owners of freehold property worth £40 a year or more who had failed to take up the order of knighthood at the coronation of 1626. Although the knighthood scheme undoubtedly had a basis in law it was clear that the Crown was reviving an ancient usage purely for fiscal purposes; moreover, the retention of the medieval qualification of £40 a year meant that many gentlemen (and indeed yeomen) who had no real pretensions to knighthood found themselves caught up in the net. To make matters worse the knighthood scheme represented the heaviest form of taxation imposed on the landed interest during the reign of Charles I: the middling gentry, for example, paid their compositions at the rate of £20, £30, £40 or even £50. Not surprisingly the money came in comparatively slowly and there were many requests for abatements. In October 1630 the Privy Council summoned before them twelve Yorkshiremen who had either failed to answer a summons from the northern commissioners or had deliberately refused to compound. These included Sir William Constable, who was a baronet but not a knight, and Thomas Maleverer of Allerton Mauleverer (both of whom were justices of the peace), William Ingleby of Ripley and Henry Darley, the heir of Sir Richard Darley of Buttercrambe.[1]

Although the North Riding had provided little resistance to the forced loan, it was in this part of the county that the most serious opposition to Wentworth and his government was encountered during the early years of his lord presidency. Writing to Wentworth in August 1629 Christopher Wandesford contrasted the goodwill of Sir William Gascoigne of Sedbury with the enmity of many of his fellow gentry in Richmondshire who had supported Savile at the last election. Sir William (he suggested) was worth cultivating in view of 'the neare combination of all this Cuntry against you partly for malice...partly for religion'. In the main this Catholic hostility must be attributed to the fact that Wentworth, as receiver for the northern recusant revenue, was exacting much higher composition rents than Savile had done:

---

[1] *Cal.S.P.Dom. 1629–31*, 175–6. *Y.A.S.R.S.*, lxi, 89–107. Sheffield Central Library: Strafford Letters, xii. Sir Henry Savile to Wentworth, 27 November 1630 and Thomas Littell to Wentworth, 4 April 1631. P.R.O., Privy Council Registers, P.C.2/xl/137.

thus in October the lord treasurer informed him that there were reports that he was proceeding 'with extreem rigor' in settling the recusant revenue.[1] The first North Riding landowners to cross swords with the lord president were Thomas Lord Fauconberg, a kinsman of the Earl of Sunderland, his son Henry Bellasis and his brother-in-law Sir Conyers Darcy who, as we have seen, had acted as North Riding collector for the loan on privy seals in 1626[2]. Although Fauconberg had Puritan relatives (among them Sir Conyers Darcy) he himself was a Catholic and much of his support in the North Riding came from the disgruntled recusant gentry. Besides the religious factor, however, there was a strong element of personal animosity. In 1628 Fauconberg quarrelled with Christopher Wandesford over a projected marriage between Wandesford's ward Thomas Danby and one of Fauconberg's daughters. Instead of going up to Cambridge, as his guardian had intended, the young heir had ridden to Newburgh Priory to treat with Fauconberg but on hearing of this Wandesford intervened and in the end persuaded him to marry his own daughter Catherine.[3] Subsequently, in February 1630, Wandesford told the lord president that Sir Thomas Layton of Sexhow had

this last weake (presuming I suppose of the difference betwixt faucolnebridge and me) moved me by letter to set att libertye one Hewardyne a kinsman of his committed to the house of Correction by the sole warrant of Sir Connyrs Darcye upon the desyre of ffaulconbridge opposed by Hewardyne in the taken up of a Comon in Cleveland...urging withall both the illegallitye of this act of darcys and the great oppression of faucolnebridge who by this meanes sought to rend away the inheritances of poore men.

Magistrates who abused their authority could expect no mercy from Wentworth and as a result of this report Sir Conyers was summoned before the Council of the North, severely reprimanded and fined for his misdemeanour.[4]

In November 1630 Wentworth heard that Fauconberg had drawn up a petition to the king charging him with injustice. Fauconberg and

[1] Sheffield Central Library: Strafford Letters, xii. Earl of Portland to Wentworth, 13 October 1629, and xvi. Christopher Wandesford to Wentworth, 5 August 1629. See above, 202.
[2] Above, 287.
[3] Sheffield Central Library: Strafford Letters, xvi. Christopher Wandesford to Wentworth, 13 November 1628.
[4] Sheffield Central Library: Strafford Letters, xvi. Christopher Wandesford to Wentworth, 14 February 1629(–30). Rushworth, ii, 161 and viii, 144–5.

Darcy appear in fact to have been conspiring, with the help of fabricated evidence, to engineer Wentworth's downfall but after considering the allegations the Privy Council completely exonerated the lord president. On 6 March 1631 Fauconberg was committed to the Fleet prison and remained in custody until the beginning of June when he agreed to sign a written acknowledgement of his fault. In the meantime his son Henry Bellasis had also been called before the Privy Council to answer a charge of publicly insulting the lord president. When Bellasis made his appearance on 6 April his behaviour was so unsatisfactory that the Council had no choice but to send him to the Gate House prison. A month later he was released after promising to make a humble submission before Wentworth and the Council of the North.[1]

In September 1631 there was a serious incident in the North Riding which might have had fatal consequences. While out riding Christopher Wandesford, accompanied by his brother-in-law Mauger Norton and a few servants, came face to face with Henry Bellasis and a party of 'nere twenty gentlemen and there followers' who included Sir Hugh Cholmley of Whitby (a nephew of Lord Fauconberg), Sir Francis Ireland of Crofton and Marmaduke Cholmley of Brandsby (both of whom were Catholics). Bellasis accused Wandesford of being primarily responsible for the differences between Wentworth and his father and attempted to provoke him into fighting a duel. For a time it looked as though the two parties might come to blows but in the end the incident passed off with nothing more than strong words.[2] There can be no doubt, however, that Lord Fauconberg had much greater support in the North Riding (where, after all, his estates were situated) than the lord president whose main territorial interests were in the West Riding. During the period of 'Thorough' Wentworth had only a handful of supporters, at least of any standing, in the North Riding: Thomas Lord Fairfax of Emley, Christopher Wandesford, Sir John Gibson of Welburn and Sir William Pennyman of Marske.

While Lord Fauconberg drew his support mainly from the North Riding he also had several close relatives among the West Riding squirearchy, including his uncle Thomas Lord Fairfax of Denton, his

[1] Sheffield Central Library: Strafford Letters, xii. Sir Arthur Ingram to Wentworth, 6 November 1630, and Sir William Pennyman to Wentworth, 26 February 1630(-1). H.M.C. Coke MSS, i, 420. Acts of the Privy Council 1630–1, 248–51, 259, 271, 285, 292–3, 318, 345–6, 373. R. R. Reid, The King's Council in the North, 414–16.

[2] Sheffield Central Library: Strafford Letters, xvi. Christopher Wandesford to Wentworth, 23 September (1631).

brother-in-law Sir William Lister of Thornton and his son-in-law Sir
Henry Slingsby of Scriven. Although there is no evidence to suggest
that the Fairfaxes were implicated in Fauconberg's plot against the lord
president they were certainly on good terms with the Bellasis family
and on one occasion when Henry Bellasis had been summoned to the
King's Manor by Wentworth Sir Ferdinando Fairfax (Lord Fairfax's
heir) had felt obliged to accompany his kinsman. This association with
the Bellasis faction inevitably aroused Wentworth's suspicions and his
relations with the Fairfax family began to turn noticeably cooler. In
October 1632 he reprimanded Sir Ferdinando and two of his fellow
justices for the manner in which they had handled the case of Francis
Steele, chief constable of the wapentake of Claro, who had been found
guilty of misappropriating public money. Wentworth's main complaint was that in 'so public and important a business' they had gone
ahead without acquainting the Council of the North, to which Fairfax
replied that he recognised the desirability of such consultation 'but to
make it a thing of absolute necessity, and solely to depend on their
directions, had not been formerly done'. In other words, Fairfax was
defending the authority of the justice of the peace against what he
regarded as the unwarrantable encroachments of the Council of the
North. Although Wentworth's quarrel was mainly with Sir Ferdinando
he was also involved in a property dispute with the elder Fairfax.
Wentworth was clearly anxious, however, to reach a settlement before
taking up the reins of government as lord deputy of Ireland because in
January 1633 we find him inviting Lord Fairfax to visit him at Gaw-
thorpe Hall with a view to composing their differences.[1]

While the lord president was fighting the intrigues of the Bellasis
faction he was also superintending the collection of knighthood
compositions. During the course of 1631 a considerable number
of Yorkshire gentry continued to hesitate over compounding and
as a consequence fines were levied on their estates. At this stage
the main opponent of the knighthood scheme was James Maleverer
of Ingleby Arncliffe, a Puritan squire, who attempted to challenge
the legality of the proceedings. When Maleverer appeared before
the barons of the Exchequer he told them that if his plea was unsuccessful he would be willing to accept their ruling in the matter of

[1] *Fairfax Correspondence*, i, 164–5, 231, 245–8, 255, 278. Sheffield Central Library:
Strafford Letters, xviii. Sir Edward Osborne to Wentworth, 5 December 1638. *Y.A.S.R.S.*,
liv, 25.

a fine. The judges, however, not only rejected his suit but urged on him the necessity of coming to terms with the northern commissioners and in the end he paid heavily for the courageous stand which he had taken.[1]

In refusing to compound for knighthood James Maleverer no doubt acted with the secret encouragement of Sir David Foulis of Ingleby, another Cleveland landowner, who in 1632 made strenuous attempts to rally opposition to the knighthood scheme. One of the Scottish gentlemen who had accompanied James I into England, Sir David had held the office of cofferer to Prince Henry and through his interest at court had acquired a substantial estate in the North Riding.[2] During the early years of Wentworth's lord presidency he served both as a deputy lieutenant and a justice of the peace (and in the years 1626 to 1629 he was also *custos rotulorum* for the riding).[3] According to the lord president Sir David's agitation against the knighthood scheme was not prompted by any personal malice towards him: it was primarily due to the fact that he had recently been called upon to account for a large sum of money, amounting to £5000 or £6000, which he had kept in his hands ever since he had relinquished the office of cofferer.[4] What Sir William Pennyman called 'the Scotch faction' consisted of a group of Cleveland gentry, including Sir David's eldest son, Henry Foulis, and his kinsman Sir Thomas Layton of Sexhow and Thomas and James Chaloner of Guisborough.[5] So far as can be seen they had no direct link with the Bellasis faction.

At a public meeting held in Sir Thomas Layton's house in July 1632 Sir David exhorted the gentlemen present to have nothing to do with the knighthood scheme. The Yorkshire gentry, he declared, 'had been in time past accounted and held stout-spirited men, and would have stood for their rights and liberties... but now in these days Yorkshiremen were become degenerate, more dastardly and more cowardly than the men of other countries... James Maleverer was the wisest and worthiest man in the country... a brave spirit, and a true Yorkshireman'.

---

[1] P.R.O., Exchequer, Accounts Various, E.101/682/35. Rushworth, ii, 71, 135–6.
[2] See above, 86.
[3] P.R.O., Chancery, Crown Office, Docquet Books, Index 4211, ff.206, 265 .
[4] Sheffield Central Library: Strafford Letters, xxi, 97. *Lord Somers's Tracts*, iv, 198. *Cal.S.P.Dom. 1631–33*, 430.
[5] There are references to the Chaloner connection in Strafford Letters, xv. Sir William Pennyman to Wentworth, 9 March 1635(–6), and xvi. Richard Winne to Wentworth, 4 March 1635(–6).

Sir David and his son also alleged that Wentworth had misappropriated some of the knighthood fines which had been collected. Although this was completely without foundation an unfortunate error in the Exchequer made it appear that the lord president had in fact been withholding money. Through an oversight Sir Thomas Layton, then sheriff of Yorkshire, was instructed to levy fines on a number of landowners who had already compounded. Sir Thomas carried out these instructions without consulting the commissioners and his officers performed their duties with some severity, taking 'great and oppressive fees' from the men who had been double charged. On hearing of these proceedings the Council of the North summoned him to appear and explain his actions but Sir David advised him to ignore the summons, arguing that the Council had no power to send for the sheriff in this way and that the office of a justice of the peace 'was above the Council at York, the one was by Act of Parliament, the other was made but by Commission'. While Sir Thomas was still considering whether to obey the summons he was arrested by a pursuivant and brought before the Council.[1]

When Sir David heard that the lord president had been informed of his activities he sought first to make his peace with Wentworth and then to muster as much support as possible in Whitehall. Wentworth, however, was determined to make an example of him as a means of curbing that 'humoure and libertye I find raign in thes partts, of observing a superiour commande noe farther than they like themselves, and of questioning any profitt of the crowne, called upon by his majesty's ministers, which might inable itt to subsiste of itself'.[2]

While Sir David's fate was still in the balance there were two further incidents of direct concern to the Council of the North, both involving North Riding gentry. In November 1632 Sir Thomas Gower of Stittenham, a justice of the peace, was arrested in London by the serjeant-at-arms and a pursuivant employed by the Council of the North. In a letter to the Privy Council the lord president and some of his fellow councillors explained that at one of the quarter sessions Sir Thomas had 'spoken publiqly very scandalous words against his Majesties Attorney here; and indeed thorow him, fixed a great imputation upon us all'. After promising to answer the charge before the Council he had gone into hiding and could not be brought in even

---

[1] Rushworth, ii, 215–20. Sheffield Central Library: Strafford Letters, xxi, 97.
[2] *Lord Somers's Tracts*, iv, 198.

though the serjeant-at-arms had searched his house on several occasions. 'The beginninge of this last Terme', they continued, 'hee went upp to London...and there quarters himselfe in Holburne, closse by others of the like affections; where it seemes they, their children and followers soe demeane and declare themselves against this government, as we heare they are there wantonly termed the Rebels of the North.' Although the letter does not name these northern rebels they must clearly have included Lord Fauconberg who was reported to have gone up to London at the end of September. Sir Thomas Gower was in fact a distant relative of Fauconberg and his heir appears to have been a close associate of Henry Bellasis.[1] Immediately following his arrest Sir Thomas petitioned the Privy Council for his release, claiming that the Council of the North had no authority outside its specific area of jurisdiction. In February 1633, however, the Privy Council rejected his plea and he was sent up to York to make his submission before the Council of the North. As a result of this case a new set of instructions was issued conferring on the Council of the North the same powers as were enjoyed by the Court of Star Chamber.[2]

The second incident occurred in May 1633 when Sir John Bourchier of Beningbrough ordered the destruction of some fences in the new royal park which Wentworth had created in the forest of Galtres. Sir John was one of several neighbouring landowners who had been involved in disputes with the Crown over alleged encroachments and rights of common within the forest. In February 1632 he had been granted an area of moorland in compensation for 'all his pretence of title' but in spite of this he had continued to pester the lord president with demands for a further grant.[3] Another factor which may have influenced him was Wentworth's treatment of his brother-in-law, William Scudamore of Overton. As we have already seen, Wentworth had entered into possession of the manor of Overton by virtue of a mortgage and extent on the property and (according to Scudamore) had enclosed within the new park of Galtres an extensive area of land which belonged to the manor.[4]

[1] P.R.O., S. P. Dom., Charles I, S.P.16/ccxxvi/1. Knowler, i, 76. *Acts of the Privy Council 1630–1*, 259, 271.

[2] *Cal.S.P.Dom. 1631–3*, 442–3, 469, 538. P.R.O., Privy Council Registers, P.C.2/xlii/291, 452–3. Rushworth, viii, 137–9. S. R. Gardiner, *History of England 1603–1642*, vii, 239.

[3] Knowler, i, 86, 88, 91. P.R.O., S.P.Dom., Charles I, S.P.16/ccxi/31.

[4] See above, 150.

In July 1633, while the Foulis and Bourchier cases were still pending, Wentworth finally took up his appointment as lord deputy of Ireland, leaving the government of northern England in the hands of Sir Edward Osborne who was made vice-president of the Council of the North. Sir Edward was a brother-in-law of Christopher Wandesford and a close friend of the lord president. In official circles he was regarded as a man who could be trusted implicitly: in June 1633, for example, Sir John Coke told Wentworth that in his estimation he was 'a young man of good Understanding, and Counsellable, and very forward to promote his Majesty's service'.[1] In spite of his removal to Dublin Wentworth still retained his office of lord president of the Council of the North and was in frequent correspondence with his deputy about northern affairs.[2]

In November 1633 Sir David Foulis, Sir Thomas Layton and Henry Foulis were tried in the Star Chamber. Having been found guilty Sir David was ordered to pay a fine of £5000 to the Crown and damages of £3000 to Wentworth, imprisoned in the Fleet (where he remained for seven years) and removed from all his offices. Of the other defendants Henry Foulis was fined £500 and committed to prison for a brief period while Sir Thomas Layton was dismissed from the case on the grounds that there was insufficient evidence against him.[3] In the following month Sir John Bourchier stood trial before the Council of the North, was fined £1800 (later reduced to £1000 through Wentworth's intervention) and kept in prison until October 1634.[4]

In December 1633 Wentworth wrote to Sir John Coke about the case of Brian Stapleton of Myton, a North Riding magistrate and a kinsman of Lord Fauconberg, who had refused to contribute to the muster master's fee. Stapleton, he told him, was a factious, ill-affected person who had been unwilling at first to compound for his knighthood and who did nothing but 'brabble and tyrannise over his poor neighbours'; in short, he was 'as arrant a saucy Magna Charta man as in all the Country'. In order to teach Stapleton a sharp lesson Wentworth suggested that he should be summoned before the Privy Council and

[1] Knowler, i, 91.
[2] This correspondence is preserved among the Strafford Letters at Sheffield Central Library.
[3] Rushworth, ii, 215–20. See also above, 138.
[4] Sheffield Central Library: Strafford Letters, xiii. Sir Edward Osborne to Wentworth, 21 August 1633, and xiv. Sir John Bourchier to Wentworth, 5 January 1634(–5). Knowler, i, 249, 281.

put out of the commission of the peace. Partly as the result of Stapleton's delaying tactics no order was made for his dismissal until July
1635 and in the meantime Wentworth's enemies managed to secure the
removal of his friend Sir William Pennyman from the North Riding
commission. When Sir William asked for an explanation the lord
keeper told him (as he related afterwards to Wentworth) that 'I had
spoken evill, scandalously, and detractingly of him...that I had used
this phrase uppon his Lordship (that my Lord Keeper would have a
snaffle put uppon him) and that I spake it to a Justice of Peace, from
whose mouth his Lordship receaved it at the first hand'. Sir William
strongly denied the charge and the lord keeper willingly accepted his
denial; he refused, however, to disclose the identity of his accuser and
this caused Pennyman to have 'a jealousy of all men, especially
Justices of the Peace'. In reporting this episode Sir William contrasted
his own case with that of Brian Stapleton: 'it may be easily discerned
how facile and propense my Lord Keeper hath beene to prejudicate my
case, and to creditt my hoodwinckt accusers; but on the other side how
deafe and incredulous he is to so open and authentick a relator as your
Lordship concerning Mr Stappleton: but this is onely my opinion, I
write it not as an instigation.' By a warrant dated 8 July 1634 Sir William was restored to his former place on the commission of the peace.[1]

In October 1634 a writ was issued for the levying of ship money on
the maritime towns. By a curious irony the man pricked as sheriff of
Yorkshire in the following month was Sir John Hotham who had
suffered imprisonment for opposing the forced loan. Sir John, however,
had in the meantime thrown in his lot with Wentworth and in May
1635 he told the lord deputy: 'I have now executed the writs for the
shippinge businesse with all the industrie and dilligence that a man
resolute and affectionate to his majesties service Could doe...and my
fellow sheriffe and I have received approbation and thanks from the
lords of the Councell by his majesties speciall Commande.'[2] In August
1635 there was a new ship money writ but now for the first time the
whole kingdom was required to contribute. Sir John, who was still
sheriff, again performed his duties with great dedication and continued

[1] Sheffield Central Library: Strafford Letters, v. Wentworth to Sir John Coke,
23 December 1633, xiv. Sir William Pennyman to Wentworth, 16 April 1634, and xv.
Lord Coventry to Wentworth, 29 June 1635. P.R.O., Crown Office, Docquet Books,
Index 4212, 127, 143, 175. Cal.S.P.Dom. 1633–4, 232, 264, 265.

[2] Sheffield Central Library: Strafford Letters, xv. Sir John Hotham to Wentworth,
5 May 1635.

to provide valuable assistance even after he had completed his term of office. In January 1637 he assured Wentworth that in Yorkshire the levying of ship money had proceeded without difficulty, 'which Considering how it was in other Counties His majestie may well Conceive your lordship's frinds and servants in this Countie have not ill ymployed theire Endeavors for his service...I have not onelie given it all the helpe I Coulde in the publique way but have used the best Interest I have with my private frinds'. So great was his determination to ensure the success of the ship money project that it had brought him into conflict with Sir Thomas Hoby of Hackness who had been anxious to have sole responsibility for assessing his own division. 'I sent him worde', Sir John related, 'that In this businesse of the shippinge I desired to Carrie it in such a way as might not onelie be Just but might avoyd all Scandal which must needs fall out preiudiciall to the service...and that I must suffer his, myne and the nearest friends I had In the worlde: Estates to be assessed in the publique way which by Experience I found satisfactorie to all. This is to him a mortall offence.'[1]

In Yorkshire the early writs of ship money aroused surprisingly little clamour and the sums charged on the county in 1635 and 1636 were collected in full, as may be seen in the following table[2]:

	1635	1636	1637	1638
sum charged on Yorkshire	£12,000	£12,000	£12,000	£4,250
amount uncollected	—	—	£1237. 15s. 6d.	£510

Before 1638 the only Yorkshire gentleman who appears to have refused ship money was Sir Michael Warton of Beverley Park, a man of Catholic sympathies and one of the richest landowners in the East Riding. Sir Michael declined to pay an assessment of £4. 4s. 6d. which had been made on some outlying property of his on the grounds that he had already been charged once at Beverley. This argument proved unavailing and in October 1635 Sir John Coke told Wentworth that when Sir Michael had been certified by the sheriff 'there wilbee that

---

[1] Sheffield Central Library: Strafford Letters, xvi. Sir John Hotham to Wentworth, 13 January 1636(–7).
[2] These figures are taken from Miss M. D. Gordon's article in *Transactions of the Royal Historical Society*, Third Series, iv, 141. For the ship money writ of 1639 see below, 315, 318.

course taken with him, as shall give noe encouragemente to the refractorines of others'.[1]

While Sir John Hotham was busily engaged in levying ship money two of his fellow deputy lieutenants in the East Riding, Sir Matthew Boynton and Sir William Constable, were planning to emigrate to New England. Both men were zealous Puritans who would have agreed wholeheartedly with Sir Ferdinando Fairfax (Sir William's brother-in-law) that they were faced with nothing less than the subversion of the established religion.[2] If, however, religious motives were a major factor these were probably not the only considerations which led them to think of emigrating. Politically the two baronets had always been associated with the Country Party and although Wentworth had appointed them deputy lieutenants it seems unlikely that they had much sympathy with his policy of 'Thorough.' Moreover, Sir William was in financial difficulties and may well have been hoping to restore his fortunes in the New World.[3]

No doubt through the influence of Henry Darley of Buttercrambe, who was involved in various Puritan colonisation schemes, the two gentlemen decided to settle with their families in southern Connecticut where Lord Brooke and Lord Saye and Sele had obtained a grant of land. In the spring of 1635 they began to make preparations for their journey but were obliged to exercise great caution because of the danger that the authorities might hear of their plans and seek to prevent their departure. In September a correspondent of John Winthrop the younger, who had newly arrived in Connecticut, informed him:

Some of the gentlemen of the north...did thinke that their would have been no notice of their purposes, and there upon assumed to send us up servants, but when they came down, found the countrie full of the reports of their going now. Those two (being Deputy leuetenants of the shire) did not dare to move any further in sending up of men for fear of increasing the reports... Our gentlemens minds remain the same, and are in a way of selling off their estates with the greatest expedicion.[4]

Early in 1636 Sir Matthew settled himself and his family in London,

[1] Cal.S.P.Dom. 1635, 290, 479, 507. Sheffield Central Library: Strafford Letters, xv. Sir John Coke to Wentworth, 26 October 1635, and Sir John Hotham to Wentworth, 17 November 1635.

[2] Fairfax Correspondence, i, 155–6.

[3] B.M., Additional MSS 40135, ff.23–4. Beverley County Record Office: Hotham MSS, DDHO/10/1. Y.A.S.R.S., lviii, 13.

[4] Massachusetts Historical Society Collections, Fifth Series, i, 213.

although (unlike Sir William Constable, who was already living there) he was still apparently undecided about the disposal of his estates. During the course of this year he was in correspondence with John Winthrop the younger on such matters as the provision of a house for his 'greate ffamilie', the welfare and employment of the servants whom he had sent over as an advance guard and the management of his herds of cattle and other livestock in which he had invested considerable money. Sir Matthew was clearly apprehensive about the possibility that Winthrop's letters might fall into the wrong hands and in February 1636 asked him to direct them to Henry Darley at the Sign of the Lamb in Gray's Inn Lane.[1]

As time went on Sir Matthew began to have doubts about the early fruition of his venture. In April 1637 he told Winthrop that because of the uncertainty of his position he did not consider it wise to be at any further charge with his stock: his servants therefore could either return to England or settle in Connecticut. Although Sir Matthew did not specify his difficulties it may be assumed that one of the main factors was a hardening of the official attitude towards the emigration of religious dissenters to New England: on 30 April, for example, a proclamation was issued stipulating that no subsidyman or person of similar financial status should embark for America without first obtaining a licence from the commissioners of plantations.[2]

In Yorkshire there was a good deal of speculation about Sir Matthew's intentions. Sir William Pennyman wrote to Wentworth in April 1637: 'Sir Mathew Boynton is about the sale of most of his land in Yorkshire, and 'tis generally conjectured how he intends to dispose of himself for the future.' Sir William's informant had sworn him to secrecy, 'inclining rather to loose parte of the value' of the property 'then it should be publicquly spoken of'. In the event Sir Matthew sold only a small part of his estate: towards the end of 1637 he settled the bulk of his land on some of his Puritan friends and relatives who were to act as trustees.[3]

When Sir William Constable finally abandoned the idea of emigrating to New England is not altogether clear, but on 17 April 1637 he managed to secure a pass enabling him and his wife, together with a

---

[1] *Ibid.*, Fourth Series, vii, 163–7.   [2] *Ibid.*, 168–9. Rushworth, ii, 409–10.
[3] Sheffield Central Library: Strafford Letters, xvii. Sir William Pennyman to Wentworth, 4 April 1637. P.R.O., Common Pleas, Feet of Fines, C.P.25(2)/523. *V.C.H.*, *N.R.*, ii, 271.

number of servants, to travel on the Continent for a period of three years. In June they crossed over to Holland where they were later joined by Sir Matthew and his family. On 5 December 1638 the vice-president of the Council of the North informed Wentworth that Sir Matthew 'is gone away togeather with all his Familye (except his eldest sonn who married the Lord Sayes daughter) to Harlem in Holland ther to remaine, wher Sir William is likewise'.[1] According to a letter written in 1640 by an Englishman travelling through the Low Countries the two families were then domiciled in Arnhem, one of several Dutch towns which had English Protestant congregations. He writes:

In Gelderland at the Citie of Arnham I received greate favors from divers worthy gentlemen of our Nation who have theire seated themselfs, especially from these Sir William Constable, Sir Matthew Boynton, Sir Richard Saltingston [Saltonstall] of Yorkshire...They have two Preachers, and this the discipline of theire Church: upon every Sunday a Communion, a prayer before sermon and after, the like in the afternoone; the Communion Table stands in the lower end of the Church (which hath no Chancel) Altar-wise, where the chiefest sit and take notes, not a gentlewoman that thinkes her hand to faire to use her pen and Inke. The Sermon, Prayer and psalme being ended, the greatest companie present theire offeringes, which amounte to about two or 3 hundred pounds a year Sterlinge.[2]

---

[1] P.R.O., Signet Office Docquets, Index 6810, 17 April 1637 and 31 July 1638 (no pagination). *Fairfax Correspondence*, i, 309. Sheffield Central Library: Strafford Letters, xviii. Sir Edward Osborne to Wentworth, 5 December 1638.

[2] C. Burrage, *The Early English Dissenters*, ii, 291.

CHAPTER XIV

Towards Civil War

In November 1637 the judges began their hearing of John Hampden's famous lawsuit in which he sought to challenge the legality of ship money. The Hampden case aroused great interest throughout the country and was a major factor in the growing resistance to the ship money levies. Sir Thomas Danby of Masham, who was sheriff of Yorkshire at the time, later wrote that these proceedings 'did much retard the service in respect of the greate expectation men had therof'. In 1638 there were many refusers in Yorkshire and when the sheriff's officers attempted to distrain their goods some men resorted to physical violence while others barricaded themselves in their houses.[1] If the denial of ship money was causing anxiety in official circles the king had even more reason to feel alarmed about the situation in Scotland where Laud's attempts to impose a new liturgy had encountered bitter opposition. For many of the king's Scottish subjects the Laudian innovations represented undiluted popery and in the National Covenant of 27 February 1638 they proclaimed their determination to stand firm in the defence of their Protestant inheritance. When news of the Scottish revolt reached England it was received with considerable satisfaction in some quarters. The king could hardly ignore such a challenge but a military campaign would place a heavy burden on his financial resources which were barely sufficient to meet his normal expenditure. Sooner or later, therefore, he would be obliged to call a new parliament.

In July 1638 John Alured of Sculcoates, who was then living in Blackfriars, was summoned to Whitehall to answer an accusation that he had openly praised the Scottish rebels.[2] Although he denied the charge it seems likely that he had made some indiscreet remarks which echoed the private sentiments of the Puritan opposition leaders, men such as Lord Saye and Sele, Lord Brooke, John Pym and Oliver St John, who were suspected of being in secret correspondence with

---

[1] Cartwright Memorial Hall, Bradford: Cunliffe–Lister MSS, Bundle 25.
[2] *Cal.S.P.Dom. 1637–8*, 558, 574.

the Scots. As members of the Providence Island Company these men were able to carry on their political activities under the cloak of Company business[1] and the young squire was probably well aware of their attitude to the Scottish rebellion since his brother-in-law Henry Darley of Buttercrambe was deputy governor and a frequent attender at the meetings held at Brooke House in Holborn. Other Yorkshire Puritans whose names appear in the records of the Providence Island Company include Godfrey Bosvile of Gunthwaite (a half-brother of Lord Brooke) who became a member in June 1634 and Sir Matthew Boynton who advanced a loan of £500 to the Company in June 1637.[2] Earlier the same year Sir Matthew's heir, Francis Boynton, had married Constance Fiennes, a daughter of Lord Saye and Sele, and for a time at least the young couple appear to have resided at Broughton Castle, the Viscount's Oxfordshire seat.[3] A further important link in this context was provided by the family relationship between Sir John Bourchier of Beningbrough and Sir Thomas Barrington, an Essex squire who had preceded Henry Darley (himself a friend of Bourchier) as deputy governor of the Providence Island Company. The two men were first cousins and it is clear that Sir John was on close terms not only with the Barrington family but with other members of their circle, in particular Oliver St John. In 1631 Bourchier had propounded a match between his fellow Yorkshireman Sir William Strickland of Boynton and a relative of the Barringtons but this was one Puritan marriage alliance which never materialised.[4]

During the course of 1638 the king sought to reach a settlement with the Scottish rebels but as a precaution he gave order that the trained bands of the six northern counties should be brought to a state of military preparedness. On 27 July Sir Edward Osborne, the vice-president of the Council of the North, held a conference of Yorkshire deputy lieutenants to discuss the implementation of the Crown's directions. All the West Riding deputy lieutenants except Lord Fairfax of Denton, who was aged and infirm, were present at the meeting but the other ridings were poorly represented, partly because of the ab-

[1] For the political role of the Providence Island Company see A. P. Newton, *The Colonising Activities of the English Puritans*, and J. H. Hexter, *The Reign of King Pym*, and for the alliance between the nobility and the bourgeoisie B. S. Manning, 'The Nobles, the People, and the Constitution', *Past and Present*, ix, 43.

[2] P.R.O., Colonial Entry Books, Bahamas, C.O.124/ii/ff. 38, 77, 85, 140, 153, 154, 197.

[3] Clay, ii, 149.

[4] B.M., Egerton MSS 2644, f.287; 2645, ff.3, 23, 175, 235, 241, 243; and 2646, f.66.

sence of Sir Matthew Boynton and Sir William Constable. Since Sir Edward was not at liberty to disclose the precise reason for these military preparations he found it difficult to convince his fellow deputy lieutenants that there was any need for haste in mustering and exercising the militia; moreover, there was a certain amount of reluctance to obey a man who had no overriding authority in the military field. Speaking for the East Riding Sir John Hotham declared that the musters could not be carried out immediately because of the harvest, while Sir William Savile of Thornhill refused point-blank to bring his troop of horse to York for training: it was his intention (he told the vice-president) to train them at a more convenient place in the West Riding. As a result of these differences there were serious delays in the training of the Yorkshire militia and Wentworth had to intervene on behalf of the vice-president.[1]

In December 1638 Sir Edward Osborne wrote to the lord deputy suggesting that Sir Thomas Metham and Sir Marmaduke Langdale should be appointed deputy lieutenants in place of the East Riding gentlemen who had emigrated to the Netherlands. In recommending Sir Thomas Metham he added:

'Tis true I have heard Sir Jhon Hotham distasts him, butt I thinke that will rather advance the service, when there is one more besides the rest, who with judgement and discreation will ballance the power he now assumes through-outt all the East Ridinge in regulatinge armes, proportioninge and levyinge the necessary charges incident thereunto, wherin though he pretend the ease of the Cuntry, yett I pray god anothr Spiritt walke nott in that shape.

In reply Wentworth agreed to Sir Thomas Metham's appointment but rejected the other nomination: 'As for Sir Marmaduke Langdale I allways tooke him to be...a Person of ill affections I am sure, to the Provinciall Power, if not to the Regall power.'[2]

By Christmas 1638 the negotiations with the Scots had completely broken down and it could now only be a matter of time before the order was given for an expeditionary force to be marched towards Scotland. Sir Henry Slingsby noted in his diary that on 3 January 1639 he went to Bramham moor 'to see the training of our light horse, for which service I myself had sent 2 horses, by commandment from the Deputy Lieuetenants and Sir Jacob Asley who is lately come down with

---

[1] Knowler, ii, 193–4, 215–6, 218. *H.M.C. Coke MSS*, ii, 189.

[2] Sheffield Central Library: Strafford Letters, x, 272 and xviii. Sir Edward Osborne to Wentworth, 5 December 1638.

speciall comission from the King to train and exercise them. These
are strange, strange spectacles to this nation in this age, that have liv'd
thus long peacably, without noise of shot or drum'.[1] While these
military preparations were going ahead, however, Sir William Savile
(who was a nephew of the lord deputy) was engaged in intrigues with
his uncle's enemies, both at court and in Yorkshire. A proud and
ambitious young man, Sir William had already been in conflict with
the Council of the North and he was in no way prepared to subordinate
himself to the authority of Sir Edward Osborne whose estate was much
inferior to his own. In December 1638 Wentworth was informed that
his nephew had declared that 'times may change and he hopes will, then
substitutes will but be as other men' and that he had told a member of
the Privy Council that at the last meeting of deputy lieutenants Sir
Edward had 'discontented all the men of qualitye imployed in those
affayres'. Not content with defaming the vice-president Sir William
attempted to secure the agreement of the Privy Council to a scheme
under which another lord lieutenant, Henry Lord Clifford, would have
been associated with Wentworth in a special commission for levying
troops in the northern counties. If this move had been successful Lord
Clifford would in effect have been in supreme control of military
affairs in Yorkshire while Sir Edward Osborne would have found himself in an extremely invidious position as vice-president. On hearing of
these intrigues the lord deputy immediately protested to the king who
accordingly gave instructions that the project should be abandoned and
on 10 February 1639 Wentworth sent the vice-president a new commission delegating to him full authority in the military field with the
title of deputy-lieutenant-general.[2]

In spite of the new authority which he had been given the vice-
president still had difficulty in securing the co-operation of Sir William
Savile and Sir John Hotham. To make matters worse the idea was conceived of replacing Hotham as governor of Hull with a professional
soldier, Captain William Legge. When the lord deputy heard of this
proposal he wrote to Secretary Windebank warning him that it could
have the most serious consequences: 'For Sir John Hotham, 'tis true

---

[1] *Slingsby Diary*, 11.

[2] Sheffield Central Library: Strafford Letters, xvi. Sir Edward Stanhope to Wentworth,
December 1638, xvii. Sir William Savile to Wentworth, 31 October 1637, and xviii. Sir
Edward Osborne to Wentworth, 5 December 1638. Knowler, ii, 254, 264, 281–2, 284,
308. *H.M.C. Coke MSS*, ii, 204.

there is somewhat more will and party than I could wish, but he is very honest, faithful and hearty, which way so ever he inclines, and to be won and framed as you please with good usage.' If he was forced to relinquish the office 'I judge it would be much worse for the service, Sir John Hotham having as much power in those parts as any other gentleman in the place where he lives, extreme sensible of honour, and discourtesies perhaps a little overmuch'. In spite of Wentworth's entreaties Sir John was removed from the governorship, an act of folly which added personal rancour to his growing disillusionment with the system of 'Thorough'.[1]

Earlier in the year 1639 there had already been indications that Sir John's attitude to ship money had undergone a radical change. In March Christopher Wandesford wrote to the lord deputy: 'I beseach you thinke whether it be fitt to putt any Imployment in the hands of Sir John Hotham nowe when he denyes to pay the ship moneyes, as by a letter dated the 29 of Januarye the sheriff Sir William Robinson advertiseth my Coosen Wandesforde both Sir John and gentlemen of the greatest Emynencye... doth'. In the event Sir John appears to have had second thoughts and it was his friend Sir Marmaduke Langdale (a loan refuser in 1627) who at this stage headed the opposition to ship money in the East Riding. Writing to Hotham on 26 March Wentworth expressed his surprise that men could deny ship money 'when the fire is kindled so near to us... I hear my old friend Sir Marmaduke Langdale appears in the head of this business, that gentleman I fear carries an itch about him, that will never let him take rest, till at one time or other he happen to be thoroughly clawed indeed; for love of Christ counsel them out of their madness'.[2]

If resistance to ship money was increasing this was not the only source of discontent among the propertied classes: they were also seriously perturbed about the military burden which the county was having to shoulder. On 14 March 1639 Sir Jacob Astley, one of the professional soldiers who had been brought in to assist, reported to Secretary Windebank that he had spent two whole days in meetings with the vice-president and the deputy lieutenants and colonels 'and your Honnour will not beleve what trubell they give me to sett them

---

[1] Sheffield Central Library: Strafford Letters, xix. Sir William Savile to Wentworth, 23 July 1639. Knowler, ii, 288–9, 307. A. M. W. Stirling, *The Hothams, i*, 31–3.

[2] Sheffield Central Library: Strafford Letters, xviii. Christopher Wandesford to Wentworth, 7 March 1638(–9). Knowler, ii, 308.

even as they shoulde be for amongst them thir be thos [that] talkes to no good purpose'. In the end Sir William Savile, Sir John Hotham, Sir Hugh Cholmley and a number of other deputy lieutenants decided to set down their grievances in writing. In a petition to the king they declared that the officers and soldiers were so poor as a result of the heavy programme of training that they would be unable to march to a rendezvous unless they were given a month's pay in advance. In a further petition they expressed their misgivings about the financial implications of an order requiring them to bring the whole militia together so that the king could review them. Pointing out that the county had already spent over £20,000 on military training they asked to be spared 'from cominge in a bodie togeather, before we shalbee commanded to march to a Rand-vous. For...it will coste neare £10,000 to call us togeather for such a purpose'. As a result the plan for a general muster was abandoned.[1]

On 30 March the king arrived at York and almost immediately orders were given for three of the Yorkshire regiments to be marched to Berwick. On receiving his instructions Sir William Pennyman lost no time in gathering his troops together and starting the long journey northwards; Sir Hugh Cholmley, on the other hand, was unable to lead his regiment because, he explains in his memoirs, 'I had caught cold and a dangerous sickness, in raising and training my whole regiment together on Paxton-Moor, near Thornton'.[2] In May Sir John Hotham, Sir Ferdinando Fairfax and other colonels of the trained bands also received their marching orders. At first there was a possibility that the departure of their regiments might be seriously delayed through lack of money, but this problem was quickly resolved: thus on 28 May Sir Ferdinando Fairfax told his father that the vice-president had sent him the sum of £500 for paying his regiment with the proviso that it should be distributed only when they were beyond the confines of Yorkshire. For the present at least the Fairfaxes appear to have been wholeheartedly loyal to the Crown, even though their relations with Wentworth had deteriorated. On 12 June Lord Fairfax wrote to his grandson Thomas who had been made a captain of horse: 'I desire you to be mindful to serve God with all your soul, and the King with all your heart...My prayers shall always be for the King and

---

[1] P.R.O., S.P.Dom., Charles I, S.P.16/cdxiv/91, 92, 93.
[2] *Fairfax Correspondence*, i, 351–2. Knowler, ii, 314–15. *Cholmley Memoirs*, 59.

the good success of the army.'[1] By this time, however, the king had decided, largely on account of his financial difficulties, to abandon the campaign and enter into peace negotiations with the Scots. The treaty of Berwick, which was concluded on 18 June, settled nothing but at least it gave the Crown a breathing-space in which to raise more money and build up a stronger expeditionary force.

In November 1639, when the annual pricking of sheriffs took place, over £1700 was still owing in Yorkshire on the ship money writs of 1637 and 1638.[2] In spite of this the king, acting on Wentworth's advice, rejected the short list of names for the Yorkshire shrievalty and instead selected Sir Marmaduke Langdale who had led the resistance to ship money in the East Riding earlier in the year. The reasons for this choice are not altogether clear, but Wentworth may have been hoping that Sir Marmaduke's attitude to ship money would quickly change when he was faced with the prospect of having to make good any short-fall from his own purse. If this was in fact Wentworth's hope it proved to be a serious miscalculation. In December the new sheriff received a ship money writ requiring him to levy the sum of £12,000 on the county but in spite of a sharp reminder he took no action for several months.[3]

Towards the end of 1639 Wentworth finally persuaded the king to call a parliament in an attempt to secure financial support for a new expedition against the Scots. The assembly, which came to be known as the Short Parliament, was not due to meet until 13 April 1640, but in the meantime a council of war was appointed and military preparations put in hand. On this occasion it was decided that the expeditionary force should be drawn mainly from the southern counties and that Yorkshire should be spared from any further charge except for the provision of 200 foot soldiers to reinforce the garrison at Berwick. Even this modest requirement, however, met with opposition from the Yorkshire deputy lieutenants who calmly informed the Privy Council that they were not prepared to act without an assurance that the coat and conduct money which the county was required to furnish for the support of these foot soldiers on their journey would be repaid in

---

[1] *Fairfax Correspondence*, i, 355–7, 362–7. *H.M.C. Coke MSS*, ii, 228–9.

[2] Cartwright Memorial Hall, Bradford: Cunliffe–Lister MSS, Bundle 25.

[3] *H.M.C. Various*, viii, 53. P.R.O., Chancery, Petty Bag Office, Sheriffs' Rolls, C.227/29. Y.A.S. Library: MD 287, rent-book entitled 'An old Booke of my fathers' (no consistent pagination).

accordance with former precedents.[1] If the gentry felt strongly about this order they soon had much greater cause for complaint. On 10 April Sir Edward Osborne received instructions that six of the Yorkshire trained band regiments were to be marched forthwith to Newcastle and the rest of the militia kept at twenty-four hours' readiness. These instructions were completely at variance with the promises which had been given earlier and even Wentworth (now lord lieutenant of Ireland and Earl of Strafford) considered that his fellow Yorkshiremen had a legitimate grievance. On 15 April he wrote to the king: 'This seems something strange as I perceive to them there, that contrary to the former Grace intended, the Charge of this second Year's War likewise is thus likely to fall upon that County to their very great Impoverishment, whilst the rest of the Kingdom at Home keep their Fingers warm in their Pockets.' A week later, when the first regiment had reached Durham, the orders for the employment of the Yorkshire militia were countermanded and immediate steps were taken to recover the money which had been distributed to the various regiments.[2]

While the gentry were complaining about the new burden of military expenditure the ship money controversy, which had been lying dormant, broke out afresh. On 11 March Wentworth told Secretary Windebank that he had heard that the sheriff of Yorkshire was attempting to alter the former assessment of ship money 'thereby to perplex the service and to disquiet, if not hinder, the levying thereof'. Accordingly he suggested that the vice-president and the Council of the North should be authorised to call the sheriff before them and command him to execute the writ without further delay. On 18 March Sir Marmaduke Langdale issued the necessary instructions to the head constables of the wapentakes, no doubt hoping that Parliament would soon relieve him of this disagreeable task. When the head constables sought to carry out these instructions they were faced with a violent resistance which was on a far greater scale than anything previously encountered. Sir Hugh Cholmley relates that he not only refused to pay his own assessment but carried the whole liberty of Whitby Strand with him while his friend Sir John Hotham headed the opposition in the East Riding. As a result Wentworth had them stripped of all their offices in the county.[3]

---

[1] *Cal.S.P.Dom. 1639-40*, 572-3. Knowler, ii, 393, 408.
[2] *Cal.S.P.Dom. 1640*, 34-5, 54, 57, 67, 68, 69. Knowler, ii, 411.
[3] Knowler, ii, 393. Sheffield Central Library: Spencer Stanhop MSS 60232. *Cholmley Memoirs*, 60-1.

In Yorkshire the parliamentary elections, which were held in early March, appear to have aroused little excitement, perhaps because at that stage no attempt had been made to collect ship money or to impose new military burdens on the county. Of the Yorkshire members who took their seats in the House of Commons there were several gentlemen who were strongly opposed both to Wentworth and to his system of 'Thorough': in particular, Henry Bellasis (the heir of Thomas Lord Fauconberg), Sir Ferdinando Fairfax, Sir Hugh Cholmley (both relatives of Henry Bellasis), Sir John Hotham and his eldest son and namesake. The majority of Yorkshire representatives, however, were moderate men such as Sir Henry Slingsby of Scriven and Brian Palmes of Lindley or close associates of Wentworth such as Sir Edward Osborne, Sir George Wentworth (his brother) and Sir William Pennyman.

In a message read to the Commons on 17 April the king made it clear that Parliament had been summoned primarily for the purpose of voting money to enable him to put down the Scottish rebellion. The Commons, however, were anxious to have their grievances settled before granting the necessary supplies. As Sir Henry Slingsby noted in his diary these grievances fell under three main heads: 'Ist greivances concerning matter of religion. 2ndly Property of goods. 3rdly Priviledge of Parliament.' In the first category the Commons included the Laudian innovations in public worship and the silencing of godly ministers and in the second, ship money, coat and conduct money, monopolies and the restraint of trade. On 5 May the king finally lost patience and dissolved Parliament, an action which Sir Hugh Cholmley considered to be ill advised 'for there were many wise gentlemen of it, and well-inclined for his and the public good'.[1]

Shortly after the dissolution Sir Hugh Cholmley, Sir John Hotham and Henry Bellasis were summoned before the Privy Council and cross-examined about certain speeches which they had made in the Commons. In the debate on 4 May (it was reported) Sir William Savile had declared that

the freeholders about him told him at his comeing, they did not care howe many subsidies were given soe that greivance of the shipp mony were taken awaye. Sir John Hotham and Mr Bellasses spake after Sir William Savile, alleadging that there were other greivances besides the shipp mony, as coate and conduct monye, and other millitary charges, which farr exceeded that of

[1] *Commons Journals*, ii, 4–5, 11–12. *Slingsby Diary*, 49–50. *Cholmley Memoirs*, 60.

shipp monye, which the countie required to be eased of, together with the shipp monye, or they durst not returne down into the Countrye. Indeede Sir John Hotham said, the millitarye charge uppon that countie was 40 thousand pounds, whereas the shipp monye was but 12 thousand pounds.

When Hotham and Bellasis declined to repeat what they had said in Parliament they were committed to the Fleet for a short period while Savile and Cholmley were forbidden to leave London without the Council's permission.[1]

Having failed in its attempt to secure parliamentary supplies the Crown endeavoured to speed up the collection of ship money which had been hanging fire while Parliament was sitting. Within a week after the dissolution the sheriffs of Yorkshire, Essex and Middlesex were examined by the attorney general 'for not collecting the shipp mony according to their severall writts, they haveing collected verie little of that monye, and have not distraynd upon any refusers'. On 29 May Sir Marmaduke Langdale received a strongly worded letter from the king ordering him, under the threat of heavy penalties, to levy the sum of £12,000 without further delay. When Sir Marmaduke continued to hesitate steps were taken to prosecute him in the Star Chamber and on 16 June he finally gave in and agreed to collect the whole amount within a few weeks.[2] Rather surprisingly, the Crown's refusal to tolerate Langdale's insubordination seems to have achieved the desired result. In July the Privy Council gave order that as a temporary expedient the large sums of ship money levied by the sheriffs of Yorkshire, Northumberland, Cumberland and Westmorland were to be used for defraying the expenses of the king's army in the North while a month later Sir Edward Osborne was writing that 'our sheriff' had recently paid in £8000. Subsequently, in January 1641, it was recorded that the ship money commissioners had received the whole of the £12,000 charged on the county by the writ of 1639.[3]

During the summer of 1640 there was growing discontent in Yorkshire over the excesses of the king's army which was now billeted in

[1] P.R.O., S.P.Dom., Charles I, S.P.16/cdliii/24. *Cholmley Memoirs*, 61. *Cal.S.P.Dom. 1640*, 166.

[2] P.R.O., Privy Council Registers, P.C.2/lii/474–5, and S.P.Dom., Charles I, S.P.16/cdliii/24. *Cal.S.P.Dom. 1640*, 120, 222–3, 308.

[3] P.R.O. Privy Council Registers, P.C.2/lii/629 and liii/90. *Cal.S.P.Dom. 1640*, 586. In her article on ship money Miss M. D. Gordon wrongly concluded that none of the £12,000 was collected (*Transactions of the Royal Historical Society*, Third Series, iv, 161).

the county. On 28 July a large number of gentlemen who were attending the York assizes met together at the house of Sir Marmaduke Langdale and decided to submit a petition to the king setting out their grievances. This petition was drawn up by Sir Hugh Cholmley and Sir John Hotham and its signatories included many deputy lieutenants and justices of the peace. After emphasising that in the previous year the county had spent no less than £100,000 in the military field the petitioners complained that they were 'oppressed with the billitting of unruly soldiers, whose speeches and actions tend to the burnding of our villages and houses, and to whose violence and insolencies wee are soe daily subiect, as wee cannott saie wee possesse our wifes, children and estate in safetie'. Since (they told the king) 'the billitting of soldiers, in any of your subiects houses againste theire will, is contrary to the aunciant lawes of this kingdome, confirmed...in the peticion of right [which had received the royal assent in 1628] wee most humbly desire...that this insupportable burthen may bee taken of from us least by theire insolencies some such sadd accident may happen as will be much displeasing to your sacrede Majestie and your loyall and obedient subjects'.[1] When this petition was read out at a meeting of the Privy Council strong exception was taken both to the substance and the choice of phraseology and Wentworth condemned it as mutinous in view of the impending threat of a Scottish invasion. In their reply the Privy Council commanded the Yorkshire gentry to be more respectful in future and to discuss their grievances with the lord lieutenant before troubling the king; denied that the military burden on the county had been as heavy as they were claiming; and told them roundly that the billeting of troops was a necessary requirement and in no way contrary to the law.[2]

According to Sir Hugh Cholmley the petition of 28 July led the Covenanters to believe that they would encounter little opposition from the Yorkshire trained bands[3] and this may well have been a factor in their decision to invade England before a new expeditionary force could be made ready. Following reports that the Scottish troops were massing near the border Sir Edward Osborne sent directions to the colonels and captains of the Yorkshire militia to be ready to march with

[1] *Cholmley Memoirs*, 61. *Slingsby Diary*, 56. P.R.O., S.P.Dom., Charles I, S.P.16/cdlxi/38.
[2] Sheffield Central Library: Strafford Letters, xxi, 203. Rushworth, iii, 1215. *Cal.S.P. Dom. 1640*, 595–7.
[3] *Cholmley Memoirs*, 61–2.

their companies at an hour's warning. In private, however, he expressed grave doubts about the loyalty of his fellow gentry. When informing Lord Conway, the governor of Newcastle, of the preparations which were being put in hand he warned him that four regiments lacked colonels and that he had been unable to find suitable replacements who were in sympathy with the king's objectives. Worse still, he feared that the Yorkshire gentry were so disaffected that the militia officers would be unwilling to march their troops beyond the county borders and might even refuse to stir at all without an advance of pay.[1] This general reluctance on the part of the ruling class of the county to assist the king against his Scottish subjects (who, it was widely felt, were simply defending their Protestant faith) is reflected in some jottings made by Sir Marmaduke Langdale in one of his rent-books. In these notes he poses a number of legal questions relating to the trained bands: for example, whether any subject of the Crown could be lawfully compelled to provide arms; whether he could refuse to march out of his county unless the enemy had entered the kingdom or if no advance of pay was forthcoming; and whether a colonel or captain had the right to relinquish his commission.[2] Such was the attitude of a man who had fought bravely in the continental wars and who was to distinguish himself as a royalist commander in the Civil War.

On 20 August 1640 the Scottish army crossed into England and three days later the king arrived in York with the intention of leading his troops in person. The day after the king's arrival he was presented with a petition from the Yorkshire gentry asking him to confirm their right to approach him direct and warning him that the militia would be unable to march without fourteen days' pay in advance. The king nevertheless persuaded them to raise the trained bands and on 25 August the colonels were instructed to bring their troops to certain nominated places of rendezvous.[3]

In the border counties the situation was becoming serious. On 28 August the Scottish forces easily defeated an English contingent at Newburn and two days later entered the garrison town of Newcastle. When news of these reverses was received in Yorkshire some men of

---

[1] *Cal.S.P.Dom. 1640*, 585–6, 588.

[2] Y.A.S. Library: MD 287, rent-book entitled 'An old Booke of my fathers' (no consistent pagination).

[3] Rushworth, iii, 1230–1. *Cal.S.P.Dom. 1640*, 626, 629, 630, 637, 642, 649. *H.M.C. Fifth Report*, Appendix, 331. *H.M.C. Sixth Report*, Appendix, 467.

property decided to remove their families to other counties. Sir Henry Slingsby the diarist wrote that after hearing of the fall of Newcastle he travelled with his wife and children to Hull and from there to the house of his brother-in-law John Bellasis in Lincolnshire. Shortly afterwards he noted:

We come not yet in Yorkshire into contribution with the Scots, for they have not yet invad'd us: but not with standing we feel the burden of the warr as well as our neighbours, by those regiments of foot and horse that are quarter'd amongst us and about us, and the Trainbands...The charge this year hath been so great to this country, by impositions and taxes laid upon it, and by the wast which is made by the souldiers that are billit'd here, that men are at a stand what course to take, or how to dispose of them selves. The fear they apprehend by that which hath befallen their neighbours in Northumberland and Bishoprick of Durham for the Scots army...hath made many both here and in Bishoprick to forsake their houses and neglect, so that it is greatly to be fear'd we shall find both the value of our lands and rents to fall and abate very much.[1]

At a meeting on 10 September the king exhorted the Yorkshire gentry to raise two months' pay for the trained bands. In reply Philip Lord Wharton, Ferdinando Lord Fairfax, Sir Hugh Cholmley and Sir John Hotham organised a petition offering a more limited contribution and calling for a parliament. At the same time they listed the economic grievances of the county:

The shippmony continyued and levyed for divers yeres last past. The vast expenses of the county the last yere, in military affaires. The biliting and insolencies of the Souldiers this summer, part of the tyme upon creditt of the Country as yet unsatisfied. The great Decay of trade. The stopp of marketts. The great charge and burthen of carriages, especially in the tyme of harvest. By all which meanes not only the common people But most of your Gentry by the failing of their rents are very much impoverished.[2]

When the lord president read this petition he took strong exception to the demand for a parliament because he knew that the king already had this possibility in mind and he considered it 'uncivill to anticipate him in point of time'. At a further meeting he managed, after a lengthy debate, to persuade a clear majority of the gentlemen present to agree that he should deliver the substance of the petition to the king without referring to the call for a parliament. Accordingly he told the king that

[1] *Slingsby Diary*, 60–1.
[2] *Slingsby Diary*, 57. Rushworth, iii, 1264–5. P.R.O., S.P.Dom., Charles I/cdlxiv/82. This petition is incorrectly dated 24 August in the calendar (*Cal.S.P.Dom. 1640*, 624).

the gentry were prepared to levy sufficient money to maintain the troops until 24 September, the day on which a great council of peers was due to meet at York. In return the king gave an undertaking that after the war the Yorkshire trained bands would be reduced from 12,000 to 6000 foot soldiers and that if any senior officers were killed in battle their heirs would be freed from all demands of wardship.[1]

According to Sir Hugh Cholmley and others who were involved in these proceedings most of the signatories of the original petition had left York before the second meeting and Wentworth's supporters mainly consisted of friends, dependants and recusants. At his subsequent trial Wentworth denied the accusation that there was a large Catholic element but it is certainly true that many who sided with him were close friends and relatives: men such as Sir William Savile of Thornhill, Sir Edward Osborne, Sir William Pennyman, Sir Thomas Danby and Sir Edward Rodes of Great Houghton. Following Wentworth's approach to the king a small group of militants attempted to submit a further petition drawing the king's attention to the demand for a parliament. This initiative, however, met with a sharp rebuff and the king sent a message to Sir Hugh Cholmley and Sir John Hotham accusing them of being 'the chief cause and promoters of all the petitions for that country' and warning them that if they 'ever meddled or had any hand in any more' he would hang them. Nevertheless when the great council of peers assembled at York it was announced that a new parliament was to be summoned for 3 November.[2]

Although the Yorkshire gentry had agreed to raise money for the trained bands there was, on the whole, little enthusiasm for the war. Worse still, the Scots had many sympathisers even in the northern counties and some persons of quality were actually in secret correspondence with their leaders. According to Clarendon, Thomas Lord Savile (the son of Wentworth's old enemy) had been in close touch with the Covenanters ever since the conclusion of the treaty of Berwick and had encouraged them to invade the country in a letter containing the forged signatures of several English noblemen. Also involved in these intrigues was Henry Darley of Buttercrambe, deputy governor of the Providence Island Company, who may well have been acting in collaboration with Lord Saye and Sele, Lord Brooke and other fellow stockholders. On 30 September Wentworth had him arrested on sus-

[1] *Slingsby Diary*, 57. *Cal.S.P.Dom. 1640–1*, 56–7, 62.
[2] Rushworth, viii, 601–32. *Cholmley Memoirs*, 63–4. *Cal.S.P.Dom. 1640–1*, 89.

picion and for two months he remained imprisoned in York Castle.[1]

Eventually recognising that he lacked the means to defeat the Scottish invaders the king took the advice of the great council of peers and opened negotiations with the rebel leaders. By the treaty of Ripon it was agreed that the Scots should be paid £850 a day until a final settlement had been concluded and that as a guarantee of payment they should continue to occupy the counties of Durham and Northumberland.[2] In the event the Scottish army did not finally depart until the late summer of 1641 and in the meantime the regiments which had been recruited in southern England remained quartered in Yorkshire, much to the discontent of the inhabitants.[3]

Once the decision to call a parliament had been announced the rival candidates were soon engaged in electioneering activities. On 26 September Ingram Hopton of Armley sent a message to one of his neighbours informing him that Sir William Savile, his colonel, intended to stand in the county election and asking him to bring in as many freeholders as possible, 'not doubtinge but that you will hold him a man soe worthy for the plaice that you shall give him your first voyces in the Election'.[4] In some of the borough elections the contest simply reflected the traditional rivalries of local families. At Knaresborough, which in 1628 had forty-six voters, the candidates were the same as in the two previous elections: Sir Henry Slingsby, Sir Richard Hutton of Goldsborough, son of the ship money judge (both neighbouring squires) and Henry Benson, one of the most substantial inhabitants of Knaresborough. Sir Henry Slingsby wrote of this election:

Sir Richard Hutton labour'd all he could to carry it by the industry of his Fathers man Moore who dwelt in the town, and I likewise by the diligence of my man Thomas Richardson who took great pains to bring the Burgesses together whom he knew would give their votes for me, he himself being one. There is an ill custome at these Elections to bestow wine in all the Town, which cost me £16 at the least and many a man a broken pate.

When the voting took place on 13 October Slingsby and Benson were declared elected.[5] At Aldborough, where the electorate was even

---

[1] Clarendon, ii, 534. *Y.A.S.R.S.*, xcvi, 74–5. *Lords Journals*, iv, 100, 102.
[2] Rushworth, iii, 1295–6.
[3] *H.M.C. Fifth Report*, Appendix, 141. *Fairfax Correspondence*, ii, 106, 112, 205–6, 208.
[4] Cartwright Memorial Hall, Bradford: Spencer Stanhope MSS, Bundle 10, Box 1.
[5] W. A. Atkinson, 'A Parliamentary Election in Knaresborough in 1628', *Y.A.J.*, xxxiv, 213. *Slingsby Diary*, 63–4.

smaller than at Knaresborough, one of the seats was virtually in the gift of Arthur Aldeburgh of Ellenthorpe who owned the manor. Richard Aldeburgh, the squire's eldest son, had represented the borough in the first two parliaments of Charles I's reign and also in the Short Parliament; it is hardly surprising, therefore, to find him elected again in October 1640. Robert Strickland of Thornton Bridge, the other successful candidate, appears to have been regarded by Wentworth as a man who could be trusted (in August, for example, he had been made a deputy lieutenant) and he probably owed his election to the fact that the lord president of the Council of the North was able to exert influence in this constituency.[1]

Apart from Robert Strickland there were only four candidates returned for Yorkshire seats who could be described as supporters of the lord president: Sir William Pennyman and Sir Thomas Danby at Richmond, and Sir George Wentworth (his brother) and Sir George Wentworth of Woolley (a kinsman) at Pontefract. At York two Puritan aldermen, Sir William Allanson and Thomas Hoyle, easily defeated Sir Edward Osborne, the vice-president of the Council of the North, and Sir Thomas Widdrington, the city recorder, both of whom had been recommended by Wentworth.[2] In the county election, which provided the most effective test of public opinion, two of Wentworth's main opponents, Ferdinando Lord Fairfax and his cousin Henry Bellasis, stood against Sir William Savile (nephew of the lord president) and Sir Richard Hutton, who presumably regarded Knaresborough as a second string. With the two popular candidates well in the lead Sir Marmaduke Langdale, the high sheriff, transferred the election from York to Pontefract, apparently in the hope that Sir William Savile would be able to muster additional support. Since Sir Marmaduke had hitherto been closely associated with the Country Party it is difficult to understand his behaviour on this occasion but whatever the reasons his attempt to influence the result ended in failure and on 10 October he was obliged to return the names of Ferdinando Lord Fairfax and Henry Bellasis as knights of the shire.[3] At Beverley there were three candidates: Sir John Hotham, who was now the undisputed leader of

---

[1] Y.A.J., xxvii, 262 and xxxiv, 31. H.M.C. Fifth Report, Appendix, 331.
[2] Cal.S.P.Dom 1640–1, 158.
[3] Ibid., 158. H.M.C. Various, viii, 54. Lord Fairfax held a Scottish peerage and was therefore not entitled to sit in the House of Lords. Sir William Savile was later returned for Old Sarum, Wiltshire.

the disaffected gentry in the East Riding; Michael Warton, the heir of Sir Michael Warton of Beverley Park who had refused to pay a ship money assessment; and Sir Thomas Metham of North Cave, one of Wentworth's deputy lieutenants who had always identified himself with the Court Party. Predictably the Puritan burgesses of Beverley voted in favour of the two Country Party candidates.[1] Of the remaining Yorkshire representatives the majority consisted of gentlemen who had actively opposed Wentworth and the policy of 'Thorough' or were later to align themselves with the more radical element in the House of Commons. These included Sir Hugh Cholmley, Sir Philip Stapleton of Warter Priory, John Hotham, John Alured and (following the enfranchisement of Northallerton and New Malton[2]) Henry Darley and Henry Cholmley, a younger brother of Sir Hugh.[3]

The Long Parliament assembled on 3 November and Sir Henry Slingsby wrote in his diary: 'Great expectance their is of a happy Parliament where the subject may have a total redress of all his grievances.'[4] At this stage there was a high degree of unanimity among the propertied classes of the kingdom. In general they were agreed that the system of arbitrary government should be brought to an end; that the Crown should be prevented from levying taxes without parliamentary consent; and that the position of Parliament should be strengthened as an essential means of safeguarding the public liberties. In a Yorkshire petition which was presented in the House of Commons on 7 November special emphasis was placed on the 'great and crying grievance' of ship money, mainly no doubt because the sheriff had been obliged in the end to make a serious effort to execute the writ of 1639.[5] Apart from the general causes of discontent there were two factors of particular concern to Yorkshiremen. In the first place, the county was still being put to the expense of billeting the king's army and there was a real danger that without regular pay the troops would stage a full-scale mutiny. On 8 February 1641 Henry Bellasis told the Commons that 'if some course weere not speedilie taken for the paiement of the Kings armie, the Northern partes and Yorkeshire espetiallie would bee plundered by the

---

[1] G. Oliver, *The History and Antiquities of the Town and Minster of Beverley*, 200.

[2] W. Notestein (ed.), *The Journal of Sir Simonds D'Ewes*, 137.

[3] For studies of the personnel of the Long Parliament see M. F. Keeler, *The Long Parliament, 1640–1641*, D. Brunton and D. H. Pennington, *Members of the Long Parliament* and A. Gooder, *The Parliamentary Representation of the County of York 1258–1832*, vol. ii.

[4] *Slingsby Diary*, 64.   [5] Rushworth, iv, 21.

souldiers therof: which armie as hee was latelie enformed did consist of about 12000 men horse and foote: and soe wee might bring the desolations of Germanie upon our selves'. So long as the English army remained in being the problem of supplying the troops with money was a recurring theme in the speeches of Yorkshire members.[1] Secondly, there was a large body of opinion, particularly within the ruling class of the county, which was in favour of abolishing the Council of the North. In the House of Commons (writes the Earl of Clarendon) Sir John Hotham, Sir Hugh Cholmley, Sir Philip Stapleton and some of the other northern gentlemen 'were marvellously solicitous to despatch the commitment of the Court of York' which they claimed was 'an illegal commission, and very prejudicial to the liberty and the property of his majesty's subjects of those four northern counties, where that jurisdiction was exercised'.[2]

Before embarking on constitutional reform the Long Parliament first took action against the king's 'evil counsellors' and other persons of consequence who had supported the Crown during the period of 'Thorough.' On 11 November John Pym moved for a committee to draw up articles of impeachment against Wentworth, and Sir John Hotham and 'some other Yorkshire men who had received some disobligation from the earl' joined in the condemnation. After attempting to take his seat in the House of Lords Wentworth was arrested and consigned to the Tower to await trial.[3] In December Sir Hugh Cholmley attacked his colleague Sir William Pennyman over his conduct as a deputy lieutenant in the North Riding. On 19 October the latter had issued a warrant to the constables instructing them to levy money for the support of his troops and to conscript anyone who refused to pay. Sir William conceded that the warrant 'might perhapps bee illegall' but pleaded justification 'by the law of necessitie and nature, in respect the Scotts were advanced to the verie skirts of Yorkeshire'. Subsequently Sir Thomas Danby, the other member for Richmond, was also called to account for certain acts which he had committed as a deputy lieutenant.[4] On 4 February 1641 Francis Nevile of Chevet, who had represented Boroughbridge in the Short Parliament, was brought to the

---

[1] W. Notestein (ed.), *The Journal of Sir Simonds D'Ewes*, 51, 58, 183, 265, 335, 432. For the method of paying the troops see P. Facer's study, 'A History of Hipperholme School from 1600 to 1914, with a Biography of its Founder, Matthew Bradley (1586–1648)' (unpublished London M.A. thesis, 1966).
[2] Clarendon, i, 315–16.   [3] *Ibid.*, i, 225.
[4] W. Notestein (ed.), *The Journal of Sir Simonds D'Ewes*, 104–5, 151–2, 326, 329.

bar of the House and charged with giving evidence to the Privy Council about the speeches made by Sir John Hotham and Henry Bellasis against the Crown's exactions. For this offence he was committed to the Tower during the pleasure of the House.[1] In threatening proceedings against all the lord lieutenants, deputy lieutenants and sheriffs who had levied taxes without parliamentary consent the Commons aroused the fears of many of the prime gentlemen of the shires. In Clarendon's view this was one of the main factors which led Sir John Hotham to throw in his lot with the popular party in the Commons. As sheriff Sir John had undertaken the task of levying ship money with characteristic energy and some at least of his fellow Yorkshiremen had not forgotten this: in January 1641, for example, Thomas Stockdale of Bilton Park reminded Lord Fairfax that 'In one of the grievances of the kingdom (the Ship money) I was a sufferer both in matter and manner; but it was in Sir John Hotham's sheriffwick, against whose rigorous and undue proceedings although I have just cause for complaint, nevertheless, observing him now a zealous patriot of his country, both in point of religion and liberty, the edge of my quarrel to himself is abated'.[2]

Among the gentry of his native county there were many who desired the downfall of Wentworth, 'that great engine...who hath...battered down [the] laws and liberties' of the kingdom 'and levelled them with the most servile nations'.[3] The House of Commons committee responsible for framing the indictment included several Yorkshire landowners who had incurred his displeasure for one reason or another, in particular Ferdinando Lord Fairfax, Sir Hugh Cholmley, Sir Arthur Ingram and Henry Bellasis. In addition, Sir David Foulis and his son Henry, Sir Thomas Layton, Sir John Bourchier and others who considered that they had been unjustly treated by the lord president supplied evidence and in some cases appeared as witnesses at his trial.[4] The impeachment proceedings began on 22 March but after a fortnight or so it became clear that the charge of high treason could not be sustained in a formal trial and on 10 April a bill of attainder was introduced in the Commons. 'Against him', Lord Fairfax told his brother Henry, 'we have framed a short Bill to convict him of treason, which was the

[1] Ibid., 322–3.
[2] Clarendon, i, 229, 239, 524 and ii, 259. Fairfax Correspondence, ii, 226.
[3] Fairfax Correspondence, ii, 104.
[4] Rushworth, viii, 14, 139, 140–4, 150, 154–5, 601–4. W. Notestein (ed.), The Journal of Sir Simonds D'Ewes, 152, 182. H.M.C. Fourth Report, Appendix, 39, 41, 45.

speedier way.' On 21 April the bill was passed on its third reading by 204 votes to 59. Of the Yorkshire representatives only six voted against the attainder: Sir Thomas Danby, Sir William Pennyman, Sir Henry Slingsby, Sir George Wentworth (either Wentworth's brother or his kinsman of Woolley), Richard Aldeburgh and William Mallory (or his son John, both of whom were M.P.s for Ripon).[1] Three weeks later Wentworth was executed on Tower Hill.

By the late summer of 1641 the Long Parliament had completed a programme of constitutional reform which commanded the general support of the propertied classes. The prerogative courts, including Star Chamber and the Council of the North, had been abolished; ship money and other types of arbitrary taxation had been declared illegal; and provision had been made for a parliament to be summoned at least once every three years.[2] In carrying out this legislative programme, however, the parliamentary leaders had deliberately shelved the controversial question of church reform and as a result many Puritans were becoming increasingly restive. On 27 May Thomas Stockdale, an ardent Calvinist, wrote in a letter to Lord Fairfax: 'Now the Earl of Strafford is removed out of the way, I suppose the other business of the kingdom will receive freer passage and quicker dispatch; and amongst the rest, that great question about ecclesiastical discipline and government of the Church by bishops.'[3] Stockdale was hoping that the Root and Branch party in the House of Commons would be able to secure the establishment of a Presbyterian system of church government but the House was sharply divided in matters of religion and little support could be expected in the Lords for any radical alteration in this sphere. In the Grand Remonstrance (which was carried by a narrow majority in the Commons on 22 November) there was a section on ecclesiastical reform which was basically Root and Branch;[4] it was, however, no more than a statement of intent which was to remain unfulfilled until the period of the Civil War.

Another factor which weighed heavily with the Puritans at this time was their fear of popery. When the Irish rose in rebellion in October 1641, partly for religious and partly for economic reasons, there were many who were prepared to believe in the existence of a general Catholic conspiracy, particularly as the rebels claimed that they were

---

[1] *Fairfax Correspondence*, ii, 81. Rushworth, viii, 59.
[2] 16 Charles I, c.i and 17 Charles I, c.viii, x, xi, xiv, xvi.
[3] *Fairfax Correspondence*, ii, 107.   [4] Clarendon, i, 424–7.

acting in support of the Crown. Joseph Lister, a Bradford clothier, wrote in his autobiography that one of his fellow Puritans 'came and stood up in the chapel door [at Pudsey] and cried out with a lamentable voice "Friends," said he, "we are all as good as dead men, for the Irish Rebels are coming; they are come as far as Rochdale...and will be at Halifax and Bradford shortly"...O what a sad and sorrowful going home had we that evening, for we must needs go to Bradford, and knew not but Incarnate Devils and Death would be there before us'.[1] The fear of an Irish invasion receded when it became clear that the newcomers were not Catholic rebels but Protestant refugees; on the other hand, there was continuing anxiety (not least among northern Puritans) about the possibility of a Catholic uprising in England. When Thomas Stockdale heard of the Irish rebellion he suggested to Lord Fairfax that all magazines should be guarded with special care; that each county should be placed under the control of a lieutenant general; and that measures should be taken to prevent 'the Popish party from conversing together, or travelling further than the next market-town'. On 23 December, however, he was writing: 'I hear of no order yet to come into the country to restrain the daily concourse of recusants: indeed the forces they are able to make out are not much considerable, yet their consultations may conduce to the prejudice both of Church and Commonwealth. Divers of the best families of them in these parts have left their own habitations, and are come to live at York'.[2]

In the early months of 1642 Thomas Stockdale helped to organise a number of Yorkshire petitions which accorded with the aims of the parliamentary leaders who were engaged in a bitter struggle with the king. These emphasised the necessity of relieving the Protestant community in Ireland, putting the realm in a state of defence, disarming Catholics and confining them to their houses, and carrying out a programme of ecclesiastical reform. The petitions are interesting not only for their subject matter but also because of the lists of signatories which have survived. In the autumn of 1640 the Yorkshire gentry had been almost completely united in opposition to Wentworth and the system of 'Thorough'; at the beginning of 1642, on the other hand, the dissidents were a much smaller and less representative group, consisting to a large extent of Puritan gentlemen, men such as Sir Matthew Boynton (who had recently returned from the Netherlands), Sir John Bourchier,

---

[1] T. Wright (ed.), *The Autobiography of Joseph Lister 1627–1709*, 7–8.
[2] *Fairfax Correspondence*, ii, 229–30, 290, 299.

Sir Richard Darley and Sir Thomas Fairfax, the heir to Ferdinando Lord Fairfax. In essence the parliamentarian party of the Civil War was already in being but the situation was at this stage relatively fluid since a number of future royalists were still sympathetic to the cause of Parliament.[1]

As his relations with Parliament rapidly deteriorated the king decided to send the Earl of Newcastle to take possession of the magazine at Hull. On 11 January, however, the House of Commons issued instructions to Sir John Hotham to use his trained bands to secure the magazine on behalf of Parliament and as a result a great quantity of arms and ammunition was brought under parliamentary control. Later Sir John was to declare:

When this Parliament was pleased first to honour me with their commands to execute the government of Hull...the state of affairs was such, as it was disputed by the wisest, whether love to a man's country, and the being of Parliament, could engage a man of so flourishing a fortune to such a hazard without some measure of foolhardiness. I saw the danger I undertook, yet well knew my duty, and how little respect or consideration my private sufferings or ruin could claim, when the whole interest of Parliaments and liberties of England were, in most men's judgements, at stake.[2]

In the following weeks the House of Commons made further encroachments on the king's military powers by ordering sheriffs and justices of the peace to put the trained bands in a state of readiness, suppress unlawful assemblies and superintend the disarming of recusants. In Yorkshire these instructions were diligently executed by Sir Thomas Gower the younger, who was then sheriff, and a group of Puritan magistrates which included Sir Thomas Fairfax, Sir Edward Rodes and Thomas Stockdale. On 12 February Stockdale informed Lord Fairfax that the sheriff and the justices who were met together at York had agreed on 'a course for ordering of the militia in such manner as may be useful in suppressing of insurrections' and were proceeding 'in full concurrence with the Parliament in all things'. Finally, on 5 March, the two Houses of Parliament issued a militia ordinance formally appoint-

[1] B.M., Egerton MSS 2546, ff.23–4. House of Lords MSS: Yorkshire petition of 15 February 1642. *Fairfax Correspondence*, ii, 349, 362, 367–73.
[2] Sir Charles Firth (ed.), *The Life of William Cavendish, Duke of Newcastle*, 8–9. Clarendon, i, 523–4. P. Saltmarshe, *History and Chartulary of the Hothams*, 141.

ing lord lieutenants who were to be answerable only to the Lords and Commons.[1]

A fortnight after the enactment of the militia ordinance the king arrived in York. In transferring the seat of government to York he was clearly demonstrating his confidence in the loyalty of his northern subjects and according to Lord Clarendon the Yorkshire gentry, with few exceptions, genuinely welcomed him, 'expressing great alacrity for his majesty's being with them'.[2] In some quarters, however, it was feared that the king was planning to use force and there was discussion at Westminster about the possibility of moving the contents of the magazine at Hull to the Tower of London. On 22 April a small group of Yorkshire gentlemen (about twenty in number) submitted a petition to the king urging on him the necessity of keeping the stockpile of arms and ammunition at Hull both for his own security and the protection of the northern counties. On the following day the king arrived at the gates of Hull with a large body of horse, his intention being to take possession of the magazine. Sir John Hotham, however, refused to admit the royal party, claiming that it would be contrary to his instructions from Parliament, and for this act of defiance he was declared guilty of treason.[3]

The petition of 22 April is of considerable significance because it represents one of the first stages in the organisation of a distinctive Cavalier party. Among the signatories were Sir Francis Wortley who had been conspicuously loyal to the Crown at the time of the Scottish invasion; Sir William Wentworth, a younger brother of the former lord president; and Sir Thomas Metham who was accused of recruiting troops among the East Riding Catholics. In the Commons the petition was roundly condemned. Most of the subscribers, it was alleged, had supported Wentworth in September 1640 when he was endeavouring to suppress the demand for a parliament.[4] In Yorkshire the leaders of the popular party were equally incensed and on 30 April the king was

---

[1] *Cobbett's Parliamentary History of England*, ii, columns 1033–5, 1083–5. *Description of Browsholme Hall, in the West Riding of the County of York*, 121–2. *H.M.C. Fifth Report*, Appendix, 7. *Fairfax Correspondence*, ii, 362, 365, 366. Clarendon, i, 570–1, 574, 577–81.

[2] Clarendon, ii, 1.

[3] *Cobbett's Parliamentary History of England*, ii, columns 1168, 1185–6. Clarendon, ii, 46–50.

[4] *Cal.S.P.Dom. 1640–1*, 62. *Cobbett's Parliamentary History of England*, ii, column 1193.

presented with a counter-petition advising him to disregard the views of Sir Francis Wortley and his fellow signatories on the grounds that they were an unrepresentative minority. Faced with allegations that he had helped to create a schism within the gentry Sir Francis felt it necessary to issue a statement in vindication of his conduct.[1]

Early in May Lord Howard of Escrick, Ferdinando Lord Fairfax, Sir Philip Stapleton, Sir Hugh Cholmley and his brother Sir Henry Cholmley were nominated as parliamentary commissioners to attend the king at York. Sir Hugh relates that in the instructions as originally drafted

we were plainly enjoined to draw the train-bands together; and to oppose the King in all things were for the Parliament's service. This I refused to accept, saying 'it were to begin the war, which I intended not,' whereupon Pym bid me draw the instructions to my own mind, which I did; but the Lord Fairfax and I departing in a coach before they could be finished, they were brought to us by the Lord Howard and Stapylton; and though not so large as at first, yet otherwise than I did assent to or could approve of.[2]

The parliamentary commissioners arrived at York on 8 May. Four days later the king told a large gathering of Yorkshire gentry that in view of the military measures which were being taken by Parliament he had decided to have a guard for his personal security. In reply some gentlemen declared that they were ready to serve him on all occasions while others expressed agreement with the proposition on the understanding that the guard could be raised by legal authority and would not include any persons who were suspect in religion. A third group, under the leadership of Sir Matthew Boynton, Sir William Constable and Sir Thomas Fairfax, contended that it was unnecessary for the king to have a special guard since he was in no danger from Parliament. To judge from the signatories of this last petition the Roundhead party (as the supporters of Parliament were now being called) had been forsaken by a few of the wealthier squires but was apparently winning new recruits, particularly among the Puritan gentry.[3]

In spite of these divisions the king summoned all the Yorkshire gentry charged with light horses to appear at York on 20 May for the purpose of providing him with a guard. On the appointed day many gentlemen 'to the number of 136 or above', together with sixty

---

[1] B.M., Thomason Tracts, 669, f.6(9) and E.153(1).   [2] *Cholmley Memoirs*, 65–6.
[3] Rushworth, iv, 615–17. B.M., Thomason Tracts, 669, f.5(24), E.147(17), E.148(4).

serving-men, all on horseback, assembled on Heworth moor where they were reviewed by the king. Initially it was decided that the king's guard should consist of fifty horsemen with Sir Francis Wortley as colonel and a foot regiment under the command of Sir Robert Strickland. In view of the persistent fear of popery the king gave order that anyone refusing the oaths of supremacy and allegiance should be rejected.[1]

On 1 June Parliament approved the Nineteen Propositions.[2] This ultimatum was totally unacceptable to the king and there now seemed little prospect of a reconciliation between Crown and Parliament.

In Yorkshire the king continued his efforts to rally support by summoning all the freeholders and copyholders of the county to a meeting on 3 June. When he arrived on Heworth moor, accompanied by a horse troop of 140 gentlemen and a regiment of foot, a great crowd estimated at between 60,000 and 80,000 was already gathered to hear his speech. The occasion, however, was not as completely successful as the king had hoped. Some sections of the crowd shouted for Parliament and Sir Thomas Fairfax, Sir Matthew Boynton and other Puritan leaders organised a petition in which they complained about the economic condition of the county, the drawing together of the trained bands and 'the daily resort of Recusants, and persons disaffected in Religion' to the court at York.[3]

As the weeks passed the king's guard continued to grow in strength. According to a news-letter from York some of those who were enlisting were papists or well-born gentlemen 'of weak, or decayed estates, who conceive civil war to be the best way suddenly to raise their fortunes equall to their discents'.[4] While the writer may well have been prejudiced there was at least an element of truth in this allegation. Two of the most prominent Cavaliers, Sir Robert Strickland and Sir Thomas Metham, had a Catholic background and were heavily indebted at this time. Unlike them Sir Francis Wortley was a staunch Anglican but his financial situation was even more desperate: indeed in 1635 he had sold the greater part of his estate to his mother, the dowager Duchess of Devonshire, for the sum of £20,000.[5]

[1] Cal.S.P.Dom. 1641–3, 322–3. B.M., Additional MSS 24475, 2. Rushworth, iv, 621–2.
[2] Clarendon, ii, 167–70.
[3] Cal.S.P.Dom. 1641–3, 334–5, 336. Y.A.J., vii, 64–6. Clarendon, ii, 198–200. B.M., Thomason Tracts, 669, f.6(29).
[4] B.M., Thomason Tracts, E.108(24).
[5] D. Scott, The Stricklands of Sizergh Castle, 135–6, 146. M. F. Keeler, The Long Parlia-

In the middle of June the king issued commissions of array with the intention of placing control of the militia throughout England in the hands of 'estated and sober men'. The list of names included with the Yorkshire commission (originally dated 18 June but reconstituted on 4 July) records the accession to the Cavalier party of a number of men who had continued to adhere to the cause of Parliament in the early months of 1642: in particular, Sir Marmaduke Langdale, Sir John Ramsden of Longley, Henry Bellasis, Sir Thomas Gower and his eldest son (the sheriff of Yorkshire), Sir William Ingleby of Ripley and Sir John Goodricke of Ribston. On the other hand, several gentlemen who were named as commissioners, among them Sir William Lister of Thornton and Sir Thomas Wentworth of North Elmsall, were to range themselves on the side of Parliament when hostilities broke out.[1]

Early in July the royalist troops began to make preparations for an attack on Hull. The king was optimistic about the outcome because Sir John Hotham had secretly undertaken to surrender the town; in the event, however, Sir John thought better of his promise.[2] On hearing that the king's forces were massing, the parliamentary committee at Hull, which included the two Hothams, father and son, and John Alured, immediately wrote to Sir Philip Stapleton, who was then at Westminster, asking for reinforcements to be despatched to help them defend the town. At the same time they suggested that Parliament should send down Sir William Strickland of Boynton, Sir Hugh Cholmley, Sir Henry Cholmley and Sir Philip himself for the purpose of strengthening the committee and rallying support among their fellow Yorkshiremen.[3] On 22 July Sir Thomas Gower the younger, writing to a relative, gave it as his opinion that the forces around Hull were not strong enough to attempt an assault on the town: in his view the king was using the Hull affair as a pretext for mustering troops. At the end of the month, after a few minor skirmishes, the Cavaliers withdrew to Beverley.[4]

With Parliament busily engaged in raising an army in southern

---

ment, 1640–1641, 355. P.R.O., S.P.Dom., Committee for Compounding, S.P.23/lxviii/72 and ccxv/23. Beverley County Record Office: Burton Constable MSS, DDEV 53/98. Sheffield Central Library: Wharncliffe MSS D92, D98.

[1] *Cal.S.P.Dom. 1641–3*, 345. Northamptonshire County Record Office: Finch–Hatton MSS 133 (no pagination).
[2] Clarendon, ii, 251–67.   [3] *H.M.C. Thirteenth Report*, Appendix i, 41.
[4] *H.M.C. Fifth Report*, Appendix, 191.

England many Yorkshire squires hastened to provide the king with money and other material support. On 30 July Sir William Pennyman was reported to have brought in a troop of horse, as 'hath most of the Gentry of this County'. Three days later Sir Thomas Gower obliged with a loan of £1500 while a news-letter of 3 August claimed that the Yorkshire gentry as a whole 'stand stiffe for the King: Sir Michael Warton knight hath lent the King £20,000, and other Yorkshire Gentlemen doe profer much'.[1] As the royalist forces increased in strength there were reports that some of the worse-disciplined elements were committing acts of violence and plundering the goods of men known to be sympathetic to the parliamentary cause. In the neighbourhood of Hull Christopher Legard of Anlaby and other Roundhead gentlemen had their houses pillaged and their livestock driven away. At Nun Monkton, near Knaresborough, a band of royalists broke into the house of George Marwood, a Calvinist squire who had recently been dismissed from the commission of the peace for disloyalty. In Marwood's absence the soldiers insulted his wife, calling her 'Puritan whore', and took all the money and plate they could lay their hands on.[2]

In Yorkshire at least the Civil War had in effect already begun but it was still an undeclared war. On 22 August this deficiency was made good when the king raised his standard at Nottingham.

[1] B.M., Thomason Tracts, E.108(37) and (40).
[2] B.M., Thomason Tracts, 669 f.6(27) and (53). *Cobbett's Parliamentary History of England*, ii, columns 1450–1.

CHAPTER XV

For King and Parliament

WRITING of the situation in Yorkshire at the beginning of the Civil War the Earl of Clarendon relates that 'the greatest part of the gentry of that populous country, and very many of the common people, did behave themselves with signal fidelity and courage to the King's service...There were very few gentlemen, or men of any quality, in that large county who were actively or factiously disaffected to his majesty'.[1] A detailed examination[2] confirms that most of the Yorkshire gentry who took sides supported the royalist cause yet the parliamentarian families were by no means an insignificant group:

total number of families in 1642	679
(a) royalist families	242
(b) parliamentarian families	128
(c) families which were divided in their loyalties or which changed sides	69
(d) families which remained neutral	240

One of the most striking features is the large number of families which maintained a precarious neutrality. In the main these were lesser or middling gentry but occasionally a major squire managed to avoid being drawn into the conflict. Mrs Alice Thornton writes of her brother George Wandesford of Kirklington who returned to Yorkshire in 1643 after spending a year on the Continent:

It must not be denied that my dear brother's affections and conscience carried him in judgement to serve his king, the church, and state, by way of armes. Yet, as things then fell out, such was his prudence for the preservation of his

---

[1] Clarendon, ii, 286, 287.

[2] The following table covers the period of the two Civil Wars, 1642–8. The main sources are as follows: P.R.O., S.P.Dom., Committee for Compounding (S.P.23), Committee for the Advance of Money (S.P.19), Commonwealth Exchequer Papers (S.P.28/138, 215 and 250) and S.P.Dom. Supplementary (S.P.46/107); J. W. Clay (ed.), *Dugdale's Visitation of Yorkshire, with Additions* and 'The Gentry of Yorkshire at the Time of the Civil War', *Y.A.J.*, xxiii, 349; and E. Peacock (ed.), *The Army Lists of the Roundheads and Cavaliers.*

family, according to his gracious majestie's command to his freinds, that he saw all was lost, and that they should sitt in quiett, and preserve themselves for the good of himselfe or sonne afterwards. So that he saw it was in vaine to strive against that impetuous streame, and involve himselfe in utter ruine willfully, when noe good could possibly be don by his service to the king, otherwaise then by our praiers and teares for him.[1]

Even outside the ranks of the neutrals the degree of commitment might be small. As the tide of battle ebbed and flowed some gentlemen gave assistance to one side and then to the other but without ever taking an active part in the proceedings. Early in the Civil War Thomas Thornhill of Fixby sent one of his tenants to fight in the king's army, promising to give him his farm if he came back alive; in 1645, however, we find him making a voluntary contribution of £80 to advance the cause of Parliament and subsequently he served as a parliamentarian justice of the peace.[2]

While some gentlemen who had initially supported the Crown went over to the side of Parliament others switched allegiance in the opposite direction. Sir Hugh Cholmley, a successful parliamentarian commander, threw in his lot with the Crown in March 1643 following the arrival of the queen at Bridlington.[3] Sir John Hotham, the governor of Hull, undertook to deliver up the town to the royalist forces but was arrested by a relative, Sir Matthew Boynton, and later executed.[4] Sir Henry Anderson of Long Cowton, another of Hotham's relations, suffered the worst of both worlds: imprisonment in York Castle by the royalists and sequestration by the parliamentarians. At one stage he drew up certain propositions which were intended to serve as the basis of an accommodation between king and Parliament but his efforts at peacemaking merely aroused the suspicions of the parliamentarian leaders.[5]

In a class so tightly knit as the Yorkshire gentry it was inevitable that political loyalties should cut across personal relationships. Two months before his defection Sir Hugh Cholmley wrote to the speaker of the House of Commons: 'But as nothing can divert

---

[1] *Surtees Society*, lxii, 59.
[2] *Cal. Committee for the Advance of Money*, 1111. B.M., Additional MSS 24516, f.71. *Surtees Society*, xl, 6.
[3] Clarendon, ii, 468.
[4] Clarendon, iii, 527–9. J. Tickell, *History of the Town and County of Kingston upon Hull*, 463–78.
[5] *H.M.C. Fifth Report*, Appendix, 107–8, 115. *Cal. Committee for Compounding*, 2334–7.

me from serving the Parliament with all fidelity whiles I am in their employment yet I profess it grieves my heart to see how these calamities increase and how I am forced to draw my sword not onely against my countrymen but many near friends and allies some of which I know both to be well affected in religion and lovers of their liberties.'[1] Such was the disruptive impact of the Civil War that in some cases the head of the family appeared on one side and his heir on the other. One of the most zealous parliamentarians in Yorkshire was Sir Thomas Maleverer of Allerton Mauleverer who raised two regiments of horse and one of foot for Parliament and was later to sign the king's death-warrant. His son Richard, on the other hand, fought for the Crown and was imprisoned for his loyalty. When compounding for his estate in 1649 he claimed that his father had kept from him an annuity of £500 a year and that there were arrears of £1700 owing to him.[2] Another parliamentarian squire, Stephen Hutchinson of Wykeham Abbey, disinherited his son on the grounds that he had become 'disaffected to the state, and thereby hath incurred my displeasure'.[3]

The political divisions within the gentry were by no means uniform throughout the county:

	North Riding	East Riding	West Riding	York
royalist families	68	44	125	5
parliamentarian families	35	37	54	2
families which were divided in their loyalties or which changed sides	15	19	31	4
families which remained neutral	77	42	110	11
	195	142	320	22

The importance of geography in determining Civil War loyalties should not be underestimated. In Richmondshire, where urban influences were weak and Catholicism was still deeply entrenched, the situation must have appeared desperate to the small minority of gentlemen who were sympathetic to the cause of Parliament. In the East Riding, on the other hand, the southern parts of the region were under the dominance of Hull which remained a parliamentarian stronghold throughout the Civil War. Clarendon writes that 'the opposite party

[1] *H.M.C. Thirteenth Report*, Appendix i, 90.
[2] P.R.O., S.P.Dom., Committee for Compounding, S.P.23/ccxv/263, 266, 267 and ccxxxvi/31, 32.
[3] *Y.A.J.*, xviii, 238–9. P.R.O., S.P.Dom., Committee for Compounding, S.P.23/ccxv/ 279, 282, 283.

was strengthened and enabled by the strong garrison of Hull, whence young Hotham on all occasions was ready to second them with his troop of horse, and to take up any well affected person who was suspected to be loyal; which drove all resolved men from their houses into York, where they only could be safe'.[1] While some gentlemen with estates in the area took refuge in York others who, on the face of it, might have been expected to support the Crown either stayed neutral or assisted the parliamentarian forces with gifts of money and plate.[2]

In the West Riding there were a number of royalist garrisons which, for a time at least, overawed the surrounding country in a similar fashion to Hull. In 1646 Francis Bunny of Newland, a Puritan gentleman, argued in a petition to the committee for compounding that 'living under the power of the Lord of Newcastle's Army in the West riding' he was forced 'to assist Commissioners appoynted to receive the Accompts of the Constables of the said Westridinge...which your petitioner could not avoid or refuse to doe unless hee would suffer his wife and children to bee ruyned, his habitacion lying neere the Garrison of Pomfrett Castle on the one side and Sandall Castle on the other'.[3] In other parts of south Yorkshire, however, it was the parliamentarians who were in a position of strength and the would-be royalists who had to ponder the implications of openly demonstrating their loyalties. One gentleman who found himself in this dilemma was Sir John Reresby of Thrybergh, near Rotherham. His son wrote that 'though his own principles lead him to be loyall, most of the gentlemen of the neighbourhood taking up arms for the Parlament, he considered for some time how to declare himselfe, but at the last was active in the commission of array to raise men for the king'. Sir John's hesitation no doubt accounts for the fact that his name was included in several commissions issued by Parliament in 1643 for the levying of money in the West Riding.[4]

The main parliamentarian region in the West Riding was the clothing area with its industrialised economy and its heavy concentration of Puritanism. Clarendon writes that 'Leeds, Halifax, and Bradford, three very populous and rich towns, (which depending wholly upon clothiers

---

[1] Clarendon, ii, 464.

[2] P.R.O., S.P.Dom., Commonwealth Exchequer Papers, S.P.28/189 and 202, East Riding accounts.

[3] P.R.O., S.P.Dom., Committee for Compounding, S.P.23/clxxviii/408.

[4] B.M., Additional MSS 28443, f.7. Sir Charles Firth and R.S. Rait (ed.), *Acts and Ordinances of the Interregnum, 1642–1660*, i, 91, 148, 230.

naturally maligned the gentry,) were wholly' at the disposition of the king's enemies.[1] Among the gentry who were seated in the clothing area the royalists heavily outnumbered the parliamentarians (and in December 1642 we find them mounting an attack on the woollen towns). In the neighbourhood of Bradford and Leeds, however, there were a number of middling squires, mainly of Puritan conviction, who took the side of Parliament, men such as Henry Tempest of Tong, Richard Thornton of Tyersall and Robert Dyneley of Bramhope.

To take up arms against a lawful sovereign, whatever acts of tyranny he might have committed, was not a step which could be contemplated lightly, least of all by members of the upper classes. In a work published during the Civil War Sir Francis Wortley, one of the most ardent royalists in Yorkshire, drew on the doctrine of the divine right of kings in emphasising the necessity of unquestioning obedience to the Crown. The true Cavalier, he wrote

conceives the King to be the Head of the Church, as it is personall, not spirituall, and hath sworne him Gods Deputy in Government...He dares not question his Authority, who is onely answerable to God, but in his heart knows him as his Vice-gerent, and knowes that to resist his power, is to resist him that gave it...He dares call his Soveraigne the Anointed of God... He conceives passive obedience always due to the power of the King.[2]

Some royalist squires may have shared these sentiments but it is unlikely that the majority subscribed to a theory of monarchy which had brought James I into conflict with the House of Commons: after all, many of them had welcomed and supported the efforts of the Long Parliament to circumscribe the royal prerogative. Nevertheless there was a wide gulf between constitutional reform and treason in arms and few men could view with equanimity either the act itself or the consequences which might flow from it. The Crown, moreover, stood for order and stability, the preservation of a hierarchic society and a hierarchic church with which most of the gentry were basically content. As Sir Francis Wortley put it, the Cavalier 'detests Parity in Church or in Commonwealth, as tending to Anarchy'.[3] In the months immediately preceding the Civil War the outlook for the Church of England appeared gloomy: religious issues were now being freely discussed in public; sectarian agitation was adding its own shrill voice to the debate;

---

[1] Clarendon, ii, 464.   [2] Sir Francis Wortley, *Characters and Elegies*, 11-12.
[3] *Ibid.*, 12.

and Parliament was threatening, in the Nineteen Propositions, to carry out a radical programme of ecclesiastical reform. Sir Henry Slingsby, who had been opposed to the Laudian innovations, wrote in his diary that whereas 'in former times it was thought greivious that conformity should be impos'd by the bishopps when the scruple should be only a Cap or a Sirples...we scruple to have root and branch pluck'd up'[1]; and indeed many who rallied to the Crown must have been alarmed at the dangers which were threatening the established Church. At the same time there was growing evidence of social unrest, often involving resistance to landlords, which gave rise to fears among the propertied classes that a civil war might result in the overthrow of their wealth and privileges, particularly if the Crown was ultimately vanquished. Although Sir John Hotham at first adhered to the cause of Parliament he was similarly concerned about the possibility of a social revolution. In the autumn of 1642 he wrote: 'I honour the King as much as any, and love the Parliament, but doe not desire to see either absolute conqueror, it is too great a temptation to courses of violence.' If peace was not restored, 'the necessitous people of the whole kingdome will presently rise in mighty numbers, and whosoever they pretend for att first, within a while they will sett up for themselves to the utter ruine of all the Nobility and Gentry of the kingdome'.[2]

Besides these general considerations there might be more specific reasons for supporting the royalist cause. Gentlemen who held offices of profit, leases of Crown property or shares in state monopolies tended to side with the king if they declared themselves at all. In seeking to justify his opposition to the plan for removing the contents of the magazine from Hull Sir Francis Wortley implied that he felt duty bound to support the king's interests because he was one of his majesty's servants and it seems likely that he had been granted an office in the royal household following its establishment at York.[3] Other royalists with similar vested interests included Sir William Pennyman of Marske who had been deprived of a lucrative Star Chamber office by the Long Parliament but who was probably still in receipt of a rent from the alum monopoly;[4] Sir Ralph Hansby of Tickhill Castle who was bailiff of Tickhill and held leases of the castle and its demesnes; and Sir Richard Hutton of Goldsborough, steward of the honor of

---

[1] *Slingsby Diary*, 121.   [2] A. M. W. Stirling, *The Hothams*, i, 64–6.
[3] B.M., Thomason Tracts, E.153(1).   [4] *Cal.S.P.Dom. 1641–3*, 200. Above, 91.
23—Y.G.

Knaresborough, whose son petitioned for a grant of the office after the Restoration.[1] In all there were twenty-five heads of royalist families who had been beholden to the Crown for part of their income either on the outbreak of the Civil War or at least up to the time of the Long Parliament. In contrast, no more than six parliamentarian gentry can be placed in this category, among them Brian Stapleton of Myton, one of the king's receivers in Yorkshire, and Christopher Ridley of Beverley who was the Court of Wards feodary in the East Riding.[2]

During the months of political unrest which preceded the Civil War the king granted titles of honour on a prolific scale in an attempt to secure or consolidate support among the propertied classes. Between January 1641 and August 1642 no fewer than thirty Yorkshiremen received baronetcies or knighthoods.[3] Several gentlemen like Sir Hugh Cholmley and Sir William Strickland of Boynton (both of whom were created baronets) refused to be influenced by the king's openhandedness and on the outbreak of the Civil War took up arms for Parliament. Most recipients, however, adhered to the royalist cause and in some cases at least may have felt themselves under a personal obligation to the Crown.

Some gentlemen had so closely identified themselves with the interests of the Crown in the period of 'Thorough' that their appearance on the royalist side can be regarded as virtually a foregone conclusion. In particular there was an inner knot of Wentworth's relatives and friends who had served under him as deputy lieutenants: Sir William Savile of Thornhill, Sir Edward Osborne (vice-president of the Council of the North from 1633 to 1641), Sir William Pennyman, Sir Thomas Danby (both ship money sheriffs), Sir Edward Stanhope of Grimston, Sir George Wentworth of Woolley, Robert Rockley of Rockley and George Butler of Ellerton. Although Sir William Savile had quarrelled with the vice-president and most of these gentlemen had signed the petitions complaining about the military burden on the county they remained basically loyal to the Crown, supported Wentworth to the

---

[1] P.R.O., Exchequer, Parliamentary Surveys, E.317/58. J. Hunter, *South Yorkshire*, i, 231. *Cal.S.P.Dom. 1660–1*, 239.

[2] P.R.O., Signet Office Docquets, Index 6810, May 1635 (no pagination) and Court of Wards, Feodaries' Surveys, Wards 5/49, certificates for East Riding.

[3] G.E.C. (ed.), *Complete Baronetage*, ii, 115, 128, 136, 149, 156, 161, 174, 176, 185, 187, 189, 194. W. A. Shaw (ed.), *Knights of England*, ii, 211, 212, 213.

very end and in some cases found themselves under attack in the House of Commons. This small group in fact represented the potential nucleus of a royalist party before such a party began to take shape in Yorkshire during the spring of 1642. In the Civil War both Sir William Savile and Sir William Pennyman died while in arms for the king and the remainder had to compound for their estates. Not all Wentworth's associates, however, declared themselves in favour of the Crown. As we have already seen, Sir John Hotham went over to the popular party in 1640 while Sir William Strickland and Sir Edward Rodes of Great Houghton (both men of strong Puritan sympathies) also took the side of Parliament, although in their case there was no specific act of defiance in the period leading up to the Civil War.

If the Wentworth group provided an element of continuity between the Court Party as constituted in the period of 'Thorough' and the royalist gentry of 1642, that section of the squirearchy which had actively opposed the lord president and his Council or had refused to pay extra-parliamentary taxes was more equally divided in its Civil War loyalties. On the one hand, Lord Fauconberg and his son Henry Bellasis, Sir Thomas Gower, Sir Marmaduke Langdale, Sir Michael Warton of Beverley Park and Sir William Ingleby of Ripley decided in the end to throw in their lot with the Crown, in most cases after maintaining links with the popular party until the early months of 1642. On the other hand, Sir John Hotham, Sir Hugh Cholmley, Sir William Constable, Sir Henry Foulis, Sir John Bourchier, Henry Darley, Brian Stapleton and James Maleverer of Ingleby Arncliffe continued to support the cause of Parliament when the Civil War broke out. In this latter group there were some gentlemen who had particularly good reason to feel antagonistic towards the Crown. Sir John Bourchier had been imprisoned and heavily fined while James Maleverer had been plunged into severe financial difficulties as a result of the distresses levied on his estate. Similarly, Sir Henry Foulis must have felt embittered at the punishment meted out to his father who, after spending seven years in prison, had died not long before the Civil War.[1]

The idea that the Civil War was pre-eminently a conflict over religion is no longer seriously entertained. Nevertheless there was undoubtedly a close relationship between religious loyalties and Civil War alignments, particularly in the case of the Catholic and Puritan gentry:

[1] See above, 303.

	Catholic families	Puritan families	Families which were partly Catholic and partly Puritan
royalist	86	24	1
parliamentarian	10	64	4
divided or changed sides	9	23	1
neutral	52	21	–
Total	157	132	6

Although there had been considerable unrest among the Catholic gentry in the early part of Charles I's reign they ranged themselves solidly behind the Crown at the time of the Scottish war in 1639. At the queen's request a collection was made within the English Catholic community for the purpose of assisting the king with his military expenditure and in Yorkshire Lord Dunbar, Sir Walter Vavasour of Hazlewood Castle and other leading recusants joined together to supervise the scheme.[1] As England moved towards Civil War it became clear that if Parliament succeeded in wresting power from the Crown the Catholics would find themselves under far heavier pressure, not only in a religious but also in a financial sense (and indeed it was not until the triumph of Parliament that recusant landowners literally forfeited the statutory two-thirds of their estate revenue). The Roundheads, for their part, appear to have been genuinely alarmed at the extent of Catholic support for the Crown although some of the accusations which originated from Puritan sources were clearly slanted for propaganda purposes. According to a Yorkshire petition of 10 May 1642 the king was being deluded by what were termed 'Romish instruments', while in a news-letter from York it was alleged that 'the Catholiques in this Kingdome give all lost, if a Civill Warre ensue not, or this Parliament is not subdued'.[2] In the face of Puritan attempts to discredit the Cavaliers by depicting them as solidly Catholic the king and his supporters were at pains to emphasise their devotion and loyalty to the established Church. To this end attempts were made to exclude men of popish sympathies from the king's personal guard and in August 1642 a group of Yorkshire royalists declared that one of their primary aims was 'the Defence of the true professed Protestant

[1] Rushworth, ii, 826.   [2] Y.A.J., vii, 74.

Religion, in opposition to Popery and Schismatical Innovations'.[1] Four days before the king set up his standard, however, it was reported from York that the recusants had been ordered to supply horsemen and arms and that many of them were resorting to church in order to qualify themselves for commissions.[2]

During the Civil War there were reports that the royalist forces in the northern counties included a substantial Catholic element. In January 1643 Ferdinando Lord Fairfax wrote to the speaker of the House of Commons: 'Amongst the Prisoners taken by Sir Hugh Cholmly at Malton, and here at Gisbrough, it is found that a great Number are Papists; and indeed the Strength of the Enemies will be found to consist much of Papists, and popishly affected; the Earl of Newcastle granting his Commissions for raising Men to Papists for the most Part.'[3] Among the Yorkshire gentry Catholicism and loyalty to the Crown were strongly linked: indeed rather more than one-third of the royalist families (86 out of 242) had Catholic sympathies and these included many of the leading recusant squires, men such as Sir Philip Constable of Everingham, Sir Walter Vavasour and Sir Philip Hungate of Saxton. Nevertheless it is noteworthy that a considerable section of the popish gentry remained strictly neutral. Moreover, several men of Catholic sympathies even went so far as to support the cause of Parliament, among them Henry Thomson of Esholt who had con-formed in 1638 after a period of recusancy and William Salveyn of Newbiggin, the heir to a convicted recusant, who had been sent in 1642 to the English College at Lisbon.[4]

During the period of 'Thorough' the Puritan gentry had never been a predominant element in the opposition groups. Lord Fauconberg was a 'Church Papist' who drew much of his support from Catholic sources.[5] Sir David Foulis, we are told, 'was never accounted inclined to the Puritans as such, but a lover of them as Englishmen, and very kind and helpfull to them in their troubles'.[6] Sir John Hotham 'was as well affected to the government of the Church of England ... as any man

[1] Rushworth, iv, 646–7.
[2] *Cobbett's Parliamentary History of England*, ii, column 1449.
[3] Rushworth, v, 125–7.
[4] Leeds Central Library: Stansfield MSS D/4/866. P.R.O., S.P.Dom., Committee for Compounding, S.P.23/xv/82 and cxv/728. J. Kirk, *Historical Account of Lisbon College*, 247.
[5] See above, 297–8.
[6] Dr Williams's Library: Morrice MSS, 'A Chronological Account of Eminent Persons &c', vol. iii (no consistent pagination).

that had concurred with' the Roundhead party, and the same could be said of his friend Sir Hugh Cholmley.[1] The other leading opponent of ship money, Sir Marmaduke Langdale, had strong Catholic connections and although he appears to have been an orthodox Anglican up to the time of the Civil War he was subsequently reconciled to the Church of Rome.[2] If, however, the dissident elements within the squirearchy reflected all shades of religious opinion it is significant that to a great extent the Puritans among them remained loyal to the cause of Parliament while others were moving over to the Cavalier party in the months of turmoil before the Civil War. As its name suggests the Roundhead party which came to the fore in the early months of 1642 was largely Puritan in character. Sir John Hotham and Sir Hugh Cholmley were still important figures on the side of Parliament but their principal colleagues were mainly persons of Calvinist sympathies, for example, Ferdinando Lord Fairfax and his son Sir Thomas, Sir Matthew Boynton, Sir John Bourchier, Sir William Constable, Sir Philip Stapleton, Sir Edward Rodes and Thomas Stockdale.

Clarendon wrote that 'very many persons of quality...who had suffered under the imputation of Puritanism and did very much dislike the proceedings of the Court and opposed them upon all occasions' supported the royalist cause when the Civil War broke out.[3] Among the Yorkshire gentry there were a number of moderate Puritans, men such as Sir Henry Slingsby the diarist, who finally ranged themselves on the side of the Crown, in some cases after associating with the Roundhead party in the early months of 1642. On the other hand, no fewer than half the parliamentarian families (64 out of 128 families) were solidly Puritan in their religious sympathies. In the main it was the Calvinist squires, the elect of God, who provided the leadership, the driving force and the endurance. The two leading parliamentarians with middle-of-the-road views on religion, Sir John Hotham and Sir Hugh Cholmley, both changed sides during the course of the Civil War but there were no defections among the Puritan gentry who headed the parliamentarian party.

In the ranks of the Yorkshire parliamentarians there were some gentlemen who had been heavily engaged in promoting the cause of Puritanism during the early seventeenth century. Sir William Strick-

[1] Clarendon, ii, 259. For Sir Hugh Cholmley see above, 261.
[2] J. Gillow, *Biographical Dictionary of the English Catholics*, iv, 123, 125.
[3] Clarendon, ii, 370–1.

land was a great patron of Calvinist ministers, as were Sir Richard Darley and his sons Henry and Richard who had also been involved in Puritan trading and colonisation schemes.[1] Sir John Bourchier was 'a serious person, an open professor of Religion, and gave Encouragement and Protection to those that did so'.[2] Sir Matthew Boynton, another zealous patron, had attended conventicles with the result that the Northern High Commission had sought, unsuccessfully, to bring him to book. Like his friend Sir William Constable (who is also said to have been persecuted for his faith) he had decided in the end to settle in Holland where he could practise his religion in peace.[3] For such men religious issues bulked large. Attempts to legislate on ecclesiastical matters had to a great extent proved abortive and in the Puritan ranks there was a sense of frustration over the lack of progress on church reform allied with a feeling of apprehension at the prospect of a Catholic uprising. In February 1642 a group of Puritan gentry, ministers and freeholders in the Cleveland region of the North Riding declared in a petition:

Whereas we know no other meanes under God to divert the iust Judgements, which he hath executed against the Church of the Laodiceans; for their luke-warmnesse in Religion, or against the Church of Thyatyra for keeping Seducers, nor to prevent our imminent dangers, but by a most necessarie and speedie executinge of the Lawes of God and the King: We doe therefore desire to certifie that we are resolved to live and dye in the faith of the Protestant Religion (knowing no other meanes of Salvation) And that we will defend it with our life and Goods...We humbly above all things desire that we may be secured, a happy Reformacion afforded, And the Lawes of God and the King without favour or delay iustly putt in execution against Papists.[4]

To the extreme Puritan the parliamentarian cause was a religious crusade or it was nothing. Interpreting the situation in Calvinist terms he regarded the conflict which was developing in the course of 1642 as a struggle between the forces of darkness and light and the ecclesiastical reforms foreshadowed in the Nineteen Propositions as the gateway to a new Jerusalem. In the summer of 1642 a Yorkshire gentleman of

[1] See above, 268, 272–3, 306, 310.
[2] Dr Williams's Library: Morrice MSS, 'A Chronological Account of Eminent Persons &c', vol. iii (no consistent pagination).
[3] See above, 308.
[4] House of Lords MSS: Cleveland petition of 10 February 1642 (calendared in *H.M.C. Fifth Report*, Appendix, 7).

Puritan sympathies wrote to a friend of his who was a member of the Long Parliament:

fruitfull blessings hath alwaies accompanied and waited upon those that have been instruments [in the service of the Church of God] as now witnesse the constant guard of Angels dayly stopping the passages of Sathan and his adherents against you; and enlarging your hearts above humane courage in all affrighting oppositions against your civill and sacred imployments wherein you have fully exprest your zealous endeavours, and hearty desires for a thorow Reformation both of Church and common wealth... you are many... many hands make light work, and the choice workmen of our kingdome also, able if need require to build a new worlde.

The Lord of Hosts, he declared, 'shall crowne your actions with trophies of everlasting fame and immortality [and] after yeares shall make report, how you have emulated the stoutest of times, and stood out to the hazard of your dearest blood for the reparing and vindicating the honour and glory of your great God, for the advancing your King, and preserving his Dominions, for the enacting lawes for freeing your Country from slavery and bondage'.[1]

In the propaganda war which was carried on during the summer of 1642 there was a striking similarity in the slogans employed by both parties. In a news-letter from York it was reported that 'the King and Parliament... speake both one language, all in words pretend the Kings Prerogative, the Priviledge of Parliament, the true Protestant religion, the Peace, the liberty and propriety of the subject, the Laws of the Land, &c. What better harmony if actions be suteable?'[2] In seeking to explain his change of allegiance in March 1643 Sir Hugh Cholmley described the original aims of the parliamentarians as follows: 'I did not forsake the Parliament till they did fail in performing those particulars they made the grounds of the war when I was first engaged, viz. the preservation of religion, protection of the King's person, and liberties of the subject.'[3] By 'the preservation of religion' Sir Hugh was no doubt referring to the defence of the Church of England against the designs of the Catholic party, for the fear of a popish plot was not confined entirely to the Puritans. Among the parliamentarian gentry both the Puritans and the orthodox Anglicans believed that they were fighting for 'the public liberties', for 'liberty and property', but it was the latter who tended to regard this as the main principle at stake. Sir

[1] B.M., Thomason Tracts, E.240 (32).   [2] B.M., Thomason Tracts, 669, f.6(27).
[3] *Cholmley Memoirs*, 67–8.

Hugh Cholmley wrote that having 'denied ship money, and shewed myself for the public liberties, I had a great esteem and interest amongst them in the Parliament'; while in his account of Sir John Hotham he described him as 'a man that loved liberty, which was an occasion to make him join at first with the Puritan party, to whom after he became nearer linked merely for his own interest and security; for in more than concerned the civil liberty he did not approve of their ways'. For a similar assessment of Sir John's motives we may turn to the diary of Sir Henry Slingsby who believed that 'he was manly for the defence of the liberty of the subject and priviledge of Parliament, but was not at all for their new opinions in Church government'.[1]

In its widest sense the expression 'public liberties', which had been one of the slogans of the Country Party, meant the privileges of Parliament, freedom from arbitrary arrest (at least for persons of substance) and the sanctity of private property, especially against the threat of arbitrary taxation. By its programme of constitutional reform the Long Parliament had set up a legislative barrier to protect these liberties from the Crown's encroachments but as the rift between king and Parliament grew wider there was mounting anxiety within the popular party over the possibility of a counter-revolution. The military plot of 1641, the Irish rebellion, the attempted arrest of the five members in January 1642, the king's removal to York, the activities of the Cavalier party in the summer of 1642, — such developments lent credence to the view that given a favourable opportunity the king and his supporters would seek to overthrow the Long Parliament and the constitutional reforms which had been enacted. Towards the end of August 1642 a group of parliamentarian gentry meeting at Otley signed a protestation condemning the military preparations at York and

the lawlesse and unpresidented presentment of the grand Iuries at the last Assize held for this County, being framed to give more strength and colour to part of their propositions, the said propositions and presentments being contrary (as we conceive) to the Lawes of the Land, and tending to the introducing of an arbitrary government, The taking away the propriety of every Subject in his estate, the liberty of the person, and the most necessary use and priviledge of Parliaments, and which is the worst of all evills to beget a warre in the bowels of the County.[2]

[1] *Cholmley Memoirs*, 65. *State Papers Collected by Edward Earl of Clarendon*, ii, 185. *Slingsby Diary*, 92.
[2] B.M., Thomason Tracts, E.116(17).

Besides the men who had been severely punished for their disaffec-
tion there were other parliamentarian gentry whose attitude to the
Crown or the court may well have been influenced by a sense of personal grievance. These included Sir William Fairfax of Steeton whose
father had seriously weakened the family estate as the result of an
extravagance fostered at court;[1] Sir William St Quintin of Harpham
who had been summoned before the Privy Council in 1634 to answer
for certain large-scale enclosures which he had undertaken to the
detriment of 'great numbers' of the king's subjects;[2] and Thomas and
James Chaloner of Guisborough who had attempted unsuccessfully to
secure from the Crown substantial arrears of an annuity of £1000
which had been granted to their father, Sir Thomas Chaloner, and his
heirs when he surrendered his interest in the alum patent.[3] As a result
of the exactions of the Court of Wards, wrote Clarendon, 'all the rich
families of England, of noblemen and gentlemen, were exceedingly
incensed, and even indevoted to the Crown'.[4] In Yorkshire some
twenty heads of parliamentarian families had once been wards of the
Crown, most of them after the Court of Wards' officials had begun to
calculate their charges on a more realistic basis. Henry Tempest of
Tong, who only attained his majority in 1642, was the second heir in
succession to be declared in ward to the king while Richard Hutton of
Poppleton may well have owed his financial difficulties, in part at least,
to the wardship system.[5] Few gentlemen, however, can have had
greater distaste for the Court of Wards than Sir John Bourchier whose
father's estate had fallen within the court's jurisdiction by virtue of his
lunacy (a condition which some Yorkshiremen believed, rather un-
charitably, to be hereditary in the family). In 1624 Sir John, who had
been granted custody of the estate, owed the sum of £2200 out of the
rents but two years later this money was still unpaid and the sheriff of
Yorkshire was instructed to attach his body and require him to give an
undertaking to appear and discharge the debt.[6]

One of the most controversial questions which has exercised
historians in recent years is the extent to which the origins of the Civil

---

[1] Sir Clements R. Markham, *Admiral Robert Fairfax*, 8.
[2] P.R.O., Privy Council Registers, P.C.2/xliv/ff.12, 75.
[3] See above, 90–1.   [4] Clarendon, i, 199.
[5] P.R.O., Court of Wards, Entry Books of Contracts for Marriages and Leases, Wards
9/cciv/ff.29 and 125, ccvi (no consistent pagination), ccvii/ff.35 and 166. *Y.A.J.*, xii, 25.
For Henry Tempest see also below 377–8.
[6] P.R.O., Court of Wards, Sheriff's Book, Wards 9/dclxxvii/f.6.

War can be explained in social and economic terms. According to one school of thought the primary cause of the Civil War was the rise of the gentry who, over the preceding century, had accumulated substantial landholdings at the expense of the Crown and the nobility. Growing rich (largely through the efficient management of their estates) they sought to win for themselves a degree of political power which was more commensurate with their stake in the country.[1] As against this there is the view that the revolutionary impulse was mainly provided by the embittered country gentry who were in financial straits as a result of their exclusion from the benefits of court patronage, which they were anxious to secure for themselves.[2]

As we have already seen, 'the rise of the gentry' is a concept which requires qualification. Although the total holdings of the Yorkshire gentry were increasing in the period 1558–1642 only a minority (less than one family in three) actually enlarged their estates in these years. More numerous were the families in decline, either irretrievably or in the course of a transitory phase: indeed over two-fifths of the gentry were in this position at one time or another.[3] If, however, there were many struggling landowners in the early seventeenth century no real link can be found between economic decay and political dissent in the period leading up to the Civil War. Sir William Constable, who was imprisoned in 1627 for refusing to contribute to the forced loan, had previously sold extensive property and was still heavily in debt[4] but he was hardly typical of the Yorkshire squires who stood out in opposition to the Crown. In the main these were men of considerable substance who owned more than they had inherited. Sir Thomas Wentworth, who was also committed to prison in 1627, was at that time in the process of increasing an estate already worth £6000 a year at his father's death.[5] His enemy Thomas Lord Fauconberg had been the richest gentleman in the North Riding until his elevation to the peerage; at the height of his struggle with the lord president we find him spending over £3000 on the purchase of a neighbouring estate.[6] Sir David

[1] R. H. Tawney, 'The Rise of the Gentry, 1558–1640'. *Economic History Review*, xi, 1.
[2] H. R. Trevor-Roper, *The Gentry 1540–1640, Economic History Review*, Supplement 1, 22, 26, 34, 42, 52.
[3] Above, 145.
[4] B.M., Additional MSS 40135, ff.23–4. Beverley County Record Office: Hotham MSS, DDHO/10/1. *Y.A.S.R.S.*, lviii, 13.
[5] Knowler, i, dedication. *Y.A.S.R.S.*, lviii, 47, 49, 64, 86, 133, 137, 155, 163, 217.
[6] P.R.O., Chancery Proceedings, Series II, C.3/425/7. See also above, 156.

Foulis owned, at the time of his intervention in the knighthood controversy, property worth more than £1000 a year, all of which had
been acquired since his arrival in England in the entourage of King
James.[1] Sir John Hotham had inherited an estate of £2000 a year and,
through advantageous marriages and other means, increased his
revenue to £3000 a year.[2] Sir Hugh Cholmley had at first been obliged
to tackle the problem of his father's debts which were both heavy and
pressing; at the time of his refusal to pay ship money, however, he
could take pride in the fact that he had significantly improved the
yield from an estate worth at the outset £1500 or £1600 a year.[3]
Finally, there was Sir Marmaduke Langdale, described in 1627 as 'a
verie rich and able man', who had spent over £12,000 on land purchase
and had thereby brought his family into the ranks of the upper gentry.[4]

In terms of landed income there were no fundamental differences
between the royalist gentry and the parliamentarian gentry:[5]

Annual income from land in 1642 £	Royalist families	Parliamentarian families
2000 and upwards	6	1
1000	27	16
750	15	6
500	28	18
250	66	41
100	50	19
under 100	50	27
	242	128

News-letters published in the summer of 1642 present what might
appear, on the face of it, to be a conflicting picture of the financial
circumstances of the Cavalier gentry. Some correspondents referred to
men of decayed estate who were hoping that a civil war would help
them to retrieve their fortunes while others wrote of the prosperous
squires who were digging deeply into their purses to assist the Crown.[6]
In fact the rising gentry and the declining gentry were both well

[1] Sheffield Central Library: Strafford Letters, xx. Richard Marris to Wentworth, 19
April 1634.
[2] P. Saltmarshe, History and Chartulary of the Hothams, 141, 144, 148.
[3] Above, 153–4.
[4] P.R.O., S.P.Dom., Charles I, S.P.16/lxviii/51. Y.A.S. Library: MD 287(b), rent-book
of Sir Marmaduke Langdale. B.M., Additional MSS 40132, 40135. Beverley County
Record Office: Harford of Holme MSS.
[5] For a discussion of sources see above, 27–8.   [6] See above, 333, 335.

represented in the royalist party. At one extreme there was Sir John Wolstenholme of Nostell Priory whose father, a London merchant and customs farmer, had built up one of the largest estates in the West Riding between 1629 and his death ten years later;[1] at the other, Thomas Wheatley of Woolley who had been so busily engaged in selling off his property that on the eve of the Civil War he was virtually landless.[2] Among the parliamentarians we also find gentlemen with estates which were sadly reduced or at least heavily burdened with debt. By the time of the Civil War Sir William Constable was almost completely dependent on the profits of a lease of the manor of Holme on Spalding Moor which he had sold to Sir Marmaduke Langdale in 1634 and immediately re-entered as tenant; since the new owner fought on the royalist side and eventually went into exile Sir William was able to take all the revenue until his death in 1655.[3] John Lambert the parliamentarian general inherited his financial difficulties from his father. When Josias Lambert died in 1632 he left an estate worth £300 a year which was heavily encumbered not only with a mortgage but also with long disadvantageous leases. In all, his debts amounted to £1200 and in addition, since the heir was then a minor, the family had to come to terms with the Court of Wards.[4] Another parliamentarian, Nicholas Girlington of Temple Hirst, was attempting shortly before the Civil War to recover the entailed family estate which his father had conveyed to a relative while he was still a minor. About 1638 he managed to gain possession of the Temple Hirst property and in the Commonwealth period succeeded in establishing his title to the manor of Girlington which had been sequestered for the delinquency of his cousin Christopher Girlington. In these proceedings the committee for compounding were informed that both men were poor but that Christopher had always supported the king while Nicholas was a loyal parliamentarian.[5] If, as alleged, some of the Cavaliers were hoping to gain financially from a civil war there may well have been parliamentarian gentry who

[1] B.M., Additional MSS 24470, f.39. P.R.O., S.P.Dom., Committee for the Advance of Money, S.P.19/cxx/179.

[2] *Harleian Society*, xxxviii, 596. P.R.O., S.P.Dom., Committee for Compounding, S.P.23/ccxvi/543, 545, 547. *Y.A.J.*, xii, 25, 26.

[3] B.M., Additional MSS 40135. f.24. F. H. Sutherland, *Marmaduke Lord Langdale*, 209. *Y.A.S.R.S.*, ix, 82.

[4] P.R.O., Court of Wards, Feodaries' Surveys, Wards 5/49 and Entry Book of Petitions, Wards 9/ccxviii/f.271. J. W. Morkill, *Parish of Kirkby Malhamdale*, 155–7.

[5] H. K. G. Plantagenet-Harrison, *The History of Yorkshire*, i, 439. P.R.O., S.P.Dom., Committee for Compounding, S.P.23/lxxxix/20, 22, 31, 53.

had similar expectations. Such benefits might flow from the expropriation of landowners who had chosen the wrong side; from the confiscation (in the event of a victory for Parliament) of Crown or church property; or from the impact of such a major upheaval on existing mortgages and recognizances. In the final analysis, however, the economic position of the parliamentarian gentry as a group was basically sound. Between one-third and one-half of the families represented had increased their estates by one means or another since the accession of James I, while on the eve of the Civil War scarcely more than one family in ten was experiencing financial difficulties. Besides the major landed families which had been adding to their holdings there were also many families of medium income which had been gaining ground. Thomas Stockdale, one of the most active Roundheads on the eve of the Civil War, had bought the Bilton Park estate in 1630 for the sum of £1880; in addition, we find him acquiring the rectory of Farnham and property in Knaresborough.[1] Thomas Westby of Ravenfield had joined with his father in the purchase of lands and tenements in Ravenfield which were said to be worth £300 a year.[2] Thomas Lister of Westby had been in ward to the king but immediately after attaining his majority spent £1100 on the acquisition of the Lower Hall and its demesnes in Gisburn.[3]

On the whole, the parliamentarian gentry were in better financial circumstances than the royalist gentry although in absolute terms the latter included a larger number of rising families[4]:

	Royalist gentry	Parliamentarian gentry
(a) total number of families	242	128
(b) families which increased their estates, 1600–42	76	54
(c) families which sold considerable property, 1600–42	61	23
(d) families which were in financial difficulties, 1638–42	60	14

[1] Leeds Central Library: Bilton Park MSS, BL 16. P.R.O., Chancery Proceedings, Six Clerks' Series, C.10/72/45.
[2] P.R.O., Chancery Proceedings, Six Clerks' Series, C.7/82/61.
[3] H. L. L. Denny, *Memorials of an Ancient House: A History of the Family of Lister or Lyster*, 205. P.R.O., Court of Wards, Feodaries' Surveys, Wards 5/49.
[4] These figures are to a certain extent overlapping since the families which were in financial difficulties in the period 1638–42 included a number of families which were selling or buying property in the early seventeenth century.

Although the gentry who benefited from offices of profit, patents or leases in the gift of the Crown were more inclined to take the royalist than the parliamentarian side, the total number of families which had such financial interests was comparatively small;[1] and indeed only twenty of the rising families which appear in the above table (fourteen royalist and six parliamentarian families) owed their advance in any way to these sources of income. The preponderance of 'mere land-owners' on both sides, the low proportion of parliamentarian families in financial straits and the considerably higher degree of indebtedness among the royalist families: such evidence conflicts with the theory that the division within the gentry had its roots in a continuing struggle between the prosperous haves and the declining have-nots. While there was undoubtedly keen competition in Yorkshire for local offices of profit, this was far from being simply a product of economic decay[2]; nor is it possible to find any clear link with the growth of political opposition during the early seventeenth century. In December 1628 George Radcliffe of Overthorpe, a lawyer who was hoping to obtain the office of king's attorney in the North, wrote to his wife that Lord Wentworth, his friend and kinsman, had been appointed lord president of the Council of the North, and he went on: 'I am told a new way for the atturney's place, which if it hold will cost me nothing; but howso-ever, one way or other, I shall be very likely to have it, for my Lord is more eager of my beinge there than I myselfe am.'[3] Radcliffe's expecta-tion was fulfilled but he and Christopher Wandesford were virtually alone among Wentworth's beneficiaries in having appeared in active opposition to the Crown. Although such men as Sir John Hotham and Sir Matthew Boynton were appointed deputy lieutenants following Wentworth's rise to power there is no evidence that they either sought or were granted any offices of profit or similar financial rewards.

It has been suggested that the political division between the royalist gentry and the parliamentarian gentry might have broadly corres-ponded with an economic division between 'those who were becoming mere rentiers, and those who were actively engaged in productive activities, whether in agriculture, industry, or trade'.[4] While there were many parliamentarian squires in Yorkshire who farmed their own

---

[1] See above, 85.   [2] See above, 88.
[3] T. D. Whitaker, *The Life and Original Correspondence of Sir George Radcliffe*, 172–3. For Christopher Wandesford see above, 87, 88.
[4] C. Hill, *Puritanism and Revolution*, 8.

demesnes and sought to develop their estates this is equally true of the royalist gentry. Among the Cavaliers there were Sir Marmaduke Langdale who was 'esteemed a serious and wise man, of most scholar-like accomplishments, and of good husbandry'; Sir Henry Slingsby the diarist who was interested in agricultural experiment; and enclosing landowners such as George Butler of Ellerton and Henry Calverley of Calverley.[1] Similarly, a considerable number of royalist squires can be found exploiting the mineral resources on their estates. Sir Francis Wortley, Sir Gervase Cutler of Stainborough and Thomas Barnby of Barnby Hall were prominent figures in the West Riding iron industry; William Bulmer of Marrick owned what was probably the largest complex of leadmines in Yorkshire; and Sir John Ramsden of Longley, Sir Thomas Danby of Farnley and Sir Ferdinando Leigh of Middleton were three of the leading colliery owners.[2]

Although common lawyers and merchants were often men of Puritan sympathies the royalist gentry contained as high a proportion of commercial and professional families as the parliamentarian gentry, even if we exclude all those who held Crown appointments:

	Royalist gentry	Parliamentarian gentry
total number of families	242	128
heads of families who were		
(a) physicians	1	2
(b) counsellors at law, recorders or attorneys	13	4
(c) merchants or tradesmen	11	6
	25	12

Taking into account the gentlemen who invested money in trading companies and younger sons who were engaged in commercial pursuits it can be said that there were in all twenty-seven royalist families and seventeen parliamentarian families with mercantile connections.

[1] T. C. Banks, *The Dormant and Extinct Baronage of England*, iii, 146. *Y.A.J.*, v, 396. For Sir Henry Slingsby and George Butler see above, 34, 37.

[2] P.R.O., S.P.Dom., Committee for Compounding, S.P.23/xcvii/705, 707, 709, cxxii/67 and clxxxvii/589, 595 and Commonwealth Exchequer Papers, S.P.28/215, order book 1651 seq., f.102. Borthwick Institute of Historical Research: York Wills, will of Sir Gervase Cutler, 23 March 1638(-9). Leeds Central Library: Ramsden MSS, RA/S1. Cartwright Memorial Hall, Bradford: Cunliffe–Lister MSS, Bundles 1 and 16. For Sir Francis Wortley see above, 64-5.

Even on this basis, therefore, there was no significant difference between the two groups of gentry.

In writing of the Civil War divisions in Somerset the Earl of Clarendon draws a distinction between the ancient county families and the *nouveaux riches* who had bought up property from members of the squirearchy but were not held 'in the same esteem and reputation with those whose estates they had'. In the main the former supported the king while the latter were solidly for Parliament.[1] If Clarendon's analysis is correct, this provides a variant of the theory that the political aspirations of the rising gentry represented the root cause of the Civil War; socially frustrated and envious of the well-established gentry, the new landowners saw an opportunity to assert themselves and take their vengeance on the county oligarchy which had rejected them. In Yorkshire a substantial minority (virtually one-third) of the families within the parliamentarian gentry had either been granted arms or entered the county since the accession of Queen Elizabeth. Among the royalist gentry there was a similar group of families but it was proportionally rather smaller:

	Royalist gentry	Parliamentarian gentry
total number of families	242	128
families which had been granted arms		
(a) 1558–1602	23	13
(b) 1603–42	10	11
families which had entered the county		
(a) 1558–1602	10	11
(b) 1603–42	25	6
	68	41

One of the most striking features about both the royalist and the parliamentarian gentry is the fact that only a minority of families were seated in the same locality in 1558 and 1642. This degree of mobility was due to a number of factors: the migration of families from other counties, the acquisition of estates by rising families, the disposal of property by families in economic decline and the emergence of cadet branches. On the parliamentarian side the proportion of families which had established themselves in this way since 1558 was particularly large: 85 out of a total of 128 families (as compared with 141 out of 242 royalist families). Among this group were the descendants of John

[1] Clarendon, ii, 296.

Robinson, a London merchant who had purchased substantial property in Yorkshire during the latter part of Elizabeth's reign: John Robinson of Ryther, the senior representative of the family, and his kinsmen Henry Robinson of Buckton, Luke Robinson of Thornton Risborough and Richard Robinson of Thicket Priory. Others included William White of Bashall, a former clerk in the Court of Wards who had acquired the Bashall estate by marriage and purchase[1]; Joseph Micklethwaite of Swine, the physician son of a York merchant who had bought an estate in the East Riding not long before the Civil War[2]; and John Bright of Carbrook whose father, a bailiff of the Earl of Arundel and Surrey and an extremely wealthy man, had been granted a coat of arms in December 1641.[3]

New entrants to the squirearchy who felt in need of social prestige might seek to gain titles for themselves and indeed a considerable number of *parvenu* landowners secured grants of knighthoods in the course of the early seventeenth century. Baronetcies, on the other hand, were expensive and there was the further difficulty that they were supposed to be available only to gentlemen of at least the third generation; but in any event some of the wealthy Puritans in particular seem to have regarded the purchase of baronetcies as a waste of money.[4] In terms of social rank the royalist gentry were, on the whole, better endowed than the parliamentarian gentry, even if we exclude those who received titles in the years 1641 and 1642:

	Royalist gentry	Parliamentarian gentry
total number of families	242	128
number of individuals with titles in August 1642:		
(a) baronets	19	5
(b) knights	39	17
	58	22
number of individuals with titles at the end of 1640:		
(a) baronets	10	2
(b) knights	29	14
	39	16

---

[1] See above, 98.
[2] G. Poulson, *The History and Antiquities of the Seigniory of Holderness*, ii, 201.
[3] See above, 19.   [4] See above, 279.

Some royalist gentlemen owed their titles to court connections, others to their kinship or friendship with Lord Wentworth who as lord deputy of Ireland had the power to create knights. In the main the future parliamentarians had no such special avenues open to them although it may be noted that three of Wentworth's knights were to take up arms for Parliament: Sir Edward Rodes (his brother-in-law), Sir Thomas Remington of Lund and Sir Henry Frankland of Great Thirkleby.[1]

If the royalists could boast of a greater degree of social eminence this did not necessarily mean that the parliamentarians were men of little standing in county affairs. Of the gentlemen who took the side of Parliament on the outbreak of the Civil War Sir John Hotham, Sir Matthew Boynton, Sir Hugh Cholmley, Sir William Constable, Sir Edward Rodes and Sir William Lister had all served as deputy lieutenants under Wentworth, although most of them had either relinquished or been removed from their appointments before the downfall of the lord president. In addition, a significant number of parliamentarians had been justices of the peace during the period of 'Thorough'. In the summer of 1640 the working magistrates on the commission of the peace included twenty-six gentlemen who were destined to support the cause of Parliament, as compared with thirty-three future royalists (though the relative strengths would no doubt have been different had there been fewer Catholics within the royalist gentry[2]). In the former group were George Marwood of Nun Monkton, William White and several other representatives of the newer county families. On the other hand, there were not a few parliamentarian gentry with incomes of £400 a year and upwards (including a handful of squires with ancient coats of arms) who may well have aspired to the commission of the peace but who never attained this peak of eminence before the time of the Long Parliament. Some of these men, such as Thomas Stockdale and George Trotter of Skelton Castle, were appointed magistrates in the period between Wentworth's overthrow and the outbreak of the Civil War,[3] while many of them sat on the commission of the peace during the Commonwealth era.

From this examination certain general conclusions may be drawn

1 W. A. Shaw (ed.), *Knights of England*, ii, 202, 203, 204.
2 P.R.O., Chancery, Patent Rolls, C.66/2858 and Crown Office, Docquet Books, Index 4212, 373, 374.
3 P.R.O., Chancery, Crown Office, Index 4212, 419, 426. 472, 475, 492.

about the factors determining the Civil War loyalties of the Yorkshire gentry. In the first place, there can be no doubt that many of the participants sincerely believed that they were fighting over important issues of principle, whether it was the defence of the king's person and authority, the safeguarding of the public liberties, the preservation of the Church of England from Puritan designs or the triumph of a Geneva-style Protestantism over both the Catholic and Laudian parties. Secondly, as in most conflicts of this nature there was a strong inter-mixture of idealism and self-interest. Thirdly, we should not under-estimate such factors as the geographical position of a man's estates, the influence of family ties and the common human failing of drifting with the tide. Fourthly, there are obvious difficulties in seeking to establish a general causal relationship between the economic circumstances of the gentry and their conduct in the Civil War. In terms of *per capita* landed income and methods of estate management there were no major differences between the royalist and parliamentarian families and, on the whole, the same can be said of their attitude to commerce and the professions. Families which held offices of profit or derived other financial benefits from the Crown were inclined to take the royalist side, but in themselves they were a comparatively minor element. There is, however, one basic fact which stands out clearly. In Yorkshire resistance to the Crown, both in the period of 'Thorough' and on the outbreak of the Civil War, was far more closely associated with grow-ing prosperity than with economic decline. At the same time it is important to recognise that the parliamentarian party embraced only one section of the rising gentry: there were in fact many successful landowners who gave their support to the Crown.

In the final analysis there were undoubtedly significant differences in the composition of the royalist and parliamentarian gentry. On the royalist side it is possible to identify two general groups with more or less predetermined loyalties. The first group consisted of some eighty Catholic families which were both socially and politically conservative. In the main these were ancient families which had long been settled on their estates and had few connections outside the sphere of the landed interest. Proud of their ancestry and their coat armour, they tended to be disdainful of the newer entrants to the squirearchy who were often men of Puritan sympathies and therefore antagonistic towards the Old Religion. Although the Catholic gentry rarely had links with the court they regarded Parliament (and particularly the Long Parliament) with a mixture of fear and detestation because of the strong anti-Catholic feeling which manifested itself in the House of Commons. The second group, amounting to some thirty families, can be roughly described as the Court Party element within the royalist gentry. The principal constituent of this group was an inner knot of Wentworth's relatives and personal friends, but it also included a number of gentlemen outside the Wentworth circle who had been associated with some of the Crown's more controversial measures or, if they had not committed themselves to this extent, were at least partly dependent on the Crown for their income. Not all these families were well-established gentry: the majority, however, were baronets or knights.

On the parliamentarian side it was the Puritans who represented by far the most important element: indeed it is difficult to see how a parliamentarian party could have developed within the Yorkshire gentry in the absence of the dynamic leadership which they provided during the fluid situation immediately preceding the Civil War. With the interests of their class intimately bound up with the fortunes of the Crown, a powerful ideology was required to induce a significant section of the gentry to engage in revolution, and Puritanism supplied this need. Besides the religious fervour which it generated, a strict grounding in Calvinist doctrine tended to breed an independence of mind which could give rise to political radicalism: thus in 1637 Wentworth wrote of the Puritans that 'the very Genius of that Nation of People leads them always to oppose civilly as well as ecclesiastically all that Authority ever ordains for them'.[1] In addition, the comparatively high degree of prosperity which distinguished the parliamentarian party may be attributed in no small measure to the Puritan virtues of diligence and thrift. Roughly half the parliamentarian gentry consisted of middling landowners and it was at this level that there was the greatest interplay of potential revolutionary factors. Most of these families were Puritan in religion and indeed in some cases had helped to establish chapels or support Calvinist preaching ministers. Few had court connections or offices of profit, but many were improving gentry who had increased their estates since the beginning of the century. In terms of social status and ancestry they were, on the whole, inferior to the royalist landowners and this may well have been a source of resentment. On the other hand, they were wealthy enough to be designated as

1 Knowler, ii, 138.

subsidymen, to be subjected to the forced loan and ship money levies and to attract the attention of the Court of Wards in the event of a minority. Since there were very few titled gentry within this group they were particularly hard hit when the knighthood scheme was launched and some of them either refused to compound or were dilatory in making their compositions. In the summer of 1642 they had to endure further tribulations when the Cavaliers ransacked the houses of gentlemen known to be sympathetic to the Puritan cause. The commissioners of array, wrote Thomas Lord Fairfax, 'so exceeded their commission by oppressing many honest people, (whom by way of reproach they called Roundheads) being for Religion, estates, and Interest, a very considerable part of the Country; that occasioned them to take up armes in their owne Defence'.[1]

[1] *Y.A.J.*, viii, 201.

APPENDIX A

The Expenses of a Leading Squire

Sir Henry Slingsby of Scriven (1602–58), who succeeded his father in 1634, ensured that his accounts were systematically maintained. As his rents and other receipts came in they were allocated to various heads of expenditure. The following tables, which show his annual expenditure in the period 1635–41, are reproduced from an account book of his in Slingsby MSS, Box D5 (Yorkshire Archaeological Society Library). The years are Old Style years, that is, they begin on 25 March.

	1635–6 £ s d			1636–7 £ s d			1637–8 £ s d		
House provision	210	5	0	367	16	0	336	1	6
Building	186	6	0	149	0	0	244	14	11
Husbandry	73	0	0	104	15	0	121	10	6
Household stuff	68	14	0	31	13	0	65	4	4
Rents, annuities, wages	299	2	0	310	0	0	301	14	8
In casualties	142	17	0	108	0	0	139	4	9
Myself	65	6	0	109	6	0	161	4	4
Purchase							40	0	0
Debt	522	15	0	447	16	2	281	0	0
	1568	5	0	1628	6	2	1690	15	0

	1638–9 £ s d			1639–40 £ s d			1640–1 £ s d		
House provision	372	19	4	297	7	8	215	5	10
Building	242	11	11	49	9	1	474	6	6
Husbandry	160	0	10	181	15	4	141	7	11
Household stuff	53	3	8	52	13	4	12	10	5
Rents, annuities, wages	164	1	5	235	18	10	210	3	11
In casualties	102	8	1	179	11	10	176	5	11
Myself	56	10	1	136	19	2	20	15	2
Purchase	40	0	0						
Debt	621	17	0	352	0	6	100	0	0
At London				200	10	2	731	10	4
	1813	12	4	1686	5	11	2082	6	0

APPENDIX B

The Economic Fortunes of Certain Families

What follows is a small selection of case histories tracing the economic fortunes of individual families broadly in the period between Elizabeth's accession and the outbreak of the Civil War. References are given only to the main sources of evidence.

Acclom of Moreby

William Acclom (d. 1568) bought the manor of Scarcroft with Shadwell and lands in Kirkby Wharfe in 1561. This transaction appears, however, to have seriously taxed his resources: in 1563 he sold part of the Kirkby Wharfe property and began to borrow heavily. At his death he held the manors of Moreby, Bonwick, Cawood and Scarcroft with Shadwell but most of his lands were extended for the payment of a debt of £120. His son John (1555–1611) became a ward of the Crown. Large-scale farming. Much of the tenanted property was let from year to year at 'the best improved rent'. Considerable litigation. Heavy indebtedness which apparently forced him to give up housekeeping: for a time Moreby Hall was let to a tenant. In 1592 he sold the remainder of the Kirkby Wharfe property and in 1607 he and his son Sir William (1582–1637) disposed of the premises in Scarcroft and Shadwell. Settlement on the marriage of the heir, 1609: (a) portion of £1000; (b) manor of Cawood settled as the wife's jointure and in addition Sir William was to receive £50 a year during his father's lifetime; (c) the remainder of the estate (anciently entailed) was to descend to Sir William and his heirs. In 1615 Sir William sold the Cawood property and settled the manor of Bonwick for his wife's jointure. The following year his sister and her husband brought a Chancery suit against him, claiming a portion of £1000. Sheep and cattle farming. In 1617 he enclosed eighty acres of waste ground in the manor of Moreby. The enclosure was thrown down and he brought a Star Chamber suit against the ringleaders. Substantial rent increases: the rent-roll of the manor of Bonwick was raised from £60 to £160 a year. At his death he left the manors of Moreby and Bonwick, together with a house in York, which produced an income of £600 a year. His personal estate was said to be worth £600 which was equal to the sum of his debts. No provision had been made for children's portions. His son John (1618–44) became a ward of the Crown. Wardship charges: fine unknown, rent 100 marks. At his death he was in considerable debt and in addition the sum of £1000 had to be raised from the estate for his daughter's portion.

(P.R.O., Chancery Proceedings, Six Clerks' Series, C.7/398/5 and C.9/6/146, and Chancery Depositions, C.21/D16/3 and C.22/759/6, 13 and 38).

Anne of Frickley

Martin Anne (d. 1589) owned the manors of Frickley and Roall. Building at Frickley Hall, 1572. Some piecemeal land-buying 1555, 1560, 1567 but he was borrowing money on recognizances at least as early as 1562. In 1581 he and his heir sold land in Hampole Stubbs, South Kirkby and Hooton Pagnell. His son George (c. 1560–1620) married an heiress and acquired the manor of Burghwallis and other property. Twenty-one-year leases. While his father had in the main been a 'Church Papist' George was for much of his life a convicted recusant. In 1591 his estate was seized for recusancy and the statutory two-thirds were leased to an outsider who had to be bought off. The rent was fixed at £26. 13s. 4d. but later increased to £40 a year. In 1613 he was said to be £394 in arrears. His financial difficulties were probably due mainly to various items of expenditure arising from his recusancy although the cost of maintaining a large family must also have been a factor. In 1604 he sold the manor of Roall. At his death the estate was worth £800 a year but it was charged with a considerable jointure for his wife (who survived until 1641) and annuities of £25 a year each to two younger sons. His son Philip (1590–1647) compounded for his recusancy in 1626. By making composition in London he was able to limit his financial liability to a rent of £20 a year although he had an estate of £500 a year in possession. Forced loan of 1627: £10. In 1629 his mother contracted to pay a rent of £35 a year for her recusancy. Knighthood composition: £20. Modest land-buying but from at least 1630 he was having to borrow money and in 1638 was raising loans on the London money market. Projected sale of property in Hooton Pagnell which broke down because of disagreement over the price. In February 1641 he settled his estate. After his death (a) certain lands were to descend to his younger son Philip, (b) two-thirds of the estate were to pass to trustees for the payment of portions amounting to £1800 and such debts as could not be met out of his personal estate. His debts totalled at least £700 in 1642 and £2400 at his death. The personal estate which he left was said to be worth £1000 and upwards.

(P.R.O., Chancery Proceedings, Six Clerks' Series, C.5/19/3 and S.P.Dom., Committee for Compounding, S.P.23/cxxix/121, 125–8, 132, 134, 136–41, 169–71).

Baildon of Baildon

Robert Baildon (1541–c. 1599) inherited the manor of Baildon and a capital messuage there which had been rebuilt in 1553. Twenty-one-year leases. Purchase of land in Baildon, 1572. In 1592 he was acting as the agent of an absentee landlord for some property in Shipley. His son William (1562–1633) began to mine coal on Baildon common about the end of Elizabeth's reign. Agreement with the other principal landowner in Baildon for the sharing of profits: his share ranged from £30 to £50 a year. Arable farming. Twenty-one-year leases. In 1618 he took as his second wife a widow who had jointure lands worth £80 a year. Litigation over a free rent, 1623–5. On the marriage of his heir William (c. 1590–1627) in 1625 he settled one-third of his estate as jointure for his daughter-in-law. At his death William the son was indebted by virtue of several judgments at common law. In 1629 the attorney of the Court of Wards alleged that his widow had made secret conveyances of the estate in an attempt to defraud the Crown. She in turn claimed that the lands were held in free and common socage and were therefore not subject to wardship. In 1635, however, the wardship and lands of her son Francis (1627–69) were granted to a servant of the surveyor of the Court of Wards for a fine of £50 and a rent of £20 a year. Assignment of the wardship first to Francis Nevile of Chevet (1636) and then to Francis Malham of Elslack (1637). During the minority the estate was in the possession of the ward's stepfather who was later accused of committing great waste. Considerable arrears of rent owing to the Court of Wards. On the eve of the Civil War the estate revenue amounted to about £350 a year.

(W. P. Baildon, *Baildon and the Baildons*).

Bamford of Pule Hill

About the beginning of James I's reign John Bamford, a Derbyshire lawyer, bought the Pule Hill estate in Thurgoland and also acquired a long lease of property at Long Ardsley. At Pule Hill he built a new manor-house. His son John (d. 1644) purchased the manor of Thurgoland in 1622. Forced loan of 1627: £5. When a survey was made in 1631 the lands at Pule Hill and Thurgoland were valued at £350 a year. His total revenue, including the Ardsley property, must therefore have amounted to £400 a year. Knighthood composition: £15. Small purchases of land in Thurgoland, 1635 and 1639, for which he paid a total of £153. By will (1644) he settled the estate on trustees for the payment of (a) portions totalling £1200 to four younger children, (b) debts in the sum of £781. 4s. od. In addition, the property was charged with a jointure of £50 a year for his wife. His son Lyon Bamford (b. 1621) was in serious financial difficulties as a result of his father's debts, his own extravagance and his losses in the Civil War. After disposing of his father's personal effects he proceeded to sell the whole of his inheritance in Thurgoland.

(Sheffield Central Library: Spencer Stanhope MSS 60264. P.R.O., Chancery Proceedings, Six Clerks' Series, C.6/116/25).

Burdett of Birthwaite

Although Thomas Burdett was a younger son his father settled the manor of Hoyland on him. His son Francis (1548–96) added considerably to his inheritance. His most notable acquisition was the Birthwaite estate (1578) which became the family seat. In his will he devised lands in Billingley, Darfield, Cawthorne and Silkstone to younger sons. His eldest son Francis (1577–1637) became a ward of the Crown. Wardship charges: fine £15, rent unknown. Sheep and cattle farming. Substantial purchases from neighbouring landowners, including the estate of the Saviles of Kexbrough. Forced loan of 1627: £10. Knighthood composition: £25. Building at Birthwaite Hall. In 1637 he settled his estate on trustees for a period of twenty-one years immediately following his death. The trustees were to pay (a) annuities amounting to some £120 a year, (b) any debts which could not be met out of his personal estate, (c) a portion of £1000 to his daughter Frances, (d) the wardship charges in respect of his heir. At his death the estate revenue was worth £800 a year. His personal estate (which was said to be worth £6000) included a coach, family portraits and a quantity of plate and jewellery. His son Francis (1617–43) was declared in ward to the Crown Wardship charges: fine £500, rent 100 marks. At his death he left unpaid debts to the value of £1600. In subsequent litigation the trustees were said to have borrowed money to discharge the wardship. It was alleged, however, that they had committed waste and enriched themselves by selling timber and granting leases at uneconomic rents in return for fines.

(P.R.O., Chancery Proceedings, Six Clerks' Series, C.5/32/96 and C.10/28/14).

Catterick of Stanwick and Carlton

Anthony Catterick (d. 1585) owned the manors of Stanwick and Aldbrough. This estate was inherited by the eldest son of his brother George (d. 1592), his own son having been passed over because he was an idiot. George Catterick, who had purchased the manor of Carlton in 1564, was a recusant from 1586 until his death. In 1589 the statutory two-thirds of his estate were leased to an outsider who had to be bought off: rent of £47. 15s. 7d. a year. Twenty years later the sum of £116. 13s. 4d. was paid as composition for his arrears of rent. His son Anthony (1563–1634) was also a convicted recusant. In 1598 he was paying a rent of £50 a year but this was subsequently reduced to forty marks a year. Fines and harassment by the Northern High Commission. Falling into serious debt, he sold the manor of Aldbrough in 1610. In 1613 he was said to owe £484. 15s. 8d. for his recusancy. Settlement of the estate, 1619. Forced loan of 1627: £13. 13s. 4d. He delayed compounding for knighthood and a fine of £40 was imposed. In 1632 he and his heir compounded for their recusancy: rents of £25 and

£15 a year respectively. At his death he left an estate worth £440 a year but it was encumbered. In 1635 his son Anthony (c. 1588–1644) brought a Chancery suit against his mother and his younger brothers seeking possession of the manors of Stanwick and Carlton in which they claimed an interest. After succeeding his father he paid a composition rent of £40 a year for his recusancy but in 1637 he conformed, probably because of heavy indebtedness. In 1638 he and his son John sold the manor of Stanwick for the sum of £4000 which he is said to have used for his children's portions. After this he was left with an estate worth £200 a year.

(W. Brown, 'The Catterick Brass', *Y.A.J.*, xix, 73. P.R.O., Chancery Proceedings, Series II, C.3/398/59).

Constable of Everingham

Sir Marmaduke Constable (d. 1575) had large estates in Yorkshire, Lincolnshire and Nottinghamshire. In 1538 he bought Drax Priory for £200 and in 1565 acquired a long lease of the manor of Acklam. Large-scale sheep and cattle farming. Twenty-one-year leases. Sheriff of Yorkshire 1573–4.He or his successor rebuilt Everingham Hall. At his death he left personal effects worth £1202. 9s. 2d. His son Sir Philip (d. 1619) had a recusant wife but was himself a 'Church Papist'. Leases varying from seven to twenty-one years with the majority in the latter category. Between 1580 and 1604 he bought substantial property, including the manors of Thorpe le Street, Drax, Arras and Wholsea. This cost him about £3000 but his land-buying may have been partly financed from the sale of his Nottinghamshire estate which had passed out of his possession before his death. In addition, he acquired a lease of church property in 1593. Sheriff of Yorkshire 1590–1. In 1613 his revenue was said to amount to £3000 a year but this was probably an exaggeration. In 1616 he made a settlement of his property on the marriage of his grandson Philip, receiving a portion of £4000 from the bride's family. Besides the heir Sir Philip had six sons and four daughters and the leases, annuities and portions which he granted them must have represented a heavy burden on the estate. No doubt because of this his son Marmaduke (1579–1632) found himself in financial difficulties and in 1622 sold the whole of his North Riding property which consisted of the manors of Skinningrove and Brotton. Leases usually for twenty-one years. In 1627 he granted a twenty-one-year lease at an initial rent of £40 but rising on a graduated scale to £60 which was to remain in force from the fifth year onwards. Knighthood composition: £80. In 1632, following the death of his father, Sir Philip Constable (1595–1664) commanded an income of about £1350 a year but there were heavy charges on the estate: (a) annuities and rent-charges (mainly payable to relatives) amounting to £399. 13s. 4d. a year; (b) debts and children's portions in the sum of £3656; (c) on compounding for his recusancy (1632) he was charged with a rent of £250 a year which would be automatically increased as certain annuities expired (in 1642 he was paying £263. 6s. 8d.). Surveys of the manors of Everingham and Thorpe le Street, 1635. New leases were generally for either seven or twenty-one years. Rent increases: in 1637, for example, the rent yield from his lands in Arras went up from £50 to £73 a year. Between 1632 and 1641 there was an increase of £138 a year in the total revenue from his Yorkshire property. Large-scale demesne farming on the Lincolnshire estate. Free grant of a baronetcy, July 1642.

(Beverley County Record Office: Maxwell–Constable MSS. *C.R.S.*, liii, 427–36).

Crathorne of Crathorne

Ralph Crathorne (d. 1593) inherited the manors of Crathorne and East and West Ness. Although his wife was convicted of recusancy he remained a 'Church Papist'. At his death his estate was worth £400 a year but it was heavily burdened with debts. The wardship and lands of his son Thomas (1581–1639) were granted to an outsider and the mother spent over £500 in securing an assignment. This involved further borrowing. In 1605 Thomas was paying an annual rent of £13. 6s. 8d. for his recusancy but he soon conformed. In 1621 his son Ralph (b. 1604) married an heiress, a union which was to lead thirty years later to the acquisition of a large estate in the East Riding. Portion of £2000. At this time the manor of Crathorne was already charged with annuities totalling £90 a year. Forced loan of 1627: Thomas paid £10. In 1629 Thomas compounded for his recusancy, paying £45 a year out of the manor of Crathorne. The following year Ralph also compounded: rent of £45 a year for the manors of East and West Ness. Both father and son paid knighthood compositions: Thomas £15, Ralph £20. In 1636 Ralph lent £1000 to a fellow Catholic in return for a rent-charge of £80 which he settled on a younger son. At his father's death the family estate was worth £700 a year but it was charged with his mother's jointure. He and his mother paid a joint rent of £90 a year for their recusancy.

(Northallerton County Record Office: Crathorne MSS. P.R.O., Chancery Proceedings, Series I, C.2 Elizabeth/N.4/49).

Danby of Masham and Farnley

Sir Christopher Danby (d. 1571) had a large estate in the North and West Ridings, together with property in Kent, Suffolk and Lincolnshire. He and his heir jointly purchased the manors of Low Ellington, Healey and Sutton in Mashamshire. His son Sir Thomas (1531–90) inherited his Catholic sympathies but, like him, was never convicted of recusancy. Large-scale pasture farming, enclosures, coalmines, stone quarries. Substantial purchases of land, including the manors of Bramham Biggin, Scruton, Pott Grange, Ellingstring and South Cave. Some of the money laid out in this way was probably derived from the sale of his property in other counties. Sheriff of Yorkshire, 1575–6. Rebuilding of Farnley Hall, 1586. At his death he left an estate worth £1500 a year but in addition his widowed daughter-in-law had jointure lands to the value of £500 a year. The estate included urban property in York, Leeds, Thirsk and the city of Durham. Settlement of the manor of South Cave on a younger son. Sir Thomas was succeeded by his grandson Christopher (1582–1624). Wardship charges: fine £126. 13s. 4d., rent £55. 4s. 10d. Corrupt steward who embezzled money, granted disadvantageous leases and generally neglected the estate. The ward himself was lacking in thrift and business ability. Considerable litigation. Although Christopher was to have received a portion of £1000 following his marriage (1607) this was apparently never paid because of the delay in settling a jointure. Heavily indebted, he mortgaged most of the estate to relatives and sold some of his outlying property, including the manor of Mowthorpe which was worth £250 a year. At the time of his death he was a bankrupt and an outlaw. His son Sir Thomas (1610–60) also became a ward of the Crown. Wardship charges: fine £800, rent £150. The estate was valued at £1554 a year but it was heavily encumbered and the widow was provided with a jointure worth at least £300 a year. The guardian, Christopher Wandesford, paid off a number of debts, discharged many burdensome annuities and considerably improved the estate. Following the death of the ward's grandmother in 1629 the Court of Wards leased her jointure lands to the guardian (at a rent of £66. 11s. 4d. a year) for the benefit of the two younger children. In 1634 Thomas Danby sold the manors of Cleckheaton and Oakenshaw which were worth £110 a year. Sheep-farming. Considerable moneylending. Division and enclosure of the open fields in Thornton Watlass, 1637. Sheriff of Yorkshire, 1637–8. Heavy expenditure in collecting ship money. In 1638 he borrowed £5000, charging his estate with a rent of £400 a year. Two years later he was required to pay the ship money arrear of £1237. 15s. 6d. which he had failed to collect, 'to his great damage'. Between 1624 and 1640 there were striking increases in the rent yield of some of his manors, in particular:

	1624	1640
manor of Farnley	£305	£414
manor of Thornton Watlass	£47	£91

On the eve of the Civil War the estate revenue (including his mother's jointure) amounted to £2300 a year.

(Cartwright Memorial Hall, Bradford: Cunliffe–Lister MSS. P.R.O., Star Chamber Proceedings, Star Chamber 8/120/2 and Chancery Proceedings, Six Clerks' Series, C.8/52/15. C. Whone, 'Christopher Danby of Masham and Farnley', *Thoresby Society*, xxxvii, 1).

Franke of Kneeton

Marmaduke Franke (d. *c.* 1563) owned the manor of Kneeton and property in Middleton Tyas and elsewhere. In 1562 he entailed the estate, apparently on the grounds that his grandson Henry, 'a very simple man', might otherwise dispose of it. Henry Franke (d. 1593) fell heavily into debt and was soon engaged in the sale of land. This process reached a climax in 1584 when he conveyed away the manor of Kneeton and all the residue of his property. His son George (1565–1607) claimed that this conveyance was invalid because of the entail. Considerable litigation. In 1586 a commission of inquiry was appointed and as a result George was awarded possession of the property included in the conveyance of 1584 subject to the payment of all his father's debts and annuities totalling £10 a year to Henry's younger children. For the speedier discharge of these debts he was allowed to sell some of his land in Middleton Tyas. Building at Kneeton Hall, 1597. The Frankes were a Catholic family and in 1604 George was presented for recusancy but apparently conformed. His son Marmaduke (1597–1666) became a ward of the Crown. Wardship charges: fine £60, rent unknown. Further building at Kneeton Hall, 1616. Marmaduke was an intermittent recusant and for a time paid a rent of £26. 13s. 4d. a year for his estate. When the knighthood scheme was launched he delayed over compounding and was fined. In 1631 he mortgaged the manor of Kneeton as security for a loan of £1000 which was later increased (1637) to £1500. In 1630 he was presented as a recusant but appears to have conformed soon afterwards. By his second marriage he acquired property in Low Worsall (jointure lands settled by a former husband) worth £35 a year. On the eve of the Civil War his estate revenue amounted to £270 a year but he was paying interest on the mortgage loan at the rate of £120 a year and none of the principal had been repaid.

(P.R.O., Chancery Proceedings, Series I, C.2 Elizabeth/II.24/42 and S.P.Dom., Committee for Compounding, S.P.23/lxxxi/139, 140, 146, 147).

Hawksworth of Hawksworth

William Hawksworth (d. 1588) owned the manors of Hawksworth, Mitton, Menston and Loftsome. Piecemeal land-buying. Long dispute over the title to the manor of Mitton. In all he had twelve children, of whom at least nine survived infancy. Portions of £100 each to his daughters. Towards the end of his life he claimed that his imprisonment for recusancy had brought him into heavy debt. His son Walter (1558–1620) married an heiress through whom he acquired Edisford Hall and further land in Mitton. Considerable litigation with a neighbouring squire. Rebuilding of Hawksworth Hall. In 1615 he bought the Fitzwilliam manor in Baildon (with mineral rights) for the sum of £1300. On the marriage of his heir Richard (1615) he entailed the estate. Demesne farming and coalmining. A number of leases granted for three lives: in his will (1619) he enjoined his son to be good to his tenants and refrain from increasing their rents. Sir Richard (1594–1658) was advised that his father had lacked the power to make leases for lives; nevertheless the existence of such leases continued to hamper his efforts to improve the estate revenue for some time. Commercial farming, coalmining on a considerable scale. Some piecemeal property buying, including a house in York and rich coalbearing land at Clayton. Moneylending, extensive litigation: in 1632 he claimed to have spent £500 on lawsuits over the differences with his wife. Estate revenue:

  1634 £1167
  1641 £1127 (apparently excluding leases for lives)
  1650 £1276

In 1641 he noted: 'If all leases was expired there being nott many in being my estate is worth p. annum: 1400 li or better.' At his death he left a personal estate worth £2100, including £860. 16s. 9d. in gold and silver.

(Sheffield Central Library: Bright MSS. W. P. Baildon, *Baildon and the Baildons*).

Hutton of Marske

The Huttons owed their establishment as a county family primarily to Matthew Hutton, archbishop of York from 1595 to his death in 1606. In 1592 he gave his son Timothy the sum of £1900 to enable him to purchase a jointure for his wife and subsequently bequeathed to him the manors of Wharram Percy and Hagthorpe, together with a number of valuable church leases. During his father's lifetime Sir Timothy (1569–1629) bought the Marrick Abbey estate (1592), the manor of Marske (1598) and considerable property in Richmond. Following his succession in 1606 his total estate revenue amounted to £1077 a year. Sir Timothy was noted for his charity and hospitality. Purchases of luxury goods in London. Bowbearer of Arkengarthdale, an office which appears to have been of negligible value. In 1605–6 he served as sheriff of Yorkshire and was fined £230 for the unsatisfactory performance of certain duties. This fine was levied in 1612 and the same year he sold the manor of Hagthorpe, worth £82 a year. In 1617, on the marriage of his eldest son, he entailed most of the estate which was then producing a total income of £1449 a year. Demesne farming. Significant increases in rent, in particular:

	1606	1616	1625
Marrick Abbey	£137	£228	£250
manor of Wharram Percy	£100	£180	£180

In his later years he had to assist his son Matthew (1597–1666) whose extravagance had brought him into heavy debt. Matthew charged the manor of Marske with a rent of £120 to one of his creditors and in 1626 sold his wife's jointure lands in Wharram Percy. Forced loan of 1627: Sir Timothy paid £20. In his will (1628) he related that he and Matthew had disposed of certain church leases which had been settled on the younger children, but on the other hand he had purchased additional land of a greater value (probably a reference to the manor of Barforth on the Moor, Durham). Provision for the payment of annuities (mainly to the younger sons) amounting to some £250 a year. At his death he left a personal estate at Marske and Richmond worth £814. This included plate, pictures and a coach. After entering into his father's estate Matthew proceeded to sell the manor of Marske (1630) and the Marrick Abbey property (1631). Both these properties had been included in the entail of 1617 and because of this Matthew's heir was able to regain possession of Marske twenty years later. In 1638 Matthew bought lands in Durham, borrowing £2000 for this purpose. On the outbreak of the Civil War his income amounted to rather more than £300 a year while his debts were well in excess of £4000.

(Northallerton County Record Office: Hutton MSS. *Surtees Society*, xvii).

Ingleby of Ripley

Sir William Ingleby (d. 1579) owned a large but scattered estate. Rebuilding of Ripley Castle, 1555. Enclosures and large-scale pasture farming. For some years he served as treasurer of Berwick and also held offices of profit in the honor of Knaresborough. Heavy indebtedness, possibly due to his expenses as sheriff (1564–5) and the cost of providing for a substantial family. During the period 1564–76 he and his eldest son sold a number of outlying manors yet in 1573 Dacre Grange was purchased. At his death he left money, goods and chattels to the value of £700. 18s. 0d. Debts owing to him £7. 10s. 0d., debts outward £630. 9s. 0d. Funeral expenses: £136. 7s. 8d. His son Sir William (1549–1618) inherited an estate which was still extensive. In addition, he had property in the East Riding which he had secured by marrying an heiress. After succeeding his father he continued to sell land but in 1592 and 1599 he purchased considerable property. Sir William was deputy steward of the royal manor of Knaresborough and high steward of the Earl of Derby's manor of Kirkby Malzeard. Acquisition of leases of Lord Derby's manors of Thirsk and Kirkby Malzeard which were worth £800 a year. This transaction proved extremely profitable but in 1604 he agreed to surrender his interest to the Earl, demanding substantial compensation. Considerable litigation with Sir Stephen Proctor of Fountains. In 1611 he bought the manor of North Deighton. Demesne farming at Ripley and North Deighton, leadmining at Bewerley. Leases mainly for twenty-one years but a number for 1000 years and upwards. Moneylending: in 1611 he lent £2000 to Christopher Danby of Masham who mortgaged the manor of Sutton as security. At his death he had money, goods and chattels amounting to £2615. 16s. 11d. Debts owing to him £3295. 3s. 4d., debts outward £1528. 6s. od. Legacies to be paid in cash: over £3000. Funeral expenses: £80. Since he died childless his estate, consisting primarily of the manors of Ripley, Broxholme, North Deighton and Brimham, passed to his nephew Sir William (c. 1595–1653). Stability and consolidation. Twenty-one-year leases. Forced loan of 1627: £20. In 1630 he refused to compound for knighthood and was apparently fined. Estate survey, 1635. In 1640 he bought Crown property known as Haverah Park, worth £80 a year, for the sum of £970. In May 1642 he was granted a baronetcy free of charge. Estate revenue: £1500 a year.

(*Calendar of Ingilby MSS, Surtees Society*, civ, 129–35. *Y.A.J.*, xxiv, 182–203).

Lister of Thornton

William Lister of Middop (d. 1582) bought and sold considerable property. His main acquisition was the manor of Thornton (1557) which became the family seat. Coalmining. In his will he settled property on one of his younger sons and granted annuities of £6. 13s. 4d. a year each to four other children. At his death he held the manors of Thornton and Middop together with a number of leases. His son Lawrence (1547–1609) had a recusant wife but was himself a conformist. In his time the family estate was kept intact but without significant addition. Although his son Sir William (1591–1650) was left a minor the right of wardship belonged not to the Crown but to the Earl of Cumberland from whom the estate was held by knight service. Marriage settlement of 1610: jointure of £200 a year (later increased to £300) in return for a portion of £1500 and two years' tabling for the young couple and their ordinary servants. This settlement was to lead to litigation between the two families in 1625. Between 1614 and 1618 he sold some of his lands in Middop and Rimington. Settlement of the estate, 1618. Later he acquired the manor of Swinden and other property worth altogether £200 a year and in addition bought further land in Thornton. Forced loan of 1627: £14. In 1629 he borrowed £1100 from his uncle Martin Lister and in return granted him a lease of property worth £200 a year which was to continue until he had received the sum of £1500. Protracted negotiations over the terms of a marriage between his son William (1612–42) and Catherine Hawksworth. In the course of these negotiations Sir William put the value of his estate at £1000 a year, of which £400 was charged with his wife's jointure and annuities to younger children. In 1637 there was a further settlement of the estate: (a) annuities of £30 each to five younger sons; (b) the heir undertook to pay his father £188 a year out of certain premises which had been settled on him until such time as Sir William received from him the sum of £2450. Demesne farming. Enclosure on the commons of Thornton,

1637. In 1639 the heir bought property in Malhamdale, worth £74 a year, for the sum of £1000.

(Y.A.S. Library: Lister–Kaye MSS. Sheffield Central Library: Bright MSS. P.R.O., Chancery Proceedings, Series II, C.3/364/41).

Meynell of North Kilvington

Anthony Meynell (d. 1576), a younger son, had acquired the manor of North Kilvington partly by inheritance and partly by purchase. Sheep and cattle farming. In 1599 he was a joint purchaser of the manor of Pickhill and Roxby, paying £950 for his half-share. His heir took part in the Northern Rebellion of 1569 but escaped with a fine. Settlement of the estate, 1572 and 1576. In the latter deed the lands in Pickhill and Roxby were settled on his second son Richard. His eldest son Roger (1536–91) married an heiress who brought him property in Thornton le Street. With the assistance of his brother Richard he acquired further land in Thornton and also bought the manor of East Dalton which was settled on a younger son. On the marriage of the heir (1587) he entailed his lands in North Kilvington, Scruton and Thornton. Heavy indebtedness, which may have been due to his 'bowntifull and liberall disposition'. At his death the estate was apparently worth £300 a year but it was seriously encumbered: (a) life annuities totalling over £80 a year; (b) a number of long disadvantageous leases; (c) half the estate had been extended on a recognizance and redeemed by his brother Richard who was still in possession in 1596. His son Thomas (1565–1653) was the first head of the family to be convicted of recusancy. In 1596 two-thirds of his estate were formally seized but he claimed that most of the revenue was taken up with his mother's jointure, annuities and debt charges. As a result the property was valued at only £5 a year. Considerable litigation over his father's debts and his own recusancy. Imprisonment and fining by the Northern High Commission. In 1604 and again in 1611 he was forced to contribute £20 to a loan on privy seals. An improving landowner, he carried out enclosures and engaged in demesne farming. In 1607 he was said to have enclosed and depopulated the village of North Kilvington. Building at Kilvington Hall, 1612. In 1612 he bought the manor of Sowerby for £650, subsequently acknowledging that he owed this purchase to his second wife (a widow and the mother of William Thwaites who sold him the property): 'if I had never married hir I had never compassed it.' There was, however, little prospect of improving the yield because the tenants had previously been granted 2000-year leases at small rents. In all, Thomas Meynell spent about £1000 on land purchase between 1612 and 1621. In 1613 he was said to owe some £750 for recusancy fines while in 1622 we find him paying at the rate of £12 a year for the statutory two-thirds of his estate. Forced loan of 1627: £8. In 1629 he and his son Anthony (1591–1669) compounded for their recusancy and were charged with a rent of £100 a year which was regularly paid up to the time of the Civil War. Knighthood composition: £25. When Anthony's eldest son married in 1637 property worth £150 a year was settled on him and his wife in return for a portion of £1000. On the eve of the Civil War the total revenue from the estate amounted to about £600 a year but it was in the possession of three generations of the Meynells and Anthony Meynell had a large family to support.

(Father Hugh Aveling (ed.), 'Recusancy Papers of the Meynell Family', *C.R.S.*, lvi, p.ix).

Monckton of Cavil

Christopher Monckton (c. 1530–1600) owned the manors of Cavil and Burland, which he entailed in 1560, and also held a lease of property at Londesborough from the Clifford family. Commercial farming. An ardent Catholic, he was both fined and imprisoned for his recusancy. In 1589 the statutory two-thirds of his estate were seized and leased back to him at a rent of £24. 6s. 6d. a year. Despite his sufferings in the cause of religion he appears to have avoided falling into serious debt. At his death the estate descended to his grandson Sir Philip (1574–1646) who was a conformist and probably, at least for most of his life, a Protestant. He married an heiress and acquired some minor property in Cheshire which included salt workings. Estate surveys. Between 1608 and the outbreak of the Civil War he considerably increased his estate in Howden by piecemeal land-buying. In addition, he purchased the manor of Little Thorpe (1620) which cost him £1800. Forced loan of 1627: £10. His son Sir Francis (b. c. 1600) farmed the demesnes of Cavil at a rent of £60 a year and also took a lease of the manor of Easthorpe from the Cliffords. Sheep farming. Estate revenue: £700 a year.

(Nottingham University Library: Galway of Serlby MSS).

Tempest of Broughton

Henry Tempest (1527–1605) had inherited the manor of Broughton from his father. An improving landowner, he consolidated his demesne grounds in Broughton and carried out enclosures on the commons. Demesne farming and horse-breeding. In addition, he mined lead on his estate, an activity which the Tempests had engaged in since at least the beginning of the sixteenth century. Twenty-one and thirty-one-year leases with fines. Purchase of the manors of Burnsall and Thorpe, 1566. In 1591 he assigned the whole estate to his eldest son, reserving only a rent of £80 a year and certain rooms at Broughton Hall. His son Sir Stephen (1555–1625) rebuilt the house in 1597. He had a large family, at least eight children surviving infancy. Probably as a means of raising portions he leased out the manor of Thorpe in several parcels for long terms of years, reserving the royalties and quit-rents. His son Stephen

(1593–1651) married an heiress (1612) through whom he acquired leases of Crown property in Roundhay. By his second wife he received a portion of £1500 but no jointure was settled. Forced loan of 1627: £9. In 1629 and 1631 he purchased the Crown estate in Roundhay, paying £2000. This resulted in considerable litigation from which he emerged victorious. Although the Tempests had always favoured the Old Religion he was the first head of the family to be convicted of recusancy. In 1629 he compounded: an annual rent of £30 for his inheritance and a further £30 for Roundhay, together with a once-for-all payment of £49 for his goods and arrears. At the same time his mother (who survived until 1648) compounded for her jointure lands: annual rent of £20. Knighthood composition: £20. Great improvements at Roundhay: clearing of woodland, enclosures, lime kilns. Repairs and to Roundhay Grange. Total estate revenue : improvements £760 a year. In April 1642 Stephen settled the manors of Broughton, Thorpe and Burnsall on trustees for a term of thirteen years. This was for the payment of (a) annuities amounting to £8. 13s. 4d., (b) debts in the sum of £728, (c) portions totalling £1600 for the younger children.

(E. B. Tempest, 'Broughton Hall and its Associations', *Bradford Antiquary*, New Series, iv, 84. Y.A.S. Library: MS 381(t). P.R.O., S.P.Dom., Committee for Compounding, S.P.23/cxvii/243–4, 250. B.M., Additional MSS 40670).

Tempest of Tong

Henry Tempest (1512–91) owned the manors of Tong and Cowling Head. Enclosure on the waste of Tong. Piecemeal sale of land in Tong, 1577–87. His son Richard (1551–1607) acquired the manor of Pillay and other lands by marriage but he had disposed of all this property before his death. After the death of his brother-in-law John Gascoigne of Thorpe on the Hill in 1590 he took over management of his estate as guardian of the heir and kept possession for fifteen years. This resulted in litigation over the sum of £1980 which Henry Gascoigne claimed from him. Enclosure. At his death Cowling Head (worth some £60 a year) passed out of the family under the terms of a settlement. When his son Richard (1577–1613) succeeded the Tong estate was worth £500 a year. Wife's portion £500. Coalmining. John Tempest (1603–23) was a minor at his father's death. Wardship charges: fine £200, rent £25. The mother, who obtained the wardship in competition with Henry Gascoigne, had to borrow the whole sum of £200. In November 1618 she put her expenditure in procuring the wardship at £492, including the fine and interest paid to moneylenders. John Tempest said to have left his estate in an embarrassed condition with a number of farms let at small rents. Personal estate worth £200 'at least'. His son Henry (1621–58) also became a ward of the Crown. Wardship charges: fine £100, rent £25. His stepfather and guardian, the Rev. Henry Fairfax, lived in Lancashire and therefore entrusted the management of the estate to a bailiff. The ward later claimed that the manor-house, the outbuildings, orchards, gardens and woods had been allowed to decay. In 1639 Henry Tempest married (against his guardian's wishes) a gentlewoman of little fortune. The same year Fairfax released his interest in the estate except for the tithes and corn-mills which he kept as security for payment of the rent to the Court of Wards. The ward proceeded to improve the estate revenue which was worth some £650 a year in 1642 (including his grandmother's jointure of £100 a year). Considerable prosperity which enabled him to engage in new building at Tong Hall.

(Cartwright Memorial Hall, Bradford: Tempest MSS. P.R.O., Chancery Proceedings, Series I, James I C.2/G14/2 and Six Clerks' Series, C.10/11/122. W. Robertshaw, 'The Manor of Tong', *Bradford Antiquary*, New Series, part xxxviii, 117).

Wombwell of Wombwell

William Wombwell (1515–77) increased his estate which in 1577 consisted of the manors of Wombwell and Thurgoland with considerable property in the surrounding area. In the decade following his father's death Thomas (*c.* 1540–1613) acquired further premises in Wombwell but also sold parcels of land in other parts of the estate. Twenty-one-year leases. His son William (1565–1622) received a portion of £1000 with his first wife. His second wife, Mary Rockley, was an heiress and under a settlement with the Rockley family (1589) he was granted a 1000-year lease of lands worth £300 a year. Subsequently it was agreed (1611) that the manors of Upper and Nether Hoyland should continue in the Wombwell family while the remainder of the property included in the lease should return to the Rockley family after William's decease. William was a man of great extravagance with a taste for litigation. Heavy indebtedness. To help him pay his debts his father sold a considerable part of his own patrimony, including the manor of Thurgoland (worth £80 a year) and premises in South Kirkby (which realised £1150). When the remainder of the family estate was settled in 1608 it was encumbered with a statute of £2000. At his death Thomas left a personal estate worth at least £1500 but there were debts to be repaid. After litigation William secured possession of lands in Hoyland worth £60 a year which his father had settled on a younger son. In 1618 he purchased a subordinate manor in Wombwell but was selling property in other places. In his will (1622) William authorised the trustees of his estate to grant twenty-one-year leases in return for fines which were to be used for the payment of debts and the augmenting of portions. Children's portions were to be raised by the sale of (a) all the Hoyland property, (b) the manor bought in 1618, unless the heir paid £600 at the age of twenty-four for the same purpose. In addition, the estate was charged with life annuities totalling £100 a year which were payable to the widow and five younger sons. His son William (1609–62) was left a minor but apparently escaped the charges of wardship because no part of his estate was held by knight service. Piecemeal sale of the Hoyland property which raised about £2600. In 1636 William was said to have paid £800 to his stepmother for her interest in the estate. Estate revenue: £600 a year.

(P.R.O., Chancery Proceedings, Series I, C.2 James I/W.3/12 and W.17/69 and Chancery Depositions, C.22/757/20. Sheffield Central Library: Bright MSS, 185(b) ix).

APPENDIX C

Personal Estates

In its widest sense the term 'personal estate' covered money and plate, company stock, debts inward, clothes and jewellery, household goods, crops, livestock and farming implements. Except where otherwise stated the value given in the following table represents the whole sum of the personal estate. In the main the rounded figures have been obtained from the records of legal cases and the more precise figures from inventories. Shillings and pence have been omitted.

The following symbols have been used:

         * minor gentry   † in financial difficulties

(1)	1559	Francis Wandesford of Hipswell	£718	Includes plate worth £26. 13s. 4d.
(2)	1566	Thomas Gascoigne of Lasingcroft	£455	Over and above his debts.
(3)	1567	*Ralph Gower of Richmond	£1024	Includes plate worth £108. 10s. 4d.
(4)	1567	Thomas Rokeby of Mortham	£486	Includes £18. 10s. 2d. in ready money, and plate worth £19. 13s. 4d.
(5)	1567	*John Thornhill of Fixby	£248	
(6)	1574	Roger Burgh of Brough	£993	Includes £7 15s. 0d. in ready money, and plate worth £20.
(7)	1575	Sir Marmaduke Constable of Everingham	£1202	Includes £5 in ready money and plate worth £47. 10s. 0d.
(8)	1579	†Sir William Ingleby of Ripley	£700	Includes £20 in ready money and plate worth £42. 6s. 8d.
(9)	1580	Godfrey Bosvile of Gunthwaite	£3000	At least.
(10)	1582	Sir Thomas Boynton of Barmston	£2454	Includes £100 in ready money.
(11)	1585	William Webster of Flamborough	£366	
(12)	1588	Sir Cotton Gargrave of Nostell Priory	£2714	Includes plate worth £282. 18s. 4d.
(13)	1595	Sir William Fairfax of Gilling and Walton	£1072	Plate and household goods at Gilling Castle. The plate was worth £393. 7s. 7d.

(14)	1597	†Thomas Tankard of Boroughbridge	£769	Includes £20 in ready money.
(15)	1603	Sir Richard Wortley of Wortley	£1181	
(16)	1607	Sir John Savile of Methley	£1346	
(17)	1610	*†Henry Beckwith of Clint	£62	
(18)	1610	John Talbot of Bashall	£554	
(19)	1612	†Richard Stapleton of Carlton	£484	
(20)	1612	*William Man of Bramley Grange	£690	
(21)	1613	Thomas Wombwell of Wombwell	£1500	At least.
(22)	1613	Richard Aldeburgh of Ellenthorpe	£951	Includes £249. os. 6d. in money and plate worth £41. 3s. 6d.
(23)	1614	†William Middleton of Stockeld	£841	Includes £3 in ready money and plate worth £81. 18s. od.
(24)	1617	Thomas Gledhill of Barkisland	£3220	Described as his goods.
(25)	1618	Sir William Ingleby of Ripley	£5911	Includes £833. 14s. 6d. in money and plate worth £252. 1s. od.
(26)	1619	†John Robinson of Ryther	£716	
(27)	1619	Christopher Maltby of Cottingham	£618	
(28)	1622	†Sir Francis Baildon of Kippax	£3000	
(29)	1623	*John Batty of Alverthorpe	£200	
(30)	1624	Sir Henry Bellasis of Newburgh Priory	£8000	
(31)	1624	*†Thomas Ayscough of Lower Newstead	£81	
(32)	1626	*Brian Franke of Alwoodley	£400	At least.
(33)	1627	*Thomas Skyers of Alderthwaite	£166	Includes £3. 6s. 8d. for purse and apparel.
(34)	1629	Sir Timothy Hutton of Marske	£814	Includes plate valued at £30.
(35)	1629	*†Francis Swale of South Stainley	£102	
(36)	1630	*Francis Gatenby of Maunby	£38	
(37)	1634	*†John Savile of Marley	£800	At least.
(38)	1634	Richard Richardson of North Bierley	£2000	At least.

(39) 1634	Richard Sunderland of High Sunderland	£8000	
(40) 1635	Thomas Parker of Browsholme	£5000	At least.
(41) 1636	Sir Arthur Ingram of Temple Newsam	£4000	Goods lost in a fire at Temple Newsam.
(42) 1637	Francis Burdett of Birthwaite	£6000	
(43) 1637	†Sir John Jackson of Hickleton	£1600	
(44) 1637	†Sir William Acclom of Moreby	£600	
(45) 1638	*Thomas Jackson of Cowling	£253	
(46) 1638	George Wentworth of West Bretton	£509	Includes plate worth £50.
(47) 1639	John Vescy of Brampton	£1000	At least.
(48) 1640	John Wilkinson of Barton	£2000	
(49) 1642	†John Redman of Water Fulford	£1069	
(50) 1642	Sir Ralph Hansby of Tickhill Castle	£3000	At least.
(51) 1643	*Edward Armitage of Keresforth Hill	£600	At least.
(52) 1643	Sir William Strickland of Boynton	£4000	Goods seized by the royalists.
(53) 1643	Sir John Hotham of Scorborough	£10,000	Includes at least £4800 in ready money.
(54) 1643	Sir Henry Anderson of Long Cowton	£2500	Money and plate seized by the parliamentarians.
(55) 1644	*John Redman of Gate Fulford	£1000	
(56) 1645	Sir Richard Graham of Norton Conyers	£600	Plate seized by the parliamentarians.
(57) Civil War period	Sir Gervase Cutler of Stainborough	£5000	Personal estate worth £4000 plundered and plate worth £1000 contributed to the royalist cause.
(58) 1646	Thomas Coundon of Willerby	£6000	Over and above debts and funeral expenses.
(59) 1647	Sir Edward Osborne of Kiveton	£2019	
(60) 1647	†Philip Anne of Frickley	£1000	At least.
(61) 1647	*Michael Fawkes of Farnley	£425	
(62) 1650	Sir Thomas Wentworth of North Elmsall	£1897	Goods and chattels. Includes plate worth £40. 13s. 4d.
(63) 1651	John Lister of Linton	£3000	At least.

(64)	1655	James Pennyman of Ormesby	£2000	At least.
(65)	1657	Sir Richard Darley of Buttercrambe	£4000	
(66)	1658	Sir Richard Hawksworth of Hawksworth	£2100	Includes £860. 16s. 9d. in gold and silver, and plate worth £32. 3s. 6d.
(67)	1658	Thomas Eastoft of Eastoft	£1192	Includes plate worth £46. 5s. od.
(68)	1659	John Savile of Methley	£14,267	Includes £10,632. 12s. 8d. in ready money.
(69)	1659	Thomas Westby of Ravenfield	£1000	
(70)	1660	Sir George Wentworth of Woolley	£1130	

SOURCES

(1) *Surtees Society*, xxvi, 131–8.
(2) P.R.O., Chancery Proceedings, Series II, C.3/70/110.
(3) *Surtees Society*, xxvi, 196–8.
(4) *Surtees Society*, xxvi, 200–4.
(5) Y.A.S. Library, Clarke-Thornhill MSS, Parcel 23.
(6) *Surtees Society*, xxvi, 245–8.
(7) Beverley County Record Office: Maxwell-Constable MSS, DDEV 66/6.
(8) *Surtees Society*, civ, 131–5.
(9) P.R.O., Chancery Proceedings, Series II, C.3/258/50.
(10) G. Poulson, *The History and Antiquities of the Seigniory of Holderness*, i, 215–24
(11) P.R.O., Chancery Proceedings, Series II, C.3/253/64.
(12) P.R.O., Duchy of Lancaster, Special Commissions, D.L.44/442.
(13) *Archaeologia*, xlviii, 123–36.
(14) Sir Thomas Lawson-Tancred, *Records of a Yorkshire Manor*, 175–83.
(15) *H.M.C. Third Report*, Appendix, 226.
(16) Leeds Central Library: MSS of Lord Mexborough.
(17) *Surtees Society*, cx, 11–12.
(18) P.R.O., Chancery Proceedings, Series II, C.3/256/82.
(19) *Y.A.S.R.S.*, l, 6.
(20) P.R.O., Court of Wards, Entry Book of Decrees, Wards 9/xciii/f.325b.
(21) P.R.O., Chancery Proceedings, Series I, C.2 James I/C.3/12.
(22) Leeds Central Library: Richmondshire Wills and Administrations.
(23) *Y.A.J.*, xxiv, 171–81.
(24) P.R.O., Court of Wards, Feodaries' Surveys, Wards 5/49.
(25) *Y.A.J.*, xxiv, 182–203.
(26) and (27) P.R.O., Court of Wards, Feodaries' Surveys, Wards 5/49.
(28) W. P. Baildon, *Baildon and the Baildons*, iii, 40.

(29) J. W. Walker, *Wakefield: its History and People*, ii, 652.
(30) P.R.O., Chancery Proceedings, Series II, C.3/364/41.
(31) Leeds Central Library: Richmondshire Wills and Administrations.
(32) P.R.O., Court of Wards, Pleadings, Wards 13/120.
(33) Nottingham University Library: Galway of Serlby MSS 12691.
(34) *Surtees Society*, xvii, 253–4. *Archaeologia Aeliana*, New Series, v, 59–60.
(35) and (36) Leeds Central Library: Richmondshire Wills and Administrations.
(37) P.R.O., Chancery Proceedings, Six Clerks' Series, C.9/6/16.
(38) Six Clerks' Series, C.7/409/61.
(39) Six Clerks' Series, C.8/89/45.
(40) Six Clerks' Series, C.8/123/33.
(41) Knowler, i, 525.
(42) P.R.O., Chancery Proceedings, Six Clerks' Series, C.10/28/14.
(43) P.R.O., Wards 9, Entry Book of Affidavits, Wards 9/dlxxii/546.
(44) P.R.O., Chancery Proceedings, Six Clerks' Series, C.9/6/146.
(45) Leeds Central Library: Richmondshire Wills and Administrations.
(46) Y.A.S. Library: Bretton Hall MSS 85.
(47) P.R.O., Chancery Proceedings, Six Clerks' Series, C.6/134/197.
(48) Six Clerks' Series, C.7/405/29.
(49) Six Clerks' Series, C.10/34/163.
(50) Six Clerks' Series, C.10/32/62.
(51) Six Clerks' Series, C.10/45/64.
(52) *H.M.C. Thirteenth Report*, Appendix, i, 102.
(53) P.R.O., Chancery Proceedings, Six Clerks' Series, C.6/191/20. T. T. Wildridge, *The Hull Letters*, 152, 161–3.
(54) *Cal. Committee for Compounding*, 2336.
(55) P.R.O., Chancery Proceedings, Six Clerks' Series, C.10/95/25.
(56) *Cal. Committee for Compounding*, 1018.
(57) P.R.O., S.P.Dom., Committee for Compounding, S.P.23/clxxx/574, 582. J. Hunter, *South Yorkshire*, ii, 267.
(58) P.R.O., Chancery Proceedings, Six Clerks' Series, C.8/106/126.
(59) J. Hunter, *South Yorkshire*, i, 143.
(60) P.R.O., Chancery Proceedings, Series II, C.5/19/3.
(61) P.R.O., S.P.Dom., Committee for the Advance of Money, S.P.19/cxx/157, 159.
(62) Sheffield Central Library: Bright MSS, BR 79(b).
(63) P.R.O., Chancery Proceedings, Six Clerks' Series, C.10/15/35.
(64) Six Clerks' Series, C.5/376/113.
(65) Six Clerks' Series, C.10/466/6.
(66) Sheffield Central Library: Bright MSS, BR 89(a).
(67) Beverley County Record Office: Eastoft of Eastoft MSS, DDBE 27/9.
(68) Leeds Central Library: MSS of Lord Mexborough.
(69) P.R.O., Chancery Proceedings, Six Clerks' Series, C.7/82/61.
(70) Y.A.S. Library: Clarke-Thornhill MSS, Parcel 24.

APPENDIX D

Households and Establishments of Servants

The number of servants represents the total establishment, both indoor and outdoor, except where otherwise stated.

The symbol * denotes a family worth £1000 a year and upwards.

			Number of Servants	Total Size of Household	
(1)	1554	*Sir Nicholas Fairfax of Gilling and Walton	30 to 40	—	
(2)	reign of Elizabeth	*Sir Richard Cholmley of Roxby	50 to 60	—	Described as men-servants.
(3)	1574	Roger Burgh of Brough	11	—	Excludes employees on the home farm.
(4)	1581	*Thomas Metham of Metham	28	—	
(5)	1600	*Sir Thomas Hoby of Hackness	14	—	Domestic servants.
(6)	reign of James I	*Sir Ralph Babthorpe of Osgodby	30	—	At least.
(7)	reign of James I	*Sir Thomas Wentworth of Wentworth Woodhouse	49	64	
(8)	August 1609	*Sir Henry Bellasis of Newburgh Priory	51	—	At Newburgh Priory and Murton Grange.
(9)	1613	Sir John Yorke of Gouthwaite	17	—	At least.
(10)	1617	Francis Stringer of Sharlston	13	—	
(11)	1632	*Sir Henry Savile of Methley	15	—	At least.
(12)	1636	*Sir Hugh Cholmley of Whitby	—	30 to 40	

(13) 1638	*Sir Henry Slingsby of Scriven	24	30	
(14) December 1638	*Sir Edward Osborne of Kiveton	—	80	This was his household at the King's Manor, York, where he governed as vice-president of the Council of the North.
(15) Candlemas 1640	Thomas Stringer of Sharlston	20	—	
(16) November 1640	*Sir Richard Graham of Norton Conyers	—	30	
(17) 1643	*Sir Thomas Danby of Farnley	22	—	
(18) 1645	Stephen Thompson of Humbleton	—	22	
(19) 1648	*Sir John Kaye of Woodsome	20	27	
(20) 1658	*Sir Richard Hawksworth of Hawksworth	24	—	
(21) Christmas 1662	*Sir Philip Constable of Everingham	30	50	Excluding the servants who came with the guests.

SOURCES

(1) *C.R.S.: Biographical Studies*, iii, 103.
(2) *Cholmley Memoirs*, 7.
(3) *Surtees Society*, xxvi, 244.
(4) Borthwick Institute of Historical Research: High Commission Act Book 1580–5, R VII/AB/17, f.98.
(5) D. M. Meads (ed.), *The Diary of Lady Margaret Hoby 1599–1605*, Introduction, 40.
(6) Foley, iii, 199.
(7) J. Hunter, *South Yorkshire*, i, 84.
(8) Y.A.S. Library: Newburgh Priory MSS, Box 3, Bundle 15, account book of Sir Henry Bellasis (no pagination).
(9) P.R.O., Star Chamber Proceedings, Star Chamber 8/19/10.
(10) Y.A.S. Library: MS 311 (no pagination).

(11) Borthwick Institute of Historical Research: York Wills, will of Sir Henry Savile, 13 June 1632.
(12) *Cholmley Memoirs*, 56.
(13) *Slingsby Diary*, 26.
(14) Sheffield Central Library: Strafford Letters, xviii. Sir Edward Osborne to Lord Wentworth, 5 December 1638.
(15) Y.A.S. Library: MS 311 (no pagination).
(16) *H.M.C. Sixth Report*, Appendix, 330.
(17) Cartwright Memorial Hall, Bradford: Cunliffe-Lister MSS, Bundle 11, account book of Sir Thomas Danby.
(18) *Cal. Committee for Compounding*, 929.
(19) B.M., Additional MSS 24467, f.250.
(20) Sheffield Central Library: Bright MSS 87.
(21) R. C. Wilton (ed.), 'A List of Guests at Everingham Park, Christmas, 1662', *C.R.S.*, xxvii, 261.

BIBLIOGRAPHY

Notes: (1) Printed collections of contemporary documents which also include a substantial commentary (as, for example, in the case of a biographical work) are shown under 'Secondary Sources'. (2) Only the more important articles are listed.

Primary Sources

I. MANUSCRIPT

British Museum

ADDITIONAL MSS, in particular

12,482	Entry book of the heraldic visitation of Yorkshire, 1665–6.
18,979	Fairfax Correspondence (Fairfax of Denton).
20,778	do.
24,439 24,463 24,466–7 24,470 24,516 24,553	Manuscripts of Rev. Joseph Hunter (material relating to Yorkshire families).
27,410–1	Manuscripts of the Calverley family of Calverley.
29,440	Memoirs of Sir John Reresby of Thrybergh, 2nd Bart.
29,442–3	Sir John Reresby's history of his family.
30,305–6	Fairfax Correspondence.
34,765	Entry book of recusants 'granted' under the Signet, 1606–11.
37,719	Commonplace book of Sir John Gibson of Welburn.
38,599	Commonplace book of the Shann family of Methley.
40,132 40,135–7 40,176	Holme Hall MSS (Constable of Flamborough and Langdale of North Dalton).
40,670	Genealogical material relating to various branches of the Tempest family.
41,168	Holme Hall MSS.

ADDITIONAL CHARTERS
1790–1   Deeds of the Fairfax family of Denton.
1797–8   do.
63,735   Holme Hall MSS.
66,608   do.
30,933   Deed of the Bellasis family of Newburgh Priory.

COTTON MSS
Titus F.1   Speech of William Strickland, 1571.

EGERTON MSS

925   Rent-book of property belonging to the archbishopric of
          York, 1580–1637.
2644–8   Barrington Correspondence (papers relating to the Bourch-
          ier family of Beningbrough).
3402   Duke of Leeds MSS (Darcy of Hornby).
3562   Thoresby Hall MSS (papers relating to the mortgaged
          estate of James Maleverer of Ingleby Arncliffe).
3568   do.

HARLEIAN MSS
4630   John Hopkinson's Yorkshire pedigrees.
6288   Surveys of Crown estates in Yorkshire, 1624.

LANSDOWNE MSS
119   Letters of James Ryther of Harewood.
153   Papers relating to recusants in the reign of James I.
608   Court of Wards precedent book.
914   Drawings of Yorkshire manor-houses, early eighteenth
          century.
988   Sir Philip Monckton's narrative of the Civil War.

Public Record Office

CHANCERY
Proceedings, Series I (C.2), Series II (C.3) and Six Clerks' Series
(C.5–10).
Depositions (C.21, C.22).
Entry Books of Decrees and Orders (C.33).
Close Rolls (C.54).
Patent Rolls (C.66).
Inquisitions Post Mortem (C.142).

Crown Office, Miscellaneous Books (C.181, C.193) and Docquet Books (Indexes 4211 and 4212).
Petty Bag Office, Miscellaneous Rolls (C.212) and Sheriffs' Rolls (C.227).

COURT OF COMMON PLEAS

Feet of Fines (C.P.25(2)).

COURT OF REQUESTS

Proceedings (Requests 2).

COURT OF WARDS

Feodaries' Surveys (Wards 5).
Indentures of Wardships and Leases (Wards 6).
Miscellaneous Books, including Books of Contracts of Wardships and Leases, Petitions, Decrees and Affidavits (Wards 9).
Pleadings (Wards 13).

DUCHY OF LANCASTER

Pleadings (D.L.1).
Depositions (D.L.4).
Rentals and Surveys (D.L.43).
Special Commissions (D.L.44).

EXCHEQUER

Accounts Various (E.101).
Bills and Answers (E.112).
Depositions (E.134).
Particulars for Grants (E.147).
Special Commissions (E.178).
Lay Subsidy Rolls (E.179).
Parliamentary Surveys (E.317).
Recusant Rolls (E.366 and 367).
Sheriffs' Accounts of Seizures (E.379).
Abbreviate of Receipts (Pells) (E.401).
Exchequer of Receipt, Miscellanea (E.407).
Land Revenue, Miscellaneous Books (L.R.2).

LORD CHAMBERLAIN'S OFFICE

Entry Books of Recognizances (L.C.4).

PRIVY COUNCIL OFFICE

Registers (P.C.2).

SIGNET OFFICE

Docquet Books (Indexes 6801–11).

STAR CHAMBER

Proceedings, Elizabeth I, James I and Charles I (Star Chamber 7 and 8).

STATE PAPER OFFICE

State Papers Domestic Series, Elizabeth I (S.P.12), James I (S.P.14), Charles I (S.P.16), Committee for the Advance of Money (S.P.19), Committee for Compounding (S.P.23), Commonwealth Exchequer Papers (S.P.28), Warrants (S.P.39).
State Papers Supplementary (S.P.46).
State Papers Colonial Series, Colonial Entry Books: Bahamas (C.O. 124).
Transcripts: Gunpowder Plot Papers (P.R.O.31/6) and Roman Transcripts (P.R.O.31/9 and 10).
Palmer's Indexes: P.R.O. Index 17,349.

College of Arms

Visitation book: Yorkshire visitation of 1612 (C.13).

Dr Williams's Library London

Morrice MSS.

Guildhall Library, London

Royal Contract Estates: deeds and rentals.

House of Lords Library

House of Lords MSS.

Lambeth Palace Library

MSS 918, 919 (Commonwealth church surveys).

Somerset House

Wills and Administrations of the Prerogative Court of Canterbury.

Beverley County Record Office

Beaumont of Carlton Towers MSS (Stapleton of Carlton, Twisleton of Drax).

Bethell of Rise MSS (Bethell, Michelburne of Carlton, Remington of Lund).
Burton Constable MSS (Constable of Burton Constable, Tunstall of Scargill, Girlington of Girlington).
Eastoft of Eastoft MSS.
Grimston MSS (Grimston of Grimston Garth).
Harford of Holme MSS (Langdale of North Dalton).
Hotham MSS (Hotham of Scorborough, Thompson of Humbleton).
Howard-Vyse MSS (Norcliffe of Langton).
Langdale MSS (Constable of Flamborough, Langdale of North Dalton, Hungate of North Dalton).
Legard of Anlaby MSS.
Macdonald of Sleat MSS (Bosvile of Gunthwaite, Wood of Thorpe).
Maxwell-Constable MSS (Constable of Everingham).
Osbaldeston of Hunmanby MSS (Osbaldeston, Westhorpe of Hunmanby, Leppington of Hunmanby).
Palmes of Naburn MSS.
Wickham-Boynton MSS (Boynton of Barmston, Griffith of Burton Agnes).

Borthwick Institute of Historical Research (University of York)
Court Books and High Commission Act Books.
Wills in the York Registry.

Brotherton Library (University of Leeds)
Wentworth of Woolley MSS.

Cartwright Memorial Hall, Bradford
Cunliffe-Lister MSS (Danby of Masham and Farnley).
Spencer Stanhope MSS (Stanhope of Horsforth, Thomson of Esholt, Greene of Horsforth).
Tempest MSS (Tempest of Tong).

Huddersfield Central Library
Whitley Beaumont MSS (Beaumont of Whitley).

Huddersfield Town Hall
Ramsden MSS (Ramsden of Longley).

Leeds Central Library (Archives Department)
Battie Wrightson MSS (Wray of Cusworth, Bosvile of Warmsworth, Berry of Hodroyd, Batty of Alverthorpe).

Bilton Park MSS (Stockdale of Bilton Park).
Gascoigne of Barnbow MSS (Gascoigne, Hungate of Saxton, Plumpton of Plumpton).
MSS of Lord Mexborough (Savile of Methley, Reresby of Thrybergh), Ramsden MSS (Ramsden of Longley).
Stansfield MSS (Thomson of Esholt).
Temple Newsam MSS (Ingram of Temple Newsam, Slingsby of Kippax).
Richmondshire Wills and Administrations.

Northallerton County Record Office

Crathorne MSS (Crathorne of Crathorne).
MSS of Lord Gisborough (Chaloner of Guisborough).
Hutton MSS (Hutton of Marske).
Hutton-Squire MSS (Conyers of Holtby).
Peirse of Bedale MSS.
Turner MSS (Layton of Sexhow, Yoward of Westerdale, Rokeby of Marske, Tocketts of Tocketts).

Northamptonshire County Record Office

Finch-Hatton MSS 133 (seen in transcript).

Nottingham University Library

Galway of Serlby MSS (Monckton of Cavil, Maleverer of Allerton Mauleverer, Ireland of Crofton, Berry of Hodroyd, Stringer of Sharlston, Savile of Wakefield, Slingsby of Scriven).

Nottinghamshire County Record Office

Savile of Rufford MSS (Savile of Thornhill).

Sheffield Central Library

Bacon Frank MSS (Franke of Campsall, Wentworth of South Kirkby, Beckwith of Ackton).
Crewe MSS (Rodes of Great Houghton).
Jackson Collection (Darley of Kilnhurst).
Spencer Stanhope MSS (Barnby of Barnby Hall, Bamford of Pule Hill).
Wentworth Woodhouse Collection: Strafford Letters and Bright MSS (Wentworth of Wentworth Woodhouse, Bright of Carbrook, Hawksworth of Hawksworth, Lister of Thornton, Wentworth of North Elmsall, Norcliffe of Langton, Wombwell of Wombwell, Wormley of Riccall).
Wharncliffe MSS (Wortley of Wortley).

Yorkshire Archaeological Society Library

Bretton Hall MSS (Wentworth of West Bretton, Popeley of Woolley Moorhouse, Savile of Wakefield).

Clarke-Thornhill MSS (Thornhill of Fixby, Calverley of Calverley, Trigott of South Kirkby).

Copley of Sprotborough MSS.

Fairfax MSS (Fairfax of Denton).

Farnley MSS (Danby of Masham and Farnley).

Farnley Hall MSS (Fawkes of Farnley, Hawksworth of Hawksworth).

Duke of Leeds MSS (Osborne of Kiveton, Wandesford of Kirklington).

Lister-Kaye MSS (Lister of Thornton).

Middleton MSS (Middleton of Stockeld).

Newburgh Priory MSS (Bellasis of Newburgh Priory, Fairfax of Gilling) (*Note*: now at Northallerton County Record Office).

Payne-Gallwey MSS (Frankland of Great Thirkleby).

Ribston MSS (Goodricke of Ribston).

Savile of Copley MSS.

Slingsby MSS (Slingsby of Scriven).

MS 178   Transcript of a journal kept by the Kaye family of Woodsome.

MS 311   Commonplace book of Francis Stringer of Sharlston and his son Thomas.

MS 329   A book of verses and essays by Sir John Reresby, 1st Bart.

MS 381(t)   Papers relating to the Tempest family of Broughton.

MS 721, MS 736,

MD 237(c)   Papers of the families of Norcliffe of Langton and Bamburgh of Howsham.

MD 175   Deeds of the families of Vavasour of Spaldington and Vavasour of Willitoft.

MD 218   Deeds of the families of Stapleton of Carlton and Percy of Stubbs Walden.

MD 248(h)   Deeds of the Wormley family of Riccall.

MD 287(b)   Rent-book of Sir Marmaduke Langdale of North Dalton.

Private Collections

Capt. M. T. Hildyard, Flintham Hall, Nottinghamshire: MSS of the Hildyard family of Winestead.

Lord Dartmouth Estate Office, Slaithwaite, near Huddersfield: Seventeenth-century rent-book of the Kaye family of Woodsome.

Documents listed in National Register of Archives Calendars which have not been seen in the original

Ingilby MSS (Ingleby of Ripley).
Newby Hall MSS (Robinson of Newby).
Vyner MSS (Mallory of Studley, Proctor of Fountains, Robinson of Newby, Wyvill of Constable Burton).
Yorke MSS (Yorke of Gouthwaite).

2. PRINTED

Acts of the Privy Council.
ALLEN, J. (ed.) *Institutes of the Christian Religion by John Calvin* 2 vols. (1935 edn.).
ATKINSON, J. C. (ed.) [*The North Riding*] *Quarter Sessions Records, North Riding Record Society* i-iv (1884-6).
AVELING, H. (ed.) 'Recusancy Papers of the Meynell Family',*C.R.S.*, lvi (1964), ix.
BACON, FRANCIS. *The Essayes or Counsels Civill & Morall of Francis Bacon Lord Verulam* (Everyman edn. 1906).
BARBER, F. 'The West Riding Sessions Rolls', *Y.A.J.*, v (1877–8), 362.
BARLOW, JOHN. *An Exposition of the Second Epistle of the Apostle Paul to Timothy, the First Chapter* (1624).
BATESON, M. (ed.) 'Original Letters from the Bishops to the Privy Council in 1564', *Camden Miscellany*, ix (1894).
BELL, R. (ed.) *Memorials of the Civil War: comprising the correspondence of the Fairfax family with the most distinguished personages engaged in that memorable contest*, 2 vols. (1849).
BONSEY, C. G. and JENKINS, J. G. (ed.), *Ship Money Papers, and Richard Grenville's Note-book, Buckinghamshire Record Society*, xiii (1965).
BOWLER, H. (ed.) *Recusant Roll No. 2 (1593–1594), C.R.S.*, lvii (1965).
BRIGG, W. (ed.) *Yorkshire Fines for the Stuart Period, Y.A.S.R.S.*, liii, lviii (1915, 1917).
BURTON, E. H. and WILLIAMS, T. L. (ed.) *The Douay College Diaries 1598–1654, C.R.S.*, x, xi (1911).
Calendar of the Letters and Papers of Henry VIII.
Calendar of Patent Rolls.
Calendar of State Papers, Colonial Series: America and the West Indies.
Calendar of State Papers, Domestic Series.
Calendar of the Proceedings of the Committee for the Advance of Money.
CALTHROP, M. M. C. (ed.) *Recusant Roll No. 1, 1592–3, C.R.S.*, xviii (1916).
CAMDEN, WILLIAM. *Britannia* (1695 edn.).

CARTWRIGHT, J. J. (ed.) 'Papers Relating to the Delinquency of Lord Savile 1642–1646', *Camden Miscellany*, viii (1883).

do. *Chapters in the History of Yorkshire* (1872).

CHALLONER, R. (ed.) *Memoirs of Missionary Priests* (1924).

CHOLMLEY, SIR HUGH. *The Memoirs of Sir Hugh Cholmley…in which he gives some account of his family, and the distresses they underwent in the Civil Wars, &c* (1787).

CLARENDON, EDWARD, EARL OF. *The Life of Edward Earl of Clarendon… Written by Himself*, 3 vols. (1761 edn.).

CLAY, J. W. (ed.) *Dugdale's Visitation of Yorkshire, with Additions*, 3 vols. (1899–1917).

do. *Roger Dodsworth: Yorkshire Church Notes, 1619–1631, Y.A.S.R.S.* xxxiv (1904).

do. *North Country Wills, 1558 to 1604*, Surtees Society, cxxi (1912).

CLAY, J. W., and LISTER, J. (ed.) 'Autobiography of Sir John Savile, of Methley, Knight, Baron of the Exchequer, 1546–1607', *Y.A.J.*, xv (1900), 420.

COATES, W. H. (ed.) *The Journal of Sir Simonds D'Ewes from the First Recess of the Long Parliament to the Withdrawal of King Charles from London* (*Yale Historical Publications*, 1942).

COLLIER, J. P. (ed.) *The Egerton Papers*, Camden Society, Old Series, xii (1840).

COLLINS, F. (ed.) *Feet of Fines of the Tudor Period, Y.A.S.R.S.*, ii, v, vii, viii (1887–90).

do. *Wills and Administrations from the Knaresborough Court Rolls*, Surtees Society, civ, cx (1900, 1904).

COMBER, T. (ed.) *A Book of Instructions, written by the Right Honourable Sir [sic] Christopher Wandesforde…to his son and heir, George Wandesforde, &c* (1777).

Commons Journals.

CROSSLEY, E. W. (ed.) 'Two Seventeenth-Century Inventories', *Y.A.J.*, xxxiv (1939), 170.

DALTON, MICHAEL. *The Countrey Justice, containing the practice of the justices of the peace out of their sessions* (1635 edn.).

DUGDALE, SIR WILLIAM. *The Visitation of Yorkshire, 1665–6*, Surtees Society, xxxvi (1859).

FERNE, SIR JOHN. *The Blazon of Gentrie* (1586).

FIRTH, SIR CHARLES, and RAIT, R. S. (ed.) *Acts and Ordinances of the Interregnum, 1642–1660*, 3 vols. (1911).

FLETCHER, R. J. (ed.) *The Pension Book of Gray's Inn, 1569–1669* (1901).

FOLEY, H. (ed.) *Records of the English Province of the Society of Jesus*, 7 vols. (1877–83).

FOSTER, E. R. (ed.) *Proceedings in Parliament, 1610* (*Yale Historical Publications*), 2 vols. (1966).

FOSTER, J. (ed.) *The Visitation of Yorkshire in 1584–5 and 1612* (1875).

FULLER, THOMAS. *The History of the Worthies of England* (ed. P. A. Nuttall) 3 vols. (1840).

FURNIVALL, F. J. (ed.) *Harrison's Description of England in Shakspere's Youth*, 2 vols. (1877–81).

GARDINER, S. R. (ed.) *Debates in the House of Commons in 1625, Camden Society*, New Series, vi (1873).

GREENWELL, W. (ed.) 'Some Lascelles Deeds and Evidences', *Y.A.J.*, ii (1873), 87.

HAWKINS, M. J. (ed.) *Sales of Wards in Somerset, 1603–1641, Somerset Record Society*, lxvii (1965).

HENSON, E. (ed.) *The English College at Madrid, 1611–1767, C.R.S.*, xxix (1929).

do. *The English College at Valladolid: Registers 1589–1862, C.R.S.*, xxx (1930).

HISTORICAL MANUSCRIPTS COMMISSION:
Third Report (Wharncliffe MSS).
Fourth Report (House of Lords MSS).
Fifth Report (House of Lords MSS, Sutherland MSS, MSS of Mr W. C. Strickland).
Sixth Report (MSS of Sir Reginald Graham, Sir Henry Ingilby and Mr F. Bacon Frank).
Seventh Report (House of Lords MSS).
Ninth Report (MSS of Mr Alfred Morrison).
Eleventh Report (Savile MSS).
Twelfth Report (Coke MSS).
Thirteenth Report (Portland MSS).
Hatfield House MSS.
Various Collections ii (MSS of Sir George Wombwell, Mrs Harford of Holme Hall and Mrs Wentworth of Woolley Park).
Various Collections viii (Temple Newsam MSS).

HODGSON, J. C. (ed.) *Six North Country Diaries Surtees Society*, cxviii (1910).

do. *North Country Diaries (Second Series), Surtees Society,* cxxiv (1914).

HOWELL, JAMES. *Epistolae Ho-Elianae* (1726 edn.).

HUDDLESTON, JOHN. *A Short and Plain Way to the Faith and Church* (ed. R. Huddleston) (1688).

HUTCHINSON, LUCY. *Memoirs of the Life of Colonel Hutchinson* (1908).

JACKSON, C. (ed.) *The Autobiography of Mrs Alice Thornton of East Newton, Co. York, Surtees Society*, lxii (1873).

JOHNSON, G. W. (ed.) *The Fairfax Correspondence. Memoirs of the Reign of Charles the First*, 2 vols. (1848).

KELLY, W. (ed.) *The Liber Ruber of the English College Rome: I. Nomina Alumnorum, 1579–1783, C.R.S.*, xxxvii, xl (1940, 1943).

KENNY, A. (ed.) *The Responsa Scholarum of the English College, Rome, 1598–1685, C.R.S.*, liv, lv (1962, 1963).

KENYON, J. P. (ed.) *The Stuart Constitution 1603–1688* (1966).

KINGSBURY, S. M. (ed.) *The Records of the Virginia Company of London*, 2 vols. (1906).

KNOWLER, W. (ed.) *The Earl of Strafforde's Letters and Despatches*, 2 vols. (1739).

KNOX, T. F. (ed.) *The First and Second Diaries of the English College Douay* (1878).

LAMBARD, WILLIAM. *Eirenarcha* (1619 edn.).

LEADAM, I. S. (ed.) *Select Cases in the Court of Requests A.D. 1497–1569*, Selden Society, xii (1898).

LEGG, L. G. W. (ed.) *A Relation of a Short Survey of 26 Counties* (1904).

LEIGH, VALENTINE. *The Moste Profitable and commendable science of surveying of Landes, Tenementes and Hereditamentes* (1577).

LISTER, J. (ed.) *West Riding Sessions Records, Y.A.S.R.S.*, iii, liv (1888, 1915).

LITTLEDALE, R. P. (ed.) *The Pudsey Deeds, Y.A.S.R.S.*, lvi (1916).

LONGSTAFFE, W. H. D. (ed.) *Heraldic Visitation of the Northern Counties in 1530*, Surtees Society, xli (1862).

Lords Journals

LUMB, G. D. (ed.) *Wills, Registers and Monumental Inscriptions of the Parish of Barwick-in-Elmet* (1908).

MACRAY, W. D. (ed.) *Beaumont Papers (Roxburghe Club)* (1884).

do. *The History of the Rebellion and Civil Wars in England...by Edward, Earl of Clarendon*, 6 vols. (1888).

MCCLURE, N. C. (ed.) *Letters of John Chamberlain (American Philosophical Society)*, 2 vols. (1939).

MEADS, D. M. (ed.) *The Diary of Lady Margaret Hoby 1599–1605* (1900).

MORRIS, C. (ed.) *The Journeys of Celia Fiennes* (1949).

MORRIS, J. (ed.) *The Troubles of our Catholic Forefathers, related by themselves*, 3 series (1872–7).

MORYSON, FYNES. *Itinerary* (1617 edn.).

NORDEN, JOHN. *The Surveyors Dialogue* (1607).

NOTESTEIN, W. (ed.) *The Journal of Sir Simonds D'Ewes, from the beginning of the Long Parliament to the opening of the trial of the Earl of Strafford (Yale Historical Publications*, 1923).

NOTESTEIN, W., RELF, E. M., and SIMPSON, H. (ed.) *Commons Debates, 1621 (Yale Historical Publications)*, 7 vols. (1935).

PALMES, WILLIAM. *Life of Mrs Dorothy Lawson of St Anthony's, near Newcastle-upon-Tyne, in Northumberland* (ed. G. B. Richardson) (1851).

PARKINSON, R. (ed.) *The Life of Adam Martindale, Chetham Society*, iv (1845).

PARSONS, D. (ed.) *The Diary of Sir Henry Slingsby of Scriven, Bart.* (1836).

PEACOCK, E. (ed.) *The Monckton Papers* (*Philobiblon Society*) (1884).

do. *A List of the Roman Catholics in the County of York in 1604* (1872).

do. 'Inventories made for Sir William and Sir Thomas Fairfax, Knights, of Walton, and of Gilling Castle, Yorkshire, in the Sixteenth and Seventeenth Centuries', *Archaeologia*, xlviii (1884), 121.

PENNYMAN, J. W. (ed.) *Records of the Family of Pennyman of Ormesby* (1904).

PERKINS, WILLIAM. *The Works* (1605 edn.).

RAINE, J. (ed.) *The Correspondence of Dr Matthew Hutton, Archbishop of York, &c, Surtees Society*, xvii (1843).

RAINE, J., jun. (ed.) *Wills and Inventories from the Registry of the Archdeaconry of Richmond, Surtees Society*, xxvi (1853).

RUSHWORTH, JOHN. *Historical Collections of Private Passages of State, Weighty Matters in Law, Remarkable Proceedings in Five Parliaments*, 8 vols. (1721 edn.).

SCROPE, R., and MONKHOUSE, T. (ed.) *State Papers collected by Edward Earl of Clarendon commencing from the year 1621*, 3 vols. (1767–86).

SOMERS, LORD. *Lord Somers's Tracts*, 13 vols. (1809–15).

STANSWELL, L. M. (ed.) *Kingston Upon Hull: Calendar of the Ancient Deeds, Letters and Miscellaneous Documents 1300–1800* (1951).

STAPLETON, T. (ed.) *Plumpton Correspondence, Camden Society*, Old Series, iv (1839).

TALBOT, C. (ed.) *C.R.S.*, liii (1961) (papers relating to Yorkshire recusants, including a book of compositions with northern recusants, 1629–32).

TAYLOR, JOHN. *Part of this Summer's Travels* (1640).

Thomason Tracts. Collection of Civil War pamphlets in the British Museum.

TURNER, J. H. (ed.) *The Rev. Oliver Heywood, B.A., 1630–72: His Autobiography, Diaries, Anecdote and Event Books*, 4 vols. (1882–3).

WHITAKER, T. D. *The Life and Original Correspondence of Sir George Radcliffe* (1810).

WHITELOCK, BULSTRODE. *Memorials of the English Affairs from the Beginning of the Reign of Charles the First to the Happy Restoration of King Charles the Second*, 4 vols. (1853 edn.).

WILDRIDGE, T. T. *The Hull Letters* (1886).

WILKINSON, JOHN. *A Treatise...concerning the office and authoritie of coroners and sherifes...court leet, court baron, hundred court, &c* (1628).

WILSON, THOMAS. *The State of England Anno Dom. 1600* (ed. F. J. Fisher), *Camden Miscellany*, xvi (1936), 1.

WINTHROP, JOHN. *The History of New England from 1630 to 1649*, 2 vols. (1859).

WORTLEY, SIR FRANCIS. *Characters and Elegies* (1646).

WRIGHT, T. (ed.) *Autobiography of Joseph Lister of Bradford, 1627–1709* (1842).

YOUNG, A. *Chronicles of the First Planters of the Colony of Massachusetts Bay 1623–1636* (1846).

YORKSHIRE PARISH REGISTER SOCIETY: various registers.

ANON. *A Catalogue of the Muniments at Kirklees* (1900).

ANON. 'Genealogia Antiquae Familiae Langdalorum', *Y.A.J.*, xi (1891), 372.

ANON. *Old Leeds Charities. The First and Second Decree of the Committee of Pious Uses in Leedes* (1926).

ANON. *The Regulations and Establishment of the Household of Henry Algernon Percy, The Fifth Earl of Northumberland* (1770).

Secondary Sources

I. GENERAL

(a) *Books*

BINDOFF, S. T. *Tudor England* (1950).

BINDOFF, S. T., HURSTFIELD, J., and WILLIAMS, C. H. (ed.) *Elizabethan Government and Society* (1961).

BLACK, J. B. *The Reign of Elizabeth 1558–1603* (1959 edn.).

DAVIES, G. *The Early Stuarts 1603–60* (1959 edn.).

Dictionary of National Biography.

GARDINER, S. R. *History of England from the Accession of James I to the Outbreak of the Civil War, 1603–1642*, 10 vols. (1896–1901).

do. *History of the Great Civil War, 1642–1649*, 4 vols. (1901).

HEXTER, J. H. *Reappraisals in History* (1960).

HILL, C. *The Century of Revolution, 1603–1714* (1961).

do. *Puritanism and Revolution* (1958).

MATHEW, D. *The Jacobean Age.* (1938).

do. *The Age of Charles I* (1951).

NEWTON, A. P. *The Colonising Activities of the English Puritans. The last phase of the Elizabethan struggle with Spain* (1914).

NOTESTEIN, W. *The English People on the Eve of Colonisation, 1603–30* (1954).

STONE, L. *The Crisis of the Aristocracy, 1558–1641* (1965).

TAWNEY, R. H. *Religion and the Rise of Capitalism* (1926).

do. *Business and Politics under James I* (1958).

WEDGWOOD, C. V. *The King's Peace, 1637–1641* (1955).
do. *The King's War, 1641–1647* (1958).

(b) *Articles*

ROOTS, I. 'Gentlemen and Others', *History*, xlvii (1962), 233.
TAWNEY, R. H. 'The Rise of the Gentry 1540–1640', *Economic History Review*, xi (1941), 1.
do. 'The Rise of the Gentry: A Postscript', *Economic History Review*, Second Series, vii (1954), 91.
TREVOR-ROPER, H. R. *The Gentry 1540–1640. Economic History Review*, Supplement 1 (1953).

2. POLITICAL AND ADMINISTRATIVE

(a) *Books*

AYLMER, G. E. *The King's Servants: The Civil Service of Charles I, 1625–1642* (1961).
BELL, H. E. *An Introduction to the History and Records of the Court of Wards and Liveries* (1953).
BOYNTON, L. *The Elizabethan Militia* (1966).
BRUNTON, D., and PENNINGTON, D. H. *Members of the Long Parliament* (1954).
COBBETT, W. *Cobbett's Parliamentary History of England*, 36 vols. (1806–20).
DIETZ, F. C. *English Public Finance, 1558–1641* (1920).
FOXCROFT, H. C. *The Life and Letters of Sir George Savile, Bart., First Marquis of Halifax*, 2 vols. (1898).
HURSTFIELD, J. *The Queen's Wards* (1958).
KARRAKER, C. H. *The Seventeenth Century Sheriff* (1930).
KEARNEY, H. P. *Strafford in Ireland, 1633–41* (1959).
KEELER, M. F. *The Long Parliament, 1640–1641. A Biographical Study of its Members (American Philosophical Society*, 1954).
NEALE, SIR JOHN. *The Elizabethan House of Commons* (1949).
do. *Elizabeth I and Her Parliaments, 1559–1581* (1953).
do. *Elizabeth I and Her Parliaments, 1584–1601* (1957).
NOBLE, M. *The Lives of the English Regicides*, 2 vols. (1798).
PEACOCK, E. (ed.) *The Army Lists of the Roundheads and Cavaliers* (1874).
WEDGWOOD, C. V. *Thomas Wentworth, First Earl of Strafford, 1593–1641: A Revaluation* (1961).

(b) *Articles*

AYLMER, G. E. 'Attempts at Administrative Reform, 1625–40', *English Historical Review*, lxxii (1957), 229.

BARNES, T. G., and SMITH, A. HASSALL 'Justices of the Peace from 1558 to 1688—a Revised List of Sources,' *Bulletin of the Institute of Historical Research*, xxxii (1959), 221.

GORDON, M. D. 'The Collection of Ship-Money in the Reign of Charles I', *Transactions of the Royal Historical Society*, Third Series, iv (1910), 141.

MANNING, B. S. 'The Nobles, the People and the Constitution', *Past and Present*, ix (1956), 43.

WILSON, J. S. 'Sheriffs' Rolls of the 16th and 17th Centuries', *English Historical Review*, xlvii (1932), 31.

3. SOCIAL AND ECONOMIC

(a) *Books*

ANDERSON, P. J. (ed.) *Roll of Alumni in Arts of the University and King's College of Aberdeen 1596–1860* (1900).

BANKS, T. C. *The Dormant and Extinct Baronage of England*, 3 vols. (1807).

BEVERIDGE, SIR WILLIAM (and others). *Prices and Wages in England from the Twelfth to the Nineteenth Century*, i, *Price Tables: Mercantile Era* (1939).

BROWN, A. *The Genesis of the United States*, 2 vols. (1890).

FOSTER, J. (ed.) *Alumni Oxonienses: the Members of the University of Oxford, 1500–1714*, 4 vols. (1892).

do. *The Register of Admissions to Gray's Inn, 1521–1889* (1889).

G.E.C. (ed.) *Complete Baronetage*, 6 vols. (1900–9).

do. *Complete Peerage*, 13 vols. (1910–59).

JORDAN, W. K. *Philanthropy in England, 1480–1660* (1959).

do. *The Charities of Rural England, 1480–1660* (1961).

KELSALL, R. K. *Wage Regulation under the Statute of Artificers* (1938).

KIRBY, T. F. (ed.) *Winchester Scholars* (1888).

MATHEW, D. *The Social Structure in Caroline England* (1948).

MAYNARD, G. *Economic Development and the Price Level* (1962).

MORRIS, F. O. *The Ancestral Homes of Britain* (1868).

NEF, J. U. *The Rise of the British Coal Industry*, 2 vols. (1932).

PEILE, J. (ed.) *Biographical Register of Christ's College, 1505–1905*, 2 vols. (1910).

PIXLEY, F. W. *A History of the Baronetage* (1900).

PRICE, W. H. *The English Patents of Monopoly* (*Harvard Economic Studies*, 1906).

ROGERS, J. E. T. *A History of Agriculture and Prices in England*, 8 vols. (1866–1902).

ROSE-TROUP, F. *The Massachusetts Bay Company and its Predecessors* (1930).

RUSSELL-BARKER, G. F., and STENNING, A. H. (ed.) *The Records of Old Westminsters*, 2 vols. (1928).

RYLANDS, W. H. (ed.) *Grantees of Arms (Harleian Society,* lxvi).

SHAW, W. A. (ed.) *The Knights of England,* 2 vols. (1906).

SINGER, C. J. *The Earliest Chemical Industry* (1948).

SQUIBB, G. D. *The High Court of Chivalry* (1959).

STERRY, SIR WASEY (ed.) *The Eton College Register, 1441–1698* (1943).

STOYE, J. W. *English Travellers Abroad, 1604–1667* (1952).

STURGESS, H. A. C. (ed.) *Register of Admissions to the Honourable Society of the Middle Temple,* 3 vols. (1949).

TAWNEY, R. H. *The Agrarian Problem in the Sixteenth Century* (1912).

THIRSK, J. (ed.) *The Agrarian History of England and Wales, iv, 1500–1640* (1967).

TURNER, R. W. *The Equity of Redemption (Cambridge Studies in English Local History,* 1931).

UPTON, A. F. *Sir Arthur Ingram, c. 1565–1642* (1961).

VENN, J. (ed.) *Biographical History of Gonville and Caius College, 1349–1897,* 3 vols. (1897–1901).

VENN, J., and J. A. (ed.) *Alumni Cantabrigienses. A biographical list of all known students, graduates and holders of office at the University of Cambridge, from the earliest times to 1751,* 4 vols. (1922–7).

WAGNER, SIR ANTHONY. *Heralds and Heraldry in the Middle Ages* (1939).

WILSON, C. *England's Apprenticeship 1603–1763* (1965).

WRIGHT. L. B. *Middle Class Culture in Elizabethan England* (1959).

ANON *A Catalogue of the Graduates in the Faculties of Arts, Divinity and Law of the University of Edinburgh* (1858).

ANON *Admissions to the College of St. John the Evangelist in the University of Cambridge,* 4 parts (1882–1931).

ANON *Masters of the Bench of the Honourable Society of the Inner Temple and Masters of the Temple* (1883).

ANON *Students Admitted to the Inner Temple 1547–1660* (1877).

ANON *The Records of the Honorable Society of Lincoln's Inn, vol. 1. Admissions from A.D. 1799* (1896).

(b) *Articles*

BELOFF, M. 'Humphrey Shalcrosse and the Great Civil War', *English Historical Review,* liv (1939), 686.

COKAYNE, G. E. 'Skinners' Company: Apprenticeships', *Miscellanea Genealogica et Heraldica,* Third Series, i (1896), 41.

HABAKKUK, H. J. 'Marriage Settlements in the Eighteenth Century', *Transactions of the Royal Historical Society,* Fourth Series, xxxii (1950), 15.

HOSKINS, W. G. 'The Rebuilding of Rural England, 1570–1640', *Past and Present*, iv (1953), 44.

KERRIDGE, E. 'The Movement of Rent 1540–1640', *Economic History Review*, Second Series, vi (1953), 16.

MERCER, F. 'The Houses of the Gentry', *Past and Present*, v (1954), 11.

4. RELIGIOUS

(a) *Books*

ALBION, G. *Charles I and the Court of Rome* (1935).

BANKS, C. E. *The Winthrop Fleet of 1630* (1930).

BIRT, H. N. *Obit Book of the English Benedictines from 1600 to 1912* (1913).

BRADY, W. M. *Annals of the Catholic Hierarchy in England and Scotland, 1585–1876* (1877).

BROOK, B. *The Lives of the Puritans*, 3 vols. (1813).

BURRAGE, C. *The Early English Dissenters in the Light of Recent Research, 1550–1641*, 2 vols. (1912).

BUTLER, C. *Historical Memoirs of the English, Irish and Scottish Colleges since the Reformation*, 4 vols. (1822).

CALAMY, E. *The Nonconformist's Memorial: being an account of the ministers who were ejected or silenced after the Restoration* (abridged by S. Palmer), 2 vols. (1775).

do. *A Continuation of the Account of the ministers, lecturers, masters and fellows of colleges, and schoolmasters who were ejected or silenced after the Restoration in 1660*, 2 vols. (1727).

COLLINSON, P. *The Elizabethan Puritan Movement* (1967).

DICKENS, A. G. *The English Reformation* (1964).

GILLOW, J. *A Biographical Dictionary of the English Catholics*, 5 vols. (1895–1902).

GUILDAY, P. *The English Colleges and Convents in the Catholic Low Countries, 1558–1795* (1914).

HALLER, W. *The Rise of Puritanism* (1938).

HAMILTON, A. *Chronicles of the English Augustinian Canonesses of St. Monica's at Louvain, 1548–1644*, 2 vols. (1904).

KIRK, J. L. *Historical Account of Lisbon College* (1902).

KNAPPEN, M. M. *Tudor Puritanism* (1939).

MATTHEWS, A. G. *Calamy Revised* (1934).

MORGAN, I. *Prince Charles's Puritan Chaplain* (1957).

NEAL, D. *The History of the Puritans*, 5 vols. (1822).

OLIVER, G. *Collections Towards Illustrating the Biography of the Scotch, English and Irish Members of the Society of Jesus* (1845).

PETRE, E. *Accounts of the English Colleges and Convents Established on the Continent after the Dissolution of Religious Houses in England* (1849).

SCOTT PEARSON, A. F. *Thomas Cartwright and Elizabethan Puritanism* (1925).

STRYPE, J. *Annals of the Reformation and Establishment of Religion and other Various Occurrences in the Church of England during Queen Elizabeth's Happy Reign*, 4 vols. (1824).

TIERNEY, M. A. (ed.) *Dodd's Church History of England*, 5 vols. (1839–43).

WELDON, B. *Chronological Notes containing the rise, growth and present state of the English Congregation of the Order of St. Benedict* (1881).

(b) *Article*

BOWLER, H. 'Some Notes on the Recusant Rolls of the Exchequer', *C.R.S.: Recusant History*, iv (1957–8), 182.

5. LOCAL

(a) *Books*

AHIER, P. *The Legends and Traditions of Huddersfield and its District*, 2 vols. (1940–5).

AMBLER, L. *The Old Halls and Manor Houses of Yorkshire* (1913).

ATKINSON, H. B. (ed.) *Giggleswick School Register, 1499–1921* (1922).

BAILDON, W. P. *Baildon and the Baildons*, 3 vols. (1912–27).

BARNES, T. G. *Somerset, 1625–1640: a County's Government during the 'Personal Rule'* (1961).

BLACK, M. W. *Richard Brathwait* (1928).

BURTON, T. *The History and Antiquities of the Parish of Hemingborough* (*Y.A.S. Extra Series*, no. 1, ed. J. Raine) (1888).

CHETWYND-STAPYLTON, H. E. *The Stapeltons of Yorkshire* (1897).

CLARKSON, C. *The History and Antiquities of Richmond in the County of York* (1821).

COATE, M. *Cornwall in the Great Civil War and Interregnum 1642–1660* (1933).

COGHILL, J. H. *The Family of Coghill, 1377–1879* (1879).

COLLIER, C. V. *An Account of the Boynton Family* (1914).

COLMAN, F. S. *History of Barwick-in-Elmet*, Thoresby Society, xvii (1908).

COMBER, T. *Memoirs of the Life and Death of the Right Honourable the Lord Deputy Wandesforde* (1778).

CROSS, M. C. *The Puritan Earl: the Life of Henry Hastings third Earl of Huntingdon, 1536–1595* (1966).

DALE, B. *Yorkshire Puritanism and Early Nonconformity. Illustrated by the Lives of the Ejected Ministers, 1660 and 1662* (ed. T. G. Crippen) (1917).

27—Y.G.

DARBYSHIRE, H. S., and LUMB, G. D. *The History of Methley, Thoresby Society*, xxxv (1934).

DENNY, H. L. L. *Memorials of an Ancient House: a History of the Family of Lister or Lyster* (1913).

DICKENS, A. G. *Lollards and Protestants in the Diocese of York, 1509–1558* (1959).

ELMHIRST, E. *Peculiar Inheritance: A History of the Elmhirsts* (1951).

EVERITT, A. M. *The Community of Kent and the Great Rebellion, 1640–60* (1966).

FACER, P. 'A History of Hipperholme School from 1660 to 1914, with a Biography of its Founder, Matthew Brodley (1586–1648)' (unpublished London M.A. thesis, 1966).

FINCH, M. E. *The Wealth of Five Northamptonshire Families 1540–1640, Northamptonshire Record Society*, xix (1956).

FOSTER, J. (ed.) *Pedigrees of the County Families of Yorkshire*, 4 vols. (1874–5).

GOODER, A. *The Parliamentary Representation of the County of York 1258–1832*, ii, *Y.A.S.R.S.*, xcvi (1937).

GOODRICKE, C. A. *History of the Goodricke Family* (1897).

do. *Ribston* (1902).

GRAINGE, W. *Nidderdale* (1863).

do. *The Vale of Mowbray* (1859).

HAILSTONE, E. (ed.) *Portraits of Yorkshire Worthies*, 2 vols. (1869).

HORNYOLD, H. *Genealogical Memoirs of the Family of Strickland of Sizergh* (1928).

HOSKINS, W. G., and FINBERG, H. P. R. *Devonshire Studies* (1952).

HOWARD, C. H. D. *Sir John Yorke of Nidderdale 1565–1634* (1939).

HOYLE, W. D. *Historical Notes of the Baronial House of Bulmer and its Descendants* (ed. G. B. Bulmer) (1896).

HUDLESTON, N. A. *Stainley and Cayton* (1956).

HUNTER, J. *Hallamshire: the History and Topography of the Parish of Sheffield* (1869).

do. *South Yorkshire: the History and Topography of the Deanery of Doncaster*, 2 vols. (1828).

INGLEDEW, C. J. D. *The History and Antiquities of North Allerton* (1858).

JAMES J. *The History and Topography of Bradford* (1841).

JEWEL, J. *The History and Antiquities of Harewood* (1822).

LAWSON-TANCRED, SIR THOMAS. *Records of a Yorkshire Manor* (1937).

do. *The Tancreds of Brampton* (1921).

LEGARD, SIR JAMES D. *The Legards of Anlaby and Ganton* (1926).

MACDONALD of the ISLES, LADY ALICE. *The Fortunes of a Family. Bosville of New Hall, Gunthwaite and Thorpe* (1928).

BIBLIOGRAPHY 407

MAJOR, H. D. A. *Memorials of Copgrove* (1922).

MARCHANT, R. A. *The Puritans and the Church Courts in the Diocese of York 1560–1642* (1960).

MARKHAM, SIR CLEMENTS R. *A Life of the Great Lord Fairfax* (1870).

do. *Admiral Robert Fairfax* (1895).

MCCALL, H. B. *Story of the Family of Wandesforde of Kirklington and Castlecomer* (1904).

do. *The Early History of Bedale* (1907).

METCALFE, T. *Medecalf* (1930).

METCALFE, W. C. and G. (ed.) *Records of the Family of Metcalfe* (1891).

MORKILL, J. W. *The Parish of Kirkby Malhamdale in the West Riding of Yorkshire* (1933).

NEWTON, J. A. 'Puritanism in the Diocese of York (excluding Nottinghamshire) 1603–1640' (unpublished London Ph.D. thesis, 1956).

NORCLIFFE, C. B. *History of the Priory and Peculiar of Snaith* (1861).

OLIVER, G. *The History and Antiquities of the Town and Minster of Beverley* (1829).

PEACOCK, M. H. *History of the Free Grammar School of Queen Elizabeth at Wakefield* (1892).

PEVSNER, N. *The Buildings of England: Yorkshire, the North Riding* (1966).

do. *The Buildings of England: Yorkshire, the West Riding* (1959).

PINE, L. G. *The Family of Wilberfoss* (1953).

PLANTAGENET-HARRISON, H. K. G. *The History of Yorkshire, i. Wapentake of Gilling West* (1879).

POULSON, G. *The History and Antiquities of the Seigniory of Holderness*, 2 vols. (1840).

PULLEIN, C. *The Pulleyns of Yorkshire* (1915).

REID, R. R. *The King's Council in the North* (1921).

RUSTON, A. G., and WITNEY, D. *Hooton Pagnell: The agricultural evolution of a Yorkshire village* (1934).

SALTMARSHE, P. *History and Chartulary of the Family Hothams* (1914).

SCOTT, D. *The Stricklands of Sizergh Castle* (1908).

SHARP, SIR CUTHBERT. *Memorials of the Rebellion of 1569* (1840).

SHEAHAN, J. J. *History and Topography of the Wapentake of Claro* (1871).

SHEARD, M. *Records of the Parish of Batley in the County of York* (1894).

SIMPSON, A. *The Wealth of the Gentry, 1540–1660: East Anglian Studies* (1961).

SMITH, A. HASSALL 'The Elizabethan Gentry of Norfolk' (unpublished London Ph.D. thesis, 1959).

SPEIGHT, H. *Nidderdale and the Garden of the Nidd* (1894).

SPENCE, R. T. 'The Cliffords, Earls of Cumberland, 1579–1646' (unpublished London Ph.D. thesis, 1959).

STIRLING, A. M. W. *The Hothams*, 2 vols. (1917).

SUNDERLAND, F. H. *Marmaduke Lord Langdale* (1926).

TAYLOR, T. *History of Wakefield: the Rectory Manor* (1886).

THORESBY, R. *Ducatus Leodiensis* (ed. T. D. Whitaker) (1886).

TICKELL, J. *History of the Town and County of Kingston upon Hull* (1798).

TURTON, R. B. *The Alum Farm* (1938).

VICTORIA COUNTY HISTORY:
A History of Yorkshire, 3 vols. (1907–13).
A History of Yorkshire: North Riding, 2 vols. (1914–23).
A History of Yorkshire: The City of York (1961).

WALKER, J. W. *Wakefield: Its History and People*, 2 vols. (1939).

WATSON, J. *The History and Antiquities of the Parish of Halifax* (1775).

WHEATER, W. *History of the Parishes of Sherburn and Cawood* (1865).

WHEATER, W. (ed.) *Old Yorkshire*, Second Series (1885).

WHELLAN, T. *History and Topography of the City of York and the North Riding of Yorkshire*, 2 vols. (1857).

WHITAKER, T. D. *A History of Richmondshire, in the North Riding of the County of York*, 2 vols. (1823).

do. *Loidis and Elmete* (1816).

do. *The History and Antiquities of the Deanery of Craven* (ed. A. W. Morant) (1878).

do. *The Life and Original Correspondence of Sir George Radcliffe* (1810).

WILSON, B. (ed.) *The Sedbergh School Register, 1546–1909* (1909).

WOOD, E. S. *The Ancient Buildings of the Harrogate District (Yorkshire Archaeological Society—Harrogate Group)* (1946).

ANON *Description of Browsholme Hall, in the West Riding of the County of York* (1815).

(b) *Articles and Pamphlets*

AHIER, P. *William Ramsden II, 1558–1623* (an offprint).

ATKINSON, W. A. 'A Parliamentary Election in Knaresborough in 1628', *Y.A.J.*, xxxiv (1939), 213.

AVELING, H. 'The Catholic Recusancy of the Yorkshire Fairfaxes', *C.R.S.: Biographical Studies*, iii (1955–6), 69, and *C.R.S.: Recusant History*, iv (1957–8), 61.

do. *Post Reformation Catholicism in East Yorkshire 1558–1790*, East Yorkshire Local History Society Publications, no. 11 (1960).

do. 'The Catholic Recusants of the West Riding of Yorkshire', *Proceedings of the Leeds Philosophical and Literary Society, Literary and Historical Section*, x (1963), 191.

BILSON, J. 'Gilling Castle', *Y.A.J.* xix (1907), 105.

BOWLES, C. E. B. 'Vescy of Brampton-en-le-Morthen in the Parish of Tree-ton, co. York, and their Descendants', *Y.A.J.*, xvii (1903), 340.

BROOKS, F. W. *The Council of the North* (Historical Association Pamphlet G25, 1953).

BROWN, W. 'Ingleby Arncliffe', *Y.A.J.*, xvi (1901), 184.

do. 'The Catterick Brass', *Y.A.J.*, xix (1907), 73.

CLAY, J. W. 'The Clifford Family', *Y.A.J.*, xviii (1905), 355.

do. 'The Gentry of Yorkshire at the Time of the Civil War', *Y.A.J.*, xxiii (1915), 349.

do. 'The Savile Family', *Y.A.J.*, xxv (1920), 1.

COMBER, J. 'The Mawdes of Riddlesden and Ilkley', *Y.A.J.*, xxiv (1917), 44.

COX, J. C. 'The Household Books of Sir Miles Stapleton Bart., 1656-1705', *The Ancestor*, ii (1902), 17, and iii (1902), 132.

DENT, G. 'Ewood in Midgley', *Halifax Antiquarian Society*, 1939, 7.

DICKENS, A. G. 'The Writers of Tudor Yorkshire', *Transactions of the Royal Historical Society*, Fifth Series, xiii (1963), 49.

do. 'The First Stages of Romanist Recusancy in Yorkshire, 1560-90', *Y.A.J.*, xxxv (1940-3), 157.

do. 'The Extent and Character of Recusancy in Yorkshire, 1604', *Y.A.J.* xxxvii (1948-51), 24.

do. 'Further Light on the Scope of Yorkshire Recusancy in 1604', *Y.A.J.* xxxviii (1952-5), 524.

ESDAILE, K. A., 'Sculpture and Sculptors in Yorkshire', *Y.A.J.*, xxxv (1943), 362.

do. 'Sculptors and Sculpture in Yorkshire', *Y.A.J.*, xxxvi (1944-7), 78, 137.

FRANÇOIS, M. ELLIS. 'The Social and Economic Development of Halifax 1558-1640', *Proceedings of the Leeds Philosophical and Literary Society, Literary and Historical Section*, xi (1966), 217.

HERRIES, LORD. 'The Constables of Flamborough', *Transactions of the East Riding Antiquarian Society*, viii (1900), 51.

JOHNSTON, N. 'History of the Family of Foljambe', *Collectanea Topographica et Genealogica*, ii (1835), 68.

KENDALL, H. P. 'Newbiggin in Egton and the Salvin Family', *Y.A.J.* xxxiii (1938), 87.

LANCASTER, W. T. 'The Family of Beeston', *Thoresby Society*, xxiv (1915-18), 245.

LAWRANCE, H. 'Pocklington School Admission Register, 1626-1717', *Y.A.J.*, xxv (1920), 53.

LISTER, J. 'High Sunderland', *Halifax Antiquarian Society*, iv (1907), 113.

do. 'The History of Shibden Hall and the Waterhouse Family', *Halifax Antiquarian Society*, xiv (1917), 53.

MACKENZIE, N. 'Sir Thomas Herbert of Tinterne: A Parliamentary Royalist', *Bulletin of the Institute of Historical Research*, xxix (1956), 32.

MARSHALL, G. W. 'The Marshalls of Pickering and their Descendants', *Y.A.J.*, vii (1881–2), 86.

PRESTON, W. E. *Official Handbook of Bolling Hall Museum* (1928).

RAINE, J. 'Marske, in Swaledale', *Y.A.J.*, vi (1879–80), 172.

RAINE, J. jun. 'The Pudsays of Barford', *Archaeologia Aeliana*, New Series, ii (1858), 173.

ROBERTSHAW, W. 'The Manor of Tong', *Bradford Antiquary*, New Series, part xxxviii (1956), 117.

ROEBUCK, P. 'The Constables of Everingham. The Fortunes of a Catholic Royalist Family During the Civil War and Interregnum', *C.R.S.: Recusant History*, ix (1967), 75.

SALTMARSHE, P. 'Some Howdenshire Villages', *Transactions of the East Riding Antiquarian Society*, xvi (1909), 1.

SHILLETO, R. J. 'The Shilletos of the West Riding', *Thoresby Society*, xxvi (1919–22), 282.

SPEIGHT, H. 'Hawksworth Hall and its Associations', *Bradford Antiquary*, New Series, ii (1905), 246.

TEMPEST, E. B. 'Broughton Hall and its Associations', *Bradford Antiquary*, New Series, iv (1921), 65.

TYLER, P. *The Ecclesiastical Commission and Catholicism in the North, 1562–1577* (privately printed, 1960).

WALBRAN, J. R. 'A Genealogical and Biographical Memoir of the Lords of Studley, in Yorkshire', *Surtees Society*, lxvii (1876), 311.

WENTWORTH, G. E. 'History of the Wentworths of Woolley', *Y.A.J.*, xii (1893), 1.

WHONE, C. 'Christopher Danby of Masham and Farnley', *Thoresby Society*, xxxvii (1936–42), 1.

INDEX

Notes: (1) In the case of Yorkshire place-names the county designation is invariably omitted. In contrast, entries relating to other English towns and villages include the name of the county except in such obvious cases as London and Norwich. (2) Families which appeared within the Yorkshire gentry may be identified by the fact that the family seat is named in all such entries.

Date Due